W9-APT-341

USING SMALL BUSINESS COMPUTERS

with Lotus 1–2–3™, dBASE II®, and WordStar®

D. G. Dologite
Baruch College
City University of New York

PRENTICE-HALL, INC., Englewood Cliffs, New Jersey 07632

Library of Congress Cataloging in Publication Data

Dologite, D. G.
Using small business computers.

On t.p. the computer languages in the subtitle are followed by the copyright symbol.
Bibliography.
Includes index.
1. Business--Data processing. 2. Microcomputers--Programming. 3. Lotus 1-2-3 (Computer program) 4. dBase II (Computer program) 5. WordStar (Computer program) I. Title.
HF5548.2.D587 1985 658'.054 85-498
ISBN 0-13-940230-6

Alternate edition published under the title of
Using Small Business Computers

Printed in the United States of America

10 9 8 7 6 5 4 3 2

ISBN 0-13-940230-6 01

Prentice-Hall International (UK) Limited, *London*
Prentice-Hall of Australia Pty. Limited, *Sydney*
Prentice-Hall Canada Inc., *Toronto*
Prentice-Hall Hispanoamericana, S.A., *Mexico*
Prentice-Hall of India Private Limited, *New Delhi*
Prentice-Hall of Japan, Inc., *Tokyo*
Prentice-Hall of Southeast Asia Pte. Ltd., *Singapore*
Editora Prentice-Hall do Brasil, Ltda., *Rio de Janeiro*
Whitehall Books Limited, *Wellington, New Zealand*

For Mother and Family

CONTENTS

INTRODUCTION

Using Small Business Computers provides business people and students with a working knowledge to use small computers. While it covers expected background and orientation material, its main focus is on the business ''applications'' of small computers. Applications are computer programs that perform user tasks, such as word processing and accounts receivable. They are the reason businesses and individuals buy small computers.

Step-by-step tutorials for ''hands-on'' experience with electronic spreadsheet, word processing, and database management applications are included. For readers without a computer or these applications, the tutorials simulate a ''you are there'' computer experience, from ''power-on'' to ''power-off.''

One-half of the book is devoted to specific business applications. The probability is very high that any business person will use from one to all of the applications covered.

The evaluation checklists that are included encourage a systematic approach to acquiring applications. They also help pinpoint application strengths and limitations.

A concluding case study designs a small computer application from scratch using an established design methodology. The methodology can be used to translate original application ideas into final working programs.

The book grew out of a need for an applications-oriented source of information for students in my Small Computers for Business course. From over fourteen years of small computer experience, I became aware of what students of small computers could most profitably study. During this time, the systematic procedures, checklists, and other materials that appear in this book were developed and industry tested.

Because computers and applications change so fast that descriptions of specific products can make a book obsolete before it is published, an effort has been made to keep the content as product independent as possible. With the tutorials, this is impossible. So representative products are used, knowing that they may be superseded in time.

The systematic approach to the use of small computers advocated, nonetheless, has been valid in the past and will continue to be valid as long as individuals and businesses use computers.

D. G. Dologite

ACKNOWLEDGMENTS

Appreciation is gratefully extended to:

- The following companies for furnishing software and other material for research: Alpha Software Corp., Ashton-Tate, Condor Computer Corporation, Douthett Enterprises Inc., Graphic Communications, Inc., Fox & Geller, Inc., IBM Corporation, Innovative Software, Lifetree Software, Inc., Lotus Development Corporation, MicroRIM, Inc., MicroPro International Corporation, Open Systems Inc. whose Software Fitness Program serves as a basis for the examples in Part III, Pacific Software Manufacturing Co., Peachtree Software, Robert J. Brady Co., Sorcim Corporation, Software Solutions, Inc., TLB, Inc., VisiCorp. Inc.
- Colleagues and students at Baruch College—City University of New York for reviewing and criticizing the text, as well as manuscript reviewers: H. Austin, Oakland Community College; R. Austing, University of Maryland; I. Englander, Bentley College; R. Matson, Schoolcraft College; D. Nielsen, Golden West College; S. Riskin, California State University—Dominguez Hills; J. F. Schrage, Southern Illinois University—Edwardsville.
- Research and student assistants for helping to construct the manuscript: S. Chia, I. Ionnides, A. Mao, Br. P. Meuten, E. Muller, B. Nagelberg, V. Sinha, M. Urban, M. Wong.

PART

understanding small business computers

Successfully using small computers in business environments comes from understanding their capabilities and limitations. Part I provides an orientation and background for understanding small computers.

Chapter 1 examines how users have implemented small computers in various work environments. It provides a perspective on ways to configure small computers to suit different work situations. Chapter 2 then examines the hardware that goes into making up a given configuration. Hardware capabilities, limitations, and trade-offs are considered.

The next two chapters describe computer programs that computerists call *software*. Software that makes the hardware work—computerists call it *system software*—is covered in Chapter 3. Software that users work with, like word processing or accounts receivable, is called *application software* and is discussed in Chapter 4.

The chapters in Part I help develop an understanding of the user–computer working relationship. Maintaining a successfully functioning system depends on it.

Part I concludes with Chapter 5 which brings earlier chapters into perspective. A selection methodology capstones the systematic approach to computer hardware and software evaluation covered in previous chapters.

1

USES AND USERS

Small business computers are probably the most significant productivity tool of our time. In the coming years, business professionals who do not harness their capability will be functioning at a disadvantage.

Innovative small shops and independent professionals can use powerful small computers as easily and cheaply as large companies. The small computer has eliminated the office technology gap that formerly was inherent in size.

This chapter explores how business professionals use small computers. It looks at single-user as well as multiuser environments. Communications over newer local area networks, as well as older wide-area networks, are reviewed. Terminology essential to functioning in these areas is introduced as needed.

A section on sources of information helps one to get informed and to keep informed about the business use of small computers. Other sections on specifying requirements and acquiring a computer conclude the chapter.

Through each section one thing becomes clear. The most important ingredient of all is the end-user, the businessperson sitting in front of the TV-like display and keyboard. The single-user environment is the fundamental building block of all other environments.

Unlike the old days, which is little more than twenty years ago, computer use was dominated by the large central computer. Individual users were appendages of its power. That trend is reversed. End-users have their own data processing power with personal small computer workstations. Figure 1–1 compares one of today's small professional workstation computers with its predecessors. It shows that the sibling is even more powerful than its parent.

Figure 1-1 Comparison (approximate figures) of an IBM large mainframe computer of only twenty years ago with an IBM small computer of the 1980s

IBM COMPUTERS

Computer Name	*IBM Personal Computer*	*System 360*
Computer Type	Microcomputer	Mainframe computer
Dates in Use	1981–present	1964–early 1970s (and some still in use)
Minimum:		
Memory (characters of storage)	16,000	8,000
Cost	$1,500	$133,000
Maximum:		
Memory (characters of storage)	1,000,000	524,000 (Model 70)
Cost	$10,000	$5,500,000
Environment	Desktop	Environmentally controlled room with raised floor for cabling, constant air cooling, and special fire protection system

COMPUTER DISTINCTIONS

In this book, small business computer means one that gives users computer power without dependence on computer experts. In terms of current computer technology, it refers to a desktop microcomputer. Office automation designers refer to it as a "general-purpose workstation," such as the one in Figure 1–2. In this book, the terms "small business computer," "workstation," and "microcomputer" will all mean a professional-level desktop microcomputer, such as the one specified in Figure 1–1 and shown in Figure 1–2.

Traditional technical classifications are *microcomputers, minicomputers,* and *mainframes* or large computers. It used to be easy to tell one from the other. They were classified by something called *word size,* the width (in "bits") of one instruction processed (covered in Chapter 2). The chart in Figure 1–3 shows how, by 1980, this distinction became blurred. Second-generation microcomputers had minicomputer word sizes and could perform like large computers of the 1960s. Simultaneously, minicomputers were assuming mainframe roles.

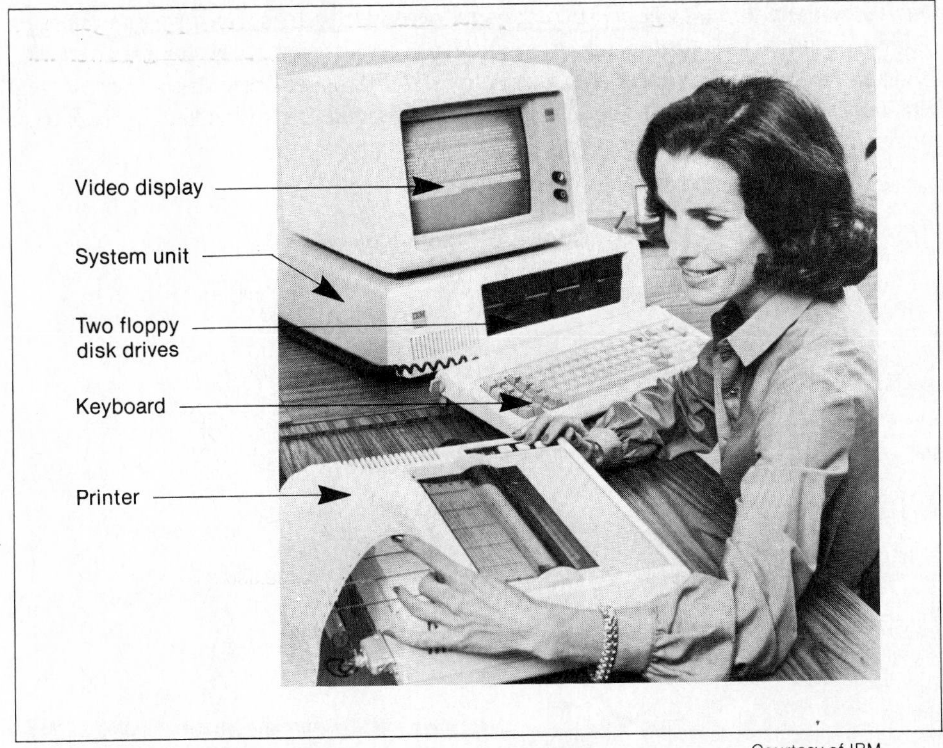

Courtesy of IBM

Figure 1-2 This typical small computer professional workstation is the IBM Personal Computer

Computer Word Size	Computer Type		
To 60 bits	Large mainframe computer	Super mini and large mainframe computer	
To 32 bits	Super mini	Mini and scientific micros	
16-bit	Mini	MICRO (second generation)	
8-bit	MICRO (first generation)		
	1975	1980	1985

Figure 1-3 Computer performance

Of the three, only microcomputers are designed to be used by one user as a self-sufficient workstation. This *stand-alone* use separates it from the other two.

Both minicomputers and mainframes are designed for multiuser use, as Figure 1–4 shows. Users have no computing power except that made available to them from

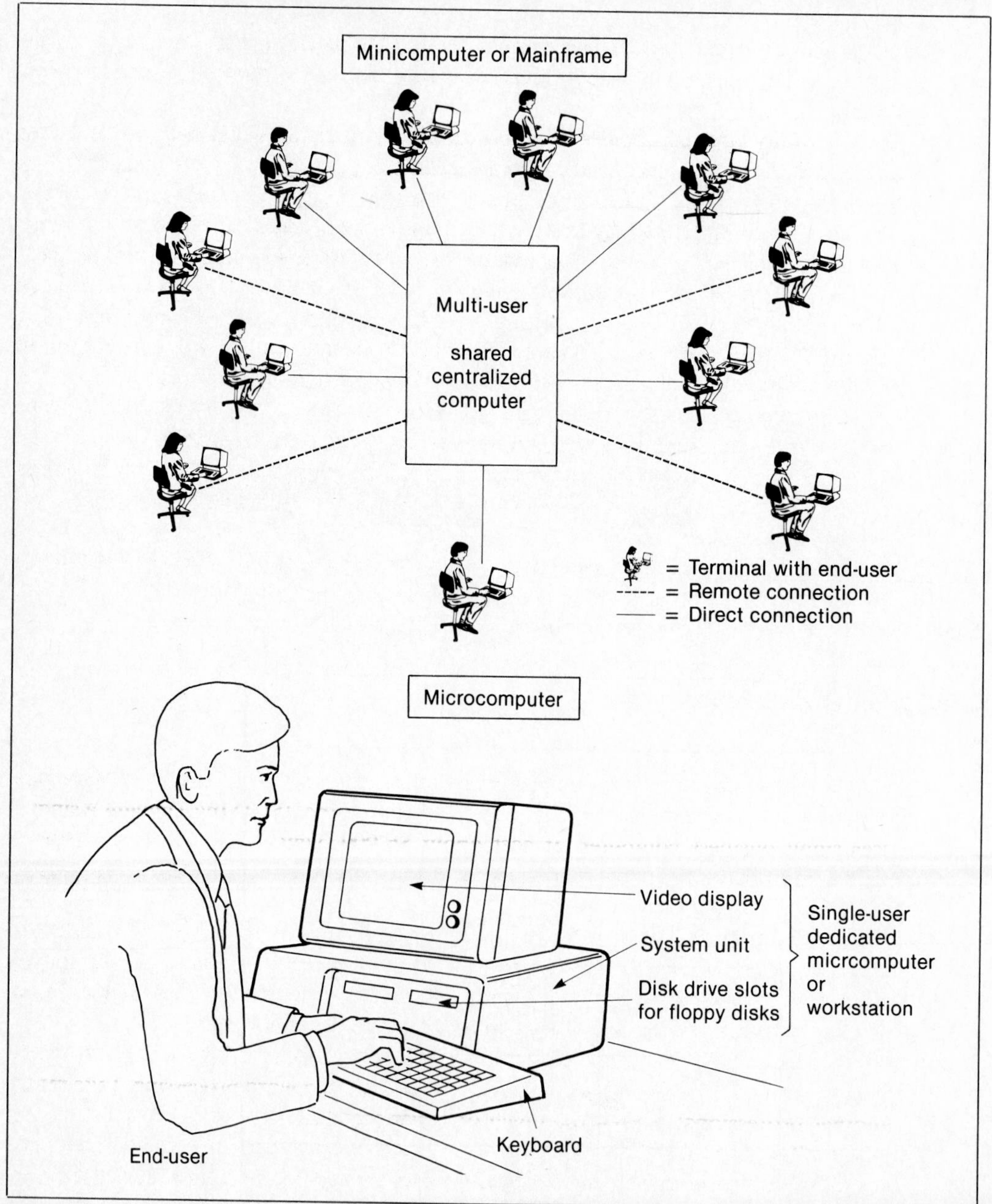

Figure 1–4 Comparison of a single-user microcomputer and a multiuser minicomputer or mainframe

the centralized computer. All users share the central computer using keyboards with TV-like displays called *terminals* or *CRTs* (*cathode ray tubes*). Such terminals that typically have no local computing capability are often called *dumb* terminals by the computer industry. End-user control is indirect and depends on the integrity of the central computer.

In an ironic twist, small computers are flexible enough to function as dumb terminals. This requires by-passing local computing power in order to *emulate* a so-called dumb terminal.

Many large companies need this capability. It enables employees to exchange information with the centralized corporate database. A *database* is an organized collection of records typically held in computer-readable form. Extracted portions of the database can be electronically transferred to a user's workstation. When the workstation's local computing power is reactivated, the user can manipulate the data as desired.

To give an example, brokers at one of the largest brokerage houses in the country all have workstations. Their workstations have been adapted to emulate dumb terminals. Whenever desired, a broker can extract client or stock information from the corporate database. Once the information is in the broker's local computer, it can be manipulated with whatever *software* the broker has. *Software* is the computerist's term for *programs* that can make the general-purpose computer do specific end-user jobs.

One job might be word processing. Brokers might electronically write letters to clients incorporating information from the database. Alternatively, they might electronically create a spreadsheet of rows and columns to calculate the return on clients' portfolios. The spreadsheet result also could be incorporated into the electronic letter. The workstation printer then prints the letter automatically.

SINGLE-USER ENVIRONMENTS

The prototype small computer environment is a single-user workstation. Mr. Williams, a marketing manager at Sporting Goods Distributors, Inc. (SGD Inc.) bought a single-user small business computer. It cost about $6,000, which falls within the typical $5,000–$10,000 range for professional-grade desktop computers. Portables that do the same thing cost less.

When he installed all the *hardware*, his workstation resembled the one shown in Figure 1–2. *Hardware* is the physical part of a computer. It contrasts with *software*, which is the nonphysical part. Hardware and software are often collectively called a *system*, although the term is often applied to each separately.

Mr. Williams wanted to do financial planning using an electronic spreadsheet. He also wanted to so some electronic report writing using word processing. Like many another professional, he felt the pinch of fewer secretaries.

To do both word processing and electronic spreadsheets, he researched and evaluated competitive software application packages. An *application* is another term for software that does an end-user task. Eventually he bought those most suited to his personal requirements.

Each application came on a floppy disk which resembles a five inch flexible phonograph record. It was accompanied by a three-ring binder containing a step-by-step User Guide. Special tutorial programs were included on the disks. They helped him learn to use the applications. They enormously shortened his learning process compared to using the manuals alone.

To use the disk-based programs, he had to transfer, or *load*, a copy of the desired disk program into the computer's memory. Memory is also called *random access memory*

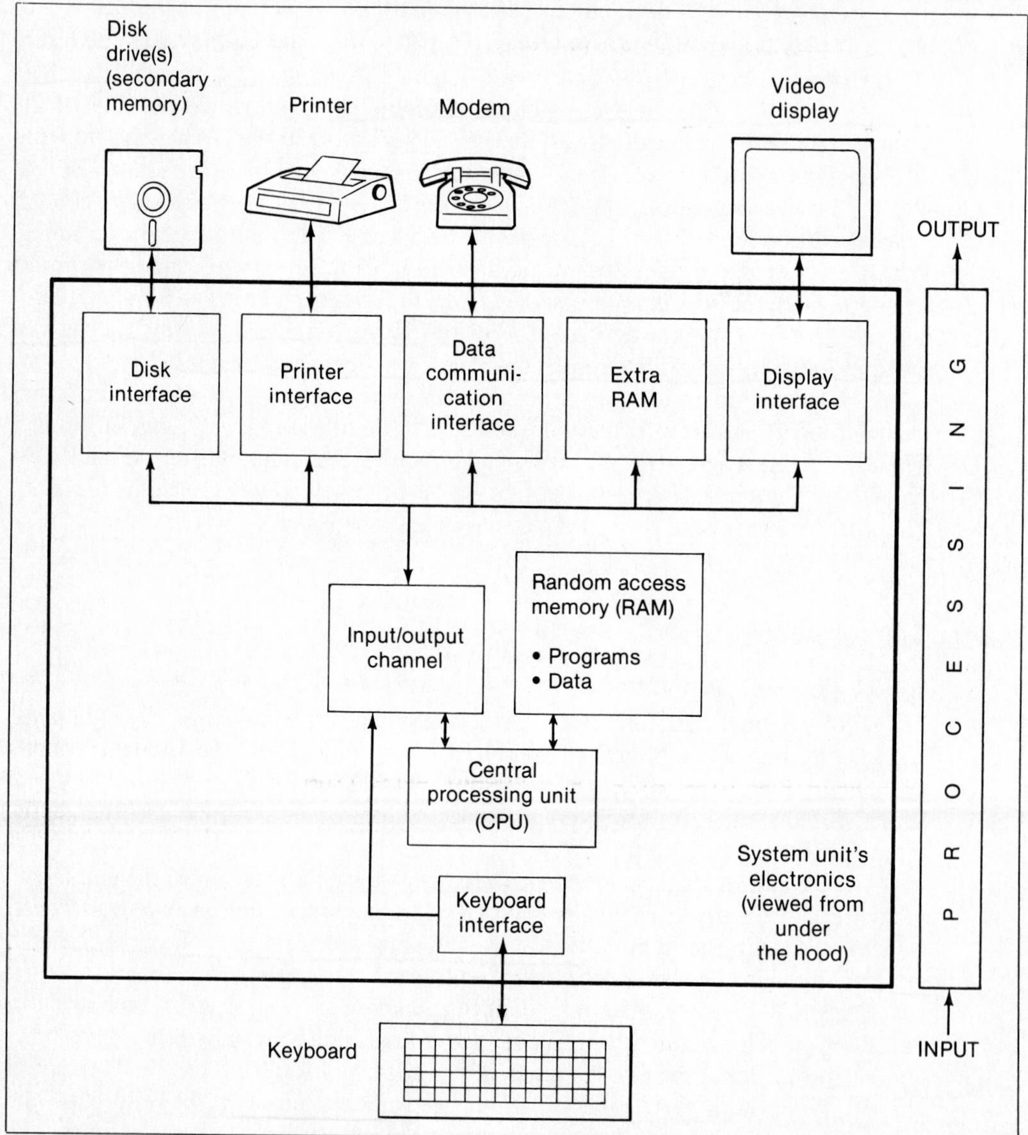

Figure 1-5 Symbolic relationship of hardware to the input-processing-output cycle

(RAM). Once the program was loaded, the computer could execute the program.

The computer's central processing unit (CPU) controls program execution. Figure 1-5 shows what goes on under the hood, so to speak, of Mr. Williams' computer. It indicates how computer operations flow from keyboarded input, through system unit processing, to final output, which presents a range of choices.

To examine a word processing application, for example, the first thing Mr. Williams does is to turn the system unit's power switch on and insert the application disk into one disk drive. A menu of options, like the one in Figure 1-6, appears on the display asking for a selection. He types E for edit, which the User Guide indicates is the option for typing a document or letter.

To put the menu on the screen, the central processing unit begins executing the first of many sequentially ordered program instructions. It fetches one program instruction at a time from the program copy in memory to act on it. If it says to display another menu on the screen, it sends the menu to the display. If the next instructions say to accept keyboard entry, the keyboard is scanned for input.

When through typing, Mr. Williams wants the document printed. He summons the menu and enters P for print. The CPU alerts the input/output controller, which wakes the printer. The CPU then transfers a copy of the document from memory to the printer. All this takes place silently and at the speed of light under the hood of the system unit.

Storing the document on disk generates a similar chain of events. The only difference is that the input/output channel controller addresses the disk instead of the printer.

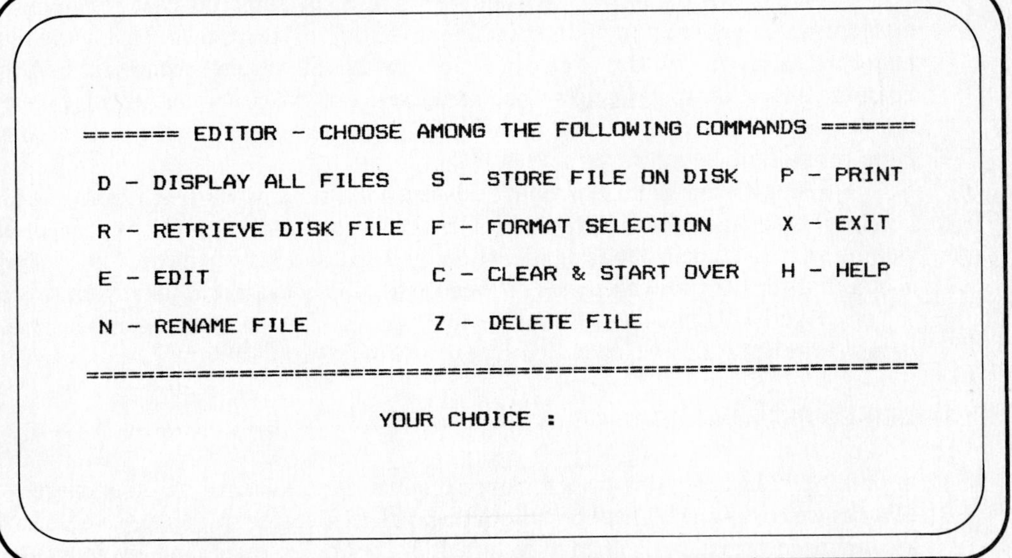

Adaptation of Volkswriter software with permission of Lifetree Software, Inc.

Figure 1-6 Sample word processing menu

Should Mr. Williams want to send the document to a remote computer, perhaps for deposit in someone's electronic mailbox, it is as easy as sending the document to his own disk drive. It takes a few more steps, but using his telephone connected to a device known as a modem (discussed in Chapter 12), the CPU sends the document over the telepone line to some other remote computer.

Events are similar at the remote computer end. The CPU is interrupted by the data communication interface. It then accepts communicated data into its own memory. In other words, the two connecting computers mirror each other in basic capability. All computers, regardless of size, function much the same way as Mr. Williams' personal workstation.

Mr. Williams subscribed to a so-called *public information utility*, sometimes referred to as a *videotex* utility, that sells electronic mail services. The service enables him to deposit mail there for traveling sales staff members. He knows they could dial into the service, using their portable computers, to read their mail on the computer display at their leisure. They also deposit mail there for him. No longer are they all engaged in telephone tag trying to find each other in the office.

The information utility is a large mainframe computer. In order to use it, Mr. Williams had to buy more software called a *data communication package*. It made his computer emulate a dumb terminal. It was no different from the software that some corporate users need to get into their corporate database.

He used the same software to dial into a large public bibliographic *on-line database* to do some market research. Doing library research from his desk saved him hours of travel and search time. By contrast, doing it manually he could not hope to have had access to so rich a store of information.

Had he wanted to, Mr. Williams could also have used his data communications software to connect to another remote workstation like his own. He had no real business reason to do so. But as an experiment, he did call to view the message bulletin board on a local computer club's small computer. The exercise was interesting to see how impossible it is for a user to perceive a difference between a small and large computer connection.

Using a message bulletin board was much like running word processing, sending electronic mail, or doing a large percentage of all computer applications. It involves viewing an initial menu, choosing an option, perhaps getting a submenu, and making another choice. These are called *menu-driven* applications and are easy for anyone to use.

Figure 1–7 symbolically illustrates the alternate ways Mr. Williams uses his small computer workstation. All have opened new ways of doing business more productively.

MULTIUSER ENVIRONMENTS

In time, SGD Inc. installed workstations similar to Mr. Williams' on other executive desks as well as in the billing and accounting offices. Because of the large volume of accounting information that had to be stored, like customer, order, and inventory item records, a so-called *hard disk* was needed. The one bought could store 20 million characters of information at once compared to less than half a million on one floppy disk.

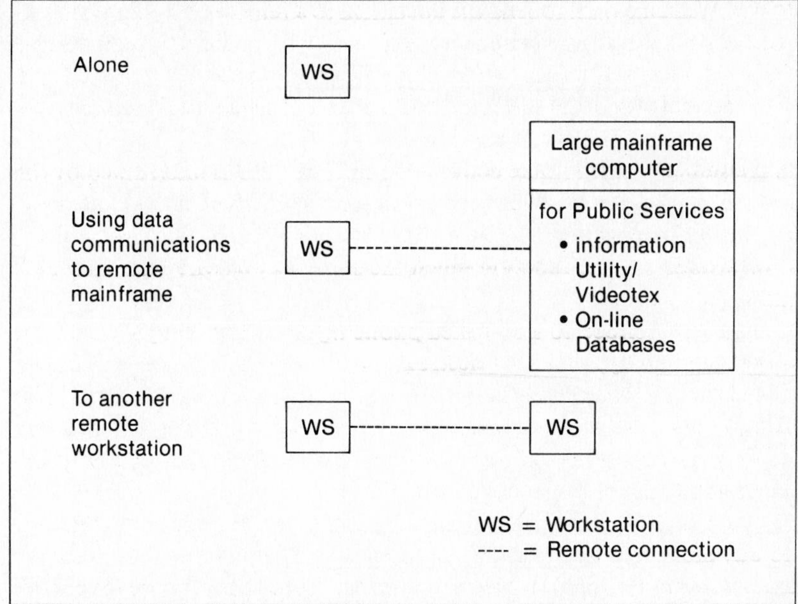

Figure 1-7 Single-user environments

Now the problem was how to share the information resident on the hard disk with the accounting workstations. All executives also wanted equal access to the latest updated company database records.

Local Area Networks

The solution was a *local area network* (LAN). It allows multiuser sharing especially of database information. It also allows sharing expensive *peripherals. Peripherals* are anything interfaced to the system unit like disk, printer, and data communication devices. Most local area networked organizations share at least disk and printer devices.

Creating a local area network at SGD Inc. required buying additional hardware and software. A network interface was needed for each workstation. It was a small board of electronics that fit into a slot next to all the other interfaces in the workstation's system unit. A physical cable linked the hardware, as diagrammed in Figure 1-8. Finally, software that was part of the deal made everything work in harmony.

Mr. Williams' personal workstation remained unchanged, as it should, by the additional capability. He was still able to have his own floppy disks or even a hard disk if he chose. He still kept his personal printer. In other words, with ideal local area networking, the integrity of the personal workstation is not violated. It still fundamentally remains a single-user workstation.

Workstation use also remains unchanged from a user's perspective. A few new commands might have to be learned, but everything else functions as it did before. Actual

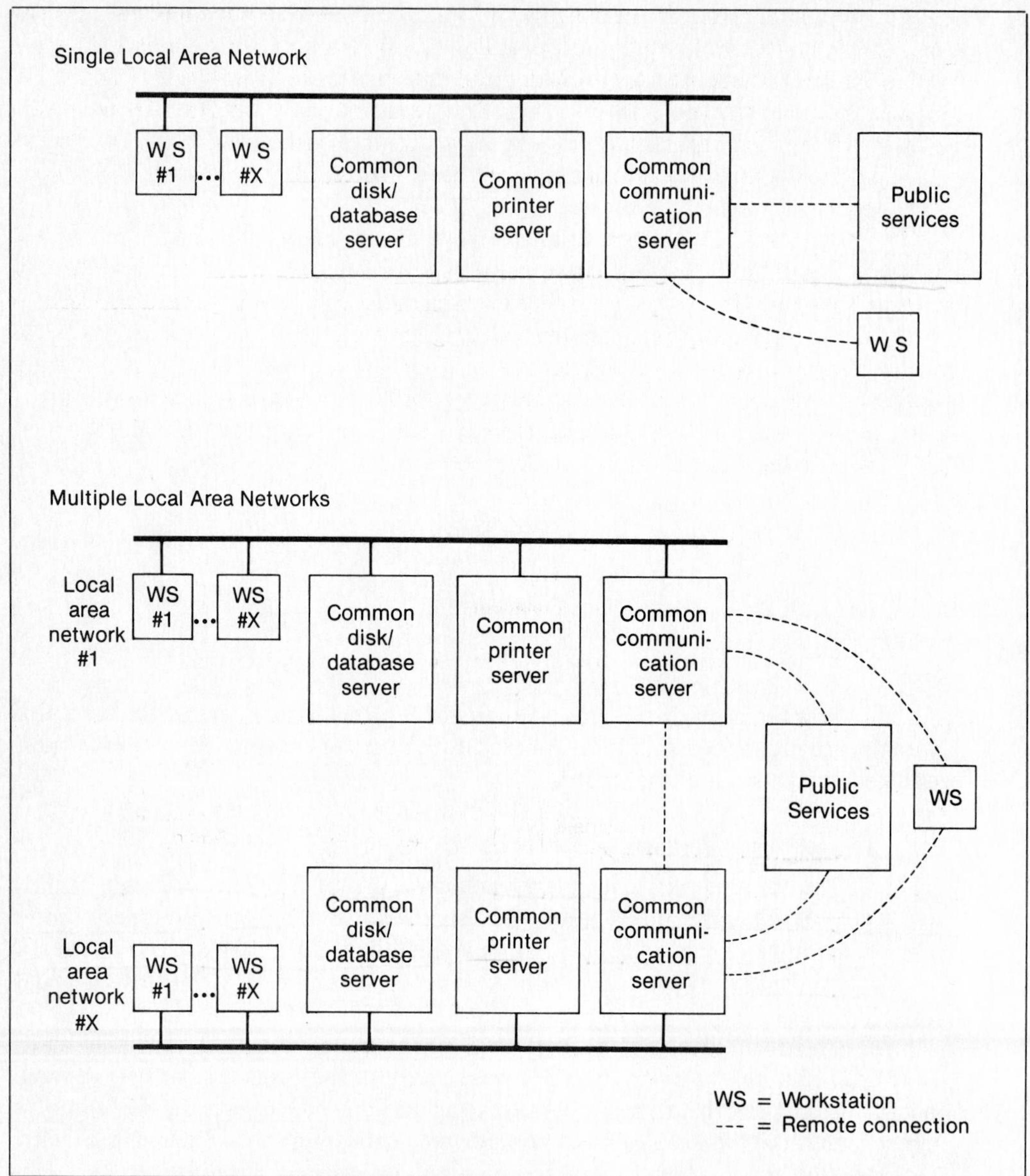

Figure 1-8 Multiuser environments for sharing data and peripherals

resource sharing is handled by software while the user remains unaware of the underlying electronics that make it all happen.

Should SGD Inc. acquire another company and install a local area network there, it could link the two. Figure 1-8 schematically shows this multiple network relationship.

Another alternative existed that SGD Inc. considered. It was a multiuser system like the computer configuration shown in Figure 1-4. The only difference is that it now had a centralized microcomputer with dumb terminals instead of a centralized mini- or mainframe computer. This setup is vulnerable should the centralized computer fail. Performance often degrades as more terminals share the same centralized computer. But for some organizations with only a few linked users, this solution may be less expensive than local area networking.

By contrast, with ideal local area networking, the failure of one workstation or server should not bring the entire network down. Adding workstations or servers should have no effect on performance characteristics in a well organized network.

For large companies, like the brokerage firm already mentioned, the networking of computers is essential to accommodate their new organizational structure. They, like other companies, have moved away from a traditional pyramid organizational structure. In the traditional pyramid organization, as charted in Figure 1-9, job functions are clearly defined and vertical reporting relationships set.

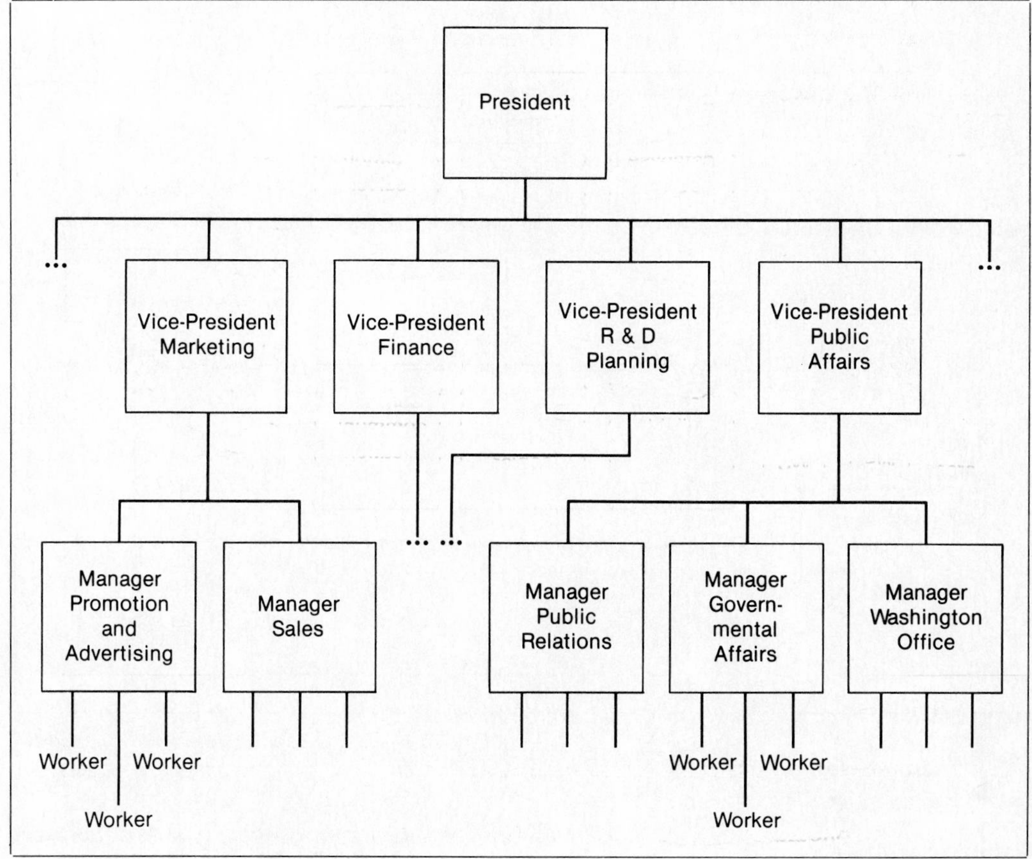

Figure 1-9 Typical pyramid organizational structure

Their new matrix organizational structure, like the one charted in Figure 1-10, is characterized by many dashed-line organizational relationships. Job functions and responsibilities spread laterally across the organization. Decisions are no longer made individually, but must be reviewed with peer groups to determine their effect on all. The result is a dramatic increase in the amount of correspondence and meetings required at all levels of management.

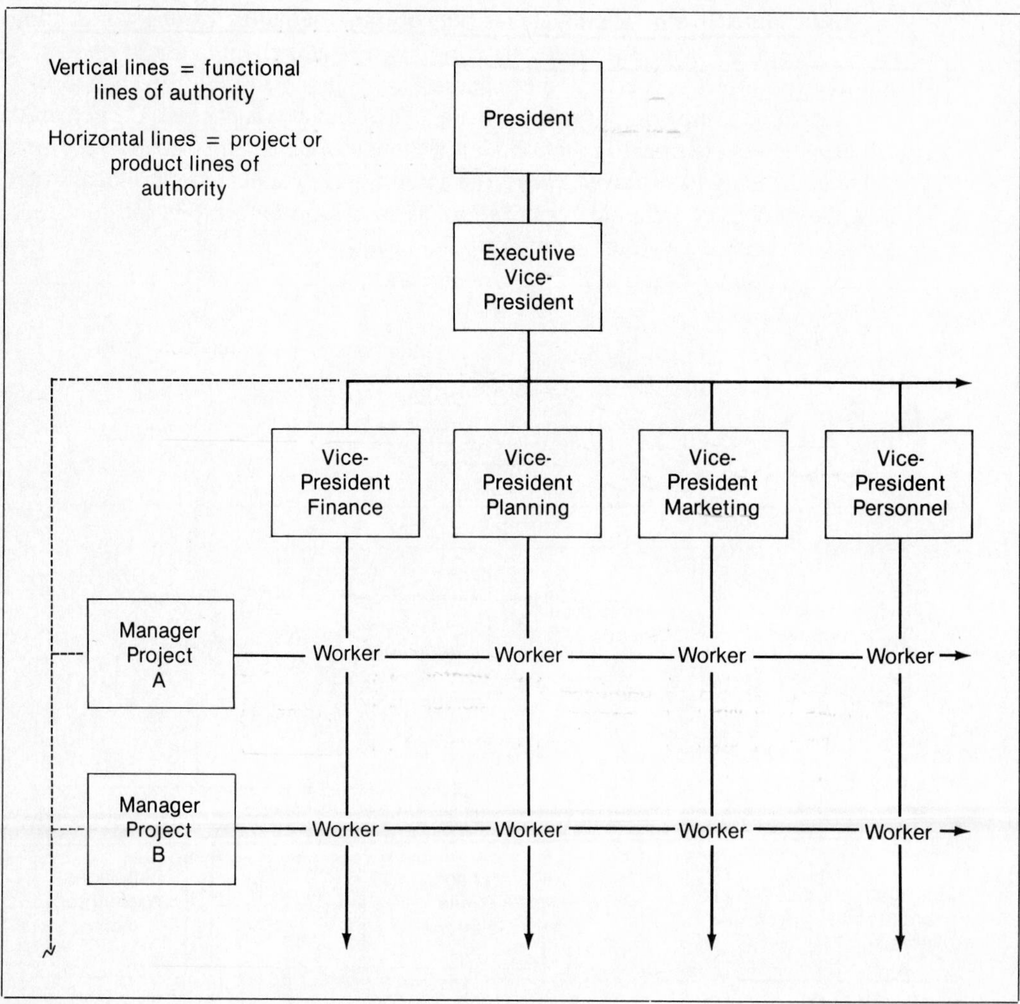

Figure 1-10 Typical matrix organizational structure

Wide Area Networks

These same executive workstations are also linked to the corporate mainframe. This remote computer link allows workstations to participate in a wide area network, as illustrated in Figure 1-11.

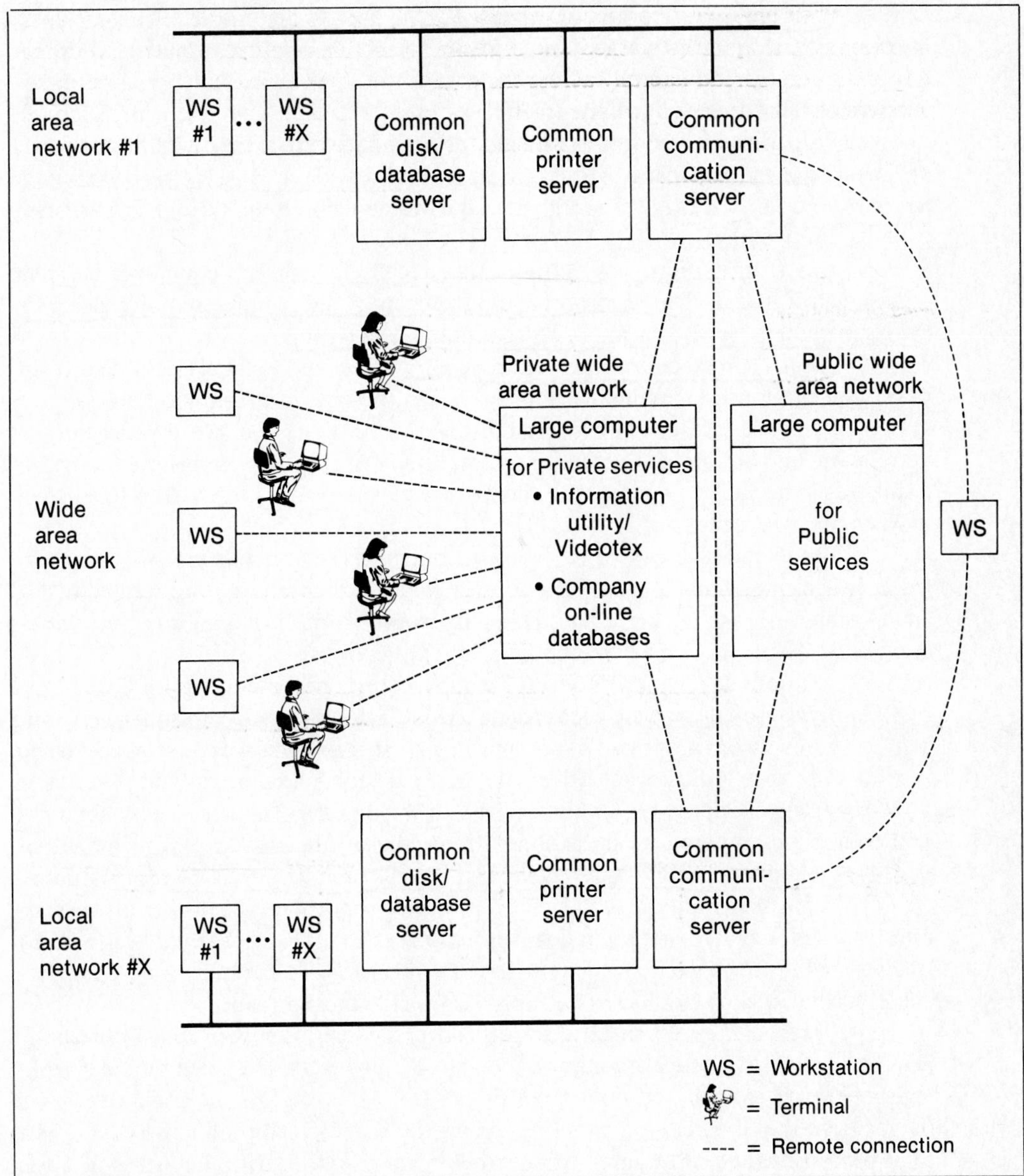

Figure 1-11 A multiuser environment that combines wide and local area networks

Part of the difference in the two networking schemes is distance and orientation. Local area networks remain confined to connecting workstations within a building or a campus. Typically they are completely microcomputer-oriented. On the other hand, wide area networks range across town, across the country, and across the globe. Typically they are mainframe-oriented.

Wide area networks are distinguished by a need to dial, as Mr. Williams does, into the vast telephone network system. Existing telephone links carry data to its destination. The largest companies have private wide area networks and privately leased telephone lines for heavy volume traffic.

Properly equipped workstations at the brokerage firm function as three separate devices: a data processor, a word processor, and a wide area networked computer terminal. The hardware savings are tangible, but the intangible benefit comes from sharing valuable information.

That information, as mentioned, is typically the corporate database resident on the mainframe. But with corporate electronic mail and computer conferencing on the mainframe as well, sharing takes on another dimension.

These services, collectively called *videotex* offerings by some, are similar to services such as those Mr. Williams enjoys through the public information utility.

One executive at the brokerage firm, for example, uses word processing to develop a memo outlining the agenda for a meeting. Through the electronic mail facility available on the wide area network, she can send the memo to interested recipients not on the local network.

The memo also can go to people throughout the organization who are away from their office. Traveling peer group members can dial into the mainframe, using any portable or home computer, to get messages from their employee electronic mailboxes. They can as easily compose and send answers.

Decisions that cannot wait for formal meetings become the subject of a *computer conference* on the private wide area network. *Computer conferencing* is an ongoing conversation between interested parties who log on at their personal convenience to add new material or to critique each other's ideas. Participants need not attend at the same time. They can participate, even while traveling, with portable computers. The chairperson of the computer conference sets deadlines for responses. The brokerage firm and others that use it claim computer conferencing significantly reduces decision-making time.

If a broker wants to send a client some electronic mail, the broker often sends it to the client's mailbox on a public information system. The client might respond by leaving mail in the broker's public mailbox at the utility. In a similar way, computer conferences could be conducted with parties outside the company.

To repeat the recurring theme, little difference exists between the way businesspersons in a large or small organization use small computers. Even common networking services are available to both types of users. A good part of the similarity lies in the fact that the small computer is the business user's personal productivity tool. The same professional needs require support whether the user works in a large organization or a one-person company.

GETTING INFORMED

Many sources exist to help potential users get informed about small business computers. They include books, periodicals, user's groups, shows, exhibitions, and conferences, among other sources.

Books

Many computer books focus on hardware acquisition. Some cover both hardware and software.

Several loose-leaf binder subscription services exist that cost one to several hundreds of dollars a year for updates. Large companies and computer consultants use them, and business libraries may carry them. One that is generally informative is *Management of Small Computer Systems* by Datapro.

Other books, periodicals, and general resource and reference material are listed at the ends of chapters in this book. All relate to the specialized topic covered in the chapter, such as data communications or electronic spreadsheets. Full publisher or supplier information is listed in Appendix A.

Periodicals

One of the best sources to keep informed is current periodicals. Most are available at local computer stores. Some useful general publications are:

Small Business Computers
Desktop Computing
Personal Computing
Interface Age

Many periodicals are dedicated to individual computer products and product lines. They cover hardware and software topics and assume a reader is somewhat familiar with the products endorsed. They aim at a more sophisticated reader and include:

PUBLICATION	PRODUCT
PC Magazine	IBM products
Personal Computer Age	IBM products
PC World	IBM products
Microcomputing 80	Tandy Corporation products

Another category of publications aims at a computer-literate reader but is not product specific. Some of these publications include:

Byte
Infoworld Newspaper
Mini-Micro Systems
Datamation
Computer Decisions

The last three in this list are free to qualified subscribers. Qualifying subscribers usually belong to organizations using several computers and have the purchasing power to support the magazine's advertisers.

User Groups

Local community user groups that began years ago as hobbyist clubs have matured to where business people attend their monthly meetings to swap problems and share solutions. Often groups are formed around product lines.

Groups usually have speakers at monthly meetings. Some invite hardware and software manufacturer representatives to talk about their products. Usually manufacturers make their products available to group members at a discount. Ongoing discount volume purchases are also usually available.

Groups often form subgroups known as *S*pecial *I*nterest *G*roups (SIGs). SIGs on data communications, corporate uses, word processing, graphics, new users, and the like reflect special interests of group members. SIGs carry on in much the same way as the parent organization. They have regular meetings with speakers and often offer specialized courses to others.

A user group newsletter keeps members informed of organization and SIG activities, officers, contact numbers, group buying deals, and meeting notices. Some newsletters resemble regular periodicals with ads and articles.

Members often contribute software to the group that is offered free to other members except for the cost of the distribution disk, or about $5. It is called *public domain software* and frequently travels from group to group. Much of it is far from commercial quality and is of interest only to programmers and hobbyists.

Companies of all sizes have adopted the idea and sponsor their own user groups. Managers responsible for the smooth integration of small computers into their organization have also banded together to form local groups. They swap ideas on how to manage the evolution of small computers into their formerly all large-computer-oriented organizations. They also look for common and shared solutions to buying, tutorial classes, and the like.

Product-specific periodicals usually carry directories listing user groups. They also give contact information. Some give group news items. Other user group information is usually available from local computer dealers.

Shows, Exhibitions, and Conferences

Computer shows, exhibitions, and conferences are often held on local, regional, and national levels. They are a good way to see a collection of the latest hardware and software available. Usually entrance fees for vendor- and user-group-sponsored events are nominal. Conferences or seminars usually feature speakers followed by audience question-and-answer sessions. Some events sponsor all-day workshops and tutorials. Fees for these services often are several hundred dollars.

Periodical directories include lists of shows, exhibits, and conferences.

Other Sources

Hardware and software manufacturers offer free literature to anyone who writes for it. Publications often have insert postcards for requesting free vendor-advertised literature. Free literature is also available at local computer stores and shows.

This literature often presents criteria for evaluation. While vendor product bias is evident, such literature can be informative. Some of it includes technical specifications that can be challenging to nontechnicians.

Manufacturers also publish directories of software and provide toll-free 800 numbers for user support. Their directories often include software produced by *third parties*. *Third party* is an industry term for independent, nonmanufacturer-developed products and services. Manufacturers are usually not directly associated with third-party suppliers.

The medical, printing, construction, wholesale, retail, and other industries inform members of computer-related topics. They do this through trade publications, professional associations, conferences, shows, and exhibits, among other outlets. No better contact exists for a new user than someone in a similar industry who already uses a small business computer.

SPECIFYING REQUIREMENTS

Specifying requirements is the first step in an orderly, systematic approach to computer acquisition. The steps are:

1. Specify business application requirements.
2. Locate software that comes closest to meeting requirements.
   - Evaluate candidate software
   - Select the best
3. Locate the hardware configuration that will secure the most benefits from the software.
   - Evaluate candidate hardware
   - Select the best
4. Implement the new system.

Mr. Williams used application checklists similar to those in this book to help specify requirements.

Mr. Williams specified, for example, that he needed a word processing application capable of doing short letters and documents under twenty pages. He required features like underlining, fixed headings, and the like.

Another user may need a word processor capable of doing 600-page manuscripts with subscripts and superscripts. Specifying needs helps focus and narrow an application software search. It also can prevent buying a disaster.

Even following application checklists to the letter, some small computer users have ended up with disasters. In some cases this stems not from an application's limitations, but from the user's failure to identify the correct problem in need of a solution.

In one case, an order processing and invoicing application was purchased to speed up an order backlog problem. The package handled all the volume the user needed with room to spare. But it did not solve the problem. It turns out that poorly maintained equipment in the machine shop was slowing down production. It caused the order backlog problem. Speeding up order processing with a small computer simply helped aggravate this situation.

Many other companies wanting to automate often do not have orderly business procedures in place. Some applications have, in fact, ended up automating inadequate procedures inherited from existing manual systems. One company first had to revise a disorderly pricing policy before any computer application could contribute to smoother operations.

Users who need help to specify application requirements can hire a professional consultant. Consultants can define business requirements and suggest ways to change internal workflow and policies to enhance productivity. They locate software that closest fits a client's business needs or can arrange for and monitor custom programming. They will further recommend the hardware configuration that would secure the most benefits from the software. Finally, they structure the conversion to the new system and assist in implementation.

ACQUIRING SYSTEMS

Users can buy small business computer hardware and software from several sources. Consultants, independent system vendors, original equipment manufacturers (OEMs), local retail stores, and mail order houses all can provide working systems.

Independent System Vendors and OEMs

Both independent system vendors and OEMs combine hardware and software, often from various manufacturers, and resell them as a *turnkey* system. Theoretically, all a user has to do to use such a system is to turn the key and go. It does require that the user first learn how to work the turnkey system.

OEM is an unfortunate name, because OEMs do not typically manufacture. They integrate hardware manufactured by others and usually add application software. Software is either their own custom product or a commercial product. Sometimes OEMs and independent system vendors are appropriately called *turnkey vendors* or *system integrators*.

When invited, a turnkey vendor typically does a *feasibility study*. From the vendor's viewpoint, this study determines if available vendor software fits user requirements. It also verifies whether a user has money to pay and is ready to sign a contract.

The software they sell is usually accounting-related and not available over-the-counter at local retail stores. Often it is also industry-specific. Some vendors have spent years selling computer systems to users in one or more industries.

This approach requires a considerable investment of user time as each vendor in turn examines present operations. But the exchange with vendors quickly educates a user about small comptuers and their applications.

These vendors can be found through industry contacts, professional trade association listings, other users, and listings found in such software directories as:

Directory of Microcomputer Software, Datapro.

ICP Software Directory, International Computer Programs.

PC Clearinghouse Software Directory, PC Clearinghouse.

Software Catalog: Microcomputers, Imprint Software. Also available in an on-line database through DIALOG.

Many directories are not readily available because they cost over $100 each. They also have the problems of containing only a fraction of the software on the market and carrying out-of-date listings. Consultants subscribe to them or can direct interested persons to where they might be available.

Local Retail Dealers

Local computer retail stores carry hardware and software for the do-it-yourself user. Some offer service as well. In many cases, the hand-holding they can provide to a new user more than makes up for the higher prices charged compared to mail order buying.

Mr. Williams, and most new computer users, appreciate the concept of hand-holding. One of the limitations of using computers is the personal commitment needed to learn how to use them. Some users need hours to set up and use the hardware and software, others require weeks, and some never get going. On his way to reaching a comfort level where he was productive, Mr. Williams needed telephone and in-person store visits to get through some easily resolved start-up problems.

Mr. Williams bought his first workstation from a local dealer. The dealer also carried all the professional support software he needed, such as a choice of word processing, electronic spreadsheet, and data communication packages.

In comparison shopping he found that stores concentrated on certain hardware and software products. One store did not carry a top-of-the-line computer, he learned later, because they could make no profit on it. Another store did not carry a popular word processing product because none of their sales staff knew how to use it. Other stores, he learned, gave terrible after-sales support. So he found picking the right dealer as critical as selecting the right product.

Mail Order

Mail ordering is cheaper but can leave one without the personal support especially needed by new users. Everything a workstation needs to function is advertised for sale in the computer periodicals already mentioned. Some manufacturers offer their own product catalogs.

Some mail order houses offer an 800 toll-free telephone number. Where it exists, this makes mail order buying a more viable alternative. It is especially useful for buying software by the more seasoned computer user.

Hardware is another story. If mail order hardware malfunctions, it may be rejected for service by a local dealer. It could mean shipping the malfunctioning part for repair. If that takes one week, a user must evaluate the trade-off of being *down,* a computerist's term for not working for a length of time.

A disadvantage of using computers is that they do malfunction. Stories exist where disks and printers figuratively, as well as literally, go up in smoke at critical moments.

Even a computer out of service for a few hours can render certain users helpless. This occurred to one user without a compatible backup unit who wanted to run off spreadsheets and pie charts for a meeting that afternoon. All data was adequately supported with a security set of backup disks. But the computer did not work. Reproducing material manually was impossible unless the meeting was postponed a week. The hopeless feeling that overcomes anyone in such a position is debilitating.

Putting hardware on a service maintenance contract with the manufacturer or an independent service company is usually needed. Service companies typically offer carry-in repair with a 48-hour turnaround. They also offer a pickup alternative that costs more for the same 48-hour service. The most expensive option is on-site service, but many businesses need this. With such service malfunctioning parts are replaced and repairs take only a couple of hours at most.

The problem is that service contracts do not usually cover nonstandard or unpopular hardware. Some mail order hardware is nonstandard, and so it will have to be return-shipped for service. As long as a user is aware of the alternatives, an informed buying decision is possible.

Company In-House Stores

Large companies that encourage individual professional use of small computers occasionally have in-house stores. Their purpose is to control the brands of computers and software purchased so that a level of software and hardware compatibility exists. Compatibility enables the swapping of software at least by disk if workstations are not networked. This is important where brokers, for example, have written customized software that is useful by others.

Company in-house stores also provide customary retail store services and supplies. Some conduct tutorials and offer maintenance service.

SELF TEST

1. Describe the difference between a small business computer, as the term is used in this book, and a minicomputer or mainframe computer.
2. What is the difference between a terminal and a video display?

3. Describe the environment options available to a single user.
4. Compare the networking of multiple users in a campus-like environment versus those in a large corporate environment.
5. Describe sources available to help a potential user get more informed about small business computers.
6. Identify the steps associated with an orderly systematic approach to computer acquisition.
7. Describe five sources for acquiring a small computer.

EXERCISES

1. *C. Davidson Case.* After Charles Davidson bought a small business computer, he found many computer publications interested him. Instead of subscribing to all of them, he asks you to investigate which ones are available at the library.
   a. Make a list of all the computer periodicals your library subscribes to.
   b. Classify the periodicals according to the following categories:
      General business-oriented publications
      Product specific publications
      Computer-literate audience publications
   c. Examine one periodical from each category and identify article topics that overlap across publications.
   d. Pick one topic and read it in all three publications. Make a summary of your investigation that specifies for each article:
      - Publication examined and article title
      - A short summary with a note about readability and a list of things you did not understand

   Recommend which of the three you think would be most helpful to a new computer user.
2. Mr. Davidson liked your library investigatory work and asked you to do another project. This involved finding out about the local computer user group.
   a. Visit a local computer user group meeting. Write a report on what transpires there. Make a list of what you did not undertand.
   b. At the end of your computer study, review the list to see how many items you can answer yourself.
3. Visit a local computer show, exhibition, or conference. Make a written or oral report about your field trip. Include in the report:
   - Hardware you liked the best and why
   - Software you thought would be especially useful for personal productivity enhancement

RESOURCES AND REFERENCES

Resources and references are listed throughout the text of Chapter 1.

Books

BARCOMB, DAVID, *Office Automation,* Digital, 1981.

BLUMENTHAL, SUSAN, *Understanding and Buying a Small-Business Computer,* Sams, 1982.

COHEN, JULES A., *How to Computerize Your Small Business,* Prentice-Hall, 1980.
HEISER, DICK, *Real Managers Use Personal Computers,* Que, 1983.
International Microcomputer Dictionary, Sybex, 1983.
ISSHIKI, KOICHIRO R., *Small Business Computers: A Guide to Evaluation and Selection,* Prentice-Hall, 1982.
MADRON, THOMAS, *Microcomputers in Large Organizations,* Prentice-Hall, 1983.
MCCALEB, ROBERT B., *Small Business Computer Primer,* Dilithium, 1982.
Management's Guide to Desktop Computers, Dartnell, 1983.
Microcomputer Market Place, Dekotek, 1983.
SEGAL, HILLEL and JESSE BERST, *How to Select Your Small Computer,* Prentice-Hall, 1983.
SKEES, WILLIAM D., *Before You Invest in a Small Business Computer,* Lifetime Learning, 1982.

Loose-Leaf and Other References

Automated Office Solutions, Datapro.
EDP Solutions, Datapro.
Electronic Office Management and Technology, Auerbach.
Reports on Office Systems, Datapro.

Periodicals

Data Processing Digest
MIS Week
Office Administration and Automation
The Office
Popular Computing
Reference
Small System World
Today's Office

2

HARDWARE

Few enormous differences exist between small computers in the same category. To build one, manufacturers, even IBM, take the same basic raw parts, assemble them, and put them into a system-unit type box. But each manufacturer's design team makes compromises in terms of features offered, overall performance, and price. Price usually dictates overall level of performance. To stay in the targeted price range, one team may decide to remove one feature in order to add another considered more essential. Users must decide which combination works best for them.

This chapter describes the basic hardware components of a personal professional-level small business computer. It follows Mr. Williams' systematic approach to the hardware buying decision. In doing so, it explains the relevance of each component. Components covered include the system unit and its peripheral devices, such as keyboard, display, disk drives, and printer. It reserves discussion of data communication and graphics hardware for separate chapters in this book.

SYSTEM BOARD

Mr. Williams' buying research convinced him of the need to buy a state-of-the-art small computer. He fully understood that anything he bought would be obsolete by the next regular new-product announcement. But probably the new product would be a different package of the same technology, if he chose right.

At the time he bought, a *16-bit* computer was considered state-of-the-art. What did "16-bit" mean? It referred to the processing power of the *central processing unit* (CPU). The CPU physically resides on the system board inside the floor of Mr. Williams' system unit. A diagram of the system board, often called the *motherboard,* appears in Figures 2–1 and 2–2.

Central Processing Unit

The system board contains a web of electronic circuity that controls all computer actions through the central processing unit. As Figure 2–1 shows, it consists of a tiny 16-bit microprocessor. Its fingernail size is concealed by a plastic housing measuring less than two inches by one inch. It resembles a centipede with its forty tiny gold pins that stick out underneath to attach it to the system board circuitry. The pins mesh

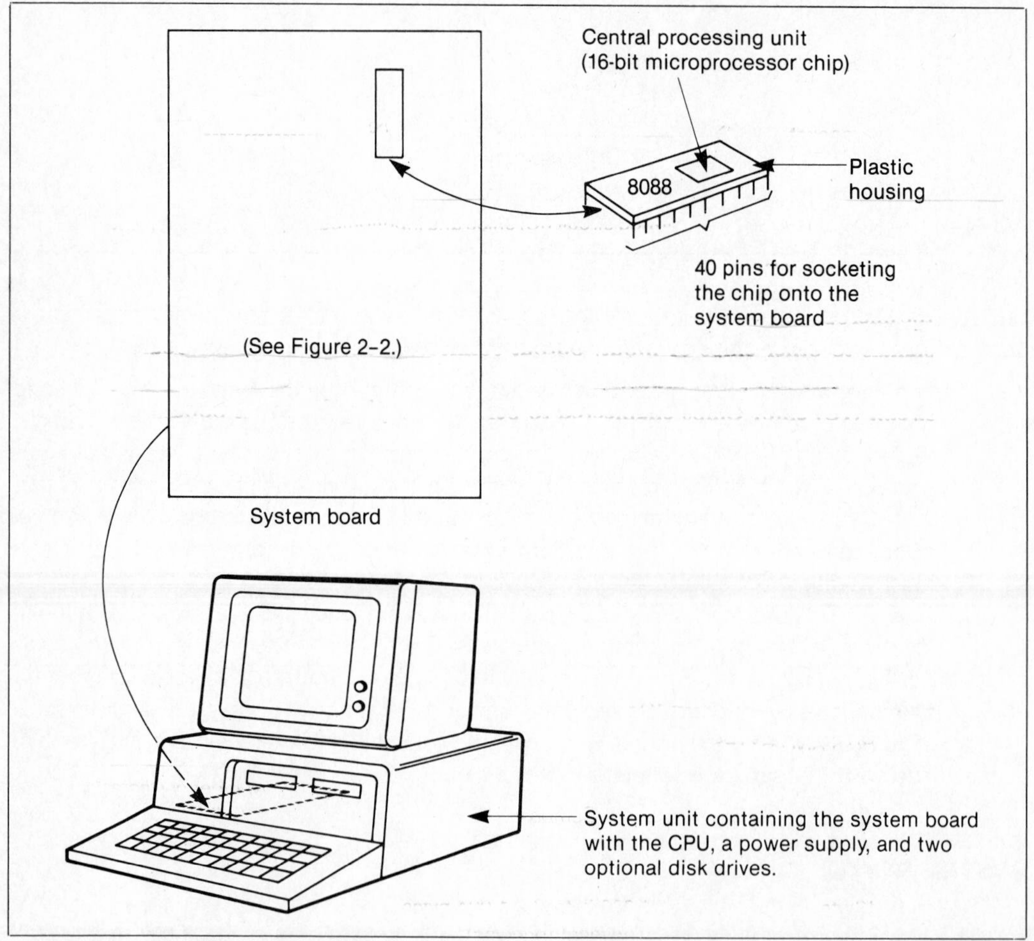

Figure 2–1 Relationship of system unit to system board to central processing unit.

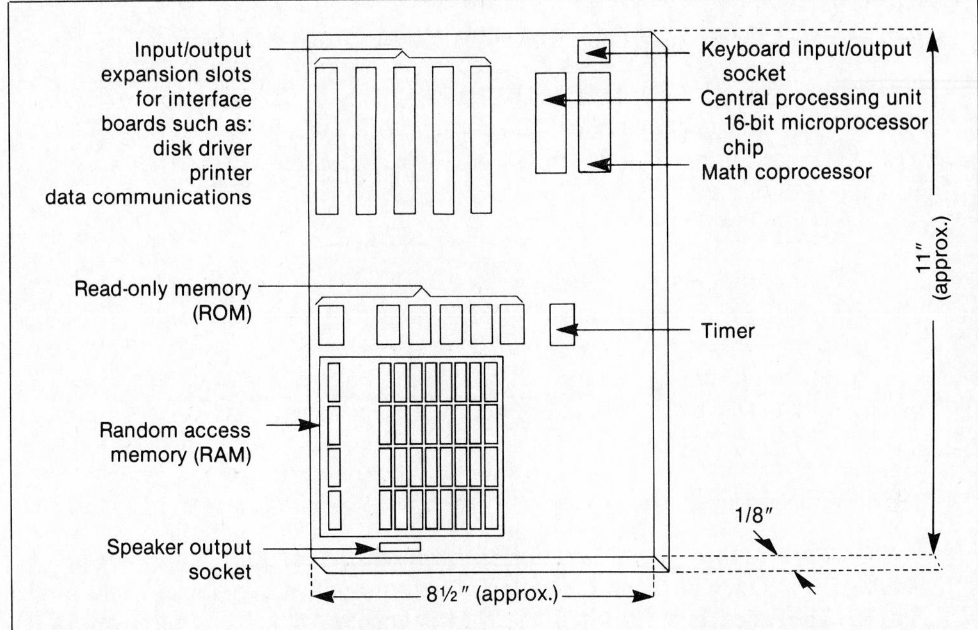

Figure 2–2 Diagram of selected integrated circuit (IC) chips and input/output expansion slots on the system board of the IBM Personal Computer. The actual size of the system board measures approximately 8½ × 11 inches (1/8 inch deep).

the microprocessor's circuitry with the circuitry on the system board. The pins send control signals to other chips or input/output connectors elsewhere on the board.

The computer industry calls the microprocessor, made of silicon, an *integrated circuit* (IC) chip. Chips engineered to perform varying functions populate the system board as shown in Figure 2–2.

Mr. Williams' CPU chip is called a 16-bit chip because it processes information 16 bits at a time. The computer deals only with *bits,* on or off electronic pulses that, in 8-bit combinations, have special meanings.

In order to process the letter "A," for example, after it is typed, it is converted to on and off signals, as shown in Figure 2–3. On or off states, illustrated by 1's and 0's, are all the computer understands. Its two states are called a *binary system,* and one digit is a *binary digit,* or *bit*. A group of eight bits is called a *byte*. The following table helps clarify the bit and byte relationship:

BITS AND BYTES

Unit	*Composed of*	*Number of Characters It Can Store*
bit	1 or 0	none
byte	8 bits	1
Kbyte	1,000 bytes (or 1,024 bytes without rounding)	1,000
64 Kbytes	64,000 bytes	64,000
Mbytes	1,000,000 bytes	1,000,000

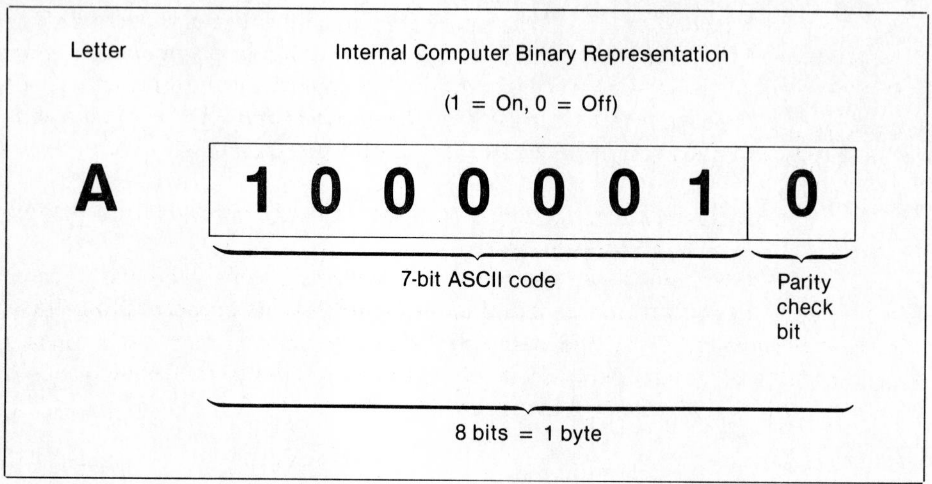

Figure 2-3 Internal computer binary representation of the letter "A" using the ASCII code

A *byte* is the fundamental unit the computer works with. It is made up of 7 bits that are a binary code representation of letters, numbers, characters, and special controls. The code scheme is called *ASCII* (pronounced ASSkey), an acronym for the *A*merican *S*tandard *C*ode for *I*nformation *I*nterchange. All small computers follow this code standard. The full code is available in Appendix B.

A final bit in an ASCII byte is the parity bit. It is a control bit to check on the accuracy of the byte. In the example in Figure 2–3, the *even parity* bit is 0. Because the one bits already add up to an even number, no parity bit needs to be added for an *even-parity* check. Any ASCII code not reconciled with its parity bit causes the computer to detect an error and halt operations because of a potential garbage data problem. It does not happen often with today's highly reliable microprocessors.

Parity checking is not a fool-proof checking technique. If two ASCII bits are reversed, the parity system would never detect the garbage data problem. Some computers use other accuracy tests to insure a high level of reliability.

Second-generation 16-bit small computers process two bytes at once. They are more powerful than first-generation 8-bit computers and work two to ten times faster than their 8-bit counterparts. The original Apple II computer that propelled small computer use is an 8-bit computer. Newer products like the Apple Corporation's Lisa, Tandy Corporation's Radio Shack TRS-16, Digital Equipment Corporation's Professional 325 and 350, and the IBM Personal Computer are all 16-bit computers. Popular 16-bit microprocessor chips are the Intel 8088 and 8086. The Motorola 68000 is a 32-bit chip used in the TRS-16 where it processes mostly 16-bit program instructions.

The number of bits a computer processes at once is called its *word size*. *Word size* is a classic way to compare computer performance. The chart in Chapter 1, Figure 1–2, shows the rapid advance in computer technology and performance as measured by word size. One *Computerworld* ad sums up the rapid small computer evolution this way: "If the auto industry had done what the computer industry has done in the last 30 years, a Rolls-Royce would cost $2.50 and get 2 million miles-per-gallon."

Scientifically oriented 32-bit computers are poularly called *number-crunchers*. Because scientific applications typically are *process-bound* to manipulate complex formulas, the 32-bit processing speed is appropriately applied. On the other hand, commercial business applications are typically *input/output-bound* with heavy data entry and printing. Increasing processing speed does not necessarily show up in increased performance.

In business applications, getting data in and out of the computer faster presents a greater challenge than processing speed.

Some 16-bit computers, like the one Mr. Williams bought, have what is called an *optional math coprocessor,* as indicated in Figure 2–2. Its purpose is to off-load number-crunching tasks from the main CPU. It can calculate numbers faster than the CPU—sometimes one hundred times faster—making a significant contribution to computer performance with some applications.

Memory

Mr. Williams had to decide how much *random access memory* (RAM) to buy. Random access memory is the place in the computer where programs and data must be resident before they are processed by the CPU. The amount of memory he bought depended in part on the largest application program to be resident there simultaneously with the *operating system* software. The *operating system* is part of *system software* and is covered in Chapter 3. It is necessary to make application software work.

Memory is temporary, volatile storage. If the computer power is turned off, everything in it is lost. That is why programs and data are permanently stored in familiar binary format on other nonvolatile devices, like floppy and hard disks. Whenever a program is needed, a copy of it is first loaded from a disk into memory and then processed.

Mr. Williams intended to use one package that required 256 Kbytes of memory. Memory requirements are published with software packages. The computer he bought came with 64 Kbytes, so he had to purchase the remainder as add-on memory. At the time, every 64 Kbytes increment cost about $50.

The first 64 Kbytes that came with the computer purchase price was located right on the system board, as shown in Figure 2–2. Each memory chip held 2 Kbytes, so the *on-board memory* added up to 64 Kbytes. The remainder came on another smaller board, like the one shown in Figure 2–4. It physically had to be placed in one of the *expansion slots* of the system board, as shown in Figure 2–2. *Add-on memory board* circuitry is interfaced with the system board's circuitry through pins, much like those on the CPU chips.

In Figure 2–2 there seems to be one chip too many in each of four rows which hold 16 Kbytes each. The chip on the left is performing a constant self-test on the other memory chips.

Every byte in random access memory, as the name implies, is randomly addressable. The CPU can instantly access any one of the 256,000 locations Mr. Williams' program requires. Each location stores 8 bits, or the equivalent of one character.

Eight of the CPU's pins are assigned to carry 8-bit data, 1 bit per pin, to its storage at a given RAM addresss location. Computerists distinguish this circuitry as the *data bus* versus the *address bus*. Twenty separate CPU pins are used to address memory

Courtesy of Amdek

Figure 2-4 An add-on memory expansion board populated with RAM integrated circuit (IC) chips, as well as chips for other functions

locations. If each address pin can carry one of two states, a total of 20 to the second power gives it an address capability of over one million locations. A chart listing the powers of two, which is useful when working with computer memory increments, is given in Appendix C.

Data passed on the data bus back and forth to memory locations could be program instructions or data, like characters in a letter prepared with a word processing application.

Other determinants of the amount of memory Mr. Williams needed were personal. He had to estimate the size of the largest electronic worksheet he would be creating. His application stored an entire worksheet in memory. Fortunately, his application gave suggested memory sizes compared to worksheet row and column dimensions.

His word processing application was also memory dependent. The more memory available, the larger the document that could be processed as a single unit without artificial linking.

Unlike random access memory or RAM, ROM is unchangeable or nonvolatile. ROM is *read-only memory,* and it comes preprogrammed with instructions that do not disappear when the power is turned off. Usually ROM contains utility routines collectively referred to as the *BIOS,* for basic input/output system. BIOS programs control the presentation of characters on the screen, give the keyboard keys their special control capabilities, and provide a small resident program to start the computer.

Powering up the computer from scratch is referred to as a *cold boot,* with the term coming from an old expression to "pull yourself up by your bootstraps." ROM is known to contain the *bootstrap program*. *Cold* and *warm system booting* refer to whether one starts a program with the machine off or already powered on.

Expansion Slots

Expansion slots are also called peripheral slots. They mainly provide a link between the computer's peripherals and the CPU. *Peripherals* are devices connected to the computer's system board, such as disk drives, printer, and a modem for data communications. Sometimes an expansion slot is used to expand RAM. Sometimes expansion options on one system, like data communications, are built into another without requiring an expansion slot.

All interfacing occurs through circuit boards like the one shown in Figure 2-4. All look similar, whatever their interfacing function. The one shown in Figure 2-4 is referred to as a *multifunction* board because of the variety of things it is wired to perform.

Users buy *multifunction boards* to conserve precious expansion slots. Some manufacturers provide expansion chassis that expand the number of slots available. Interface boards are variously called *adapters,* boards, *circuit boards,* and *cards.*

Buying a new peripheral usually means acquiring an interface board, floppy disk program, and a User Guide. The program generally gets patched into the operating system software. This gives the operating system new knowledge of the attached peripheral and enables passing appropriate jobs to it. Dealers often install interface boards and patch the software.

KEYBOARD

The keyboard that came with Mr. Williams' small business computer is shown in Figure 2-5. It is a typical keyboard on a professional-level small business computer. The familiar alphabetic keyboard resembles a normal typewriter keyboard. This similarity helped shorten the learning curve because he was somewhat familiar with typing.

If completely unfamiliar with typing, he could have used one of several disk

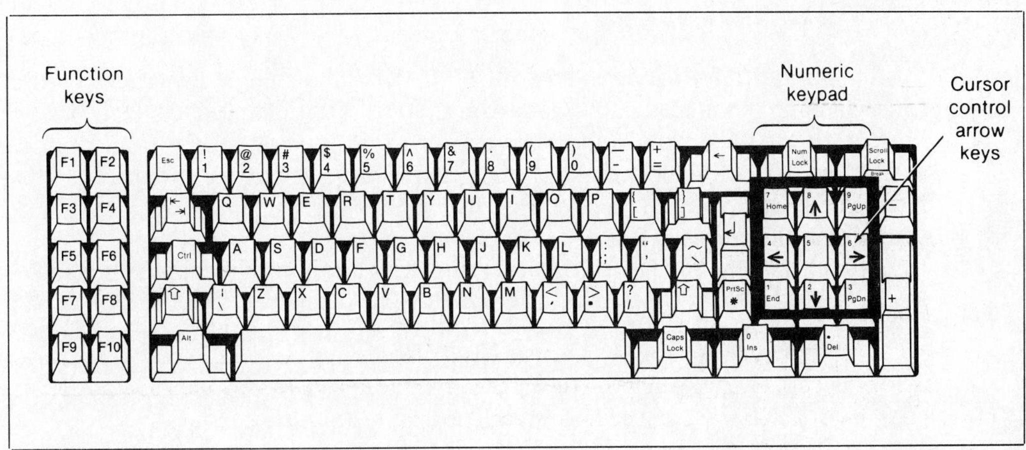

Courtesy of IBM

Figure 2-5 Typical keyboard with function keys, numeric keypad that incorporates cursor control arrow keys, and auxiliary keys.

tutorials on keyboarding. Many applications do not, however, require a great deal of keyboarding skill. Word processing is an obvious exception.

The separate *numeric keypad* is for speeding data entry in many numeric-oriented applications. In order to use the number keys, the NUM LOCK key must be depressed.

The keypad also contains the cursor control keys. The cursor is the tiny underscore or blinking box on the display. It always indicates the position where the next typed character will appear. Arrow keys move it right, left, up, and down around the screen.

In menu-driven applications, the cursor usually rests after a user prompt like "Type number of selection:__." It indicates a keyboard entry is needed. When doing word processing, Mr. Williams uses the cursor control keys to move the cursor rapidly to the place in the text where a change is to be made. Just holding the key down longer than one stroke timing causes a repetitive action of the key. Holding the right arrow cursor control key down, for example, zooms the cursor to the right. The facility to move the cursor all over the display and make changes is often called *full-screen editing*.

A new group of keys Mr. Williams learned were the *function keys*. Some keyboards have them across the top of the keyboard. Often they are called *program function keys* and referenced in tutorials as F1, PF1, or whatever number applies. Programmers call them *soft keys* because their functions are controlled by software.

One word processor Mr. Williams used, for example, has F10 as the key that cancels the last action. The F5 and F6 keys mark the beginning and end of a block of text that needs to be moved elsewhere. Some word processing and other packages allow users to redefine function key actions.

Another application uses the same keys differently. It gets confusing at times. To help remember function key assignments, some users attach labels to keys as reminders. Computer stores sell cardboard templates that overlay function keys and have a place to write memory-jogging labels.

Requirements Planning

Since all information entered into SGD Inc.'s accounting system is keyboarded, some planning was needed. How many data entry workstations need to be active at one time to get the daily work done? The answer to this question came from counting keystrokes. The documentation to the accounting package provided pictures of input screens and descriptions of input entries. By counting them all one character at a time, a keystroke figure was available for data entry purposes.

For example, one SGD Inc. order entry transaction requires approximately 200 keystrokes. At 400 orders a day, that comes to 80,000 keystrokes (400 × 200). A data entry operator can average 10,000 to 12,000 keystrokes an hour. If a conservative average of 10,000 keystrokes an hour is used, it would take 8 hours to enter orders every day. Since errors need correction, and operators take breaks, a 25-percent buffer might be added. That makes order entry a daily 10 hour job for conservative planning purposes.

Alternate solutions are either one workstation with two work shifts or two workstations with two operators on the same shift. With two workstations, one would be free several hours to process payroll, word processing, or whatever. The second workstation could function as a backup should the other malfunction. A simplified version of SGD Inc.'s keystroke plan is given in Figure 2–6.

Work flow also influences workstation requirements. At SGD Inc., workstations are needed in billing, accounting and warehouse areas. Since the warehouse load is light at about 2 hours a day, that workstation could serve as a further backup to the other two.

Some single-user workstations cannot be used while printing is in progress. Available workstation entry hours have to be reduced, in such cases, by the number of print hours required. Alternately, some *print-spooler* software can be acquired. This permits keyboard entry and printing to occur simultaneously.

Seasonal and other fluctuations could influence planning figures. Accounting gets more accounts receivable checks at the beginning of the month than at any other time. These fluctuations need to be assessed in workstation requirements planning.

Expansion or growth also needs consideration. If workstations are networked, another workstation can easily be added if the workload increases. If a single- or multiuser centralized system is considered, more careful calculations need to be done to be sure the hardware supports planned growth.

The following list summarizes how SGD Inc. systematically approached the evaluation of workstation needs:

1. List keystroke count by transaction type at each location.
2. Multiply counts by the number of similar transactions needed daily.

Figure 2-6 A simplified keystroke plan

WORKSTATION REQUIREMENTS PLANNING WORKSHEET

Keyboarded Transaction	*Location*	*Characters in One Transaction*		*Daily Number of Transactions*		*Total Keystrokes*
Order entry	Billing	200	×	400	=	80,000
Inventory receipts confirmation	Warehouse	150	×	150	=	22,500
Cash disbursement	Accounting	100	×	100	=	10,000
Cash receipts	Accounting	110	×	300	=	33,000
						145,500

SUMMARY BY LOCATION

	Billing	*Accounting*	*Warehouse*
Total keystrokes	80,000	43,000	22,500
Add 25% overhead	20,000	10,750	5,625
	100,000	53,750	28,125
Divide by 10,000 (conservative keystroke estimate per hour)	÷10,000	÷10,000	÷10,000
Total workstation requirement hours	10	5.3	2.8

3. Summarize keystroke counts by workstation location.
4. Add an estimated overhead factor to get a new total by location.
5. Divide the preceding totals by 10,000 (or another estimate of keystrokes per hour) to get total workstation hours by location.

Daily figures by workstation guide the planning. Often one lightly loaded workstation can off-load another, or it can be considered a backup. Having a backup could pay for itself in unlost billing days. Or it might be needed for less critical monthly and annual data entry jobs, like an annual inventory update to the database.

DATA ENTRY ALTERNATIVES

Alternatives to keyboard data entry include, among others, a pointer device called a *mouse, touch-sensitive displays, light pens, optical devices,* and *voice.* All require specialized software to integrate with a given computer and end-user application.

The *mouse* is a pointing device that functions much like the cursor control keys. One example of the many varieties is shown in Figure 2–7. As the mouse is physically moved around the desktop, the cursor moves. The device is often marketed to professionals who have an aversion to keyboarding.

Figure 2-7 Example of a mouse data entry device

Courtesy of The Mouse House

Those who use their professional workstation as a constant work tool find any diversion of the hand from the keyboard disruptive. The mouse, however, is found useful by those making a transition from manual to computer use, as well as by the occasional computer user.

Touch-sensitive displays, like the mouse, divert the hands from their most productive position on the keyboard. Such a display is activated by touching the screen and blocking the light in an X-Y coordinate on a display grid, as shown in Figure 2–8. Some futurists predict it will replace the mouse for professional and occasional use. Its use is already important in educational and graphic applications.

A *light pen* works with a grid pattern similar to the touch-sensitive display. The difference is that light emitted from the pen activates a grid's cell. The light pen is an indispensible tool to engineers in *computer-aided design* (CAD) applications. Its use as a painting device is covered in Chapter 7.

As they become less expensive, *optical character recognition* (OCR) and *bar code* recognition input devices are being used with small computers. Low-cost OCR readers start at $1,000 and usually recognize only one type style. The OCR-A style,

Courtesy of Hewlett-Packard, Inc.

Figure 2-8 Touch-sensitive display

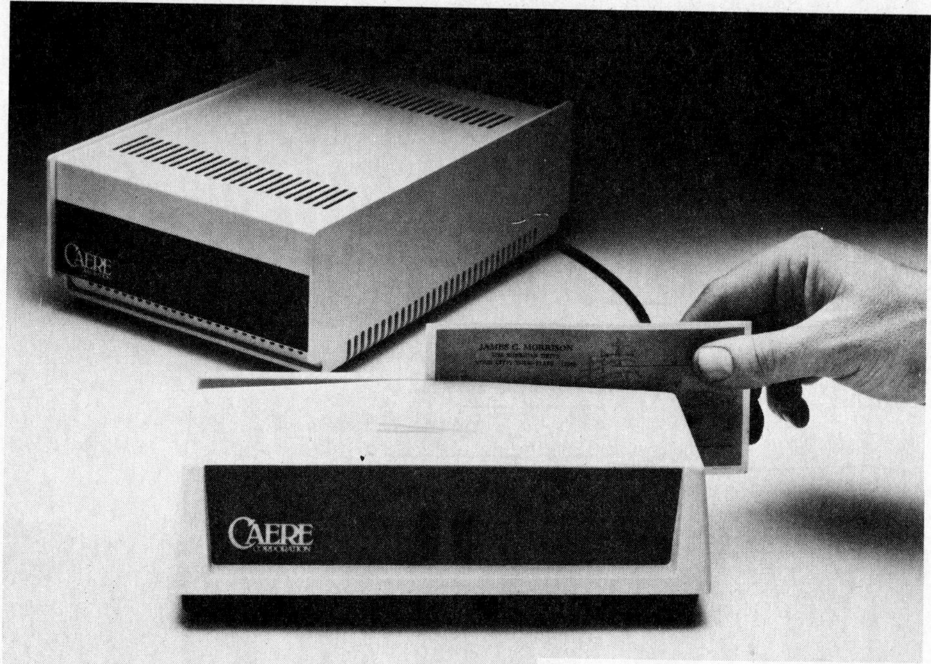

Courtesy of Caere Corporation

Figure 2-9 Optical character recognition (OCR) slot reader and sample of OCR-A type character style

```
OCR A  Size I

0123456789  ¬#$%'*! ABC
DEFGHIJKLMNOPQRSTUVWXYZ
```

endorsed by the American National Standards Institute, is shown in Figure 2–9, along with an OCR reader. Such a reader is suitable for applications requiring only one line of characters to be read from a document.

The bar code wand shown in Figure 2–10 reads various types of printed digital bar codes. One code is the Universal Product Code (UPC) found on retail products. Bar wands sell for as little as $200. Both bar code and OCR readers usually require custom software with post-recognition logic to interpret codes and integrate them into end-user applications.

Of all the so-called *exotic input and output devices, voice* shows the most promise in many applications. *Voice recognition,* or making the computer "understand" human speech, is different from *voice response* or *synthesis,* which is getting a computer to "speak." Both add efficiency and appeal to business applications.

Voice recognition uses a microphone for sound input, as shown in Figure 2–11. It remains limited in accurately interpreting human words and requires large amounts of computer memory to process.

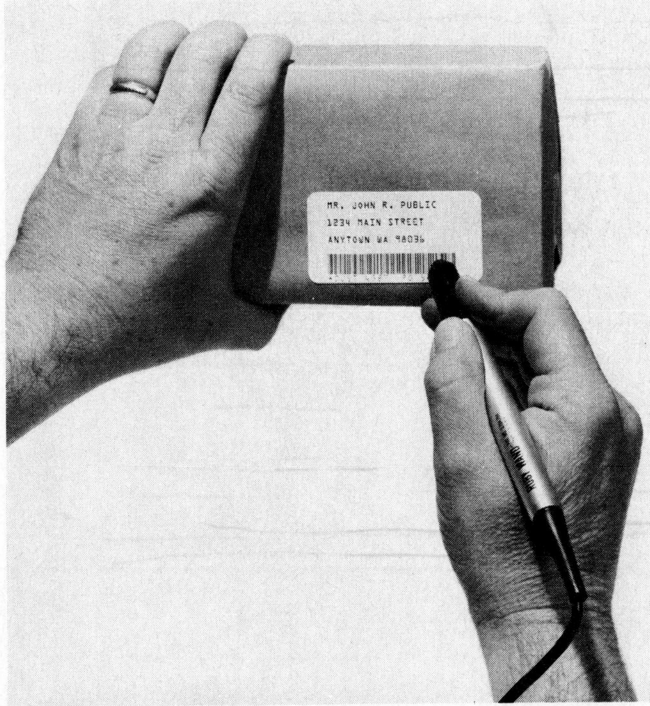

Courtesy of Intermec

Figure 2-10 An example of the Universal Product Code being scanned with a bar code reader wand

Most voice systems available today are speaker-dependent: each operator must train the system to recognize his or her voice patterns. This involves repeating words or phrases six or seven times. The words are digitized and stored as data on disk. Later, when the word is spoken as a command to the computer, the sound pattern must match one of those previously stored. After a match, the program continues sequentially to perform whatever it was designed to do.

Most of these systems are also called *discrete word recognizers* because a user must pause very slightly between words or phrases. Inputting command words or phrases can involve awkward repetition and mismatches.

Some researchers predict efficient voice recognition devices are years away from serious commercial use. At least one small computer vendor, however, demonstrates a voice recognition feature it claims is a natural language interface to command the computer to do one's bidding.

The same small computer also offers voice mail. Voice mail is a combination of voice recognition and voice response. To get the voice message into the computer, messages are spoken as before into a microphone and then digitized and stored on disk. But voice mail does not have to be multirecorded and complexly prepared for searching and matching as a command does. It only involves the digitization of recorded voice, which is a well developed technology. In this application, a memo from the boss is audible in the boss' own voice on playback.

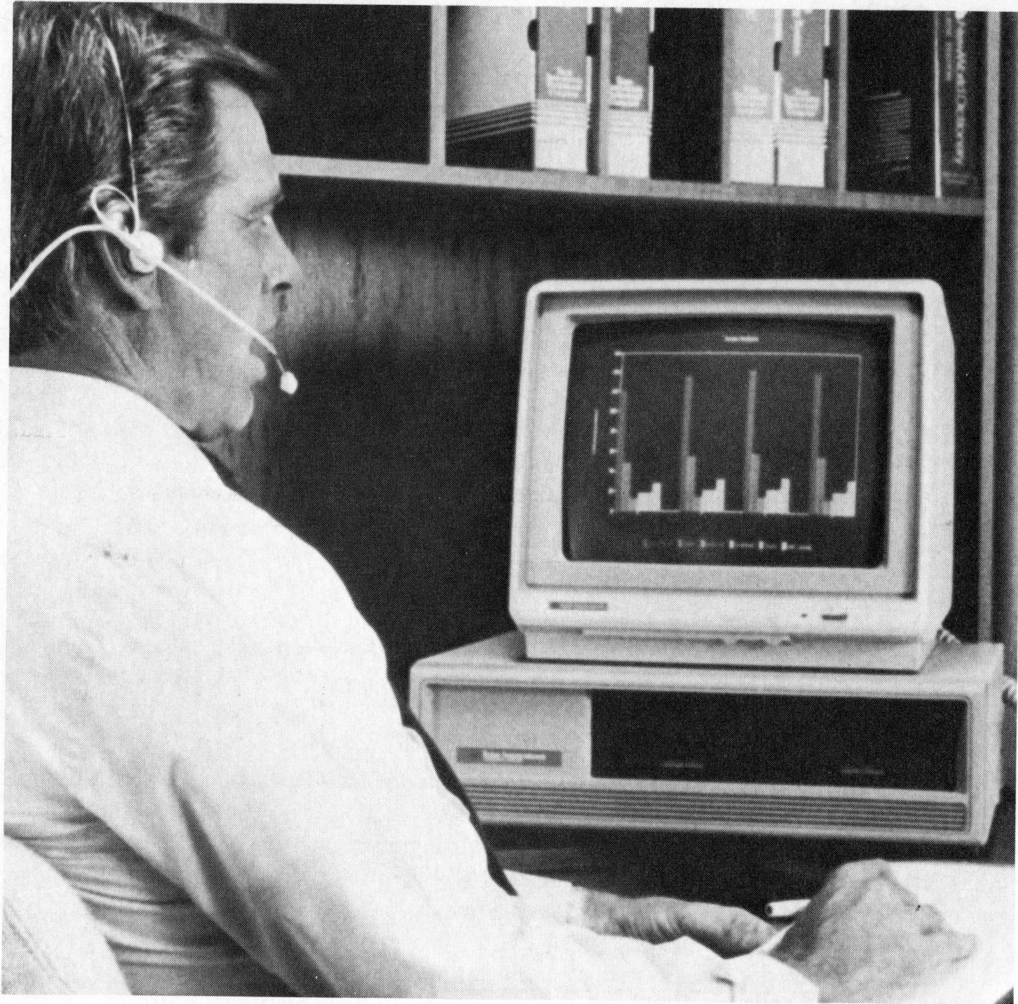

Figure 2-11 Using voice recognition input

Courtesy of Texas Instruments

Voice response computer applications play back anything that is prerecorded and digitized through a *voice synthesizer,* which recreates sound. Even children's toys have for years successfully used one of several known sound synthesis techniques. Its continued use in business computer applications, along with more developed voice recognition schemes, seems inevitable.

DISPLAY

When he initially bought his computer, Mr. Williams had to select a display. One green display, called a *monochrome monitor,* was considered standard. As the name "monochrome" implies, it is a one-color display. *Monitor* refers to the fact that it is on a one-channel cable attached directly to the system unit.

An alternate choice would be a color monitor, called an RGB (for red, green, blue) monitor. But after running a word processing package on one, he decided against color. The application ran slower because of design tradeoffs that some color monitors require. Higher-quality, expensive color monitors do not have the same text character image limitations.

Mr. Williams selected an amber monochrome monitor (about $300), instead of the green. Both colors are reportedly easier on the eyes after prolonged use than black-and-white monitors. He also bought a special stand to tilt the monitor to whatever comfort-viewing position he chose. He also had to buy an interface board for the monitor. He bought a color interface adapter in anticipation of someday getting a color display. The board also drove his monochrome display.

Each character on his display appeared in an 8 × 8 dot matrix, as shown in Figure 2–12. His display had only one-dot descenders for the lower-case characters like j, p, and y. It is less attractive to read than characters with two-dot descenders. But he made

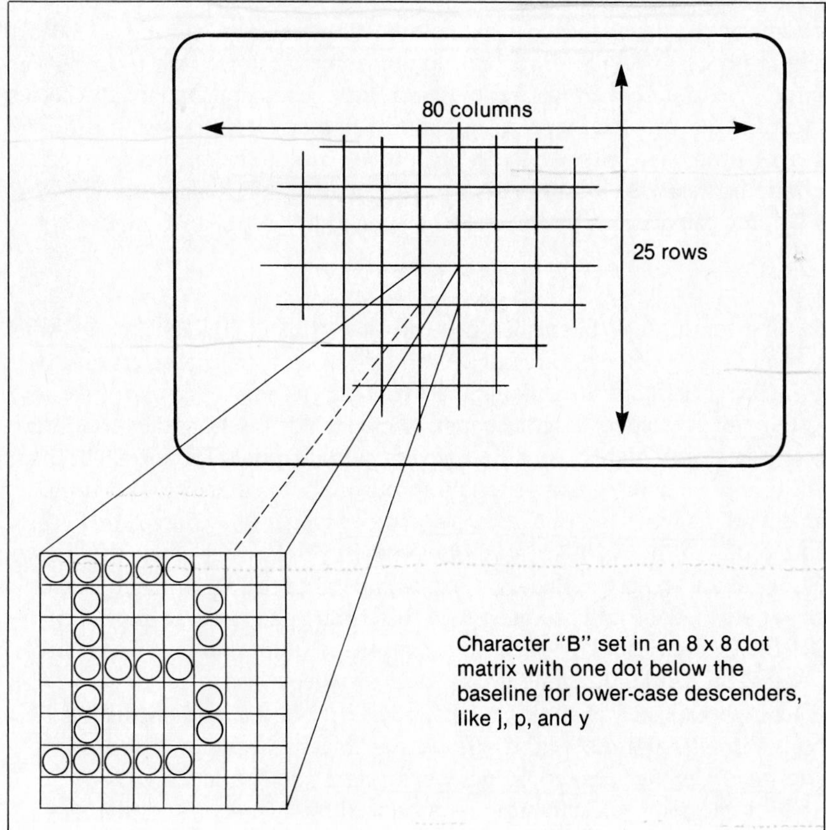

Figure 2–12 Symbolic display screen layout with a single character enlarged for detail

the trade-off knowingly when he chose the color interface board. The monochrome board sent better-looking characters to the display but could not be used for graphic aplications.

Mr. Williams' screen could display 80 columns by 25 lines. Although this is normal, some displays offered 80 columns by 66 lines. These displays function as full-page word processing screens, easily accommodating the entire contents of an 8½ × 11-inch sheet of paper, which is 85 characters by 66 lines. With one-inch margins all around, the content is fully visible. The display turns on its side for horizontal viewing of wide spreadsheets. Some opponents argue that viewing large chunks of material at one time is less efficient than viewing it in more manageable smaller portions.

PRINTERS

Making a printer choice among the hundreds available was not simple. When purchasing this peripheral, Mr. Williams first examined his requirements for print quality: in general, the better the print quality, the more expensive the printer. He also had to determine the print volume.

In addition to knowing his computer application requirements, he had to learn the basics about printers to do informed shopping. He heard stories about others who bought printers, then found their word processing package did not support it. Another printer he heard about broke down every other day. In many installations, the printer is the most error-prone hardware device. Many are not built to be pushed for seven or eight straight hours a day. As a cautionary measure, Mr. Williams planned some extra time in his volume calculations and decided he wanted a very reliable product.

Type

The first thing Mr. Williams learned was that printers are classified as either impact or nonimpact. Typewriters are impact printers. They form characters on a page by striking the paper being printed. Nonimpact printers put images on paper through methods that do not involve striking the paper. These include ink jet and laser printers, among others. They offer higher speeds but are not as appropriate for normal business document printing. They have more specialized purposes, such as color printing.

Impact printers offer *formed character* and *dot-matrix* type characters. Formed characters are produced by *daisy wheel* or *thimble*-type print head elements, as shown in Figure 2–13. Characters are molded, one on each petal of the daisy wheel. The little 4-inch diameter wheel constantly spins. When the correct character at the end of the spike reaches the twelve o'clock position, it is hammered onto a ribbon, which strikes the paper. A *thimble* works the same way as a daisy wheel.

A daisy wheel printer changes character styles by physically changing the daisy wheel. Wheels slip into and out of their protective housing in the print-head.

A dot-matrix impact printer composes characters with dots arranged in a matrix, much like that on the display. Characters are produced by software that controls pins, which are activated against a ribbon, as shown in Figure 2–14. A comparison of dot-matrix and formed characters appears in Figure 2–15.

Thimble element
(Courtesy of NEC Information Systems)

Daisy wheel element
(Courtesy of Qume Corporation, a subsidiary of ITT Corporation)

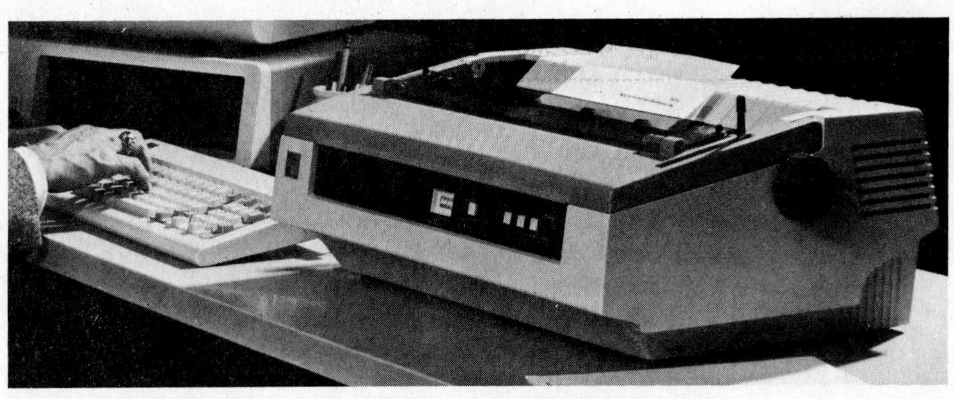

(Courtesy of NEC Information Systems)

Figure 2-13 A formed character letter-quality printer. Such printers use either a daisy wheel or a thimble element to produce fully formed characters

For correspondence, many users want a low-speed formed character printer, which is often also called a *daisy wheel, letter-quality,* or *solid font character printer.* For the higher-speed printing of bills, mailing labels, or rough drafts, users often get a dot-matrix printer. This is what Mr. Williams began with.

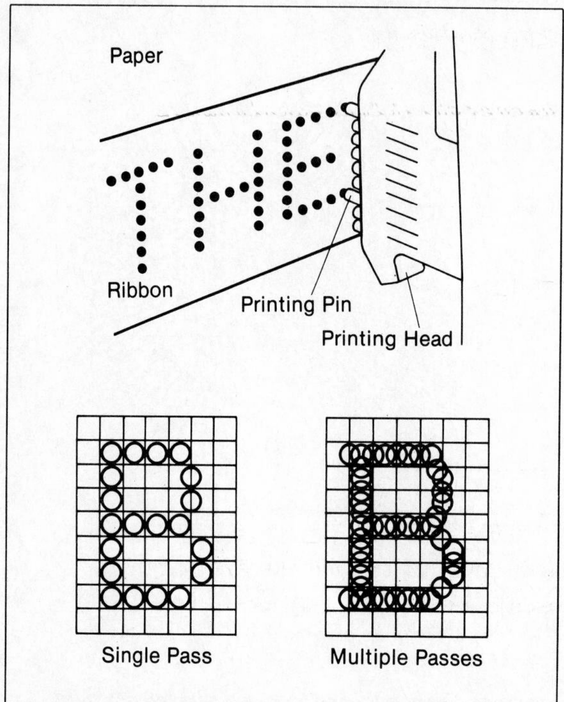

Figure 2-14 Dot-matrix printing head (above, left). The letter "B" formed by a (left) dot-matrix printer after one pass and after multiple passes

Multifunction Dot-Matrix Printers

When SGD Inc. began to use more computing, their applications included 10-percent correspondence, 50-percent bills, statements, checks, and other routine external mailings, and 40-percent internal company reports. They bought one of the more flexible multifunction dot-matrix printers. These printers produce both standard, or rough-draft dot-matrix output as well as letter- or correspondence-quality output. Through combining repeat print passes and various pin-head arrangements, such as those shown in Figure 2–16, they produce varied results. Specification for one such printer included:

Quality	*Dot Matrix*	*Speed in Characters-per-Second*
Letter	18×48	40
Memo	9×15	100
Rough-draft	9×7	220

Some dot-matrix printers do pin-controlled or dot-controlled graphics and character size manipulation. Character width or *pitch width,* which is measured in *characters-per-inch* (cpi), is often called *character font*. Some printers allow selections from a panel located on the front of the printer.

FORMED CHARACTER EXAMPLES

Script characters

ABCDEFGHIJKLMNOPQRSTUVWXYZ abcdefghijklmnopqrstuvwxyz
1234567890

Pica characters

ABCDEFGHIJKLMNOPQRSTUVWXYZ abcdefghijklmnopqrstuvwxyz
1234567890

DOT-MATRIX EXAMPLES

Standard characters

ABCDEFGHIJKLMNOPQRSTUVWXYZ abcdefghijklmnopqrstuvwxyz
1234567890

Boldface characters

ABCDEFGHIJKLMNOPQRSTUVWXYZ abcdefghijklmnopqrstuvwxyz
1234567890

Expanded characters

ABCDEFGHIJKLMNOPQRSTUVWZYX
abcdefghijklmnopqrstuvwxyz
1234567890

Condensed characters

ABCDEFGHIJKLMNOPQRSTUVWZYX abcdefghijklmnopqrstuvwxyz
1234567890

Figure 2-15 Comparison of formed and dot-matrix printed characters

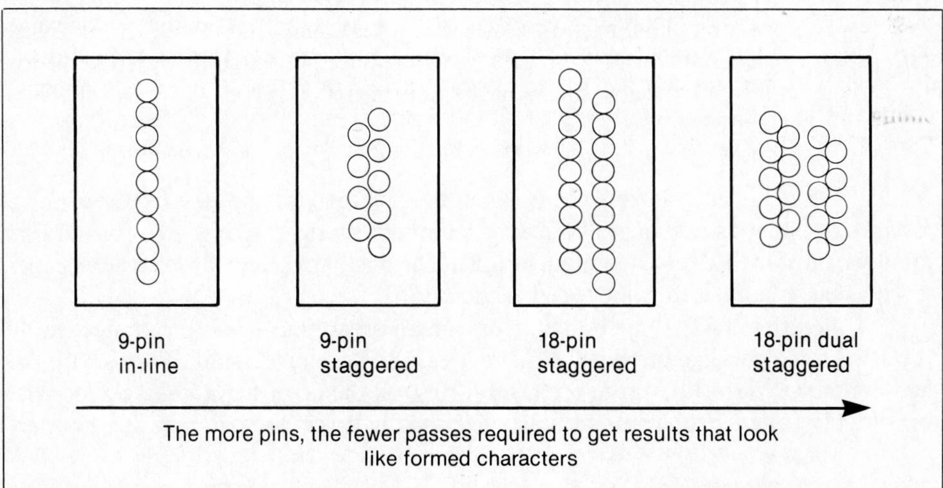

Figure 2-16 Examples of dot-matrix pin-head layouts

Another concern is the amount of text stored in printer circuitry prior to actual printing. A common buffer size is 2 Kbytes, or about 1⅓ double-spaced pages. Some printers offer a 48-Kbyte buffer so that entire documents can be dumped there. This frees the computer to do other tasks while printing takes place.

The technique is called *print-spooling*, as mentioned. If a printer does not have built-in spooling available, software packages and multifunction interface boards can provide it. It is a common feature on multiuser centralized systems.

The ease of interfacing a printer to the computer is another evaluation criterion. Either of two connectors are common. One is called the *Centronics* interface for parallel printers. Dot-matrix printers generally read data one full character at a time, or 8 bits in parallel. The other connector is the RS-232-C for serial connection. Formed character printers usually read characters slower in serial fashion, or one bit at a time.

Speed

For businesses requiring fewer than 20,000 printed pages a month, printers rated in characters-per-second speeds are satisfactory. They are called low-speed printers compared to those rated in lines-per-minute. Some line-rated printers take the same amount of time to print a 1- or 132-character line.

Wide printers print 132 characters, a carry-over from the standard-width paper used for most mainframe computer printouts. This width often is still needed for small computer accounting application reports.

On the other hand, dot-matrix printers can speed over a partial line and get on to the next one. The ability of the print-head to determine the quickest route to its next printing position is called *logic seeking*. This technique makes it difficult to compare the true speed of such printers. Speed is further enhanced with bidirectional printing. In order to print in both directions, a buffer has the next line waiting. It gets printed from right to left, immediately after a normal left-to-right line.

Complicating planning further is the fact that published manufacturer speed ratings are usually considerably faster than that produced in actual service. This is due to carriage returns, line feeds, and signals about buffer status.

Paper Feed

When buying printers, Mr. Williams made sure they handled continuous-form tractor-fed paper as well as single-sheet friction-fed paper. In-house reports and lists are done on standard stock computer paper. The company's regular letterhead paper is sheet-fed as needed to print correspondence.

Preprinted forms are bought from a mail order house. It is recommended by the accounting package provider to make it easy to have professional forms with the least amount of effort. Custom-designed forms, on the other hand, take a good deal of time. They often require professional design and time to get computer spacing accurate.

Other Printers

Line printers are considered the heavy volume end of the printer market. They are most often found in mainframe computer environments. But low-end line printers in the 300- to 1,000-lines-per-minute class are used in small computer environments that generate over 20,000 pages per month. A summary list of printer types by application category appears in Figure 2–17.

Ink jet and photographic printers, as well as plotters, are considered in Chapter 7, "Graphics."

Cost of Ownership

Total printer cost includes purchase price, maintenance, and supplies over the life of the printer. Most users keep printers more than five years. They show significant differences in cost of ownership because of maintenance costs. They are not designed, generally, for a 100-percent *duty-cycle,* which many users overlook. This is the printer industry's term for the amount of time a printer actually creates documents, not the time the printer is powered up.

For example, a printer with a 25-percent duty cycle actually prints two hours a day (25-percent of an eight-hour workday), even though it is on during all eight hours.

Figure 2-17 Printer types by application category

Applications	*Printer Category*	*Speed*	*Price ($)*
1. Typewriter quality (no graphics) Executive correspondence Legal briefs Manuscripts "Image" documents	Formed character low-speed	12–80 cps*	600–4,000
2. Draft quality Electronic spreadsheets Bar charts (graphics) Accounting data Control lists and reports Nonimage documents and correspondence	Dot-matrix low-speed	200 cps	500–2,000
3. Both #1 and #2	Dot-matrix multifunction		2,000–3,600
	• near letter-quality	150 cps	
	• draft quality	900 cps	
4. High-volume printing (over 20,000 sheets/month)	High-speed:		
	• formed character	150–3,000 lpm*	7,000–100,000
	• dot-matrix	150–600 lpm	3,000–17,000
	Electrostatic	300–18,000 lpm	5,000–170,000
	Xerographic/laser	800–60,000 lpm	18,000–400,000

*cps = characters per second; lpm = lines per minute

Figure 2-18 Print requirements planning worksheet

	NUMBER OF PRINTED LINES			
	DAILY		MONTHLY	
Accounting Application	*Letter Quality*	*Draft Quality*	*Letter Quality*	*Draft Quality*
Invoices	550			
Invoice register		75		
Customer statements			3,200	
Aged trial balance				2,000
Other Applications				
Word processed letters,	400	400		
Electronic spreadsheets	200	400		
Total Lines	1,150	875	3,200	2,000

Example 1:

Daily total lines	1,150
Average characters/line	× 80
Total characters	92,000
Formed character printer working at 80 characters-per-second	÷ 80
Total seconds	1,150
	÷ 60
	19 minutes

Example 2:

Daily total characters	92,000
Multifunction dot-matrix printer working nearly at letter-quality speed of 150-characters-per-second	÷ 150
Total seconds	613
	÷ 60
	10 minutes

Example 3:

Daily total characters	92,000
Multifunction dot-matrix printer working at draft-quality speed of 900 characters-per-second	÷ 900
Total seconds	102
	÷ 60
	1.7 minutes

Example 4:

Daily total lines	1,150
Line printer—300 lines-per-minute	÷ 300
	3 minutes

A duty cycle of 25-percent, with about 40-percent of each page devoted to text, is average for many printers. It is a safe figure for printer planning purposes.

Requirements Planning

In order to determine SGD Inc.'s print requirements, Mr. Williams listed every document printed. A simplified version of his planning worksheet is given in Figure 2–18. He also distinguished the quality of print required and the frequency of each document.

Information for the worksheet comes from documents and reports illustrated in application User Guides. Counting the number of lines, including headings, on documents provides figures. Some things require estimates, like the number of daily word processed lines. Some on-demand management reports need to be lumped together and listed as a daily estimate. Long-term requirements also need consideration.

The daily print volume is the most important requirement to satisfy. Often it needs to be further split out by location. SGD Inc.'s long-range plan was to have a printer located right in the warehouse to print shipping documents.

Once a working line count is determined, alternative printer solutions can be evaluated. For illustration purposes, four alternatives are developed for the simplified example given in Figure 2–18.

SGD Inc.'s printing needs were far more extensive than given in the example. Their choice of a multifunction dot-matrix printer served their larger print needs. Some individuals, like Mr. Williams, continued to rely on their low-speed dot-matrix personal printers.

DISKS

The workstation Mr. Williams purchased came with floppy or hard disk drives. He began with two built-in floppy disks and later upgraded his system with a separate hard disk.

Unlike volatile random access memory, which loses its contents on power cutoff, disk storage is nonvolatile. This means anything stored will not disappear until specifically erased.

Floppy Disks

Floppy disks come in assorted 3-, 5-, and 8-inch sizes. A 5¼-inch disk is common and costs about $5. It is made of mylar flexible plastic, which gives the name *floppy* to the disk. The mylar is housed in a protective envelope, as shown in Figure 2–19. A magnetic oxide coating on the disk is magnetized or not to represent binary 1's and 0's. A read/write head, similar to one on a record player, is positioned over a specific *track* and *sector* of the disk. Once positioned, it can either read digital information stored there or write it.

If a user glues a label over the *write-protect notch,* it signals the disk drive not to accept write-overs, which would destroy stored data. Mr. Williams write-protects original copies of application software to avoid inadvertently damaging his investment.

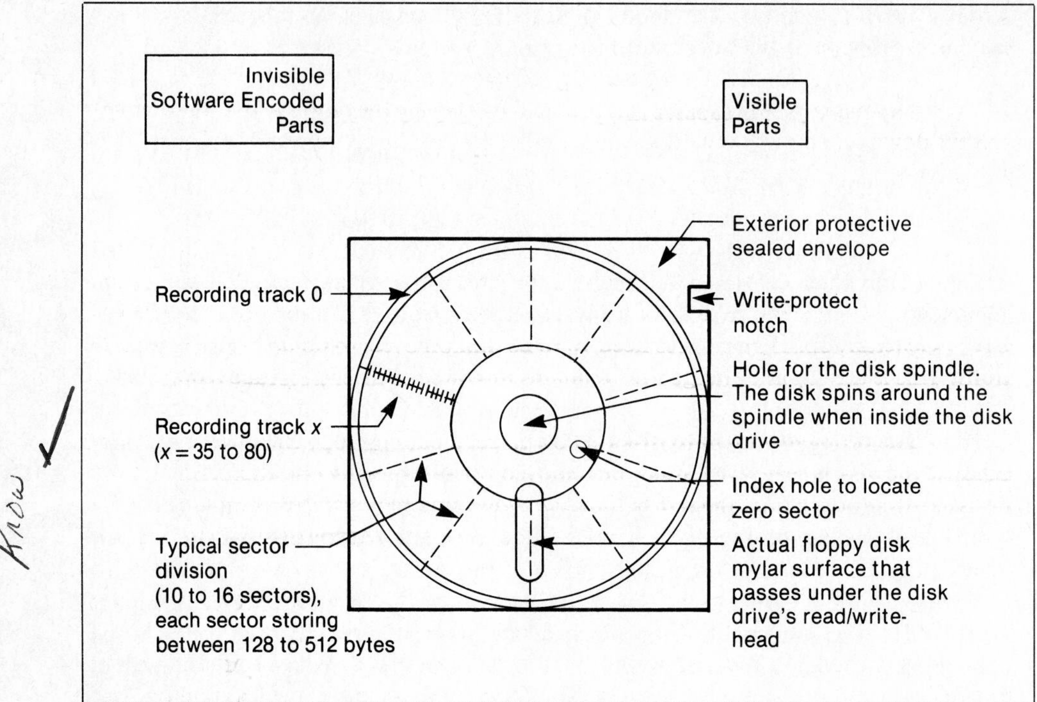

Figure 2-19 Floppy disk

One typical 5¼-inch floppy disk has 320,000 bytes of storage space. It is a double-sided, double-density disk. Floppy disks usable only on one side are called single-sided, like a typical 5¼-inch 160,000 byte disk. *Density* refers to the data storage capacity of a disk. A double-density disk has twice the storage capacity of a single-density disk.

Half-height or *thinline* disk drives fit two drives in the space of one regular-size drive. In a two-disk drive system, this can instantly double disk storage capacity from 640,000 bytes to 1,280,000 bytes. Often half-height drives are cheaper than regular drives.

RAM Disks

A pseudo disk is a *RAM disk*. Mr. Williams partitioned off part of RAM and, in effect, declared that it function as a speedy floppy disk. He did this because his word processing package normally made many switches of information from the floppy disk to the RAM, every time certain actions were required. These disk accesses visibly slowed down work continuity. Once he transferred the entire application from the floppy to the so-called *memory* or *speed* disk, it worked at internal machine speed. It made a big difference to his document composition progress.

Using RAM disk software assumes that enough memory is in place for partitioning. Often with a RAM disk the need for a second floppy disk drive evaporates. Some users prefer to buy more memory rather than a second floppy disk drive or even a hard disk. At least one manufacturer sells software and enough memory boards to emulate an 8-million-byte disk.

The main drawback with memory disks is that everything is lost if the power fails. Battery backup devices solve this problem by keeping the power active long enough to shut down gracefully. Whether using a memory disk or not, battery backup is considered necessary by some small computer users.

Hard Disks

Hard disks, often called *Winchester* or *fixed* disks, are rigid metal platters, often 5¼-inches, sealed in their drive. Data storage capacity ranges from 5 to over 100 million bytes. Generally small businesses need 10 to 20 million bytes to do accounting applications. This is the capacity range Mr. Williams migrated to after a storage requirements analysis.

The problem with hard disks is how to get a backup copy for safety purposes. Because the disk is sealed, it cannot be removed for safekeeping elsewhere. Some solutions to this problem are floppy disk, *tape cartridge,* and *removable disk,* among others.

When he bought a hard disk, Mr. Williams rejected floppy disk backup as being satisfactory only for the smallest hard disk and the most patient users. Disk swapping gets tiresome and is error-prone. It is a possible solution, however, for *selective backups* where only files updated since the last update are backed up.

Anyone who uses a hard disk still needs a floppy disk drive as a transfer medium to get purchased software onto the hard disk. Purchased software is sold on floppy disks.

SGD Inc. bought a hard disk with a built-in tape cartridge for backup. It took six minutes to make a backup of a 15-million-byte hard disk without operator intervention and with data transfer verification. To contrast, if done with floppy disk, it would take about fifty 320,000-byte floppies. Removable disk cartridges have speed characteristics like tape cartridges.

Disk capacities, prices and technology are constantly changing. A sampler of Mr. Williams' disk storage alternatives is available in Figure 2–20. Futurists predict the advent of optical disk storage in the gigabyte, or billions of bytes, range.

Video cassette recorders (VCR) are being used for hard disk backup. They can store as many as 100 million bytes on a single video cassette. But they take hours to save or restore a complete video cassette's worth of data, with all users denied access while backup is in progress.

Disk Backup

Why is disk backup such a critical issue? One story Mr. Williams heard from an industry associate convinced him of its value.

Consider the case where a new insurance company employee failed to follow daily backup disk procedures. It was summer and due to an air conditioning overload, there was a drop in power causing a temporary brown-out. The read/write disk head reacted by wiping out a portion of the disk, making the data on it unusable.

If a backup disk was available that reflected records as of the end of the previous day, only one day of reentry would be needed to restore records. Without a current backup

Figure 2-20 Sampler of disk storage

Type	*Data Storage Capacity Ranges (K = 1,000 bytes) (M = 1,000,000 bytes)*	*Price Ranges ($)*
Floppy Disk Drives		
Internal housing		
3.5-inch	875 K–1 M	225–300
5.25-inch—full height	160 K–1.6 M	265–1,300
5.25-inch—half height	900 K–3.6 M	300–1,200
Separate Housing		
5.25-inch	640 K–800 K	500–1,300
8-inch	1.2 M–6 M	1,300–1,600
Hard Disk Drives		
Internal housing or external subsystems		
3.9-inch	5.3 M	1,500
5.25-inch	5–40 M	1,600–5,000
External subsystems with removable cartridge backup		
5.25–inch	5 M removable with 5 M fixed	1,800
	to	
	15 M fixed	4,500
8–inch	10 M fixed with 10 M removable	7,300
	to	
	80 M fixed with 10 M removable	16,200
With tape backup	6–40 M	3,100–6,600
With 1-M floppy disk backup	5–30 M	4,500–12,400
Backup Only		
Hard disk to video cassette recorder	100 M	800 (interface only)
Tape cartridge	20 M	4,000
RAM disk		
Software	160–512 K	50–225
Interface board and software	512 K–1 M	1,000–3,000

available, records would have to be recreated from whenever the last backup occurred. In this case it was two weeks ago. Two weeks worth of transactions had to be reentered to bring the disk records current. The cost of the restoration, in terms of labor, lost time, and poor morale, could not be estimated.

Many backup schemes are advocated by many software manufacturers. A common one used is called the grandparent-parent-child technique, as diagrammed in Figure 2–21. Users begin the backup procedure by having three disks available. After the first day, disk #1 is copied to disk #2. The second day disk #2 is used and backed

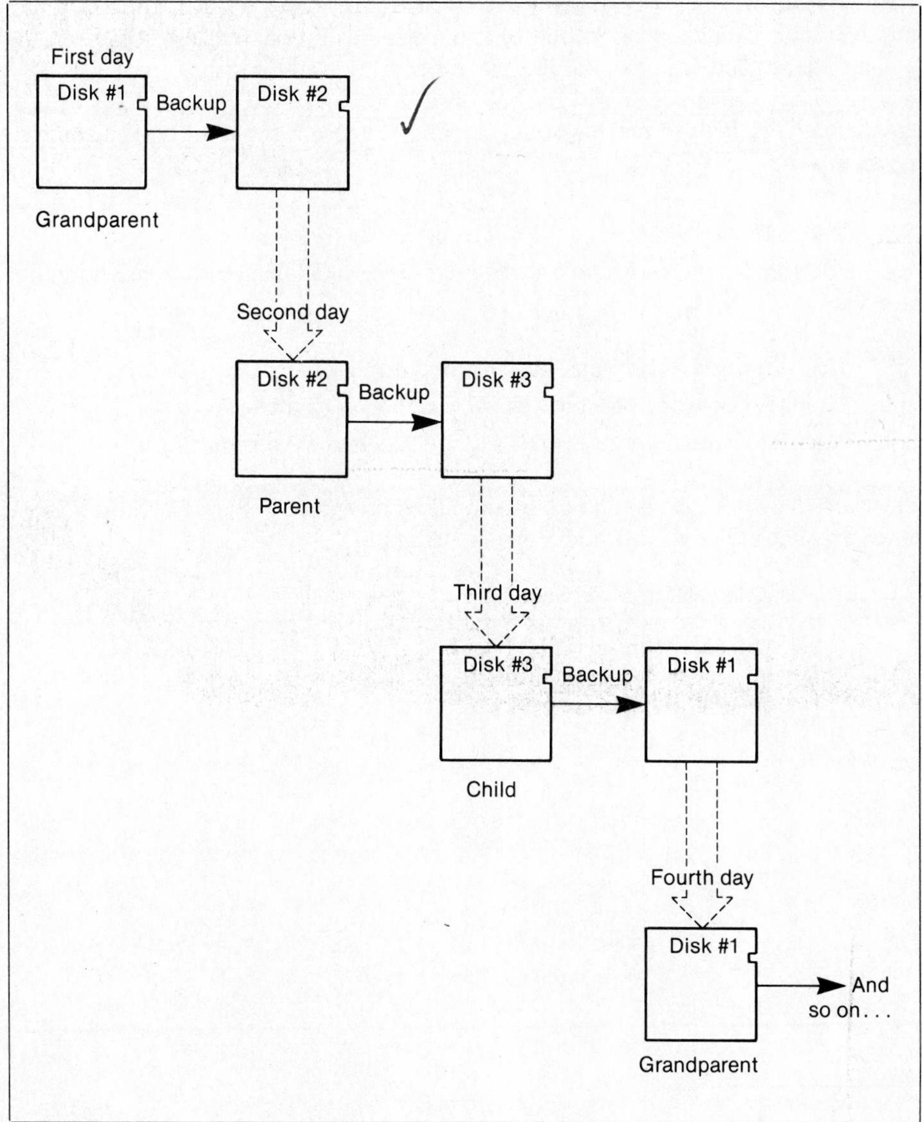

Figure 2–21 Grandparent-parent-child backup technique

up to disk #3 at the end of the day. Disk #3 is used the third day, and the backup cycle begins again on the fourth day with continual backup disk rotation.

If both the current disk and current backup disk fail, there is always one other disk to try from the previous day. Assuming it works, only one day of work is lost. This system requires a careful record or log attached to each backup disk. The log should indicate who backed up the disk, the time and date done, and what files were backed up.

Some users make an extra end-of-week backup disk to store off-site. Should a real disaster occur, there is some assurance of being only one week behind. Additional insurance requires that paper printouts of files, periodically updated, also be stored off-site. This includes critical material like customer and inventory lists.

Originals of program disks should also be safely stored off-site. Experienced users use only originals to make working copies. They store copies of documentation off-site as well.

Requirements Planning

To determine hard disk storage requirements, Mr. Williams followed a standard forumula:

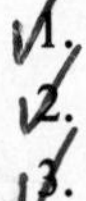

1. List all programs and data to be stored on disk.
2. List the disk space occupied by each item as a character count.
3. Add the character counts and add an estimated expansion factor.

He developed a worksheet similar to the simplified one given in Figure 2–22. It helped him to arrive at a disk storage requirement figure.

Figure 2–22 Disk requirements planning worksheet

Storage Item	*Average Characters*		*Volume*		*Total*		*Application Programs*		*Total*
Company Database									
Customer record	300	×	4,000	=	1,200,000	+	72,000	=	1,272,000
Accounts receivable									
Open items record	100	×	16,000	=	1,600,000	+	64,000	=	1,664,000
General ledger record	100	×	500	=	50,000	+	84,000	=	134,000
Other Applications									
Word processing documents	3,000	×	400	=	1,200,000	+	170,000	=	1,370,000
Electronic spreadsheets	3,000	×	400	=	1,200,000	+	160,000	=	1,360,000
System Software									200,000
Subtotal									6,000,000
Allowance for growth and workspace									× 2
Total character requirement									12,000,000

Some information for the worksheet comes from application User Guides. It gives the amount of storage programs require.

For accounting applications, documentation also gives character counts for each record type. The critical step here is to translate the company's long-range plans into database expansion numbers. Is there to be a promotion to get many new customers? Is there a plan to increase inventoried items? When these and other planning issues are resolved, figures could be incorporated into the worksheets. The expansion factor could be applied to each item individually or to a group of items. The example takes the group approach.

Estimating storage for word processed documents and electronic worksheets involves reusing printer assumptions about average document and worksheet length. Document retention periods should be established. When several users share the hard disk, the final storage figure should consider all users' document storage needs.

To simplify planning word processing storage needs, SGD Inc. used the following disk storage chart as a guide:

DISK STORAGE

Disk Space Used	*To Store*
1 byte (8 bits)	One letter or symbol
1,500 bytes	One double-spaced typewritten page with an average of 250 words (1,500 characters and spaces)
30,000 bytes	20 typewritten pages
150,000 bytes	100 typewritten pages
5,000,000 bytes	Over 3,400 typewritten pages

For economic or security reasons, it may not be necessary to keep everything *on-line* at once. *On-line* means immediately accessible for user data processing. Hard disk planning usually assumes all computer data and programs are resident at all times on the disk.

Floppy disk planning is different. If the inconvenience of loading a floppy disk is not a problem, word processed documents can be stored one per disk, if desired. The same is true of worksheets.

Planning is needed, however, for integrated accounting applications using floppy disks. Usually it is unnecessary to keep all records and programs on-line at once. Accounts payable and payroll, for example, are probably not needed when orders are processed.

It requires finding from the software documentation the mininum on-line program and data storage required per application. If an order entry application is to update open order, customer, and inventory item records during the processing of one transaction, then the application program and all relevant database records must be available on the computer disk drives at once.

EVALUATION

After evaluating hardware and software options, Mr. Williams originally bought a single-user floppy disk system. His order and bill looked like the one in Figure 2–23. Eventually he added a color display, and the company established local area networking adding a hard disk and a faster multifunction printer. Because of careful shopping, his system accommodated all without problems.

Two checklists guided his systematic hardware evaluation and selection. One checklist helps evaluate individual characteristics about *components*. A *component* is one part of the hardware, like the video display or system unit, that goes into making a complete working small business computer. Another checklist helped evaluate generalities about the hardware, like cost and maintenance. Both checklists are needed for *each* component. They are given in Figures 2–24 and 2–25.

To give an example of checklist use, when Mr. Williams evaluated system units, he used the Hardware: General Checklist to guide the evaluation of product generalities. This included learning about a manufacturer's reputation and installed user base. He checked manufacturer stability to be sure the company would still be in business in three to five years to both upgrade and maintain his unit.

The General Checklist also prompted finding who would maintain the unit if the manufacturer did not provide service. In his case, the manufacturer would not service the entire unit because the add-on memory interface board and the amber display

Figure 2–23 Single user stand-alone floppy disk system

Hardware	*Purchase Price*
Basic 64 Kbyte system including system unit and keyboard	$1,355
Additional 192 Kbyte add-on memory on a multifunction board including a clock with a serial and parallel port for modem and printer interfacing	530
Dot-matrix printer, 132 columns wide	840
Printer cable	55
Amber monochrome display	300
Display interface board	300
Two 5¼-inch 320 Kbyte disk drives	1,058
Disk drive interface board	220
Modem	530
Modem cable	35
	$5,223
Third-party on-site maintenance service contract	$65/month

were manufactured elsewhere. So he found an independent company that serviced the entire unit, offering on-site maintenance within eight working hours of a service call.

The General Checklist also prompted checking hardware reliability. Hardware manufacturers frequently publish a mean time between failure (MTBF) as well as a mean time to repair (MTTR) figure for their products. The hard disk SGD Inc. eventually bought had a MTBF of 10,000 power-on hours to failure and 30 minutes to repair. The figures indicated four years of projected reliable use.

It was a different story for floppy disks drives. In general, with heavy use, he could count on a disk failure every six months, which he did experience. With his service contract, if a disk fails, the service vendor simply replaces it on-site. The service company then either repairs the disk or sends it out for repair. When returned, it is reused at another customer installation.

Before getting an on-site service contract, Mr. Williams tried the carry-in service to his local store. But his second disk failure took three trips, each costing a lost half-day of work. In addition, the second disk failed during the repair of the first one. When it all worked again, he called an independent maintenance service contractor, who had a good reputation, to take the complete service burden off his hands.

It also was important to find that, in one case, upgrading from one hard disk to a larger model required other hardware and software changes. This made one piece of equipment less desirable than another.

Such findings supported specific facts on individual hardware components. The Hardware: Component Checklist helped him detail specifications for everything from the system unit to the printer.

Figure 2-24 Hardware: General Checklist

Component: ______________________

	A	*B*	*C*
Product name	________	________	________
Model number	________	________	________
Manufacturer	________	________	________
Cost	________	________	________

Items to Check	*Rating (Scale: 1 = poor to 10 = excellent)* A	B	C
General			
Ease of use	____	____	____
Product reputation	____	____	____
Number installed:			
In country	____	____	____
In user's local area	____	____	____
By vendor company	____	____	____
Local user references	____	____	____

Figure 2-24 (continued)

Items to Check	*Rating (Scale: 1 = poor to 10 = excellent)* A	B	C
General			
Easy to follow User Guide	_______	_______	_______
Manufacturer:			
Reputation	_______	_______	_______
Length of time in business	_______	_______	_______
Reliability:			
Published mean time to failure	_______	_______	_______
Published mean time to recovery	_______	_______	_______
Length of warantee period	_______	_______	_______
Diagnostic self-test available	_______	_______	_______
Upward compatibility:			
Several larger/better models available now	_______	_______	_______
Upgrade cost	_______	_______	_______
Other hardware retained as is	_______	_______	_______
Software retained as is	_______	_______	_______
Payment terms available	_______	_______	_______
Rental available:			
Renewal provisions	_______	_______	_______
Payments credited toward purchase	_______	_______	_______
Deposit required	_______	_______	_______
Shipping/delivery costs	_______	_______	_______
Other related costs	_______	_______	_______
Delay between order placement and delivery	_______	_______	_______
Cancellation provision	_______	_______	_______
Installation			
Who is responsible	_______	_______	_______
Steps required	_______	_______	_______
For each step, requirements for:			
Time	_______	_______	_______
Personnel	_______	_______	_______
Power, cables, etc.	_______	_______	_______
Other environment or facility needs	_______	_______	_______
Additional costs	_______	_______	_______
Site preparation responsibility	_______	_______	_______
Who is responsible for successfully interfacing components in multivendor situations	_______	_______	_______
Who tests to insure hardware is successfully installed	_______	_______	_______

Figure 2-24 (continued)

Items to Check	*Rating (Scale: 1 = poor to 10 = excellent)* A	B	C
Maintenance			
By manufacturer	_____	_____	_____
By another company:			
Length of time in business	_____	_____	_____
Service reputation	_____	_____	_____
Number of accounts serviced	_____	_____	_____
List of hardware serviced	_____	_____	_____
Number of accounts using hardware concerned	_____	_____	_____
On-site maintenance contract:			
Guaranteed time between service request and response	_____	_____	_____
Average time to repair	_____	_____	_____
Flat-fee maintenance contract:			
Cost	_____	_____	_____
All parts and labor included	_____	_____	_____
Pickup and delivery included	_____	_____	_____
Guaranteed pickup time after call	_____	_____	_____
Guaranteed delivery time after pick-up	_____	_____	_____
Carry-in service:			
Per call parts and labor charge	_____	_____	_____
Guaranteed pickup/delivery time	_____	_____	_____
Address of nearest service location	_____	_____	_____
Local user references	_____	_____	_____
Written policy about level and quality of service	_____	_____	_____
Loaner hardware provided	_____	_____	_____
Emergency backup facilities available	_____	_____	_____
Written policy about backup service	_____	_____	_____
Service provided at other locations	_____	_____	_____
Subtotal	_____	_____	_____
Divide by number of items rated for average rating	_____	_____	_____

Transfer Average Rating to Selection Summary: Hardware, Figure 5-2.

Information for individual component evaluations came mainly from specification sheets and User Guides that come with purchased components. Loose-leaf reference services like *Datapro Reports on Microcomputers* are also helpful.

Users, user group and trade association contacts, periodical product reviews, and shows, covered in Chapter 1, are other hardware information sources.

Figure 2-25 Hardware: Components Checklist

Items to Check	*Rating (Scale: 1 = poor to 10 = excellent)* A	B	C
System Unit			
Product name A: ________	B: ________		C: ________
Central processor:			
Word size	____	____	____
Coprocessors available	____	____	____
Number of operating systems available:			
Single-user	____	____	____
Multiusers on centralized computer	____	____	____
Number of users	____	____	____
Local area networking	____	____	____
Random access memory:			
Minimum	____	____	____
Maximum	____	____	____
Increment size	____	____	____
Interface expansion slots:			
Number available	____	____	____
Number needed for basic functions	____	____	____
Expansion chassis available	____	____	____
Number of disk types and drives supported	____	____	____
Number of printers supported	____	____	____
Number of data communication ports	____	____	____
Keyboard			
Product name A: ________	B: ________		C: ________
Detached from system unit for ease of use	____	____	____
Familiar key arrangement	____	____	____
Numeric keypad	____	____	____
Programmable function keys	____	____	____
Display			
Product name A: ________	B: ________		C: ________
Screen:			
Size	____	____	____
Antiglare surface	____	____	____
Area:			
Columns	____	____	____
Rows	____	____	____
Color:			
Monochrome	____	____	____
RGB (red, green, blue)	____	____	____
Size of character dot-matrix	____	____	____
Number of descender dots	____	____	____

Figure 2-25 (continued)

Items to Check	*Rating (Scale: 1 = poor to 10 = excellent)* A	B	C
Display			
Brightness	______	______	______
Contrast	______	______	______
Portable	______	______	______
Printer			
Product name A: ______	B: ______	C: ______	
Quality:			
Dot-matrix:			
Character density (number of dots)	______	______	______
Formed character	______	______	______
Multifunction	______	______	______
Line	______	______	______
Other: ______	______	______	______
Speed	______	______	______
Bidirectional printing	______	______	______
Logic-seeking	______	______	______
Buffer size	______	______	______
Print-spooling	______	______	______
Duty cycle rating (handles work volume)	______	______	______
Interface compatibility (parallel or serial)	______	______	______
Paper feed:			
Pin/sprocket/tractor	______	______	______
Friction	______	______	______
Paper size (minimum/maximum dimensions)	______	______	______
Carbon copies—maximum	______	______	______
Graphics	______	______	______
Built-in character set(s) adequate	______	______	______
Options:			
Expanded type	______	______	______
Condensed type	______	______	______
Italic type	______	______	______
Bold type	______	______	______
Underline	______	______	______
Superscript	______	______	______
Subscript	______	______	______
Pitch (number of characters per horizontal inch)	______	______	______
Lines per vertical inch	______	______	______
Change character set	______	______	______
Maintenance:			
Ease of changing paper	______	______	______
Ease of changing ribbon	______	______	______
Noise level	______	______	______

Figure 2-25 (continued)

Items to Check	*Rating (Scale: 1 = poor to 10 = excellent)* A	B	C
Disk			
Product name A: ______ B: ______ C: ______			
Capacities available	______	______	______
Access speed	______	______	______
Operating system compatible	______	______	______
Desk space occupied	______	______	______
Backup:			
Media provided or available	______	______	______
Program included	______	______	______
Selective backup	______	______	______
Interface controller:			
Requires expansion slot	______	______	______
Number of drives per controller	______	______	______
Compatible with a variety of RAM disks	______	______	______
Buffer size	______	______	______
Detects and corrects errors	______	______	______
Ease of:			
Start-up procedure	______	______	______
Adding drives	______	______	______
Changing of drives	______	______	______
Repeat the next two steps for each component or a group of components as needed.			
Subtotal	______	______	______
Divide by number of items rated for average rating	______	______	______

Transfer average rating to Selection Summary: Hardware, Figure 5-2.

SELF TEST

1. What are the major functions contained on the system board?
2. What does bit mean? ASCII? Parity check?
3. Describe the difference between first- and second-generation microcomputers.
4. What is the function of RAM versus ROM?
5. Compare the data bus and the address bus functions.
6. What is an interface board? What does it look like? Where does it go on the system board?
7. List the steps needed to evaluate workstation requirements.
8. Identify three alternate data entry devices to a keyboard. What applications are these devices best suited for?
9. Compare the two major alternatives in impact printer technology.
10. What information is needed to plan printer requirements?

11. Compare floppy, hard, and RAM disk advantages and disadvantages.
12. Describe one floppy disk backup scheme.
13. Outline a formula to establish disk storage requirements.
14. Why are two checklists given in Chapter 2 to evaluate hardware?

EXERCISES

1. *Weatherton Grain Company Case.* Assume you are in charge of estimating hard disk data storage needs for the Weatherton Grain Company. Some of your investigation turns up the following:

Storage Item	*Average Characters*	*Volume*
Inventory item record	200	100
Customer record	300	2,000
Word processing documents	1,500	200

   Assume the application programs take up an average of 125,000 characters each. So far, what are Weatherton's disk storage needs? Assume the preceding list is the full requirement. If so, what would a final storage figure need to include?
2. Using the least expensive dot-matrix and formed character printers you can find, get printed examples like those shown in Figure 2–15. Do the same for the most expensive printer in each category. Write a report comparing the result of this investigation.
3. Find three recent advertisements for multifunction interface boards. Make a list of features contained on each. Divide price by the number of features offered to determine average cost per feature. Identify the worst value and justify why.
4. *M. Jonas Case.* Mike Jonas is an independent businessperson who decided to buy a professional-level desktop computer. He plans to use it mainly for personal productivity enhancement. If Mr. Jonas used the hardware list in Figure 2–23 as a guide, what hardware changes do you think he would make? What price changes would he find?

RESOURCES AND REFERENCES

See also Chapter 1, Resources and References.

DE VONEY, CHRIS AND RICHARD SUMME, *IBM's Personal Computer,* Que, 1982.

Directory of Independent IBM Personal Computer Hardware and Software, InfoPro.

Guide to Personal Computing, Digital, 1982.

IBM-PC Expansion and Software Guide, Que, 1983.

MCWILLIAMS, PETER A., *The Personal Computer Book,* Prelude, 1982.

SACHS, JONATHAN, *Your IBM PC Made Easy,* McGraw-Hill, 1983.

WEBSTER, TONY, *Microcomputer Buyer's Guide,* McGraw-Hill, 1983.

WILLOUGHLY, WILLIAM EDWARD AND NANCY FOSTER JACOBS, *The ABC's of the IBM,* Sybex, 1983.

ZAKS, RODNEY, *Microprocessors,* Sybex, 1983.

ZAKS, RODNEY AND AUSTIN LESEA, *Microprocessor Interfacing Techniques,* Sybex, 1982.

ZAKS, RODNEY, *Your First Computer,* Sybex, 1980.

3

SYSTEM SOFTWARE

Users typically view their interaction with a small business computer as a very direct link to hardware, as shown in Figure 3–1. Hardware is the visible part of a computer system, so the view is natural. Logically, the user is several layers removed, from the computer's viewpoint, as also shown in Figure 3–1. Two layers of software intervene, the application and system software layers. This chapter concerns the system software layer.

As Figure 3–2 implies, this chapter concerns the three levels contained within the system software layer. They are the operating system, utilities, and language processor levels.

Users of packaged applications often have little direct interface with system software, except for the utility level. Those who write programs from scratch know the three system software levels well.

OPERATING SYSTEM FUNCTIONS

The operating system is the centerpiece in the collection of programs known as system software. It handles input and output functions as well as supervises program execution and memory.

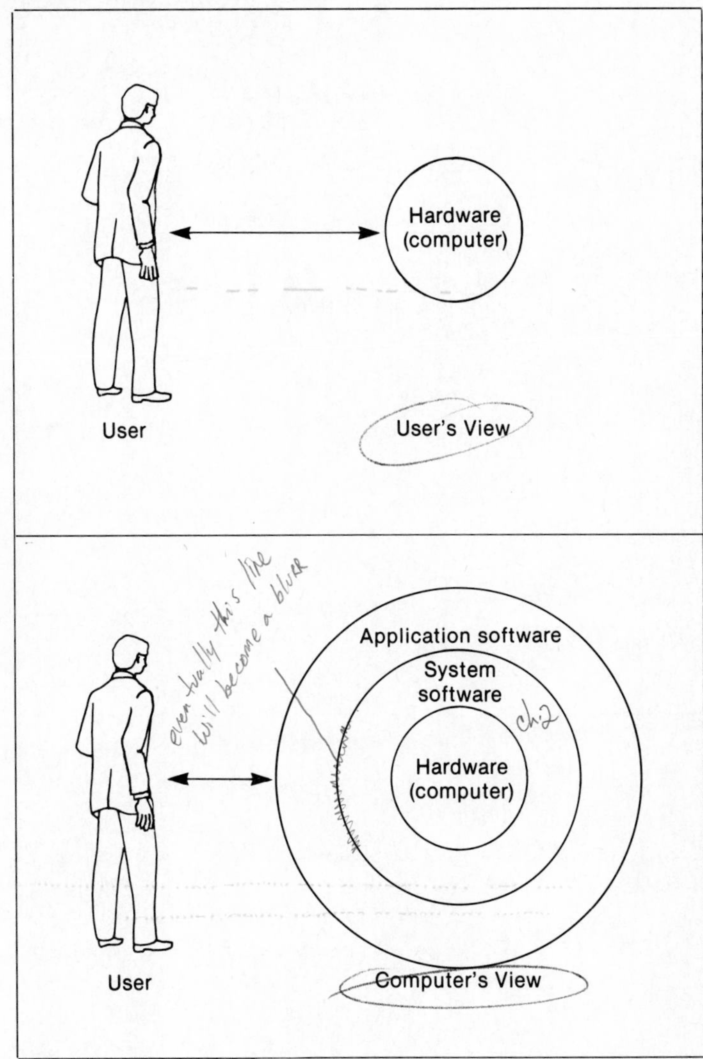

Figure 3-1 Comparison of user's and computer's views of computer interaction

Peripherals Input and Output Handling

Users assemble hardware peripherals to suit their needs. One may use floppy disks and another hard disk. Both use the same application software. One solution that lets the same software work on variously configured hardware is the operating system.

Operating system software has a variable and a fixed part. Most applications are written to work only with the fixed part, often called the disk operating system (or DOS, pronounced daus). It services application programs with such logical functions as opening and reading files.

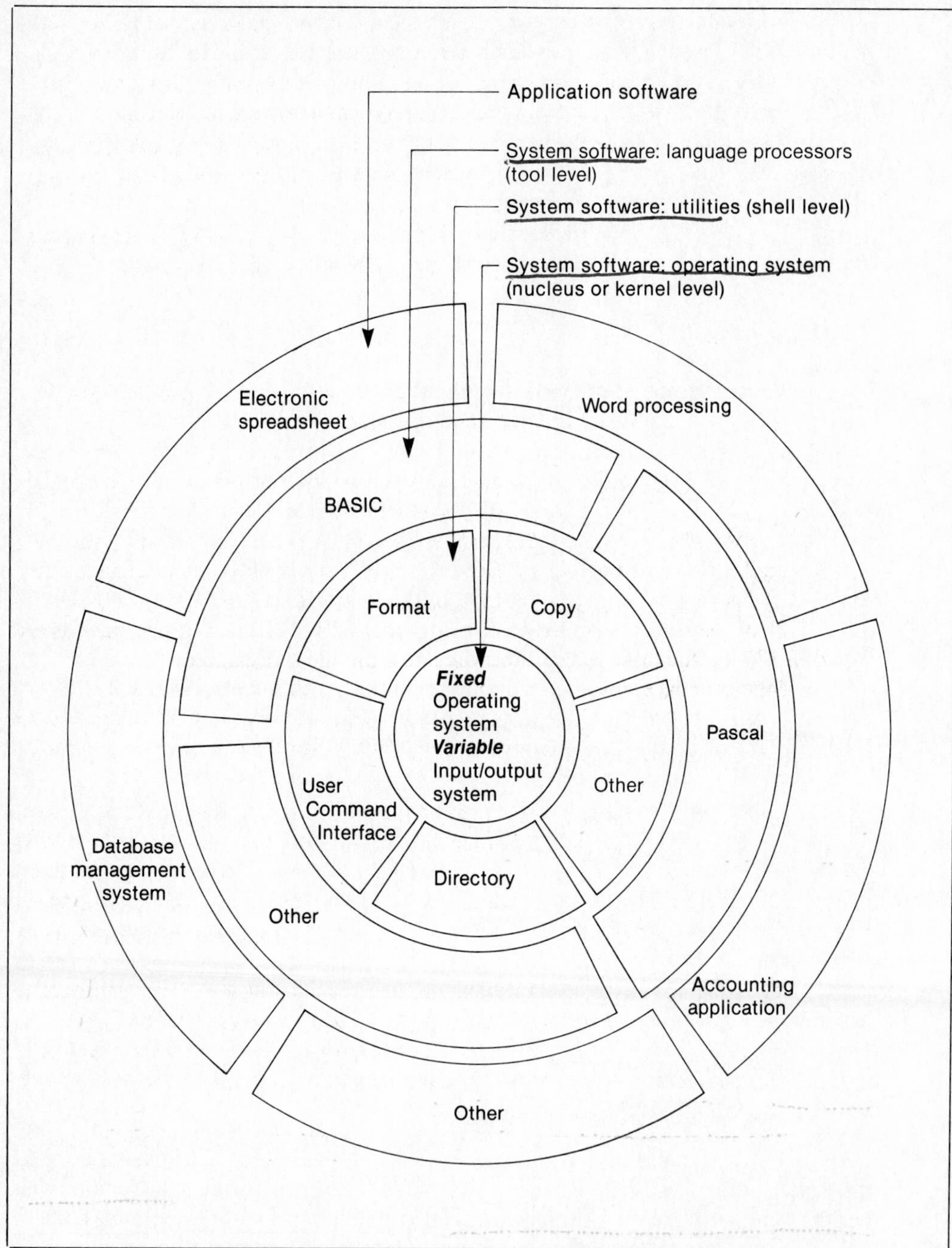

Figure 3-2 One version of the software hierarchy

The variable part of the operating system is often called the BIOS, for Basic Input/Output System. It services application programs by transferring information back and forth with physical peripheral devices. This part of system software helps to keep application software free from handling physical hardware interfacing.

The ability of an application to remain aloof from hardware is called *machine independence*. This feature makes the software *portable*. It can be used across a range of hardware as long as the operating system is the same.

The CP/M (Control Program for Microcomputers) operating system initiated the widespread trend to application portability. It works on 8-bit computers.

Supervisory Control

Beside its linking or device-handling function, the operating system acts as a traffic cop, supervising what gets executed and when.

If an application in process needs a record, like a customer's account, the operating system fetches it from a disk file. First the operating system halts processing temporarily until the record is retrieved. If a nonexistent record is asked for, it notifies the application, which can take corrective action. If no error control is programmed into the application, the operating system takes over and usually suspends execution. The user is notified of the problem through the operating system's utility software.

The operating system uses a directory that tells it where customer records are stored in files on the disk. It also supervises how the file is organized.

Memory space allocation is another operating system control function. It places programs separate from data and treats each differently. For programs, it fetches sequential instructions that the central processor works on one at a time. If the central processor needs data, it knows where it is temporarily stored awaiting use.

Operating systems use various memory management techniques to make random access memory appear larger than it actually is. An application may be sold as needing a minimum of 64 Kbytes of random access memory. In reality, the program may be 128 Kbytes. In order to execute in a 64-Kbyte memory space, some memory management techniques are required. Techniques known as *program overlays, swapping* or *virtual memory,* and *memory banks* are common.

The *program overlay* technique chains one program segment onto another. For example, a program might begin by displaying a menu and asking for a processing choice. Depending on the user's choice, a new program segment could be called from disk to overlay the menu program segment. Once in memory, the chained program executes until, perhaps, the user types an exit signal.

The exit signal could cause the program segment in memory to chain back to the menu program. On recall from the disk, it overlays whatever was previously in memory. This overlay technique can repeat as needed. On floppy disk systems, the disk exchanges usually cause noticeable delays.

Swapping or *virtual memory* works much like program overlays. The difference is that transfers occur according to dictates of the operating system, not the application program. Usually this technique is used in centralized multiuser operating systems.

A *memory bank* technique allows the central processor to switch between addressing different physical banks of memory. Switching provides additional memory to one user or separate memories to several users. This technique allows users to share memory through partitioning, with each user's area inaccessible to others.

To review, the supervisory functions performed by the operating system to keep the computer running smoothly are:

Memory space allocation control
File management control
Process control

OPERATING SYSTEM ENVIRONMENTS

Major differences in how the operating system exercises process control are evident in single-tasking, multitasking, and multiuser operating system environments.

Single-Tasking

A single-tasking operating system is the kind Mr. Williams used. It accommodated one user at a time. He could only do one thing at a time, whether it was an electronic spreadsheet, a word processed document, data communications, or whatever. If he wanted to print a document he had to wait to resume work until the printing was done. More than a few times, the wait inconvenienced him.

He found an application program, called a *print-spooler,* that allowed him to print and enter simultaneously. The application was allocated to *foreground* processing, as a computerist would say, while printing occurred in the *background*.

One popular single-tasking operating system for 16-bit microcomputers is MS-DOS. MS stands for Microsoft, the company that wrote the software. When IBM put MS-DOS on their Personal Computer, they called it PC-DOS.

System and application software are usually sold by version number, like PC-DOS 2.0. The number reflects different upgrades of the software. The difference between PC-DOS 1.1 and 2.0 is an upgrade that mainly supports hard disk file management.

Should anyone trade up to the new operating system, all application software written for PC-DOS 1.1 can also be used on 2.0. This is called an *upward migration path* or *upward compatability*. It is highly desirable, and more software manufacturers are emphasizing this migration compatability in their ever evolving and maturing products.

Otherwise, to upgrade to an incompatible operating system requires buying new software to work with it—in effect, trashing all old software. Users with heavy investments in application software and learning do not willingly change to an operating system that is incompatible with their present software.

Another single-tasking operating system is CP/M-86. The 86 refers to the microprocessor chip it works with, the Intel 8086. This operating system by Digital Research is a 16-bit version of CP/M.

Some guidelines Mr. Williams used to choose his operating system included a good product reputation, a large established user base, and a variety of desirable software products available for it.

Multitasking

Multitasking operating systems seems to turn one computer into many. Computerists would call the technique creating *virtual machines* or *screens.* This is the kind to which Mr. Williams eventually migrated.

Business professionals do multiple concurrent tasks all the time. By using the *windowing* concept, as shown in Figure 3–3, a display is dynamically divided into a number of rectangular areas. Each is called a window. Each window has all the capabilities of a single display. A user can edit a document with a word processor in one window, examine an electronic spreadsheet in another, and create a bar chart of the spreadsheet in a third.

By moving the cursor into a window or command line, a user indicates which of several active processes is intended for use. Output from one window can be directed to another window and different processes can be interconnected to carry out multiple functions. Mr. Williams found he was far more productive than with his single-tasking operating system.

Some microcomputer multitasking operating systems are based on the minicomputer model called Unix. It is not unusual, therefore, to find microcomputer versions with names like Xenix, Venix, Micronix, and QNX. Tandy Corporation's System 16, the Fortune 32:16, and Apple Corporation's Lisa computers all use the Xenix operating system by Microsoft.

Multiuser

Multiuser operating systems allow more than one user to share a single physical small business computer system. They look and work just like the minicomputer and mainframe model shown in Figure 1–4. They also use dumb terminals, if desired.

Many multitasking systems are also multiuser systems. The Unix and Pick operating systems are larger computer models for new small computer versions.

A professional associate of Mr. Williams uses a multiuser system. His multiuser microcomputer system is more limited in growth potential. His supports under 16 terminals versus under 256 for minicomputers. Memory and hard disk storage capacity are also more limited.

Often, like minicomputers, actual and theoretical numbers vary. The number of terminals connected varies based on how heavily each terminal is used and when performance becomes sluggish.

Many cases exist where a user reaches the practical growth limit and still needs more users connected. If no larger capacity computer is available, it could mean starting a new cluster. Sharing files between clusters could be a problem unless a networking

IBM 3270 Personal Computer, Courtesy of IBM, Inc.

Figure 3–3 A multitasking system with windows, showing two electronic spreadsheets and one graphics process in progress

capability is available. Networking is discussed in Part V of this book.

Another alternative to a multiuser growth problem is to begin fresh with the minimum configuration of a much larger-capacity computer. While this provides growing room, the operating systems may be incompatible. It may not be desirable to trash the old software and to begin training all over.

In any system with multiusers, file access permissions can be specified for the file owner and for each authorized user. Four file protection permissions are often available. A *read* permission allows access, but no file updating authority. *Write* permission gives a user update privileges. *Append* allows a user to add new records to a file. The *execute* permission means the file contains a program instead of data and that the user with this permission can run the program. By combining these permissions a file can be classified for any user as read and execute only, read and append only, and so on.

Multiuser operating systems also prevent two users from trying to update the same customer record at the same time. The feature that prevents this is called *record locking* or *lock-out.* A locked-out user is given an option to wait or to resume with something else. Such systems, like most other operating systems, also time and date stamp files, indicating when the last access or update occurred.

UTILITIES

Mr. Williams uses system software directly through its utilities. They are a collection of separate programs mainly to manipulate files and directories.

With his simple single-tasking floppy disk system, he learned system software commands to format and copy disks as well as view a directory of disk files. The A> prompt on the display as shown in Figure 3-4 alerts him to the fact that he is interfacing with the system software level. Users typically identify this as the operating system prompt.

Format

Blank floppy disks are unusable until formatted. *Formatting* a disk partitions tracks of the disk into sectors and gives address information to each sector. The partitioning of sectors is unique to each operating system. With a number of operating systems

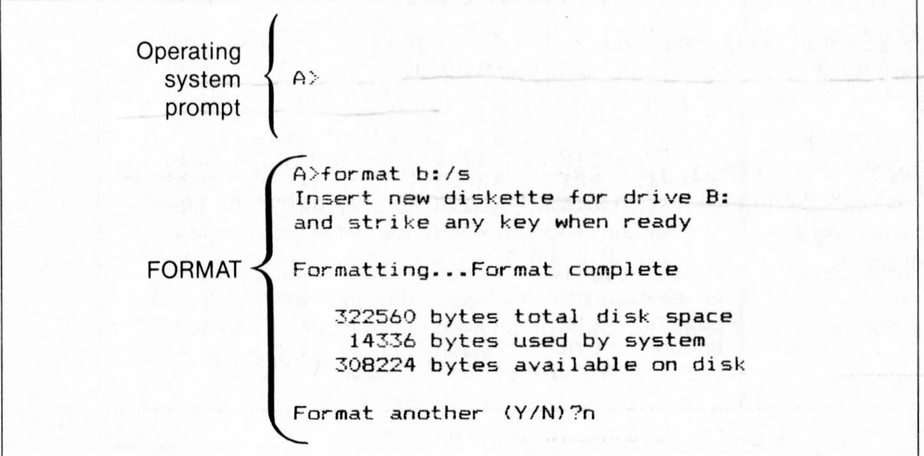

Figure 3-4 Some system software commands and responses

The direct access technique allows an application to directly retrieve any record requested, as long as the record number is known. In a real estate billing application, tenant numbers that are equivalent to record numbers for 1 to 100, for example, are available instantly by typing the desired number. One disadvantage is that if only tenant #1 and #100 are active, the file management subsystem automatically reserves record slots 2 to 99, which is wasted disk space.

Another disadvantage is that some key record identifiers are non-numeric or out of simple ascending numeric order. Some examples are apartment 2A, or inventory part number XTC 423, or the first six digits of a customer's last name. To find where such a desired record is stored, a programmer must devise an indirect method of associating a key identifier with a record number. Once the record number is known, a direct access can occur.

One common indirect method is to establish an index file of key search items matched with associated record numbers. This is called the *keyed* or *indexed file access technique,* as illustrated in Figure 3–9.

In the example in Figure 3–9, assume a user enters apartment number 2A. First an index file containing only apartment numbers with associated record numbers is sequentially searched for 2A. When 2A is found, the record number becomes known. It now is possible to make an immediate direct access to record number 3. The smaller index file is created when the full master file is initially built.

Indexing requires more programmer skill to manage and extra disk space to store the index. It also often requires more memory because usually the entire index is transferred into memory whenever an application using it is executed. The index table

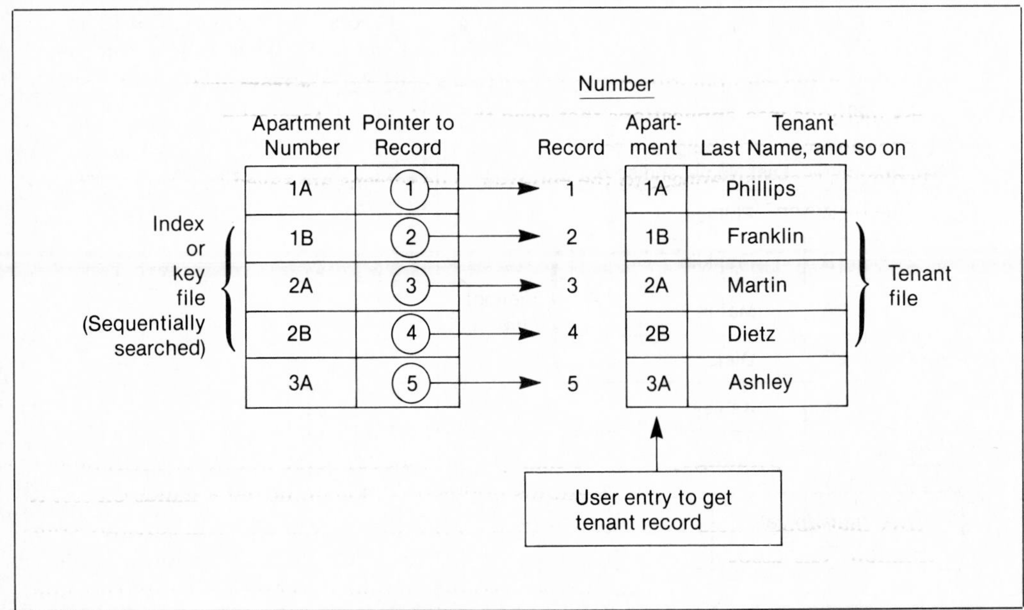

Figure 3-9 Indirect access to records in a random access file

can then be searched at internal machine speed instead of slower disk speed. All index maintenance due to record adds, changes and deletes must be programmed.

A second file technique usually offered along with random access is *sequential access*. *Sequential* files must be searched from beginning to end sequentially to locate any record requested, as implied in Figure 3–9. The technique, therefore, is inappropriate for large files containing records that users randomly request. Especially when floppy disk is used, search time can require seconds, which seems very long to anyone at the keyboard waiting to update a record.

A few advanced systems offered an index sequential access method (ISAM). This technique works like the indexed method already described, except the programmer is relieved of writing the file-handling code. Periodically, however, a user of an ISAM file may find it necessary to run a program to untangle the web of pointers that automatically build up and that can slow performance.

Programmer Tools

System software usually provides features for both inexperienced programmers and professional application developers. These include editors, which are crude versions of commercial word processors. Their objective is to facilitate the typing and correction of lines of program code. Some programmers ignore the built-in editor and develop code with a favorite word processor as long as the word processor makes readable files available to the language processor.

An assembler language and related debugging tools are usually available to programmers who like to work close to machine code.

Some programmer tools or productivity aids are available as optional purchases. Two examples are programs to eliminate the tedious jobs of writing file manipulation code and screen formatting.

A file manipulation package can free a programmer from writing index file access methods into applications that need them. A screen formatting package can give a programmer the ability to design or "paint" input and output screens right on the display as they will appear to the end-user. The screens are saved in a screen file and called by the application as needed. Both tools help reduce application development time and may help design better applications.

EVALUATION

Evaluating system software is necessary to uncover limitations to specified requirements. A single-user operating system, for example, will not support a multiuser environment.

When Mr. Williams bought his floppy disk system, he did a hands-on test to verify that applications he wanted worked on the hardware and system software combination. His associate also did hands-on testing when buying a multiuser system. Although it was not possible to run the maximum terminal complement at full throttle, he tried to exercise the system with several terminals running. Both talked to other users with similar systems to get their evaluations.

Some advocate that it is impossible for a novice to evaluate system software. Mr. Williams felt it certainly was not as straightforward as evaluating applications. Since he wanted a single-user system that was widely accepted, he realistically felt only a modest effort should be expended on evaluation. If the system, however, is for more than one user, or if it involves multitasking or will be used for application development work, its features must be examined closely.

The System Software Checklist that appears in Figure 3-10 is designed to assist in the evaluation effort. It should be supplemented with the General Software Checklist and the Hands-on Test Checklist given in Chapter 4.

Figure 3-10 System Software Checklist

Candidate Packages Names:

A: ______________________

B: ______________________

C: ______________________

Check "must have" items.		Rating (Scale 1 = Poor To 10 = Excellent) A	B	C
	Operating System			
___	Variety of desirable application programs available	___	___	___
___	Works on a larger computer	___	___	___
	Computer model	___	___	___
	Conversion tasks required to upgrade	___	___	___
___	Single-tasking	___	___	___
___	Multitasking	___	___	___
	Maximum tasks supported	___	___	___
___	Intertask communication	___	___	___
___	Tasks can start/stop/suspend other tasks	___	___	___
___	Windowing	___	___	___
___	Multiuser	___	___	___
	Maximum supported	___	___	___
___	Multitasking	___	___	___
___	Password security	___	___	___
___	File permissions	___	___	___
___	Record-locking	___	___	___
___	Date and time stamps	___	___	___
___	Separate directories	___	___	___
	Memory management:			
	Space occupied	___	___	___
	Space addressable	___	___	___
___	Swapping supported	___	___	___
___	Program overlay/chaining	___	___	___
___	Memory bank addressing	___	___	___
	Peripheral management:			

Figure 3-10 (continued)

Check "must have" items.	Rating (Scale 1 = Poor To 10 = Excellent) A	B	C
Operating System			
___ User-installable device drivers	___	___	___
___ Print spooling	___	___	___
___ Remote communication support	___	___	___
___ Mixed floppy and hard disk on one unit	___	___	___
Language Processors			
___ Variety of languages available	___	___	___
Length of time available	___	___	___
___ Programmer tools available	___	___	___
File access techniques:			
___ Sequential	___	___	___
___ Random or direct	___	___	___
___ Indexed sequential (ISAM)	___	___	___
Subtotal	___	___	___
Divide by number of items rated for average rating	___	___	___

Transfer Average Rating to Selection Summary: Software, Figure 5–3.

SELF TEST

1. What is the function of each layer in the system software hierarchy?
2. Identify the difference between the fixed and variable parts of the operating system.
3. Give an example of how the operating system exercises supervisory control.
4. Name two techniques that make memory appear larger than it really is.
5. What are two potential limitations of single-tasking environments?
6. What is multitasking?
7. Describe a file security scheme in a multiuser system.
8. List four utilities and their functions.
9. Give an example of pipelined tasks. Identify the filters and the pipe.
10. How is an interpreter different from a compiler?
11. Describe, using an example, two kinds of direct access.

EXERCISES

1. *Kristen Company Case.* The Kristen Company is installing a multiuser operating system and needs an appropriate hierarchical directory structure. Using Figure 3–6 as a guide, lay out a structure that would be suitable to support three vice-presidents. Each is

responsible for two managers. In addition, each maintains separate directories for word processing and electronic spreadsheet files.

2. Read three recent articles about small business computer multitasking operating systems. All three articles could be about one operating system or several. For each operating system, list the features available in each system software layer. If several are used, compare features to make a determination about which one is the superior product.
3. Locate and execute a disk-based tutorial similar to one listed in the Resources and References section of Chapter 3. Make an outline of the steps in the learning sequence. Prepare an oral or written report on what you learned and how you learned it. Conclude the report with your evaluation of the tutorial's effectiveness.

RESOURCES AND REFERENCES

Operating Systems

ASHLEY, RUTH AND JUDI FERNANDEZ, *PC DOS: Using the IBM PC Operating System,* Wiley, 1983.

CORTESI, DAVID E., *Inside CP/M: A Guide for Users and Programmers,* Holt, 1982.

DAHMKE, MARK, *Microcomputer Operating Systems,* McGraw-Hill, 1981.

ETTLIN, WALTER A. AND GREGORY SALBERG, *Microsoft BASIC Made Easy,* McGraw-Hill, 1983.

FOX, DAVID AND MITCHELL WAITE, *Pascal Primer,* Sams, 1981.

GRANT, CHARLES W. AND JON BUTAH, *Introduction to the UCSD System,* Sybex, 1983.

KING, RICHARD, *IBM-PC DOS Handbook,* Sybex, 1983.

LOMUTO, ANN N. AND NICO LOMUTO, *A Unix Primer,* Prentice-Hall, 1983.

MURTHA, STEPHEN M. AND MITCHELL WAITE, *CP/M Primer,* Sams, 1980.

THOMAS, REBECCA AND JEAN YATES, *A User's Guide to the UNIX System,* McGraw-Hill, 1982.

TIBERGHIAN, JACQUES, *The Pascal Handbook,* Sybex, 1981.

TOWNSEND, CARL, *How to Get Started with MSDOS,* Dilithium, 1981.

ZAKS, RODNEY, *CP/M Handbook with MP/M,* Sybex, 1980.

ZAKS, RODNEY, *Introduction to Pascal* (including UCSD Pascal), 2nd ed., Sybex, 1983.

Pascal Language (for BASIC, see Chapter 18 Resources and References)

BOWLES, KENNETH L., *Beginner's Manual for the Pascal System,* McGraw-Hill, 1980.

HUME, J.N.P. AND R. C. HOLT, *UCSD Pascal: A Beginner's Guide to Programming Microcomputers,* Reston, 1982.

PRICE, DAVID, *Pascal: A Considerate Approach,* Prentice-Hall, 1982.

Disk-based Tutorials

ATI Training Power-IBM PC-DOS, ATI.

HEBDRICKSON AND DIETZLER, *The Instructor Self-Teaching Software for the IBM-PC,* QED, 1982.

How to Use Your IBM Personal Computer, Cdex.
IBM PC DOS 2.0, Cdex.
PC Tutor, Comprehensive.
Teach Yourself Concurrent CP/M, DELTAK.
Teach Yourself the IBM PC, DELTAK.
Teach Yourself PC-DOS, DELTAK.
Understanding Personal Computers and Their Applications, Cdex.

Other Learning Aids

Getting Started on Your IBM PC, videotape, DELTAK.

4

APPLICATION SOFTWARE

Application software is the most important ingredient of any small computer system. Application software makes the hardware perform a meaningful end-user task like word processing or order processing and billing. It is so important that informed users shop for application software first. Then they buy hardware that the software runs on.

Most of this book is devoted to application software. This chapter covers general topics related to all application software. It defines application types and what to consider in the buy-versus-build-from-scratch application controversy. A major section concerns evaluating application software.

TYPES OF APPLICATION

The term *application* software, as mentioned earlier, comes from the fact that such software *applies* the computer to end-user purposes. Common *applications* of small computers to specific end-user tasks include:

PROFESSIONAL SUPPORT APPLICATIONS

Word processing

Database management systems

Electronic spreadsheets
Graphics
Data communications

ACCOUNTING APPLICATIONS

Order Processing
Accounts Receivable
Inventory
Purchasing
Accounts Payable
Payroll
General Ledger

INDUSTRY-SPECIFIC APPLICATIONS

Real Estate Management
Building Contractor Job Costing
Dentist Billing

Most application software for small computers is bought as preprogrammed *packages,* ready for immediate use. Preprogrammed application packages are also variously called *canned, off-the-shelf,* and *over-the-counter* software.

PROFESSIONAL SUPPORT APPLICATIONS

Professional support applications are those generally retailed over-the-counter at local computer stores. They are designed to help business professionals accomplish five of their most important functions: writing, information retrieval, calculating, planning, and communicating.

Mr. Williams uses word processing to facilitate his writing tasks and database management systems to retrieve information from personal files as well as company files. He uses data communications to communicate with his business peers through a local area network. Data communications are also used to reach remote computer banks of stored information at a public information utility.

For the planning and calculating function itself, he uses an electronic spreadsheet. Of the many available, VisiCalc stands out as the single product that generated, in 1979, the era of the small computer as a professional's support tool. VisiCalc's name itself suggests its use as a visible calculator. Often he converts spreadsheets to graphic form for presentation to others or for further analysis purposes.

Some software vendors combine several functions into one integrated package. Examples are Lotus 1-2-3, Symphony and Framework. Lotus combines electronic spreadsheet, database file management, and graphic functions. On the other hand,

Symphony and Framework include all the same functions and further include word processing and data communications. Such packages are called *multifunction or integrated application packages.*

A *multifunction package* allows a user to move freely among applications. Often the video display splits into several smaller displays or windows. Each window reflects work with a different function.

One of Mr. Williams' business associates works with such a package. It is not unusual for her to be developing a spreadsheet when a phone call interrupts. The phone call results in a need to type a quick memo using the word processing function in a separate window. The memo is to include a pie chart of the spreadsheet figures being completed. The pie chart is reviewed in a third window. Systems like this, flexible enough to accommodate such a professional worker pattern, are becoming more prevalent as small computers become more powerful.

One advantage of an all-in-one, or multifunction, applications package is that only one set of commands must be learned to use all functions. One disadvantage, however, is that such packages so far tend to offer fewer features than comparable stand-alone products in each application area. This trend is expected to reverse as new packages emerge.

Multifunction applications usually require a large memory to execute. For example, one requires 320 Kbytes of memory. This compares with usually under 128 Kbytes for stand-alone applications.

Without a multifunction package, users must learn a new set of commands and procedures for each application. This often complicates the learning experience, which can be weeks to master a single function like electronic spreadsheets or word processing. Usually it takes only hours, however, to learn the basics.

This lengthy start-up problem has spawned an entire industry of application learning aids. They range from on-screen tutorials to prepared disk exercises, to audio and video training aids. A review of the list of learning aids at the end of the Electronic Spreadsheet Chapter 6 gives an idea of the extent of available support.

Another of Mr. Williams' friends uses a *family* of related *stand-alone packages.* Such an example includes the MicroPro family of products which includes WordStar, a word processor, CalcStar, an electronic spreadsheet, and InfoStar, a database management system, among others. Commands are the same throughout the suite of programs.

The biggest disadvantage to using stand-alone packages is switching applications. Movement between packages requires the normal quitting of one task, saving the active file, and removing the disks on a floppy disk system. Then the new application must be loaded from disk to memory and started from scratch. Many find this routine tedious and disruptive to a busy work pattern. Disk removal is eliminated when using a hard-disk system.

Mr. Williams found a solution to simplify application switching. He bought an add-on package that functioned as a shell allowing him to use any application desired. DesQ and The Integrator are examples of products that integrate any off-the-shelf packages. StarBurst is a shell that integrates only the MicroPro family of stand-alone products.

When using the shell he could activate any desired application. It made concurrent use of multifunctions feasible. It also allowed him to retain his investment, both in cash and learning, in his old familiar software.

The cost of professional support applications can be several hundred dollars apiece, but function and price vary enormously. For example, one word processing package costs $50 and another $600. One data communication package is distributed free, but its author requests a $35 contribution from satisfied users. The package easily surpasses another that performs fewer functions at $150. One database management package costs $100 and another $3,500. Whereas one can be used to create a full accounting system, the other is useful as a rolodex or index card file replacement.

Multifunction application packages cost about $500 to $2,000. Some have only two functions, others more. They also vary enormously in features available.

ACCOUNTING APPLICATIONS

Accounting applications help keep accurate records of the cash flowing into and out of a business. This information is vital to SGD Inc. and all other businesses to monitor the health of the organization. It also enables management to make informed short and long range planning decisions.

SGD Inc.'s General Ledger application summarizes the cash movement that other applications feed it. Accounts Receivable identifies customer payments or cash flowing into the company. Accounts Payable identifies checks written or cash flowing out of the company.

Accounting applications also include sales order processing and invoicing or billing as well as inventory control and purchasing, among other functions. They primarily help expedite repetitive, often complex, procedures associated with "doing business as usual." At SGD Inc. that usually is processing sales orders, billing customers for shipped orders, purchasing new inventory and paying for the new stock.

SGD Inc. and most other organizations like the fact that in an integrated accounting application, database records used by one application are available to others, as shown in Figure 4–1. One advantage of integration is that database information integrity is retained. Since only one copy of a record exists to be used by all applications needing it, decisionmaking in all areas is uniformly based on the same information.

Another advantage is that data need to be entered into the database only once to be usable by any application. Once entered it automatically gets filtered to wherever it is needed. This reduces clerical time and error by eliminating transaction re-entry.

Accounting applications can range in price from a few hundred dollars for one application to as much as $15,000 for a package of all integrated applications. Less expensive packages are retailed through local computer stores. The majority of accounting software, however, is sold through independent software integrators and turnkey vendors who provide training and follow-up support.

When accounting packages are generalized enough to be used by many industry types they are often called *general* or *cross-industry accounting packages*. An example is an accounts receivable package that can be used by a manufacturer as well as by a contractor.

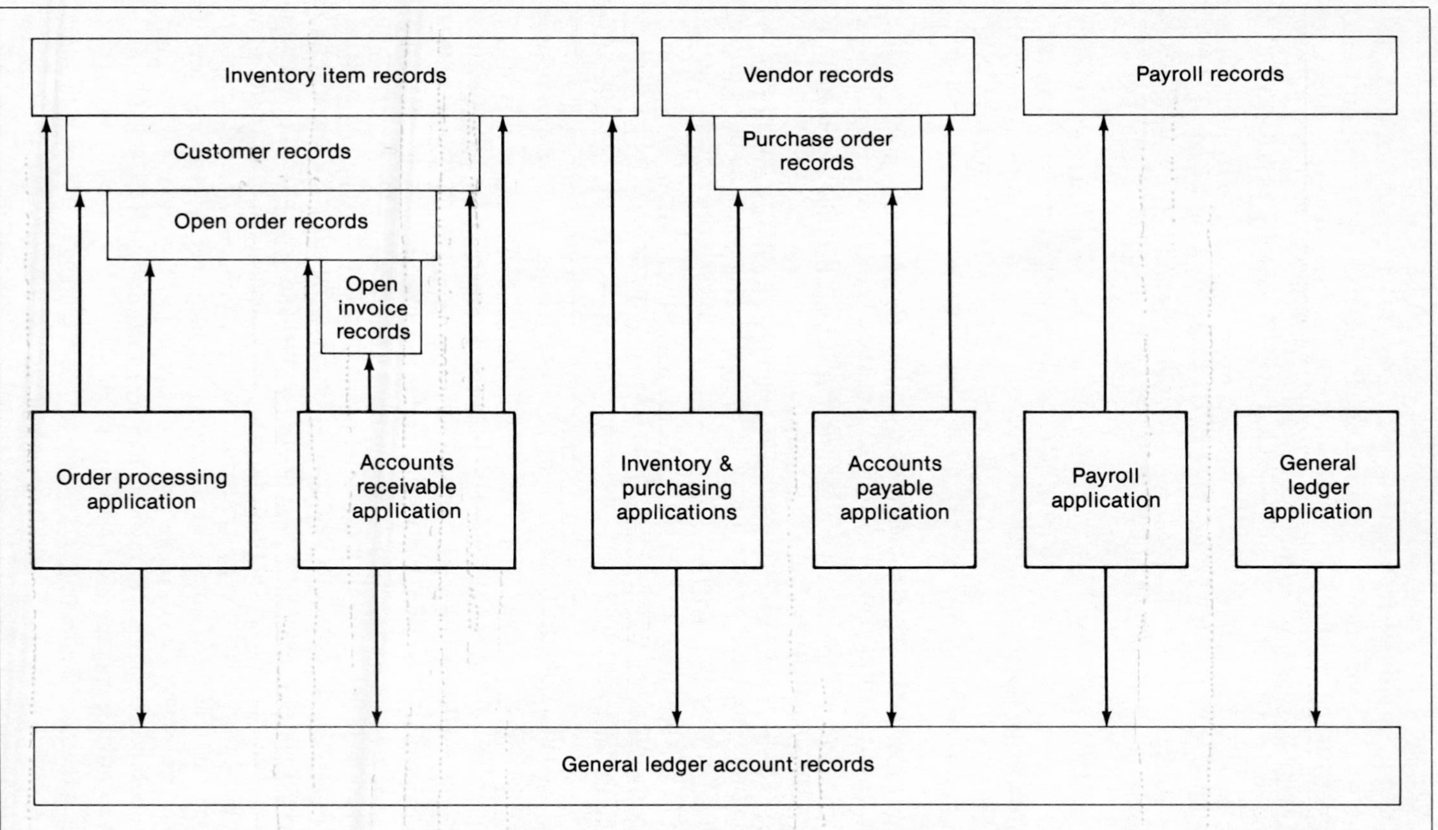

Figure 4-1 Relationship between database records and applications in an "integrated" accounting package

INDUSTRY SPECIFIC APPLICATIONS

Industry-specific application examples are real estate management, building contractor job costing, and dentist billing. Usually they integrate both operational and accounting functions and are sold as turnkey systems.

Computerists classify industry-specific application software as *vertical* packages. This is because one package caters to only one industry segment. On the other hand, they call general accounting packages *horizontal* packages. This is because such packages are broadly sold across industry types.

SGD Inc. eventually bought an integrated accounting package that was not specifically designed for the distribution industry. They were in the sporting goods distribution business, and a horizontal package met most of their needs.

One nursing home successfully installed an industry-specific application. Their turnkey vendor had been selling software to nursing homes for years. Industry needs were well planned and provided for in the package.

Individual peculiarities were handled in a professional way. The program asked start-up questions. Answers to the questions effectively set switches, or *parameters,* allowing preprogrammed routines to function or not. The way the package anticipated user demands evidenced a strong industry familiarity.

On the other hand, a service company that bought an industry-specific package had an unsuccessful installation. The package, it turns out, was custom-designed for one company and now was being recycled to others. It evidenced peculiarities designed to please the first company that had the software made from scratch.

Package inadequacies were not uncovered earlier because of an unsystematic approach to package evaluation. A hands-on test of the software was not done. The user watched a vendor demonstration. Vendor-directed demonstrations are usually flawless by design. Much time and money was lost refitting the package for practical use. In addition, the user had to get involved with programmers, system specifications, and other detail associated with creating or modifying software from scratch.

Most industry-specific packages begin as custom designs for one customer. Vendors who decide to resell a package normally market test it before launching new sales. Testing is done with the cooperation of several users who participate in what the computer industry calls a *beta test*. It is a package debugging and refinement period.

Mr. Williams understood the importance of a thoroughly debugged and industry-sensitive package. He knew users who had to salvage the chaos created by a poor package choice. This is largely avoided when approaching the package-buying decision with a *caveat-emptor* or let-the-buyer-beware attitude.

MAKE OR BUY

SGD Inc. found an integrated accounting package to suit its needs. Other companies may not be as fortunate. Alternatives that present themselves in such a situation include:

Compromise requirements to fit a preprogrammed package

Modify an existing package

Program the application from scratch

Use a database management package as an alternative to programming from scratch

A major disadvantage of packaged software is that it probably is not an exact fit to user needs. Faced with such a situation, there are several possibilities. One advocates that if 80 percent of the package fits, then modify the other 20 percent of user requirements to make use of the package as is. With the most inexpensively retailed software, that is highly realistic.

A word processing package under $500, for example, may fit "must have" requirements, but it falls short on the "would like to have" requirements. Compared to the benefits that computerized word processing can bring to any writing effort, the trade-off decision is not hard to make. Also, since the software is sold "as is," there is no possibility to modify the package.

Turnkey packages generally can be modified, especially if they are databased systems. But the cost of modifying that last 20 percent could cost more than building the software from scratch. A conservative view is that, if the data exists, modification is possible. If the data exists nowhere, probably it is best to forget modification.

Consider, for example, that a user wants a year-end profit report by item. If profit figures by item for the past twelve months are available, a program can be written to print the report. On some database managed systems, users could probably generate the report themselves.

But if data are not available, a major programming effort might be needed, especially in nondatabased systems. The change could cost more in money, time, and grief than building the software from scratch.

If a desired application is not available packaged, however, it may be necessary to design and code the application programs from scratch. An application generally consists of many interrelated programs. It is common, nonetheless, to refer to a single application as simply a program.

Getting a custom application may require hiring a programmer-analyst or software house to do the detailed technical development work. Computerists refer to this work, listed below, as the program development life cycle:

Specify requirements

Design programs

Code programs

Test and debug, or correct, programs

Use and maintain programs

As soon as an application is implemented, revisions are inevitable. This leads to respecifying requirements and beginning the cycle over again.

Many application packages have taken many so-called "man-years" of development time before being usable. Any custom effort requires a substantial investment of time, money, and talent to make it work. An example of such an effort is the subject of Part V of this book.

Figure 4–2 compares features of package and custom application software. Custom software is flexible since it is designed solely to please one user. Usually custom software is also more efficient because it is not encumbered with options designed to please a broad user population.

On the other hand, preprogrammed packages are more economical and quicker to install and use than custom applications. Typically no professional staff is required to run packages, and user documentation is available. Rarely does documentation get done in a custom software effort.

Users could develop custom applications with far less time and expense with a database management package. Mr. Williams' sister-in-law did this for some rental properties she managed. She created a tenant billing application.

Database management systems that can be used by noncomputerists still require the development of all screen displays, reports, and database record designs. Sometimes professional assistance is used for this work. But the results can be swift and measured in days and weeks. This compares to months of effort typically required to do the same thing from scratch.

The chapter on database applications in Part V of this book gives an actual example of what is required to bring up a small custom application from scratch, using one commercially available database package.

To summarize, the hierarchy of application software acquisition choices, in terms of the best investment of user time and money, is:

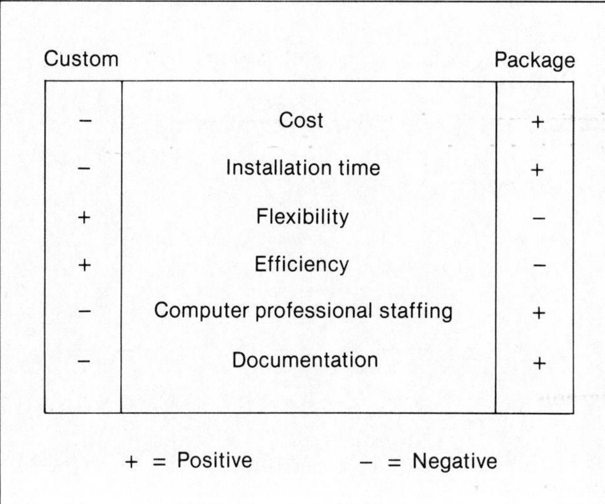

Custom		Package
–	Cost	+
–	Installation time	+
+	Flexibility	–
+	Efficiency	–
–	Computer professional staffing	+
–	Documentation	+

+ = Positive – = Negative

Figure 4–2 A comparison of custom versus packaged application software

Buy a packaged application
Modify an existing package (usually possible with turnkey systems)
Use a database management package
Program from scratch

EVALUATING APPLICATIONS

To support a systematic evaluation of application software, checklists are provided. Two are the General Software Checklist and Hands-on Test Checklist. They are appropriate for any software evaluation. Two more are for turnkey systems only. They are the Turnkey Checklist and the Reference Questionnaire.

Like many other checklists, those described in this book are designed to be amenable to modification for individual needs. They function best as a departure point for thoughtful investigation and evaluation.

General Software Checklist

The General Software Checklist in Figure 4-3 is a guide to prescreening candidate packages. It encourages a check of published reviews or articles about an application. Articles and reviews abound for retailed application software. Often reviews shed revelatory insight on package performance and ease of use.

Figure 4-3 General Software Checklist

Candidate Packages:

	Name	*Supplier*	*Cost ($)*
A:	______	______	______
B:	______	______	______
C:	______	______	______

Items to Check	*Rating (Scale: 1 = Poor to 10 = Excellent)* A	B	C
Package			
Cost	______	______	______
Package reputation	______	______	______
Package supplier reputation	______	______	______
Published evaluation reviews	______	______	______
Recommendations of other users	______	______	______
Length of time available	______	______	______
Number of installations	______	______	______
Number of upgraded versions	______	______	______
Cost and procedure to upgrade to new version	______	______	______
Maintenance charge	______	______	______

Figure 4-3 (continued)

Items to Check	*Rating (Scale: 1 = Poor to 10 = Excellent)* A	B	C
Program backup copy procedure	______	______	______
Compatability with installed/planned hardware/operating system (minimum RAM, screen size and color range, number and type of disk drives, printer support)	______	______	______
Other add-on hardware/software required	______	______	______
Availability	______	______	______
Cost	______	______	______
On-screen tutorial	______	______	______
Availability of other learning aids	______	______	______
Documentation			
User Guide/Manual with index	______	______	______
Report and screen examples	______	______	______
Procedure for:			
Operation	______	______	______
Start-up	______	______	______
Data backup	______	______	______
After-Sale Support			
Supplied by purchase source	______	______	______
Hot-line (800 telephone number) to package supplier	______	______	______
User newsletter or other information service	______	______	______
User group established	______	______	______
Old versions still supported	______	______	______
Subtotal	______	______	______
Divide by number of items rated for average rating	______	______	______

Transfer Average Rating to Selection Summary: Software, Figure 5-3.

If reviews are uniformly dismal, it may save a hands-on test entirely. Uniformly good reviews, however, are not uncommon, even for bad software. Reviewers have publication loyalty and other biases influencing judgment. So while reviews are helpful, they should be regarded as opinion and not as fact.

On-line databases of published articles and reviews are available. One information utility that offers software directory searches also offers article searches. Article searches give publication references with summaries of articles. Based on the summaries, one could decide if a thorough reading of source articles would be informative.

The General Software Checklist also rates package reputation. Information for this rating can come from reviews as well as from computer dealers, user group members, and other sources.

Current users can provide valuable insight to after-sale support. Do competent people respond to phone inquiries? Are old versions of the product still supported? How often are new versions issued? Can new upgrades be obtained through the mail or a dealer? How much do upgrades cost?

Application literature and package documentation often provide information for checklisted items. Documentation for packages sold at computer retail stores can usually be examined at the store free of charge. As one dealer warns, "If you can't understand a User Guide after reading it for fifteen minutes at the store, it won't make any more sense when you use it later."

Documentation can often be purchased separately. It is a good investment for a thorough investigation of a seriously considered package. Some companies deduct the cost from the price of software, if later purchased.

Documentation should include an index and examples of use. Evidence of a written tutorial is good, but an on-screen one is even more helpful. Step-by-step procedures for start-up, operations, and data backup should be clear. The Guide should list supported operating and hardware systems as well as other environmental limitations.

Program backup copy procedures can be important if the application is distributed on disks that are *copy protected,* or uncopyable. The copy problem is an unresolved one in the small computer marketplace. It is designed to inhibit the illegal proliferation of proprietary software. Until the copy problem is resolved, a legitimate purchaser of business programs should do everything possible to prevent any downtime occurring from faulty program disks. Sometimes this involves buying a backup copy, if none is supplied, immediately after purchasing the original software.

Hands-on Test Checklist

Many software products are poorly designed and therefore tedious and costly to use. To avoid being encumbered with poorly designed software, a potential user should evaluate the software by doing a hands-on test. The Hands-on Test Checklist in Figure 4–4 is provided for this purpose.

When test data are collected for hands-on testing of an application, the exercise is called an informal *benchmark test*. The prepared data are repeatedly used to test all candidate packages. The primary areas that get scrutinized in such a test are performance and ease of use.

Mr. Williams assisted in the hands-on test of SGD Inc.'s integrated accounting package. He specifically had an interest in the order processing and invoicing part of the package. Both he and Ms. Fenton, the office manager and bookkeeper who initially was to operate the system, conducted the test. They first described on the Hands-on

Figure 4-4 Hands-on Test Checklist

Candidate Packages:

	Name	*Test Date*	*Test Location*
A:	______	______	______
B:	______	______	______
C:	______	______	______

Items to Check	*Rating (Scale: 1 = poor to 10 = excellent)* A	*B*	*C*
Performance and Function			
Data entry for (describe):			
1. ______	______	______	______
2. ______	______	______	______
3. ______	______	______	______
Screens for:			
1. ______	______	______	______
2. ______	______	______	______
3. ______	______	______	______
Printed copy for:			
1. ______	______	______	______
2. ______	______	______	______
3. ______	______	______	______
Database file maintenance for:			
1. ______	______	______	______
2. ______	______	______	______
3. ______	______	______	______
Periodic routines, if applicable	______	______	______
Audit trail controls, if applicable	______	______	______
Data backup procedure	______	______	______
Ease of use			
On-screen tutorial	______	______	______
User Guide/Manual	______	______	______
Computer response time	______	______	______
Prompts:			
User-friendly	______	______	______
Logical	______	______	______
Consistent	______	______	______
HELP routines	______	______	______
Easy EXIT routines	______	______	______
ERROR correction routines that do not deadlock processing	______	______	______

Figure 4-4 (continued)

Items to Check	*Rating (Scale: 1 = poor to 10 = excellent)* A	B	C
Screen formats:			
Clear and uncluttered	______	______	______
Consistent	______	______	______
Other			
(The following procedures should be known even if not tested or not in the User Guide)			
Recovery from:			
Memory full	______	______	______
Program aborts	______	______	______
Saving to a full disk	______	______	______
Writing to or reading from a damaged disk section (or sector)	______	______	______
Printer jams	______	______	______
Subtotal	______	______	______
Divide by number of items rated for average rating	______	______	______

Transfer Average Rating to Selection Summary: Software, Figure 5–3.

Test Checklist those transactions, screens, reports, and database update capabilities they required of any order processing application. Among other items, their checklist included:

DATA ENTRY FOR:

1. A new order
2. A change to items ordered
3. A change between item quantity ordered and item quantity shipped

SCREENS FOR:

1. An unshippped customer order
2. A backorder

PRINTED COPY FOR:

1. Pick ticket
2. Invoice
3. Sales Journal

DATABASE MAINTENANCE FOR:

1. Adding a customer "ship to" address
2. Changing the item pricing structure

An extra copy of the checklist is necessary to list other related items.

After the checklist is filled out, the actual test begins. In this case, testing is done at a turnkey vendor's demonstration room.

They were assured that their test would not be done with a specially prepared demonstration version of the package. They were aware that demonstration packages are often known to be skillfully crafted showpieces. Usually such "demos" do not accurately represent real processing or response timing.

Response time is the time from when a user types the last key of an entry to the time the computer displays the first letter of a reply. Response time is important because, when attention is allowed to flag, productivity goes down. Demos occasionally shield all the nitty-gritty processing steps that could interfere with an acceptable response time. They must be uncovered, however, in order to make an informed comparative study.

Where hardware is available, a package can often be tested in the convenience of one's workplace. Such packages may require first paying the full purchase price. In return there is a policy that refunds are paid within thirty or sixty days if not satisfied with the package.

With no expert guidance available, this approach could take considerable test time and effort. One integrated accounting package conservatively estimates it takes ten hours to do the introductory tutorial exercise.

Often a demo disk is included with this sales approach. These demo disks typically are exact copies of their originals. The only difference is that database capacities are limited to a few records each for test purposes only. These are completely valid copies for hands-on testing purposes.

In the SGD Inc. company case, it is decided to test normal new order entry as well as a change to an existing order. To do this Ms. Fenton first powers up the system. Only a password and date are required to start operations. Then a few customer and inventory records are loaded with test data so information is available to do normal order processing.

Since no on-screen tutorial is available, Ms. Fenton has the User Guide for assistance. Data entry procedures are followed, but deliberate errors are committed to test error recovery and "help" routines. While many professional support applications designate one key that functions as a help key, none is available on this accounting package.

Fortunately errors are displayed in plain English and include clear instructions for recovery. Some less satisfactory software produces error messages in code that requires looking up a translation and recovery procedure in a manual. Some unsophisticated software comes to a dead halt and requires expert help to resume.

Entering the actual new order, as well as a modification, provides further opportunity to examine the prompts that guide operator entry. The test reveals prompts that are unintimidatingly free of computer jargon or codes. They are also logical and consistent, which also means they are easy to follow and eventually learn.

Prompts also appear in the same screen location and require familiar responses. Responses do not shift arbitrarily, for example, from a "YES" to a "Y" to a carriage return for indicating a positive response. Once a response pattern is established, it is consistently used.

The prompting technique used to enter or type data has a strong effect on operator training time and motivation. Some suggest that the longer it takes to learn an application, the less desirable the software is. Certainly the number of features and functions in a package make a difference in learning time. But while some packages can be intuitively learned in hours, others need days and weeks.

Mr. Williams then selects from a menu of choices to display a customer's order. He reaches the processing level desired through several submenus. In some systems, menu selections can be entered so rapidly by an experienced user that menu screens are bypassed entirely. This is a desirable feature. Alternately, a user can choose the level of menu help desired. The experienced level might suppress all menus.

Unfortunately, the screen Mr. Williams retrieves is so cluttered that the order shipped date seems obscure. Some reports he prints are also so full of code letters and abbreviations that they are almost uninterpretable. He wanted screen and report designs to be clear and easy to use.

The Sales Journal, which he prints after invoices, looks just fine. It serves as a permanent control list of all invoices printed during the last print run. Control totals on the Journal match the ones manually prepared to cross-check application computation accuracy.

Continuing the test, Ms. Fenton tries end-of-period routines to be sure periodic computer totals match manual test totals. She heard a story about one innocent user who worked with an application from a July installation through December 31 only to find the year-end totalling routine never worked.

Finally, backup procedures are examined. This procedure is a daily event with accounting systems, and can be very time-consuming. Some systems have very elaborate multidisk swapping procedures that are highly error-prone. Some do the same thing with built-in system control to guard against error. Others transfer data to different storage media. A hands-on test of this event prevents any unpleasant surprises during possible future use.

When the test is completed, a total average score is calculated. It is used to compare all packages being evaluated.

Hands-on testing is also appropriate for evaluating custom software. Then the test is usually called *acceptance testing*. It often is a much more highly structured event. For example, test data may be prepared by computer experts to test as many alternate processing paths as feasible.

Turnkey Checklist

Turnkey systems are generally put together by system integrators for specific industries. They include functionally integrated applications that profoundly change the way business is normally done. In the case of one printing industry turnkey system, changes affect everything from over-the-phone job estimating to shop floor employee and machine productivity analyses. Major job training and realignment is necessary for both the professional and office staff to change from manual to automated methods of operation.

Acquiring such systems are major organizational commitments. A bad choice with a turnkey system can have disastrous results and is known to even cause business failure.

Answers to items on the Turnkey Checklist, given in Figure 4–5, come from vendor literature, system documentation, other users, and knowledgeable industry contacts. They also come from direct questioning of the vendor.

Figure 4-5 Turnkey Checklist

Candidate Systems:

	Name	*Turnkey Vendor Name and Phone*
A:	______	______
B:	______	______
C:	______	______

Items to Check	*Rating (Scale: 1 = poor to 10 = excellent)* A	B	C
Application Software			
Length of free warranty period	___	___	___
Period begins after an agreed-upon acceptance test	___	___	___
Period specifies a level of continuous performance	___	___	___
Procedure to correct program errors:			
Before warranty expires	___	___	___
After warranty expires	___	___	___
Associated costs (should be none until after warranty expires)	___	___	___
New documentation supplied	___	___	___
Other documentation:			
Program source code (or is it held by a third-party)	___	___	___
Dictionary of all data items	___	___	___
Diagrams of workflow sequence	___	___	___
Program modifications:			
Done by supplier who wrote software	___	___	___
Cost policy provided	___	___	___
Time guidelines provided	___	___	___
Payment terms available:			
Tied to an installation schedule	___	___	___
Tied to an acceptance test that progress has been achieved	___	___	___
Software maintenance:			
Written policy on level and quality of service	___	___	___
Provided at remote installations	___	___	___
Charges for multiple copies of application or operating system software	___	___	___

Figure 4-5 (continued)

Items to Check	*Rating (Scale: 1 = poor to 10 = excellent)* A	B	C
Hardware			
Degree of vendor relationship to hardware manufacturer (such as manufacturer's distributor versus independent sales organization)	______	______	______
Larger computer available now to run software as is	______	______	______
Description of components provided with both required and growth capacities for:			
System unit	______	______	______
Random access memory	______	______	______
Disk	______	______	______
Backup hardware	______	______	______
Display	______	______	______
Other: __________________	______	______	______
Costs:			
Hardware	______	______	______
Hardware delivery	______	______	______
Site preparation	______	______	______
Supplies	______	______	______
Insurance	______	______	______
Other: __________________	______	______	______
Warranty period:			
Length of time	______	______	______
Begins when	______	______	______
Vendor			
Time in computer business	______	______	______
Time in vendor business	______	______	______
Time servicing user industry	______	______	______
Number of customers	______	______	______
Customer references in same industry in local area	______	______	______
Other computer hardware products sold	______	______	______
Other application software products sold	______	______	______
Types of businesses sold to	______	______	______
Support staff numbers:			
Programmers	______	______	______
Trainers	______	______	______
Maintenance technicians	______	______	______
Other	______	______	______
Assistance provided, as well as estimated time, charges, and procedures for:			
Specifying requirements/feasibility study	______	______	______
Installation planning	______	______	______
Hardware installation	______	______	______
Application software installation	______	______	______
Application training	______	______	______

Figure 4-5 (continued)

Items to Check	*Rating (Scale: 1 = poor to 10 = excellent)* A	B	C
Vendor			
On-site training service	_____	_____	_____
Custom programming	_____	_____	_____
Recent financial statement supports company stability	_____	_____	_____
Bankruptcy or computer litigation history	_____	_____	_____
Contract terms negotiable	_____	_____	_____
Written checklist responses can be attached to contract	_____	_____	_____
Model contract provided for examination	_____	_____	_____
Subtotal	_____	_____	_____
Divide by number of items rated for average rating	_____	_____	_____

Transfer Average Rating to Selection Summary: Turnkey System, Figure 5–4.

The application software section of the checklist addresses package modification and maintenance. Relatively inexpensive software can become costly if the user requires modifications, and the user may find modifications are impossible with some packages.

Since businesses operate in a dynamic environment, viewing accounting or industry-specific software as "frozen" is a misconception. Many managers with a payroll package have been faced with implementing a new tax or adding a new box to the employee W–2 form. New government regulations require that the payroll program be flexible. Business grows, and new procedures come along that inevitably require software additions. It is important to fix responsibility for these changes. Who does them and what are the costs?

Ideally the company, person, or people who wrote the software are in the best position to make changes. But if the software developer is no longer available, a substitute approach is needed.

If a reputable software house designed and programmed the application, it ordinarily can provide competent follow-up support for its products. But if a moonlighter put together the package and has since disappeared, support can be a problem. So can custom program requests.

Turnkey packages also are known to use less well-known operating systems. Some have latent program errors that need maintenance. So checking the status of the operating system supplier is as critical as checking the application supplier.

Another section of the checklist raises the issue of payment terms and warranty. Vendors may try to get full payment when the software is installed. But what about a case where the software was not fully operational for three months? The financial burden should not fall on the user. Payment should follow a no-cost period, referred to as an *unconditional warranty period,* when package performance is proven. This period should begin only after an agreed-upon performance test is passed. During this period, any program corrections required to make the package operational in the user's installation should be made by the vendor regardless of cost.

After that, payments should follow an agreed-upon schedule tied to progress milestones. When one company acquired its turnkey system, it contracted for the following payment schedule:

PAYMENT AMOUNT	SCHEDULED MILESTONES
5%	Contract signing
5%	Delivery of the hardware
5%	Delivery of the documentation and a copy of the software package
15%	Installation and successful operation of system on user site
45%	Acceptance by user, or not later than 30 days after installation
25%	Expiration of the warranty period or the expiration of the free maintenance period

The company executed tests at each phase before payment was made. With a sizable percentage of payment withheld to the end, the user retained the vendor's interest in keeping the installation running smoothly.

The question about obtaining a copy of program code, or human-readable source code, listings are also raised in the checklist. Consider, for example, that Sporting Goods Distributors depends entirely on a turnkey vendor for all software maintenance. The firm has no access to program code. Soon, new tax changes must be made in the packaged payroll application.

Suppose the software vendor has entered bankruptcy proceedings and all assets, including the package program code, are secured. If the code is resident with a third-party, or escrow, agent, the agent can determine to release the code to users. With this arrangement, a user at least can find software assistance to execute the modification needed. The precaution of checking on the availability of program code could avoid serious operational problems.

Checking on whether or not software runs unchanged on a larger computer is further disaster insurance. Many first-time users seriously underestimate system growth. In one extreme case, all computer capability was exhausted in only six months. Since no larger computer existed in the hardware line, the user had two choices. One was to cut back on the number of database records needed and make do with less. The other was to abandon the investment in hardware, software, and training, and to start all over with a new system. Either way, the decision is painful if no growth path is available.

Many of the items on the Turnkey Checklist quickly become understandable in their subject context. One is the hardware concern for a vendor backup facility. Should a serious malfunction occur that takes days instead of hours to repair, one needs to know that processing, and often the business itself, can carry on.

Checklist items requesting "time" and "number" information try to determine if some kind of track record is already established for software, hardware, and vendor services. Without a track record in these areas, a new user should be suspect. On the other hand, a user might choose to be a test site for a turnkey vendor's product in exchange for a price break.

The small computer business is volatile and transient. There are many new ventures, start-up companies, business failures, acquisitions, and so forth. To avoid being left with an incomplete or unusable system, users should closely analyze the balance sheet, company history, and financial stability of candidate turnkey vendors. Further, a potential user should visit a vendor's facilities and meet the people who might be handling the system installation and maintenance. If the vendor also supplies the hardware, it is not unreasonable to check out the physical parts inventory and backup facilities.

Some items on the Turnkey Checklist are for information purposes. Items that check what other application packages or hardware a vendor sells are informative in relation to the turnkey system of interest. If many different products are supported, for example, and the vendor staff is lean, maybe there is cause for concern. If only one turnkey product is supported, on the other hand, maybe the concentration of resources could benefit a user. A careful balance of all factors in the total vendor picture is needed to rate some of the vendor checklist items.

Reference Questionnaire

It is informative to cross-check vendor and package claims with user references who have valued experience. The Reference Questionnarie given in Figure 4–6 helps to get this information.

Figure 4-6 Reference Questionnaire for turnkey system

Turnkey System Name: ____________________ *Reference Company Name and Address:* ____________________

Contact Name and Phone: ____________________

Application software

Application software used?

Is it easy to use?

Does it do everything expected of it?

Does it handle your transaction volume within normal working hours?

Is it free of program errors?

- Number of errors found?
- Correction procedure?
- Time and cost to fix?
- Was new documentation supplied?

Figure 4-6 (continued)

Application software

Is documentation easy to use?
  Is it accurate?
  Is it thorough?
Are audit controls satisfactory for your accountant?
Is the backup procedure adequate?
  Time required to do backup?
Time to install application software?
  Was it done on schedule?
Training time required?
  Was it done on schedule?
  Was it done on-site?
  Was it competent and complete?
Number of new versions since installation?
  Procedure, time, and cost to install new version?
  Was new documentation supplied?
Program change or modification experience?
  What was changed?
  Who did the change?
  Where was it done?
  Was it done on schedule and according to budget?
  Was the result satisfactory?
Custom programming experience?
  What was programmed from scratch?
  Who did the change?
  Where was it done?
  Was it done on schedule and according to budget?
  Was it satisfactory?

Hardware

Computer model used?
  For how long?
Disk capability adequate?
Print capability adequate?
Number of workstations in use simultaneously?
  Slow response time experience?
  Solution to the response time problem?
Hardware installation done on schedule?
  Unanticipated hardware needed?
  Environmental changes required?
Has any upgrade been made to a larger computer
  model or more power peripherals?
  How soon after installation?
  What hardware and costs were involved?
  Hardware breakdown experience?
  Best and worst response time for a service call?
  Best and worst time to complete a repair?
  Is service competent and complete?

Figure 4-6 (continued)

Vendor

Why did you buy from this vendor?
Would you recommend this vendor to others?
Other vendor assistance/experience (with cost) for:
  Specifying requirements?
  Planning for installation?
  Analyzing and designing custom programs?
  Programming?
  Hot-line help for operators?
  Backup facility use experience?
    Adequate?

System in General

Any unanticipated:
  Expenses?
  Problems?
  Benefits?
Are security controls adequate?
Any operator turnover experience?
  Reason?
What level of technical knowledge is required to use and maintain the system?
Would you buy this system again today?
Would you recommend it to others?

Rate Reference Information on:	*Rating (Scale: 1 = poor to 10 = excellent)*
Application satisfaction	_______
Hardware satisfaction	_______
Vendor satisfaction	_______
System in general	_______
Subtotal	_______
Divide by 4 for average rating	_______

Consolidate all Reference Questionnaire ratings into one average rating figure for transfer to Selection Summary: Turnkey System, Figure 5-4.

Continuing their evaluation, Mr. Williams and Ms. Fenton question users. These users are references supplied by the vendor. Mr. Williams is prepared for "setups," or users who have been prepared by the vendor to give all the right answers.

Mr. Williams invites users to lunch. After getting to know each other better, a "truth-speak" session begins. In some cases the truth is devastating whereas in others it is reassuring.

One concern is with processing time. There is a question about whether SGD Inc.'s volume of processing actually can be handled in a seven-hour day. Guidelines are needed to avoid the sort of problem encountered by one company that needed to enter 300 orders a day. After the system was installed, it turned out the company needed a 12-hour work day to do daily processing. While others may not process the same mix of transactions, they at least offer a touchstone for volume planning.

Users also can provide valuable information on centralized multiuser system degradation. Each multiuser computer has an upper limit of workstation connections. In practice, however, the working limit is lower. It shows up in poor system performance because of factors such as the number of concurrent users and applications competing for system resources. Learning the practical limit of workstations can be vital to the selection process.

Users also can supply important insights on correcting software failures. For example, at one user site, a disk problem wiped out some programs, because no program code existed, even on backup disks. The vendor was in Chicago and the user in Dallas. If Mr. Williams and Ms. Fenton called, they would hear how human error and transportation breakdowns made things very uncomfortable. Such users provide insight to determine the nature, quality, speed and reliability of maintenance.

The acid test for any package is to ask references if they would buy the same package today. Their answer to that and other questions about software, hardware, and vendor support can be informative.

Mr. Williams and Ms. Fenton round out their evaluation process by actually visiting some user sites. Seeing the system in a production environment is worth the trip. On one visit, for example, they observe that the order processing workflow needs two office staffers. The procedure is, nonetheless, highly efficient and might be a solution at SGD Inc. The visits also shed light on such mundane things as form paper use and other supply needs.

Procedure

To conduct a systematic evaluation of application software, the specific application of interest often is evaluated first. Specific application checklists are included in various chapters of this book devoted to the various applications.

If an application meets user requirements, then further package scrutiny is pursued. The checklists in this chapter support this continued evaluation.

There is no right or wrong order to using checklists or evaluating packages. The checklists help insure that all important evaluation areas are covered.

Each checklist has space to make subjective item ratings, as well as an average rating. A final average is transferred to a Selection Summary, such as those given in Chapter 5. All checklist scores end up on the summaries where a final average helps determine the single best package or turnkey system to acquire.

SELF TEST

1. Identify three types of computer software applications, and give specific examples within each type.

2. Compare the advantages and disadvantages of stand-alone versus multifunction application packages.
3. What is an integrated accounting package?
4. What is an industry specific package?
5. If an application package cannot be found to meet a user's specifications, what alternatives does the user have?
6. Compare the advantages and disadvantages of custom versus packaged application software.
7. What program development steps are required to get custom application software?
8. Rank the hierarchy of application software choices available to a user in terms of the best investment of time and money.
9. Describe the use of the following in evaluating application software:
   General Software Checklist
   Hands-on Test Checklist
   Turnkey Checklist
   Reference Questionnaire

EXERCISES

1. *Yates Salon Supply Center Case.* Yates Salon Supply Center wants to implement a payroll application on its existing small business computer. Mr. Cooper, the company financial officer, located the payroll directory listings in Figure 4–7 in a product-specific periodical directory. The listings seemed little more than product announcements. He had to request literature and documentation to learn if applications were candidates for further evaluation.

   His specific payroll requirements include: 75 employees, 6 department/divisions, 5 fixed payroll deductions, and multiple-state tax calculations. Based only on the information available in Figure 4–7:
   a. Which payroll packages do you think should be examined further?
   b. Which package(s) address the issue of:
      Customization
      Source code availability
      Update
   c. If Mr. Cooper's long-term intention is to integrate payroll with the general ledger package, which product would be investigated further?
2. *Bethesda Nursing Home Case.* Bethesda Nursing Home wants to automate their manual patient billing system. They purchased a small business computer for $10,000 to do this. This was their first venture into computing. However, after one year of trying to program their system, they gave up on the whole project. During that year, they also spent $15,000 on programming fees to a free-lance programmer to implement a system they never used. Discuss alternate strategies Bethesda could have used when originally deciding to automate their patient billing.
3. *Ajax Corporation Case.* A financial officer at Ajax Corporation wants to install a workstation with professional support applications.
   a. Locate two multifunction packages. Use the General Software Checklist to evaluate them.
   b. Recommend one package you think would be worth a hands-on test and explain why.

Payroll #1

Handles 200 employees in 99 departments. Employees can work in multiple states under five different pay rates. Also handles vacation, sick, and nontaxable pay rates. Included are federal and state unemployment tax and six deduction fields. *(List Price: $495, manual and demonstration disk $50)*
Requires: 64K (other requirements not available).

Payroll #1 Company
P.O. Box M1047
Mountain View, CA 94043
(415) 444-4444

Payroll #2

Stores 200 employee records on double-sided floppy disk. User manual included. Menu-driven. At additional cost, customizing is available. *(List Price: $49).*
Requires: 64K, one disk drive, printer.

Payroll #2 Company
3028 Silver Lane
Ann Arbor, MI 48106
(313) 333-3333

Payroll #3

This payroll program provides for 300 employees distributed to a maximum of 15 divisions. Thirty deduction types and five taxable categories are available. Federal and state income taxes for all 50 states are built-in through tax formulas. Updates are available at a modest charge. Printed output includes: checks, check register, W-2 forms, quarterly and summary reports. While it is written in UCSD Pascal, the UCSD Pascal system is not required. Hard disk compatible. *(List Price: $394)*
Requires: 64K, two disk drives, printer.

Payroll #3 Company
22 Hammel Dr.
Garden Grove, CA 92641
(714) 777-7777

Payroll #4

Provides for 150 employees for every 100K of disk storage. This allows space to copy the master file on the disk if automatic backup is used. Details of each pay period are retained through a self backup feature.

Handles situations like reimbursing employees for out-of-pocket expenses, paying bonuses, keeping track of vacation time, loans, advances and repayments. Includes custom state and local tax calculation programming. Programs are designed for rapid reprogramming. Original commented program source code is included, along with the tax tables.

To eliminate errors, input data goes through a double-keying procedure, if necessary.

Other features include: up to 10 department names per disk, up to five automatic fixed deductions with a different amount for each department, and up to five special pay amounts or deductions for each employee each period. *(List Price: $400)*
Requires: 48K, two disk drives.

Payroll #4 Company
P.O. Box 735
Bellingham, WA 98226
(206) 222-2222

Payroll #5

Designed for novice users, includes five modules: payroll, contractor, restaurant, farm and piecework. Prints checks and W-2 forms. Allows automatic posting to the Job Cost and General Ledger programs by the same manufacturer. Users maintain federal tax changes, FICA limits and percentage changes, FUTA limit changes, state unemployment limits, and state income tax changes. *(List Price: Each module $595)*
Requires: 64K, two disk drives, 80-column monitor, 132-column printer.

Payroll #5 Company
P.O. Box 1301
Clearwater, FL 33575
(813) 888-8888

Figure 4-7 Simulated directory listings from a product specific periodical

RESOURCES AND REFERENCES

See also Chapter 1, Resources and References.

Application Software Solutions, Datapro.
Application Software Reports, Auerbach.
Guide to Computer Program Directories, U.S. National Bureau of Standards.
"How to Buy Software Packages," Datapro, 1983.
Microcomputer Index, article abstracts, Microcomputer Information Services. Also available online through DIALOG.
OnLine Micro-Software Guide and Directory, Online. Also available through DIALOG.
Packaged Software Buyer's Guide, Management Information.
Packaged Software Reports, Management Information.
PERRY, WILLIAM E., *Microcomputer Software Selection Guide,* QED, 1983.
Sourcebook: Small Systems Software and Sources, Information Sources.
VisiOn, VisiCorp, 1983.
VisiSeries, VisiCorp, 1983.

5

IMPLEMENTATION ISSUES

Surrounding the phases of acquiring computer hardware and packaged software are related implementation issues. Those covered in this chapter are identified in Figure 5–1. They include determining budget guidelines and cost-justifying a computer purchase. Covered also are issues related to the use of professional support during the acquisition phases.

This chapter also brings together all the evaluation checklists in the book. They are collected on separate Selection Summaries used for hardware, software, and turnkey system selection.

Once the best selections are made, installation begins. Often it involves going from manual to automated procedures. Conversion needs preplanning for success. The use and maintenance of an installed system then requires monitoring. It helps detect symptoms that signal when a renewed acquisition cycle is appropriate.

BUDGET GUIDELINES

How much does one need to budget to benefit from using a small business computer? The answer is whatever can be cost-justified by the benefits of automation. As a rule of thumb, companies like SGD Inc. in the distribution business spend anywhere from

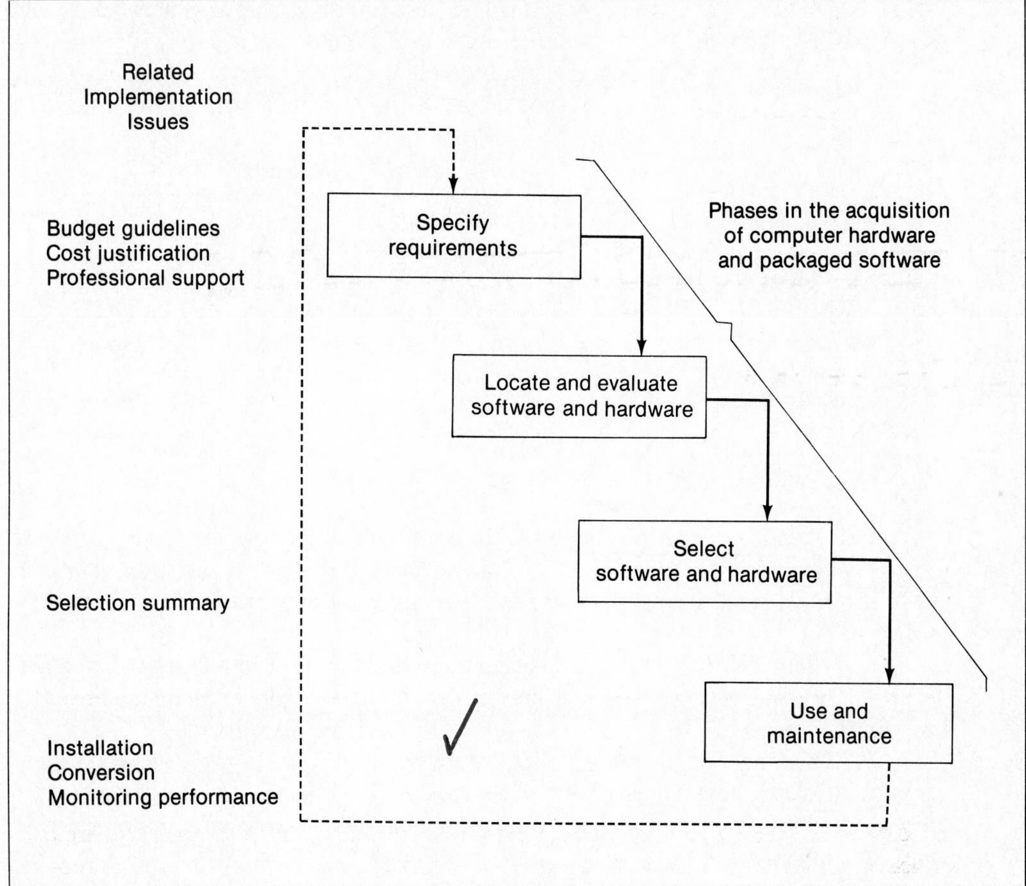

Figure 5-1 Implementation issues related to the phases of computer system acquisition

1 or 2 and as much as 4 percent of their annual gross sales on a computer system including hardware, software, supplies, and related maintenance expenses. On the other hand, service-oriented businesses tend to spend almost twice as much.

A typical single-user professional workstation cost breakdown might be:

	WORKSTATION COST RANGE	
Item	*Minimum*	*Maximum*
System unit, keyboard, video display, modem, and disk drives	$3,500	$14,000
Printer	600	3,500
Software	1,000	6,000
Totals	$5,100	$23,500

Wide area network interfacing is assumed in these figures. Local area networking can add anywhere from $500 to $5,000 more per workstation.

To give a simplified example, assume SGD Inc.'s gross sales are $1 million. Going by the rule of thumb, Mr. Williams should plan to budget the following for workstations:

	BUDGET EXPENDITURE	
	Minimum	*Maximum*
Gross sales	1,000,000	1,000,000
Budget factor	× .01%	× .04%
Budget	$10,000	$40,000
Minus allowance for related expenses (10–65%)	.35%	.35%
	$3,500	$14,000
Available for workstations	$6,500	$26,000

Related expenses are budgeted to cover things like hardware and software maintenance contracts. When SGD Inc. had only Mr. Williams' workstation, they paid $350 annually for hardware maintenance. No maintenance was needed for off-the-shelf software.

When SGD Inc. moved into using accounting applications and local area networking, the maintenance picture changed. Both hardware and software maintenance contracts averaged 10 to 15 percent a year of the original investment.

When he was a solitary user, supplies like extra floppy disks, computer continuous-form stock paper, printer ribbons, disk file holders, and the like added up to less than $500 a year. Once accounting applications were added, supply expenses mounted quickly.

Other expenses that might be involved include:

Extra cables, electrical outlets, and proper lighting

Installation costs, including delivery and new office furniture and files

Site modification

Conversion cost of entering information from the old system, if needed. (Accounting systems require this as do many others like legal word processing applications. All contracts, letters, forms, and other documents must be entered into the system before they are useful. One legal firm hired office temporary help to do this. It cost them $5,000 over two months to convert.)

Personnel costs, including hiring and training expenses

Security costs for affixing hardware to prevent theft, and for a safety deposit box or vault at another location to store backup copies of magnetic media and sensitive printed documents

Insurance

Finance charges
Consultant fees
Depreciation
Legal fees if advice is needed for vendor contracts and negotiations

COST JUSTIFICATION

In many cases cost justification of a workstation investment produces figures that recommend a very swift payback period. This enables a company to spend much more than rule-of-thumb amounts would recommend.

If SGD Inc. plans to amortize Mr. Williams' original computer investment over three years, the annualized cost is:

	WORKSTATION COST RANGE	
	Minimum	*Maximum*
Total cost	$10,000	$40,000
3-year amortization	÷ 3	÷ 3
Annual cost estimate	$3,333	$13,333

Although five years is the normal amortization period for computer equipment, some companies prefer to realize a shorter payback period. This is mainly because of the fast pace of technological obsolescence in computers. SGD Inc. looked on Mr. Williams' single-user workstation as a pilot test. They wanted a shorter payback period and planned to add other applications and workstations after the first year.

Soft Dollars

A technique called *value-added* is frequently used to justify automated systems for professional or management workers. With this technique, the addition of automated systems assumes performance or productivity improvement. Improvement gets measured in *soft dollars*. *Soft dollars* are those that a company can recapture based on increased productivity. They do not decrease a company's immediate expenses. They do, however, help pay for the system over the long term.

From talking with others, from hands-on testing, and from other sources, Mr. Williams estimated he could prepare marketing budgets and forecasts in half the time it now takes him to do them manually. If he now spends about four hours a week, automation would give him two hours a week more for other work. Assume his $40,000 annual salary climbs to $48,000 with fringe benefits. The soft dollar savings can be calculated approximately to be:

$48,000/year = $923/week (52 weeks)
35 hours/week = $26.37/hour
2 hours/week = $52.74 savings/week
$52.74 × 52 weeks = $2,742 savings/year

While this does not cover the minimum payback expected, other intangible benefits cover the remainder to be cost justified.

Defining or evaluating productivity means considering unmeasurable factors such as quality of work. Mr. Williams admits that he often accepts the first solution to a problem when developing at least an alternate strategy would be useful. With the encouragement of an easy-to-use electronic spreadsheet for marketing analyses, he now does creative problem solving by building more sophisticated numerical models of problems. He feels his decision making has become more effective as a result. He claims one of his better marketing strategies resulted in well over a $3,333 increase in sales revenue.

Higher quality of work, employee job satisfaction, and morale remain largely intangible, unquantifiable benefits. Other intangible benefits, like Mr. Williams' access to external on-line economic and marketing databases for more informed decision making, also enhance quality of work. These considerations all influenced the original buy decision at SGD Inc.

The development of SGD Inc.'s company database, with the addition of accounting applications, resulted in similar unmeasurable benefits. Mr. Williams and his fellow workers found that the availability of previously inaccessible information stimulated new productive ideas. It encouraged more coordinated and cooperative planning. The difference was reflected in the company's growing profit and reduced expenses.

One legal firm measured increased productivity in the hours lawyers saved not having to proofread legal documents prepared by a word processing application. Using a traditional typewriter, every revision of a document has to be reread since the document is completely retyped. With word processed documents, lawyers only proofread those portions that are changed. Time saved can be measured and used as a soft dollar justification.

Through one study a firm determined that their lawyers spent four hours a week proofreading documents. It assumed using word processing could cut this time in half, giving each lawyer two more hours a week for other work.

Assume for this example that the lawyers in question had the same salary as Mr. Williams. The annual cost savings is $2,742, using exactly the same calculation as before.

If one workstation produces word processed documents for only four lawyers, it could be justified in one year. This payback period could be reduced even further if other soft dollars are calculated. They might include decreased secretarial proofreading time, decreased document preparation time due to reusing standard *boiler-plate* paragraphs, and decreased lawyer waiting time for revisions to be completed.

Supporting arguments for further justification concern the impact of lost company image if a document goes out with obvious errors. Another is the impact of delayed documents on project progress and scheduling.

Hard Dollars

Other techniques used to justify automated systems are *expense reduction* and *cost avoidance*. Both result in *hard dollar* savings. *Hard dollars* are monies currently being spent or planned for upcoming years. These are direct dollars going for measurable expenses.

A classic example of reduced expenses concerns personnel. Assume SGD Inc.'s bookkeeper spends 16 hours a month sending out customer statements. The bookkeeper also spends 12 hours a month doing payroll. A computer is estimated to reduce this time by 75 percent to 7 hours for both. If the bookkeeper's salary is $8 an hour, there is a savings of $2,016 a year.

Most new computer installations do not result in reducing permanent staff, except in assembly line jobs. Instead, in office and professional environments employee time is almost always refocused on other work activities. Usually the introduction of office automation results in freeing time for more job-enriched tasks. The computer takes over the repetitive, mundane chores it excells at.

Often a computer can help to avoid hiring new help due to company growth. One fabric manufacturer grew 200 percent in two years without having to add office staff. It required that the computer purchase included such long-range growth forecasts.

Most companies find the accounting applications are easiest to quantify for cost justification. Reducing the inventory investment is a good example. Automated inventory control can help prevent expensive idle inventories from building. A business with good controls can keep on hand only what is needed. A $300,000 inventory reduced by just 5 percent results in a $15,000 savings.

Likewise, $300,000 of outstanding accounts receivables reduced by just 5 percent due to better billing procedures results in $15,000 cash that can be reinvested elsewhere. Or, it could mean $15,000 less that has to be borrowed just to meet normal operating expenses.

When SGD Inc. installed their accounting applications, they were able, through better procedures, to:

Reduce their inventory investment
Reduce outstanding accounts receivable
Reduce bad debt accounts

In general the company experienced an average 50-percent reduction in clerical time on all bookkeeping tasks. This was in addition to:

Better cash flow management
Better customer service
Increased sales due to better identification of high-profit versus low-profit items

Depending on a company's financial situation, it may be better to rent equipment than to buy it. A company's tax consultant is a good adviser on the best way to go and why. With Mr. Williams' system, the tax benefits on a purchase reduced the total system cost by as much as 46 percent over its five-year depreciable tax life. Both depreciation and an investment tax credit on the purchase price cut the total true cost of the equipment almost in half.

Besides tax benefits, when doing more sophisticated analyses, companies also consider costs associated with staff training time and expenses. Even costs associated with the diversion of executive time from normal duties is calculated. In some cases, diverted executive time can be considerable and should be monitored before it becomes a problem. Companies also use sophisticated techniques like evaluating the present value of future income and expenses to evaluate new investment strategies.

PROFESSIONAL SUPPORT

Some users require the professional skills of a computer consultant to convert to automated systems. Selecting a consultant should be as carefully approached as selecting a business partner. Usually a formal contract is needed to bind the working relationship between client and consultant. The following section discusses the consultant relationship, contract, and the request for a proposal document that a consultant usually prepares.

Computer Consultants

Computer consultants provide three basic services: special expertise, extra help, and an objective outside opinion. SGD Inc. hired one with special expertise when they moved into local area networking. SGD Inc. did all the preliminary work of specifying requirements and evaluating available systems. They wanted an expert's objective outside opinion on what they thought was a good solution. The expert was then retained to oversee the installation of the network.

The services of consultants with special skills are normally the easiest to justify. In a case like SGD Inc.'s, the company had a short-term need for an unusual ability. While the price paid seemed high, it had to be compared with alternative trade-offs. One is that it would be unwise to try to hire and keep such a specialist. Not only would hiring be costly and time-consuming, but, once found, such an employee would become bored and leave soon after the project ended. Another reason was that the risk of making a poor system choice was an untenable alternative.

Having worked with consultants before, SGD Inc. knew that they needed lots of help to understand a company's needs and wants. Only then can they provide informed advice. SGD Inc. also knew that consultants do not make management decisions. That responsibility falls with the client company.

To choose the right consultant, SGD Inc. sent their requirements to several candidates recommended by industry contacts. They asked for proposed solutions to their requirements. From returned proposals they were able to determine how consultants understood SGD Inc.'s industry and special company requirements. From resumes, reference checks, and interviews with persons doing the actual consulting work, they found a consulting firm.

To help screen computer consultants, a checklist similar to the vendor part of the Turnkey Checklist in Chapter 4 was used. To screen a consultant's references, a questionnaire similar to the Reference Questionnaire in Chapter 4 was used. When hiring a vendor or consultant, a user's aim should be to insure that the candidate has substantial experience. The experience should be supported with successes that references can verify.

SGD Inc. found that consultants charge anywhere from $200 to $1,500 a day and more. Normal rates fell into the $400 to $800 a day range, not including transportation and incidental expenses.

Contracts

SGD Inc. negotiated a fixed-cost contract. This procedure required a solid definition of the deliverable result expected. Project completion date and acceptance conditions also needed to be defined prior to contracting.

They rejected a time-and-materials contract offer. This type of contract is open-ended. Experts suggest this is not for unsophisticated computer users. It is mainly used when a contract is for the purpose of augmenting existing staff.

Whether dealing with a computer consultant or a turnkey vendor, negotiating contract terms is part of the relationship. The objective is to make it less expensive for the consultant or vendor to perform than not to perform.

The best way for a user to have some control is to tie payment to a progressive schedule of deliverables. An example of one was offered in Chapter 4 for a turnkey system. If a contract is to be negotiated for custom software development, progress payments are more involved. Guidance on preparing such a contract and others is available in the Resources and References section at the end of the chapter.

SGD Inc. was like many users who call together a contracting team consisting of the company's legal counsel, accountant or financial advisor, and resident computerist. Only one person, however, is given control of the negotiation process.

A user is at an advantage during the negotiation phase. Once an agreement is signed, the user loses leverage to the contractor and has only the conditions of a well constructed contract to protect the business if things begin to sour.

Some main contract clauses in any computer related contract are:

Scope of the contract: establishes the commitments made by each party to the other. The work to be done or end product sought needs to be explicit as do the expected time schedule and deliverables expected.

Cost and payment schedule: includes what is a chargeable expense and the reimbursement procedure.

Cost additions: defines how changes and additions to fixed-cost contracts are handled.

Limitations of liability: fixes who is responsible for exactly what, an especially critical clause if multiple contractors or suppliers are involved in a project.

Criteria to measure performance: quantitatively defines what constitutes contract fulfillment, such as the installation of a local area network that provides a response of three seconds or less 80 percent of the time, with fifteen workstations in operation.

Issues of ownership: legally defines ownership of products developed during the contracted project. This is especially important in contracts for custom software development work.

Provision for termination of contract: provides some continuity of knowledgeable support personnel in case of consultant or vendor business termination.

Remedies and arbitration: avoids litigation in case of breach of contract.

A good contract should encourage an open discussion of problems at an early stage. It should also give both parties an opportunity to remedy them before they become the basis for litigation. While the contract protects all parties legally, its focus should be on a practical approach to achieving a finished job that is beneficial to all.

One consultant highlights the importance of a good contract with the following story. In a case brought to court, a turnkey vendor was proven to be incompetent. The vendor almost drove the client into bankruptcy. Still the ruling favored the vendor. The basis for the ruling was that the wording of the contract excluded performance as a condition of payment.

Computerists warn new users to be aware that as far as contracts go, "If it's not in writing, it doesn't exist." Any verbal deals are worthless unless every detail is available on a contract as well. Computerists also warn against being coerced into using a vendor's standard contract. Typically they are heavily slanted in the vendor's favor.

Request for Proposal

The document SGD Inc.'s consultant prepared and sent to local area network vendors for bids was called a *request for proposal* (RFP). The document consisted of:

Cover letter
Description of SGD Inc.'s business background and computer budget
Software requirements
Hardware requirements
Service support requirements
Request for vendor's professional and financial background with documentation

The RFP spelled out what everyone agreed would be an ideal local area network.

In many cases, RFPs are a collection of checklists, similar to those found throughout this book, with a cover letter and company description. Users can prepare their own RFPs. But a computer project budgeted for under $20,000 may find many vendors not interested.

For projects where RFPs are appropriate, they serve several purposes. One is to force vendors to respond to requirements on prepared forms or in a predefined way. This simplifies the final evaluation. It compels vendors to be specific about system features, performance claims, support, and training. All documented answers typically are incorporated into a final contract.

Another purpose of the RFP is to save time. Documents can be sent to several vendors at once. Since they are in a uniform format when returned, they can be easily compared. When the top few bids emerge, only a few repetitive interviews to evaluate potential contractors need be conducted.

RFPs also reduce the chance of a misunderstanding between contract parties. This can reduce the potential for disagreements and lawsuits.

HARDWARE AND SOFTWARE SELECTION

Mr. Williams, like computer consultants he has worked with, aims for a systematic approach to selection. Usually this involves using checklists, like those found in this book, to help order the evaluation process. Once evaluation is complete, selecting the best hardware and software becomes one additional mechanical step.

Although an attempt is made throughout the book to make checklists complete, they still need to be tailored to individual situations. Only a potential user can know what the hardware and software requirements are for their business needs. Checklists help to understand what computer systems can do. As new products emerge and as new features are added, changes need to be made to update checklists.

The extra step from evaluation to selection involves combining checklists that relate to one selection process and recalculating a combined rating. The Selection Summaries in Figures 5–2 through 5–4 serve as convenient worksheets for this final step. A perfect candidate would have an average rating of 10. Rarely will this happen.

Figure 5–2 summarizes the selection process for hardware. Ratings from the Hardware General and Components Checklists found in Chapters 2, 7 and 12 are transferred there. Sections need to be completed for each component acquired separately and for which several competing products are evaluated.

Figure 5–2 Selection Summary: Hardware

	Candidates		
	A	*B*	*C*
Component #1: ____________			
Candidate names	____	____	____
Hardware: General Checklist rating	____	____	____
Hardware: Component Checklist rating	____	____	____
Subtotal	____	____	____
Divide by 2 for average rating	____	____	____
Final ranking (1st, 2nd, 3rd)	____	____	____
Component #2: ____________			
Candidate names	____	____	____
Hardware: General Checklist rating	____	____	____
Hardware: Component Checklist rating	____	____	____
Subtotal	____	____	____
Divide by 2 for average rating	____	____	____
Final ranking (1st, 2nd, 3rd)	____	____	____

Figure 5-2 (continued)

	Candidates		
	A	B	C
Component #3: ______________			
Candidate names	_____	_____	_____
Hardware: General Checklist rating	_____	_____	_____
Hardware: Component Checklist rating	_____	_____	_____
Subtotal	_____	_____	_____
Divide by 2 for average rating	_____	_____	_____
Final ranking (1st, 2nd, 3rd)	_____	_____	_____

Figure 5-3 summarizes the selection process for software. System software is considered separately from application software. It requires that the System Software Checklist rating from Chapter 3 be transferred to the summary.

Figure 5-3 Selection Summary: Software

	Candidates		
	A	B	C
System Software:			
Candidate names	_____	_____	_____
System Software Checklist rating	_____	_____	_____
General Software Checklist rating	_____	_____	_____
Hands-on Test Checklist rating	_____	_____	_____
Subtotal	_____	_____	_____
Divide by 3 for average rating	_____	_____	_____
Final ranking (1st, 2nd, 3rd)	_____	_____	_____
Application #1: ______________			
Candidate names	_____	_____	_____
Application Checklist rating	_____	_____	_____
General Software Checklist rating	_____	_____	_____
Hands-on Test Checklist rating	_____	_____	_____
Subtotal	_____	_____	_____
Divide by 3 for average rating	_____	_____	_____
Final ranking (1st, 2nd, 3rd)	_____	_____	_____
Application #2: ______________			
Candidate names	_____	_____	_____
Application Checklist rating	_____	_____	_____
General Software Checklist rating	_____	_____	_____
Hands-on Test Checklist rating	_____	_____	_____
Subtotal	_____	_____	_____
Divide by 3 for average rating	_____	_____	_____
Final ranking (1st, 2nd, 3rd)	_____	_____	_____
Application #3: ______________			
Candidate names	_____	_____	_____

Figure 5-3 (continued)

	Candidates		
	A	*B*	*C*
Application #3: ________________			
Application Checklist rating	______	______	______
General Software Checklist rating	______	______	______
Hands-on Test Checklist rating	______	______	______
Subtotal	______	______	______
Divide by 3 for average rating	______	______	______
Final ranking (1st, 2nd, 3rd)	______	______	______

Specific application ratings, on the other hand, will come from many different chapters and checklists. Only those being evaluated need have ratings transferred for summary selection purposes.

All software needs to be supported with ratings from the General Software Checklist and the Hands-on Test Checklist. Both are needed for every piece of software being considered. They are from Chapter 4.

Finally, Figure 5-4 summarizes the selection process for a turnkey system. This is a more elaborate selection procedure. It involves combining appropriate results from Figures 5-2 and 5-3 with other ratings. The other ratings come from the Turnkey Checklist and Reference Questionnaire in Chapter 4.

Figure 5-4 Selection Summary: Turnkey System

	A	*B*	*C*
Candidate Names	______	______	______
Turnkey Checklist rating	______	______	______
Reference Questionnaire rating	______	______	______
Local Area Network Checklist rating	______	______	______
* System Software Checklist rating	______	______	______
* Application ratings:			
1. ________________	______	______	______
2. ________________	______	______	______
3. ________________	______	______	______
* Hardware component ratings:			
1. ________________	______	______	______
2. ________________	______	______	______
3. ________________	______	______	______
Subtotal	______	______	______
Divide by *X*** for average rating	______	______	______
Final ranking (1st, 2nd, 3rd)	______	______	______

* Ratings come from Figures 5-2 and 5-3.

** *X* should be the number of "rating" items filled in above.

Generally more than one Reference Questionnaire will be used for a turnkey system evaluation. It is necessary, therefore, to get an average rating of all Questionnaires for a single vendor. This single average rating needs to be transferred to the Selection Summary.

This selection method is simple to use and easily understood by others. It is only one of several systematic techniques used to select hardware, software and turnkey systems. Another popular technique assigns weights to each item being evaluated. Rating points are then multiplied by weights to arrive at a total score.

Selecting small computer hardware and software is not a simple task. Users who specify and procure a system in the same logical manner applied to any major capital investment, and who diligently evaluate and monitor every phase of the acquisition process, reap the benefits later. Ultimately, it is the user's responsibility to make sure things go right. It is the user's money that is at risk, and it is the user who will pay if things do not go right.

INSTALLATION

Some installations of hardware or software never seem to go right. From his own experience, Mr. Williams advises others to expect the best but prepare for the worst. He suggests that, if hardware is to be delivered in two weeks, plan on four to six weeks to avoid disappointment. Then when it does arrive, plan on extra time before it actually works.

Site Preparation

Before new computer workstations were scheduled to arrive, SGD Inc. used something like the Preinstallation Checklist in Figure 5-5 to guide preparations.

Figure 5-5 Preinstallation Checklist

Scheduled hardware arrival date: ______________

	DATE
Physical Site	*Completed/Available*
Workstation space for:	
System unit (including disks and display)	______
Printer and printer stand with continuous form paper feed and paper catcher	______
Other devices	______
Storage space for supplies:	
Software User Guide/Manuals	______
Cartons of continuous-form paper	______
Floppy disk file containers	______
Backup disk storage	______
Dedicated power line	______
Other cables	______
Adequate power outlets (3-prong)	______

Figure 5-5 (continued)

Scheduled hardware arrival date: ________________

	DATE
Physical Site	*Completed/Available*
Telephone jack for direct connect modem	________
Workstation adjustable lighting	________
Supplies	
Floppy disks	________
Cleaning kit for disk drive	________
Floppy disk file containers	________
Hard disk backup media	________
Stock computer paper, continuous-form	________
80 columns wide	________
132 columns wide	________
Preprinted continuous-form paper	________
Printer ribbons	________
Replacement daisy wheels or other printer parts	________

The Preinstallation Checklist focuses on physical site planning and supplies. Mr. Williams recalls his first unplanned installation. No one told him that several 3-prong plugs would need outlets or that he needed a telephone jack for the direct connect modem. When the computer arrived on his desk, he found he needed a special stand for the printer that allows continuous-form paper feeding with a paper catcher.

Lighting needed adjustment because of an unpleasant reflected glare on the screen. Eventually he had to find storage space for paper, disks, and manuals.

With some preinstallation planning and preparation, some frustration could be eliminated. The larger the installation, the more necessary it is to do careful preinstallation planning.

Mr. Williams used a hardware *self-diagnostic disk* that came with his hardware to check it out. The *diagnostics* tested each piece of hardware in turn, like the memory, keyboard, display, disks, printer, and modem. At selected points, while the diagnostic program was operating, the display would indicate what was being checked and how it checked out. Only the modem did not check out. After rereading the User Guide, he discovered all it needed was the power turned on. After that, the diagnostic program worked smoothly.

Acceptance Testing

In a turnkey system installation, the process of checking out hardware and software is known as *acceptance testing*. This can become very formalized, and occasionally special software is used to put a system through its paces. Turnkey contracts generally detail each test that will be run to determine system acceptability. If response time is under three seconds 80 percent of the time with fifteen workstations in use, for example, the system may fail to perform as specified. If so, a vendor normally would be given an opportunity to remedy the problem.

On the other hand, retail store software comes packaged with a so-called "as-is" limited use license. A buyer either uses it as is or not. The software provided does not even guarantee its ability to perform. That is why a careful check of acceptable features and performance is required before money changes hands.

CONVERSION

When SGD Inc. installed accounting software, it first had to convert all manual records to magnetic media. The task was formidable, as it usually is.

SGD Inc. was warned against the hazards of trying to "put everything on the computer at once." Experience shows this spells disaster. Computerizing means changing the way business is done. The last thing needed in most businesses is to change all aspects of a business at once. Tasks need to be done in priority order. SGD Inc. decided to begin with the least critical task first in order to give everyone time to adjust to the new system.

In order to make a smooth transition to the automated system, the project leader used a Conversion Checklist such as the one in Figure 5-6. It covered such areas as training, data entry, and parallel operations. All areas were supported with assistance by the turnkey vendor.

Figure 5-6 Conversion Checklist

Application: ____________________
Project leader: ____________________
Scheduled dates: Begin ____________________
End ____________________

	ESTIMATED DATE		ACTUAL DATE	
	Begin	*End*	*Begin*	*End*
Training				
Managers	______	______	______	______
Data entry personnel	______	______	______	______
Data Entry				
Determine source of data	______	______	______	______
Gather data	______	______	______	______
Keyboard data	______	______	______	______
Parallel Testing				
Computer as backup to manual processing	______	______	______	______
Manual as backup to computer processing	______	______	______	______
Complete cut-over	______	______	______	______

Training

Both accounting system data entry operators and company managers should be trained to use the system. They require different training orientations.

Where orientation and training are not handled carefully, valued employees have quit and even sabotaged new equipment. SGD Inc. correctly determined that the best way to prevent such negativism was to involve employees as early as the requirements specification phase. Their technique was successful as it usually is wherever tried.

Since management and future operators at SGD Inc. were involved in the evaluation and selection process, as they should be, training went smoothly. All were familiar with what the system was expected to do. User Guides were made available to everyone to prepare themselves for hands-on training.

The User Guide helped to orient managers about reports and their use. Managers only had to be trained in how to make inquiries and to generate reports. This was handled on a private basis with each manager.

Data Entry

Training on how to enter orders, customer payments, inventory receipts, and the like was offered to data entry operators. At first they entered only sample data. When they felt comfortable with the operations and learned how to correct errors, they entered *live data,* or real orders, payments and other information.

They also had to enter all customer account records, inventory item records, general ledger account records and other company database information. The task is often called *initializing* the database or building the database files. The conversion project leader had to determine what data was to be entered. Once established, actual data needed to be collected, grouped, and control totalled for entry in batches.

By entering small controlled groups of information, the project leader could be sure the system would not be flooded with bad information. Computerists refer to this as GIGO, or "garbage in means garbage out." If bad information is uncontrollably allowed into a system, everything out of the system will also be bad information.

Parallel Testing

Once data is entered, parallel testing begins. This is the period when the manual and computer systems function together for comparison purposes. Many companies, including SGD Inc., had to ask personnel to work overtime and to come in on weekends to accommodate the double workload. Some hire temporary help for parallel testing as well as for the initial data entry work.

Many vendors recommend parallel tests of one to three months. Some companies cannot afford the people and financial burden of more than a few weeks of parallel operations. However long, testing should force periodic closings and run month-, quarter-, and year-end reports. The procedure would uncover any problems in this critical processing.

Some systems cannot be run in parallel, like one that does something never done before. The point of the parallel test is to verify system performance. Once confident about performance a switch or *cut-over* to computer operation is appropriate. Turnkey vendors recommend the continued use of manual processing as a backup procedure for up to two months.

SECURITY AND PERFORMANCE MONITORING

Part of the ongoing monitoring involves audit and security control. Security procedures at SGD Inc. are carefully observed and supported by off-site backup disks, printouts, and documentation. They also conduct surprise audits and rotate data entry personnel. Passwords are changed often. Their procedures are normal in a well administered data processing based organization.

Keeping a written log of problems, both for hardware and software, can help resolve maintenance problems. At SGD Inc., each time a malfunction occurs, everyone is trained to record it in their workstation Performance Log Book.

Log books many times are responsible for revealing patterns that help avoid more troublesome problems later. Problems with faulty cable connections, disks, and printers often begin with tell-tale symptoms. Symptoms might be anything abnormal, like repeated disk read errors. When these problems are observed and recorded, maintenance trouble-shooters often can solve problems easier.

Cases are recorded where log books have been accepted as valid evidence in litigated computer cases. In one case they proved the inadequacy of vendor maintenance.

Monitoring performance helps determine when a system needs upgrading. Backup procedures that take hours to do and work that constantly needs overtime scheduled to complete are not symptoms that get recorded in a log book. When observed they indicate problems that need attention. Some may require new computer-based solutions, but some may need other administrative action.

By monitoring changes in day-to-day computer activity, one has a better chance to avoid potential problems. One also has the basis to plan future needs and ample time to be sure plans are turned into reality before crises occur.

When it looks like automation might solve a new problem or create a new opportunity or enhance productivity in new ways, an acquisition cycle begins again. As shown in Figure 5–1, it starts with specifying requirements. Once begun, the acquisition cycle follows a natural path until one actually uses the small business computer in another new productive way.

SELF TEST

1. What rule-of-thumb guidelines have been used for setting computer budgets?
2. Identify five expenses in addition to hardware and software, that need consideration when allocating funds.
3. What technique is commonly used to cost-justify computers for professional workers?

4. What are soft dollars? Hard dollars?
5. Describe some unmeasurable factors that should be considered when cost-justifying a computer installation for a professional worker.
6. Identify some possible benefits of computerized accounting.
7. What three basic services do computer consultants provide?
8. At what point in negotiating a computer contract does the user have the most advantage?
9. Describe three clauses that typically appear in computer contracts.
10. What is contained in an RFP?
11. Describe the purpose of the Selection Summary for software.
12. List some areas that need attention to prepare a physical site for a computer installation.
13. What is acceptance testing?
14. Describe the three main tasks accomplished in the conversion process.
15. What is the value of a Performance Log Book?

EXERCISES

1. If one budgets 65 percent for incidental related expenses under both a $10,000 minimum and $40,000 maximum cost ranges, what is left to buy workstations? Is it adequate under the minimum budgeting plan?
2. List the steps used to calculate an annualized soft dollar saving to cost-justify a word processing application for lawyers.
3. Read three case history articles about new small computer installations of accounting systems. Write a report including:
   - How each was cost-justified
   - Benefits of automation realized
   - Installation problems encountered
4. *Harlan Company Case.* The Harlan Company made a decision to have an accounting application programmed from scratch. You have been asked to prepare a list of special clauses that should be included in a contract with any software developer. Use books on contracting in the Resources and References section for assistance.

RESOURCES AND REFERENCES

Books

BRANDON, DICK H. AND SIDNEY S. SEGELSTEIN, *Businessman's Guide to Microcomputers: How to Select Hardware, Software, Services,* Boardroom Books, 1981.

BRANDON, DICK H., *Data Processing Contracts,* Van Nostrand, 1976.

HOFFMAN, PAUL S., *The Software Legal Book,* Carnegie, 1983.

ISSHIKI, KOICHIRO R., *Small Business Computers: A Guide to Evaluation and Selection,* Prentice-Hall, 1982.

LUEDTKE, PETER AND RAINER LUEDTKE, *Your First Business Computer,* Digital, 1983.

SEGAL, HILLEL AND JESSE BERST, *How to Manage Your Small Computer,* Prentice-Hall, 1983.

SEGAL, HILLEL AND JESSE BERST, *How to Select Your Small Computer,* Prentice-Hall, 1983.

Computer Consultants

Association of Consulting Management Engineers (ACME)
Association of Management Consultants (AMC)
Consultant Brokerage
Computer Consultant, Battery Lane
Directory of Management Consultants
Directory of Professional Consultants, Shenson
Independent Computer Consultants Association
Institute of Management Consultants

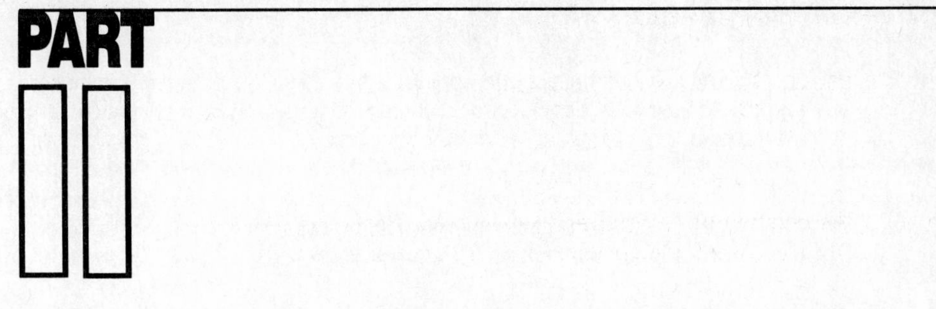

PART II

using professional support applications

Part II examines professional support applications. This software helps execute some of a business user's main activities. Electronic spreadsheet packages, discussed in Chapter 6, support the planning, budgeting, and forecasting activity.

Graphics, discussed in Chapter 7, also support the same activity. It helps a user assess volumes of data by presenting them as visual summaries versus columns of numbers. Graphics further support the communication activity through its presentation characteristics.

Word processing, covered in Chapter 8, simplifies the writing activity. It also facilitates a host of other tasks concerned with text preparation, manipulation, and storage.

None of the software in Part II produces predefined results in the form of screen displays or reports. Instead a user specifies results according to individual needs.

In order to specify results, be it a display of a quarterly budget or a printed letter, a user must tell the application what is to be done, how it is to be done, and when it is to be done. Most packages in Part II, therefore, require that a user learn a special language, procedure, or rules to "talk" to the application.

For electronic spreadsheet and word processing applications, a supplement follows the discussion chapter. It is a tutorial for hands-on experience with a representative commercially available product in the application category.

Nothing quite substitutes for actual hands-on use in the application area. To borrow the familiar proverb, "I hear and I forget, I see and I remember, I do and I understand."

If the specific tutorial software is not available, reading the supplement can simulate the hands-on experience. Because tutorial sessions are described from power-on to power-off, you may assume that you are in front of a small computer, activating workstation keys and producing the results described.

6

ELECTRONIC SPREADSHEETS

What if a scratch pad on a decision maker's desk had a memory? What if changing some critical figures on the pad results in an instantaneous recalculation of the entire spreadsheet? Electronic spreadsheets are in effect scratch pads with a memory. Their instantaneous recalculation capability allows anyone, without previous computer experience, to explore "what-if" sensitivity analyses with immediate results.

This chapter "walks through" how a decision maker uses an electronic spreadsheet. In doing so, it illustrates this computer-age tool's impact on improving personal productivity. Spreadsheet advantages and limitations are also examined, as are guidelines for evaluation.

A supplement to the chapter is a hands-on keystroke-by-keystroke tutorial for actually using a representative electronic spreadsheet.

CHARACTERISTICS OF ELECTRONIC SPREADSHEETS

Both a scratch pad and an electronic spreadsheet are convenient tools to explore problems that can be defined numerically in row and column format. Typical uses include sales projection and analysis, profit planning, cost estimating, inventory planning, risk analysis, and tax planning, among others. To compare manual and automated techniques of problem analysis, suppose Mr. Williams at Sporting Goods Distributors, Inc. prepares the table of sales projections in Figure 6–1 using conventional scratch pad, calculator, and pencil.

Now suppose Mr. Williams uses an electronic spreadsheet to do the projections. What differences would there be? The answer is initially, except for numbers in the total column, none. In other words, the burden of developing the planning model is the planner's. Primary numbers in the spreadsheet *model,* also called the *matrix,* have to be manually entered. In addition, the planner must precisely define relationships between numbers on the spreadsheet.

In Figure 6–1, for example, totals reflect the result of units times price. The relationship of the two columns is important to the electronic spreadsheet. It gets typed into the computer as a simple $c = a \times b$ formula. The formula stays hidden while a result flashes on the computer's screen.

This ability to memorize entered relationships gives the electronic spreadsheet its power. Whenever changes affecting stored relationships are made, the program instantly recalculates and redisplays updated values.

To use an example, assume Mr. Williams wants to know what effect there will be on totals if sales of Type C tennis hats fall to 300 units. With an electronic spreadsheet, typing the number for the new units is all that's needed. Instantly the total and grand total appear updated. This immediate feedback to "what-if" questions makes an electronic spreadsheet a powerful, flexible analysis tool.

ENTERING A SPREADSHEET ON THE COMPUTER

Looking over Mr. Williams' shoulder, one observes how to enter a spreadsheet. After the computer's power switch is turned on, he slips a floppy disk containing the spreadsheet program into the disk drive. Instantly the computer's screen looks like Figure 6–2, a blank spreadsheet with labeled columns and rows.

The electronic spreadsheet program, loaded from the disk into the computer's memory, could have been any one of many available. This one happens to be Lotus

	PRICE	UNITS	TOTAL
T hat A	$12.75	100	$1,275
T hat B	$10.98	200	$2,196
T hat C	$ 7.75	360	$2,790
GRAND TOTAL			$6,261

Figure 6–1 Scratch pad spreadsheet of SGD's sales projections

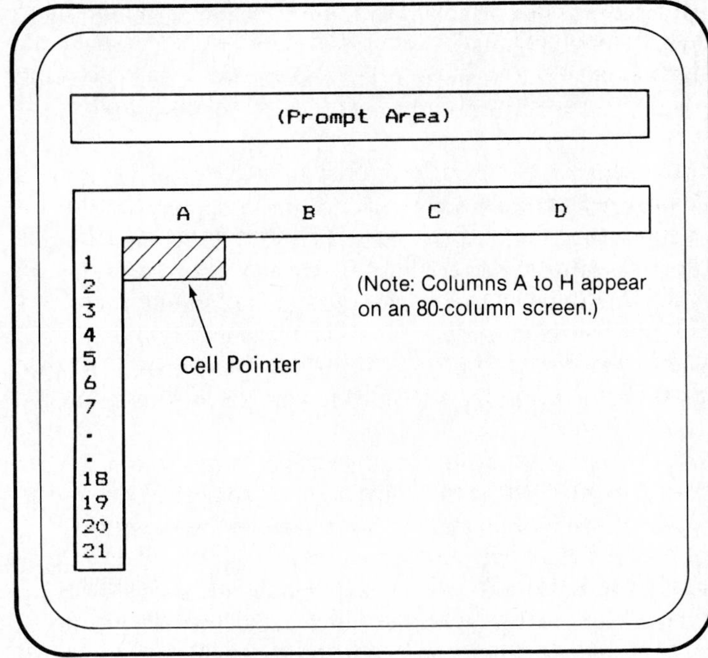

Figure 6–2 First screen of a typical electronic spreadsheet

1-2-3.* It is an interactive, cell-oriented, electronic spreadsheet. In addition to the spreadsheet, Lotus 1-2-3 also contains graphics and database management functions.

The Lotus 1-2-3 spreadsheet resembles the one in VisiCalc®. VisiCalc is the original interactive, cell-oriented electronic spreadsheet. Its appearance in 1979 sparked a software industry blitz of similar products with similar sounding names like SuperCalc, CalcStar and PlannerCalc. Such products are also called *spreadsheet simulators* and *financial modelers.*

Figure 6–2 illustrates only a small portion, or *window,* of what often is an enormous sheet of electronic paper. It is configured like an accountant's typical spreadsheet that is divided into rows and columns. Undisplayed columns and rows can be scrolled into the display area by typing arrow keys.

At the intersection of column A and row 1, called *coordinate* or *cell* A1, is the *cell pointer.* The cell pointer indicates which cell is currently activated or being considered for use.

To enter the spreadsheet shown in Figure 6–3, Mr. Williams types the down arrow key to move the cell pointer to cell A2. After typing T-hat-A, the down arrow key is used again to move to the next cell, and the next, for the following two entries.

The up and right arrow keys get Mr. Williams to the top of column B. There, he types in a column description, then uses the down arrow key to arrive at cell B2. In the next two cells, he types numbers reflecting prices. He repeats the exact same arrow

*"Lotus" and "1-2-3" are trademarks of Lotus Development Corporation. © Lotus Development Corporation, 1984. Used with permission.

movement and typing procedure as used in column B to enter column C. He concludes column C entries by typing a label, G-Total.

Descriptive labels, numbers or formulas can be typed into any cell. Column D requires the entry of formulas to calculate total amounts. Totals are the result of price multiplied by units.

Multiplication is indicated by an asterisk (*) key. So Mr. Williams types +B2*C2 into cell D2. The extra plus sign in front of B2 tells the program to read B as a formula instead of as a label. The result instantly appears in D2. The formula, meanwhile, remains in the computer's memory as cell information and is not displayed. The rest of the column is typed substituting 3, then 4, for the 2 in the formula.

The last item in the total column is the sum of all the items above it. Special functions like summation are invoked with an "@" key. The cell information is typed as @SUM(D2.D4). The range from cell D2 to cell D4 is summed and the result displayed.

The spreadsheet entry is complete. To make it look a bit neater, a command is entered to right-justify descriptive labels. Mr. Williams found command entry to be relatively easy to master. It required a lot of arrow and carriage return key typing. For example, if a return key is symbolized as a bracketed [R], he had to type /→[R]/→[R]/→[R]A1.D5[R] to right-justify all the labels on his spreadsheet.

To enter a command requires first typing the slash (/) key. It brings a menu line of command names to the prompt area. A command pointer highlights the first of several command choices. Mr. Williams types the arrow keys to move the command pointer to a desired command name. Then he types the carriage return key to indicate command selection.

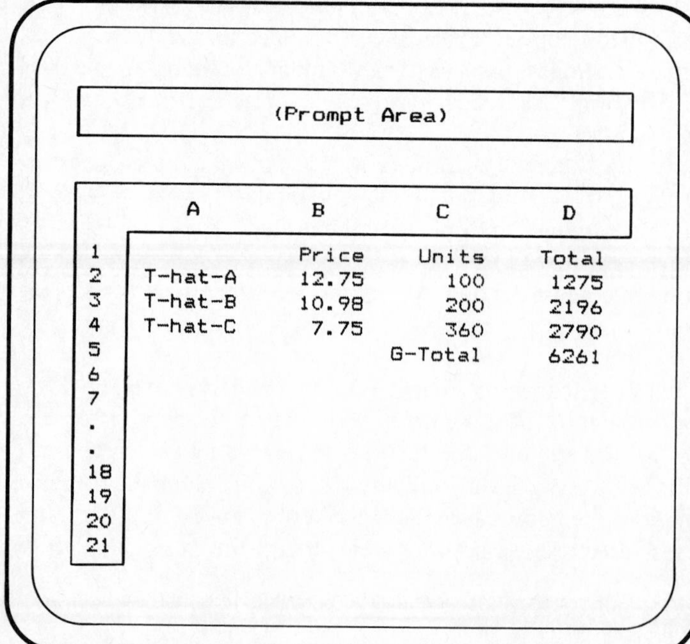

Figure 6-3 Electronic spreadsheet of SGD's sales projections

The command names he selects are: /RANGE LABEL-PREFIX RIGHT. These commands tell Lotus to fix *labels* that appear anywhere within the cell *range* of A1 to D1. The labels should be *right*-justified. They previously had a left-justify *prefix* symbol, as do all label entries. Fortunately, nothing more than arrow and carriage return keys had to be typed. The program prompted him through the necessary command sequence.

Other command sequences save a spreadsheet on a disk as a file for later use. The command sequence is /FILE SAVE. Along with the command selection, Mr. Williams types any eight-character filename he desires. To print a spreadsheet on paper, he uses the command sequence /PRINT PRINTER (cell range) GO. The cell range is the first and the last cell coordinates that mark the extreme boundaries of his spreadsheet.

As is obvious, the up-front work of electronic spreadsheet entry is often as labor-intensive as doing it manually. In addition, a planner has to learn about cell and command pointer movement, formula entry, and commands from a User Guide. While the learning effort requires time, it does not require previous computer experience.

(Prompt Area)

	A	B	C	D	E	F	G
1			Quarterly Budget - Phoenix District				
2							
3			1	2	3	4	Total
4							
5	Sales		20000	22000	24200	26620	92820
6	Cost of goods sold		10000	11000	12100	13310	46410
7	Operating profit		10000	11000	12100	13310	46410
8			--------	--------	--------	--------	--------
9	Operating expenses		8000	8800	9680	10648	37128
10	Pre-tax profit		2000	2200	2420	2662	9282
11			--------	--------	--------	--------	--------
12	Net income		920	1012	1113	1225	4270
13							
14	Growth factor per quarter			0.10			
15	Manufacturing cost factor			0.50			
16	Operating cost factor			0.40			
17	Combined tax rate			0.54			
18							
19							
20							
21							

Figure 6-4 An electronic spreadsheet of a quarterly budget

WHAT-IF SENSITIVITY ANALYSIS

The payoff for all the initial effort comes in doing what-if sensitivity analyses. To get a response to the what-if question posed earlier, Mr. Williams simply changes the units for type C tennis hats, from 360 to the dropped figure of 300. This requires moving the cell pointer and typing the units amount. Totals across and down instantly display the reduced figures.

Mr. Williams further explores whether a price-cutting strategy is worth pursuing. What if the price of type A tennis hats drops to $11.99, causing sales to climb to 150 units? Entering the new dollar and sale figures quantifies this assumption. The instantly available bottom line recommends that the strategy is worth more serious investigation.

Another planner who does sale budgets calculates quarterly sales on the basis of a growth rate from a base figure. The spreadsheet is shown in Figure 6–4. By moving the pointer to the cell in which the growth rate is displayed and changing the figure, the program automatically recalculates projected sales for budget periods. All expense and profit figures based on sales are also automatically changed.

But the electronic spreadsheet is capable of more complex analyses. One investment manager uses it to create five-year income and cash flow statements for real estate ventures. The statements created are based on about fifty revenue and cost assumptions. Any change in assumptions takes only seconds to recalculate. The user keeps changing assumptions until satisfied that an understanding is reached of which assumptions are truly critical to the situation at hand.

What users find from working with electronic spreadsheets is that assumptions once believed to be important are often demonstrated to be not as crucial as others. In one manufacturing company case, overhead costs as a percentage of gross profit proved to be more critical to the bottom line than material cost assumptions. To the planner, getting that kind of understanding about the situation was worth the investment of start-up time and money.

PERSONAL PRODUCTIVITY ENHANCEMENTS

Electronic spreadsheet features enhance a user's personal productivity. A copy feature, in particular, automatically duplicates cells across a range of rows or columns.

A business forecaster preparing a ten-year plan, for example, enters figures for only the first year's column. With a few keystrokes, subsequent columns replicate the same or incremented figures in a matter of seconds. This copy feature is a great time-saving device when preparing more elaborate spreadsheets. Equally useful is a feature to insert, delete, or move entire rows and columns. This can be especially useful when a spreadsheet is finished and it is discovered that an important calculation was omitted.

The availability of built-in functions like summation further support a user's planning productivity. Average, count, minimum, maximum, and net present value are generally available, as are engineering math functions. Many electronic spreadsheets even allow a user to construct some elementary program logic for complex spreadsheets.

Users working with large spreadsheets find the horizontal and vertical split screen

(Prompt Area)

	A B	C	D	E		J	K
1		Phoenix	Chicago	Boston	1	Atlanta	L. A.
2					2		
3	Sales	92820	55420	60000	3	60000	74500
4	Cost of goods sold	46410	24939	31200	4	30000	35015
5	Operating profit	46410	30481	28800	5	30000	39485
6		------------	------------	------------	6	------------	------------
7	Operating expenses	37128	23276	24000	7	27000	26075
8	Pre-tax profit	9282	7205	4800	8	3000	13410
9		------------	------------	------------	9	------------	------------
10	Net income	4270	3314	2208	10	1380	6169
11					11		
12					12		
13	Break-even point	0.50	0.55	0.48	13	0.50	0.53
14					14		
15	Factors used:				15		
16	Manufacturing cost	0.50	0.45	0.52	16	0.50	0.47
17	Operating expenses	0.40	0.42	0.40	17	0.45	0.35
18	Combined tax rate (all)		0.54		18		
19					19		
20					20		
21					21		

Figure 6-5 Example of an electronic spreadsheet with a vertically split screen

capability helpful. As shown in Figure 6–5, juxtaposing sections of a spreadsheet can be valuable for comparative analysis.

The ability to reuse saved spreadsheet formats is another aid to productivity. For example, if the planner saved the spreadsheet in Figure 6–3, it could be reused to calculate the simple gross pay for employees. To do so, names are typed into Column A. All that is needed is then to type hourly rate into Column B and hours worked into Column C. Totals are automatically extended by the generalized formulas originally entered and retained as cell information.

LARGE COMPANY USES

Advanced spreadsheet features help large companies promote uniform spreadsheet information collection and use throughout an organization. Large companies engage their most knowledgeable people to create budget, planning, and forecasting templates. *Template* is the industry term for reusable spreadsheet models with built-in titles and formulas. These templates are easy to use by others in an organization who only need to know how to fill in the blanks.

Template builders need not worry about template users accidentally altering formulas, titles, or any other important information. Advanced features provide protected areas for all these parts of a spreadsheet. Confidential data, which a user need not see, can also be shielded. Other desirable features, like step-by-step prompts and data checking, make advanced template features highly desirable in many firms.

A follow-up feature is the ability to consolidate spreadsheets. After various groups, departments, or divisions have completed their spreadsheet templates, information from them is combined into concise, presentation-quality reports.

There are packages that go beyond consolidating similar spreadsheets. They provide an ability to link data in dissimilar spreadsheets. Links are really commands in a master spreadsheet. The commands direct the spreadsheet to go to other specific spreadsheets to retrieve specific cell information and update the master with it.

A financial officer at another large company uses this feature. She links specific cells to the sales and cost data cells in division spreadsheets. When she retrieves the master spreadsheet from the disk, the links work instantly and invisibly. If division spreadsheets are updated before retrieving the master, the master would reflect the updated information. This useful feature eliminates the need to reenter data from one spreadsheet to another. In effect, an entire network of spreadsheet connections can be created.

SECOND-GENERATION SPREADSHEETS

Such large company features are enhancements provided by a second-generation of cell-oriented electronic spreadsheets like SuperCalc, MultiPlan, Lotus 1-2-3, new versions of VisiCalc, and others. Some are unfairly called "VisiClones" to show their parentage. Improvement can be expected to propel such spreadsheets through many generations.

One installed upgrade is the ability to name cells or blocks of cells and then use the names in formulas. For example, consider the spreadsheet in Figure 6–4 with sale items in cells C5 to F5. With some spreadsheets, these four cells could be named SALES. Then it would only be necessary to enter SUM(SALES) in cell G5. By a careful choice of names, it becomes possible to instruct the program in English rather than in formulas.

Another upgrade feature is an ability to anticipate a user's next move. For example, assume the content of one spreadsheet cell is copied to multiple columns. When moving to a new row for a new entry, the program proposes the same number of columns for copying the new entry. One spreadsheet that does this is on target better than 50 percent of the time and requires only a RETURN key response to go ahead with the move. Typing in anything else overrides the proposed response.

While one enhanced spreadsheet offers up to eight simultaneous window splits on the screen, another provides multicolored spreadsheets. If color is chosen, a blue border surrounds a yellow matrix, with positive numbers displayed in white and negative ones in red. This spreadsheet also allows viewing cell formulas as easily as data, just by asking for them to be displayed instead of data. This flexibility makes it easy to check the entire spreadsheet for errors.

LEARNING AIDS

Generally users find spreadsheet programs among the easiest computer applications to use, once the commands are learned. The commands are like a craftperson's tools, the more they are used, the more proficient one becomes in creating useful spreadsheets.

One device to simplify the learning and use of electronic spreadsheets is the inclusion of a help key. On some versions, typing the "?" key brings to the screen a list of possible entries relating to the current active cell. This is a welcome feature for any beginner or occasional user.

But laboring over hundreds of pages in a User Guide to learn to use an electronic spreadsheet can be tedious. This problem has been attacked by vendors of training software. Training software usually is supported with more User Guides and sometimes audio cassettes. Much of it includes prepared spreadsheet examples on disk. Users load the example desired and follow related exercises in the accompanying written tutorial. One spreadsheet publisher includes prepared examples on the program disk for advanced exercises. This relieves a good deal of the tedium associated with entering example after example on the way to proficiency.

Periodicals, books, and user's groups also abound to assist beginner and advanced spreadsheet users. Representative examples are listed at the end of the chapter.

Books generally offer prepared spreadsheets with entry instructions for many different needs. Often they are well worth investigating for ready spreadsheet guidance to preparing, for example, an inventory cost matrix or price earnings ratio matrix. They also provide ideas for creative spreadsheet use.

Softbooks are another learning aid. One company's softbook comes as a looseleaf binder that contains printed pages and a disk. Printed pages cover both the principal part of the book and an explanation text designed to augment the information on disk.

Some creative uses include the preparation of payroll checks. But spreadsheet applications like payroll tend to be poor cousins to dedicated accounting-oriented software. Nonetheless, creative use of the flexible electronic spreadsheet tends to be boundless.

Beginners and advanced users alike can take advantage of prepared templates sold by independent software vendors. A real estate investor, for example, bought templates to use for income property investment, mortgage loan, property depreciation, and amortization analyses. All templates can be customized by changing titles, inserting rows and columns, adjusting formulas, and so on.

PROGRAMMING-LIKE LANGUAGE-ORIENTED SPREADSHEETS

Some very sophisticated and comprehensive financial management spreadsheets are unlike the VisiCalc-type spreadsheets considered so far. This type of spreadsheet is not cell-oriented. Instead it is programming-like and language-oriented. Users construct a hierarchy of program layers, which then produce a spreadsheet on the screen. Such spreadsheets are clones of financial modeling applications offered to customers by mainframe time-sharing services. This ancestry, however, does not seem to offer any implicit advantage.

Spreadsheets based on this design model often require users to be familiar with mainframe-type computer operations and procedures. For example, users build spreadsheet models by first writing programs in a super-FORTRAN language that is often used to construct mainframe models. Programming is done completely independently of the screen or cell coordinates. Another program often must be written to format the spreadsheet with headings, proper punctuation, and the like to get presentation-quality printed spreadsheets.

These programming-like language-oriented spreadsheets are often easier to grasp from a logical standpoint—especially if the user has a background in programming. One package, in particular, has the advantage of superior graphics. A user can store graphics and charts and later display them in a color slide show sequence.

INTERFACING WITH OTHER APPLICATIONS

Graphics are possible with cell-oriented Lotus 1-2-3 or VisiCalc-type spreadsheets as well. VisiCalc's related VisiPlot generates pie, bar, and line graphs from spreadsheet information. To get the graphic result requires that spreadsheet information first be saved using the special DIF (data interchange format) file storage command.

The DIF file feature is an open interface permitting the exchange of VisiCalc spreadsheet files with any program designed to interpret them. VisiCalc's publisher and other vendors have written an assortment of applications that interface through DIF files. The assortment includes exchanges with graphics and statistical trending packages, as well as with word processing, database management, data communication, and other packages.

Often statistical packages are combined with graphics packages to display trends. Statistical packages typically include multiple linear regression, cumulative total, percent change, and various other data transformations peculiar to time series data. One manager uses the trending and graphics programs to plot the high, low, and current sales for each of a dozen branch operations. Another tracks moving averages of a stock portfolio. In each case, the benefit of viewing information in graphic form is perceived as greater than if left in tabular format.

Others use data communication programs to receive and convert files from remote databases into spreadsheet formats. Economists at one major metropolitan firm regularly receive economic data from a commercial database service one thousand miles away. The data is used in a prepared spreadsheet for forecasting. A marketing consultant who interfaces a data communication package uses it to send and receive data with clients. The data get included in spreadsheet models.

It is easy to see how valuable open interfacing can be. It could be frustrating to produce a spreadsheet that must be reentered by hand in order to be integrated into a word processing report, incorporated into statistical graphs, or sent to remote offices. Yet some spreadsheets, as well as other professional support applications, do not provide open interfacing. With a multifunction package, of course, easy interfacing is implicit among applications.

But can the spreadsheet interface with other vendor software? It is important to examine how spreadsheet functions and features fit requirements to avoid a mismatch or unpleasant surprises.

EVALUATION

Before acquiring an electronic spreadsheet, specifying requirements that must be met by the application should be defined. The Electronic Spreadsheet Checklist given in Figure 6-6 helps identify needs and provides a systematic tool for evaluating candidate packages. It needs to be backed up with both the General Software and Hands-on Test checklists provided in Chapter 4. The best way to complete an evaluation of comparable packages is to take sample manually prepared spreadsheets and actually hands-on test them with candidate packages.

Checklists, as mentioned elsewhere, are best used as a point of departure for more intense analyses. This is especially true if an acquisition involves a new small computer that will be used to run more than the spreadsheet program.

The Electronic Spreadsheet Checklist includes features that should be checked because they are not available in all spreadsheets, like the ability to vary individual column widths. Other items are listed because they vary from product to product, like the ability to recalculate a spreadsheet automatically after changes. Some programs do this for the entire spreadsheet without user intervention. Mr. Williams used one like this. Some programs, however, recalculate only from the point of change forward. This could be a problem when working with complex spreadsheets.

Some functions that are universally available, like a "growing command," have been included for reference purposes. The *growing command* allows a user to specify that one column or row will be greater than the preceeding one by a certain percentage. Such a command is useful in budget and forecasting spreadsheets.

The checklist includes some criteria not yet covered. Those needing a brief explanation are described in the following paragraphs.

Maximum size spreadsheet columns and rows should be specified to be sure a package can accommodate the largest matrix needed. But typically it is impossible to get both a column and row maximum at the same time. For example in the case of a 64 Kbyte memory VisiCalc, if one used the maximum 254 rows, the maximum number of available columns would be substantially less than the theoretical 63. Total maximum spreadsheet size is dependent on both available memory and the complexity of formulas used.

For another version of VisiCalc, on the other hand, published maximums are:

Total Memory in Kbytes	*Maximum Spreadsheet size in Kbytes*
64	22
128	86
192	150
256	214

But how does one know how many kilobytes in a spreadsheet? It requires first quitting VisiCalc, then entering an operating system command for a directory listing. The listing shows the spreadsheet filesize in kilobytes.

In the case of another spreadsheet, only 64 Kbytes of memory is used. The program's ability to link spreadsheets theoretically obviates the need for huge memory capacity.

Figure 6-6 Electronic Spreadsheet Checklist

Candidate Packages Names:
A: ______________________
B: ______________________
C: ______________________

Check "must have" items.

Must have	Item	Rating (Scale: 1 = poor to 10 = excellent) A	B	C
	Information Entry Method			
____	On-screen cell formulas	____	____	____
____	Programming-like language	____	____	____
	Maximum Size			
____	Spreadsheet columns ____	____	____	____
____	Spreadsheet rows ____	____	____	____
	Capability			
____	Consolidate similar spreadhseet	____	____	____
____	Link data from dissimilar spreadsheet	____	____	____
	Interface with Other Software			
____	Statistical trending	____	____	____
____	Graphics	____	____	____
____	Data communication	____	____	____
____	Word processing	____	____	____
____	Datebase management system	____	____	____
____	External database services	____	____	____
____	Accounting	____	____	____
____	Manufacturing	____	____	____
____	Other ______________	____	____	____
	Operational Features			
____	Split screen	____	____	____
____	Variable width columns	____	____	____
____	Formula printout	____	____	____
____	Table look-up	____	____	____
____	Global GOTO COORDINATE addressing	____	____	____
____	Store data separate from format	____	____	____
	Computational Features			
____	Net present value	____	____	____
____	Other financial functions	____	____	____
____	Square roots	____	____	____
____	Other statistical/engineering functions	____	____	____
____	Logic testing	____	____	____
____	Automatic recalculation	____	____	____
____	Growing command	____	____	____
	Format Features			
____	Align decimal columns	____	____	____
____	Format reports	____	____	____
____	Align decimal columns	____	____	____
____	Format reports	____	____	____

Figure 6-6 (continued)

Check "must have" items.	*Rating (Scale: 1 = poor to 10 = excellent)*		
Format Features	*A*	*B*	*C*
____Paginate	____	____	____
____Partial print-out	____	____	____
____Round-off numbers	____	____	____
Subtotal	____	____	____
Divide by number of items rated for average rating	____	____	____

Transfer Average Rating to Selection Summary: Software, Figure 5-3.

Another electronic spreadsheet solves the size limitation problem with a memory management technique called *virtual memory.* Usually associated with mini- and mainframe computers, virtual memory can accommodate an essentially unlimited number of entries by tapping the disk drive as extended RAM memory.

Maximum numeric digits should be specified to be sure the package can handle the largest totals expected of it. A package that can produce a maximum of only seven digits could not handle results in the hundreds of millions, which need eleven digits.

Table look-up is the ability to select values from a table. One of the more important common uses of this feature is a tax preparation application that selects rates from a tax table.

Logic testing is the ability to construct decision points and some elementary logic flow in a model. A logic function uses programming keywords like IF, AND, OR, NOT, and it is used anywhere formulas can be used. For example, if a need existed to test whether all the spreadsheet values at A1 through A5 were true and at least one of the values at D1 through D4 were true, the VisiCalc formula would look like "@AND(@AND(A1.A5),@OR(D1.D4))." This function is for advanced spreadsheet uses.

SELF TEST

1. List some characteristics of electronic spreadsheets.
2. Contrast a VisiCalc-type spreadsheet with a programmer-like language-oriented spreadsheet.
3. What information can a cell contain? Give examples.
4. What is a command? How is it invoked?
5. List some personal productivity enhancements enjoyed by electronic spreadsheet users.
6. What is a template? How do large companies use them?
7. Explain the difference between consolidating similar spreadsheets and linking data in dissimilar spreadsheets.
8. Describe some second-generation spreadsheet characteristics.
9. What kind of electronic spreadsheet learning aids are available?
10. What other applications might spreadsheet users like to interface with? Why?
11. Electronic spreadsheets have their own vocabulary. Explain: recalculation after changes, growing command, maximum size matrix, logic testing.

EXERCISES

1. *Phoenix District Case.* Assume you are the corporate financial officer in charge of designing a "fill-in-the-blanks" electronic spreadsheet template for all district offices. Use the Phoenix District spreadsheet in Figure 6–4 as a prototype of the result you want from each district.
   a. Which labels would be field protected?
   b. Which cells would contain formulas?
   c. Which cells would contains fixed numeric information?
   d. Which cells would required "fill-in-the-blanks" manual entry?
2. *Maxwell and Sons Company Case.* Mr. Maxwell's son is interested in securing an electronic spreadsheet to prepare models similar to those in Figure 6–5. Using Figure 6–5 as a guide, what are the five features you would recommend Mr. Maxwell examine most closely in a candidate spreadsheet?
3. *LBK Enterprises Case.* Ms. Jackson, an economist in the Marketing Research Department of LBK Enterprises, has an electronic spreadsheet. Now she wants to get more timely economic data from an information utility one thousand miles away. The utility offers an on-line database of its economic information. Explain what software capabilities Ms. Jackson must have to access the economic data.
4. *Ajax Corporation Case.* The financial officer at Ajax Corporation specifies the following must-have requirements, among others, for an electronic spreadsheet application:
   a. Cell-oriented
   b. Interfaces with:
      Word processing
      Graphics
   c. Consolidate similar spreadsheets
   d. Split screen
   e. Variable windows

   Locate professional support multifunction packages that have an electronic spreadsheet. Or use the packages already located from the Ajax Corporation Case Exercise in Chapter 4. Of the packages located:
   a. Which ones meet the requirements specified?
   b. Of the products that meet the requirements, which one is the superior product?
   c. Defend your answer.
5. *Ajax Corporation Case.* To continue the Ajax Corporation evaluation, use the Hands-on Test Checklist as a guide to actually test selected application products. The spreadsheet example in Figure 6–5 could be used for this test. Is the test result consistent with the product evaluation already made?

RESOURCES AND REFERENCES

Books

ANBARLIAN, HARRY, *An Introduction to VisiCalc Matrixing for the Apple and IBM,* McGraw-Hill, 1982.

BROWN, GARY D. AND DONALD SEFTON, *Surviving with Financial Application Packages for the Computer,* Wiley, 1983.

COBB, DOUGLAS FORD AND GENA BERG COBB, *SuperCalc Super Models for Business,* Que, 1983.

COBB, DOUGLAS FORD AND GEOFFREY T. LEBLOND, *Using 1-2-3,* Que, 1983.
MCLAUGHLIN, HUGH AND LEITH ANDERSON, *1-2-3 for Business,* Que, 1984.
SCHWARE, ROBERT AND ALICE TREMBOUR, *All About 1-2-3,* Dilithium, 1983.
The Power of: VisiCalc, Management Information Source, 1983.
The Power of: Lotus 1-2-3, Management Information Source, 1983.
The Power of: SuperCalc, Management Information Source, 1983.
The Power of: Multiplan, Management Information Source, 1983.
TROST, STAN, *Doing Business with 1-2-3,* Sybex, 1984.
TROST, DEBBIE, ET. AL. *How to Use SuperCalc 2,* Dilithium, 1983.
VisiCalc Advanced Version, VisiCorp.

Periodicals

Absolute Reference, The Journal for 1-2-3 Users, Que.
The Power of: Electronic Spreadsheets, Management Information Source.
SATN: The Journal for VisiCalc Users, Software Arts.
Regular columns appear in *Desktop Computing* and others.

Disk-based and Other Tutorials

ATI Training Power: Teach Yourself Lotus 1-2-3, ATI.
DESAUTELS, EDOUARD J. AND WILLIAM C. BROWN, *VisiCalc for the IBM Personal Computer,* Brown.
Lotus 1-2-3 Tutorial Disk, Lotus.
Managing Your Business with the Lotus 1-2-3 Program, Cdex.
Managing Your Business with SuperCalc or SuperCalc Program, Cdex.
Managing Your Business with VisiCalc or VisiCalc Advanced Version Program, Cdex.
Teach Yourself Lotus 1-2-3 on the IBM PC, DELTAK.
Teach Yourself Multiplan, DELTAK.
Teach Yourself SuperCalc, DELTAK.
Teach Yourself VisiCalc on the IBM PC, DELTAK.
Teach Yourself VisiTrend/Plot, DELTAK.
The SuperCalc Program, Cdex.
Using 1-2-3, McMullen and McMullen.
Using VisiCalc, McMullen and McMullen.
VisiTutor for VisiCalc, VisiCorp.
VisiTutor for VisiCalc Advanced Version, VisiCorp.

Prepared Templates

Financial Planning with Lotus 1-2-3, Sams.
VisiCalc Business Forecasting Model, VisiCorp.

Related Software Products

Business and economic external database access for VisiCalc, Data Resources.
DocuCalc and LoadCalc for VisiCalc, Micro Decision Systems.

Supplement: LOTUS ™ 1-2-3 ™ TUTORIAL

This is a keystroke-by-keystroke tutorial on how to use the electronic spreadsheet Lotus 1-2-3, produced by Lotus Development Corporation. It is written to be used as a guide while sitting at a computer. If a computer is not available, a reading of the tutorial can serve as a simulation of the actual session.

The IBM Personal Computer version 1A of Lotus is used in the tutorial. It requires the PC-DOS operating system version 1.1 or 2.0, a minimum of 128 Kbytes of memory, two disk drives and a printer.

Setup Procedure

In order to use Lotus 1-2-3, first load the Lotus program into the computer's memory as follows:

1. Open the left disk drive door (or latch) by pulling up at its bottom edge.
2. Carefully insert the Lotus disk, with its label up, into the drive. The oval cutout in the square disk jacket should enter the drive first. The label should enter the drive last. Gently push the disk all the way in and close the drive door.
3. In the same way as in steps 1 and 2, insert a preformated disk that can be used for storing completed spreadsheets in drive B. (See Figure 3–4 for format procedures.)
4. Turn the computer's switch on. The disk drive now begins to whir and click, and the red "in use" light on the drive comes on. Some initial typing is required, as follows:
   - A prompt message asks for entry of the current date. Type the date followed by a carriage RETURN (↵) key. For brevity, the symbol [R] will be used to indicate the RETURN key in the remainder of this tutorial.
   - A prompt message asks for the entry of the time. Type the time followed by the [R] key. Alternately, both the time and date entries can be ignored by typing only the [R] key in each case.
   - The Lotus main menu appears on the screen with the word 1-2-3 highlighted. The highlight is called a command pointer. To indicate selection of a command where the pointer is located, in this case at 1-2-3, type [R].
   - The message "Press any key to continue" appears. Type any key. The spreadsheet outline, as shown in Figure 6S–1, appears on the screen and is ready to accept entries.

CONTENT OF THE SCREEN

After a successfully completed setup procedure, which is frequently called *booting* the system, the screen displays the outline portion of the electronic spreadsheet. The screen can be thought of as a window into the computer's memory which contains a much larger spreadsheet.

As shown in Figure 6S–1, the spreadsheet is divided into rows numbered 1, 2, 3, and so on, and columns lettered A, B, C, and so forth. Each intersection of a row and column is a cell coordinate position such as A1, B3, D17, and the like. At each cell coordinate one can type a descriptive label, a number or a formula.

The top three lines of the screen are Lotus' control panel and prompt area. Whatever is typed at the keyboard appears on the control panel's second line before it appears in the cell. Entries move into the cell after the [R] key is typed. By watching the control panel, typing errors can be detected and corrected before they enter a cell.

The second line alternately will display command names whenever a slash (/) is typed. The first of several commands is always highlighted by a command pointer. To select a command, type the right arrow key to move the pointer to the command desired. Then type the [R] key.

The third line displays an explanation of the currently highlighted command.

Cell Entry and Cell Pointer Movement

Cell information is displayed on the control panel's first line. In the example shown in Figure 6S–1, it displays A1. If something previously had been typed into A1, the first line would display that information.

Typing an arrow key on the keyboard moves the cell pointer in the direction of the arrow. The right (→), left (←), up (↑), and the down (↓) directions should be tried for practice. For example, type → until the cell pointer seemingly moves off the right edge of the screen. New columns slide onto the screen and old ones disappear off the left edge. This is called *scrolling,* and it works in all four directions. Try it now. Typing the key labelled HOME returns the pointer to cell coordinate A1.

There is an easier way to move the cursor to coordinate G16 than to type the right arrow key six times and the down arrow key fifteen times. Instead, type the F5

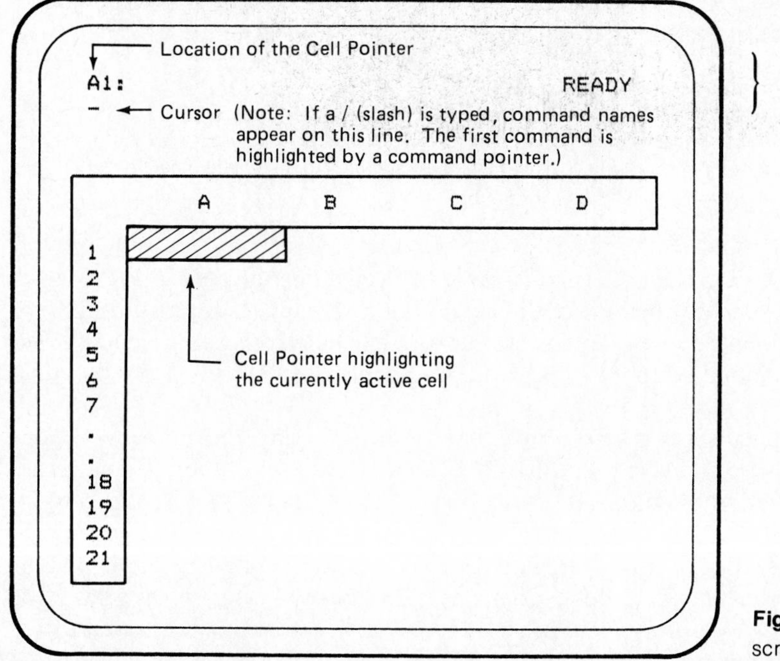

Figure 6S–1 Lotus 1-2-3® screen

function key on the left side of the keyboard. Pressing this key means "go to" in Lotus. The control panel displays ENTER ADDRESS TO GO TO. Type the desired destination coordinate, followed by the [R] key. Almost instantly, the cell pointer appears at the designated cell. For practice, try to move to G16, then move the cell pointer back to A1 again (remember to use the HOME key to return to A1).

Spreadsheet Examples

Sporting Goods Distributors, Inc. One simple example of using an electronic spreadsheet has already been described for the Sporting Goods Distributors company in Chapter 6. Enter that example first, using the step-by-step description in the text of Chapter 6 as a guide. Here are some things to remember when doing the SGD, Inc. spreadsheet.

1. Anything typed on the keyboard will not enter the computer's memory until the final [R] key is typed. Alternately, typing an arrow key serves the same function.
2. If a typing error is discovered before typing the final [R] key, use the backspace key to erase, then retype, the entry. Alternately, the ESC escape key will cancel an entry before the final [R] key is typed.
3. To replace the content of a cell with something else, type the new entry over the old one.
4. To blank out or erase the content of a cell after the final [R] key is typed requires the command sequence /RANGE ERASE (cell coordinate). To do this:

Type	*Description*
/	Starts the command mode.
→[R]	Moves the command pointer to the RANGE command and selects it.
→→[R]	Moves the command pointer to the ERASE command and selects it. Finally, the single cell coordinate or cell range of coordinates to be erased must be typed, such as B4 or B4.B12.

5. After a label is typed, it is displayed in a cell with a preceding single quote. The quote identifies it as a left-justified label. It happens automatically. Typing a double quote (") before a label will right-justify the label. Typing an exponentiation symbol (∧) before a label will center it.

The spreadsheet example in Chapter 6 provides an alternate way to right-justify all labels (see /RANGE LABEL-PREFIX RIGHT in the "Lotus Commands" section at the end of the tutorial).

ABC Food Company. Figure 6S–2 shows a spreadsheet prepared by a financial planner at the ABC Food Company. This spreadsheet assumes sales to be frozen at $15,000 a month. Expenses are $10,000 the first month and increase by 1 percent each following month.

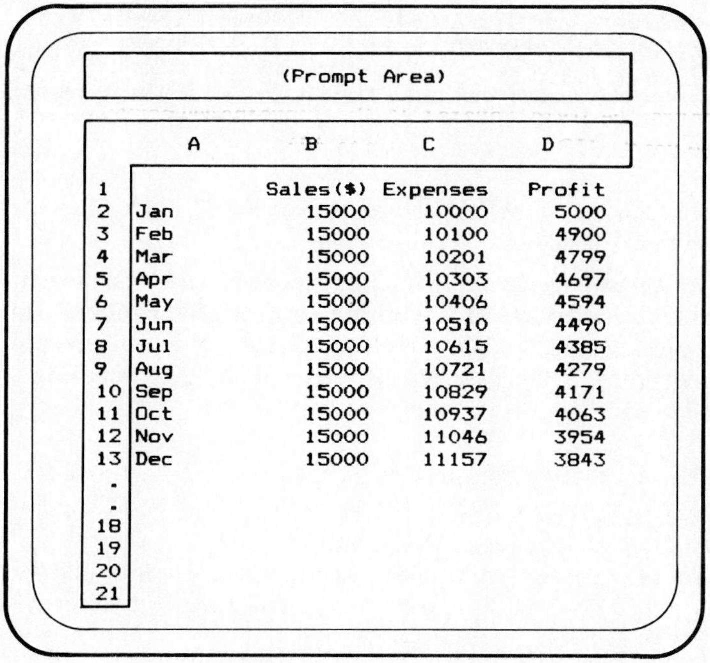

(Prompt Area)

	A	B	C	D
1		Sales($)	Expenses	Profit
2	Jan	15000	10000	5000
3	Feb	15000	10100	4900
4	Mar	15000	10201	4799
5	Apr	15000	10303	4697
6	May	15000	10406	4594
7	Jun	15000	10510	4490
8	Jul	15000	10615	4385
9	Aug	15000	10721	4279
10	Sep	15000	10829	4171
11	Oct	15000	10937	4063
12	Nov	15000	11046	3954
13	Dec	15000	11157	3843
.				
.				
18				
19				
20				
21				

Figure 6S-2 ABC Food Company profit planning spreadsheet

The COPY command is introduced in this exercise to simplify cell entry. The display screen should be closely watched when using the COPY command to observe the instantaneous copying.

As shown, Figure 6S-2 has no decimal numbers. The /WORKSHEET GLOBAL FORMAT FIXED 0 command was used when the example was finished to remove all decimal places. To make your own exercise look like Figure 6S-2, the command keystroke sequence is given at the end of the example.

Steps to prepare the ABC Food Company spreadsheet are:

1. Follow the "Setup Procedure" above. Alternately, an old Lotus spreadsheet can be wiped out in order to start fresh with a new spreadsheet. The command sequence /WORKSHEET ERASE YES does this. The keystrokes for this command sequence are given in the "Lotus Commands" section at the end of this tutorial.
2. Use the down arrow (↓) to move the cell pointer to A2.
3. Type titles for the twelve months. To do this, type: Jan ↓ Feb ↓ Mar ↓ Apr ↓ May ↓ Jun ↓ Jul ↓ Aug ↓ Sep ↓ Oct ↓ Nov ↓ Dec[R].
4. Type a new column label for SALES($) and indicate the January amount. To do this type: [F5]B1[R]Sales($)↓15000[R].
5. Use the COPY command, instead of typing $15,000 eleven times, to put $15,000 in the cells for the remaining eleven months. The steps to do this are:

Type	*Description*
/→→[R]	Starts the COPY command. (Note: If an arrow key is held down too long, it may end on a different command than the one planned.)

[R]	Selects the current cell as the one to copy FROM. In advanced spreadsheets, entire ranges are used as the source range for copying FROM. In this example, only the one cell where the cell pointer is now located, will be copied.
B3.B13[R]	Indicates the range of cells which is to be copied TO. In this example, it is cell B3 to B13. This entry must be closed with the [R] key.

6. Type the expenses label and enter the January value $10,000. To do this, type: [F5]C1[R]Expenses↓10000↓.
7. Next increase expenses 1 percent each month. In this case, different amounts are expected each month. It requires a special entry at cell C3 to reflect the increase. To do this, type: 1.01*C2[R]. The formula tells the spreadsheet program to multiply the amount in C2 by 101 percent. With the formula now in place, it can be copied for each month as follows:

Type	*Description*
/→→[R]	Starts the COPY command.
[R]	Selects the current cell as the one to COPY FROM.
C4.C13[R]	Indicates the range of cells which is to be copied TO. In this example, it is cell C4 to C13.

8. Establish the final label. To do this, type: [F5]D1[R]"Profit↓. The double quote right justifies the label.
9. Indicate the first formula for PROFIT = SALES − EXPENSES at cell D2. The cell coordinates are B2 for SALES and C2 for EXPENSES. To do this, type: +B2−C2[R].
10. Finally, copy the formula in the rest of the column as follows:

Type	*Description*
/→→[R]	Starts the COPY command.
[R]	Selects the current cell as the one to copy FROM.
D3.D13[R]	Indicates the range of cells which is to be copied TO. In this example, it is cell D3 to cell D13.

11. To remove all decimal digits, type: /[R][R][R][R]0[R].

Lotus Commands

Lotus commands are invoked by typing a slash (/). Typing a slash generates a command menu on the second line of the control panel. Commands are selected by moving the command pointer to a desired command and typing the [R] key. Alternately, commands could be invoked by typing a slash and the first letter of each command desired.

To undo or cancel a command sequence before Lotus has executed it, type two keys simultaneously, the CTRL and SCROLL LOCK keys. Alternately, type the ESC escape key repeatedly until the command menus vanish.

Some examples of useful commands follow. Commands are first listed by name sequence for reference, then by keystroke sequence.

COPY
/→→[R]from – range[R]to – range[R]

Copies information from one or more cells, to another cell area of the spreadsheet.

FILE RETRIEVE
/→→→→[R][R]filename[R]

Retrieves a saved spreadsheet file from the disk and displays it on the screen. This command sequence automatically displays active filenames on the third line of the control panel. A filename can be selected by moving the command pointer to the filename desired and typing the [R] key.

FILE SAVE
/→→→→[R]→[R]filename[R]

Saves the currently displayed spreadsheet on a disk under any eight-character filename specified. Valid filename characters are: A to Z, 0 to 9, and the underscore symbol (__).

PRINT PRINTER RANGE GO
/→→→→→[R][R][R]cell range[R]→→→→→→[R]

Prints the spreadsheet in the specified cell range on the printer. After printing finishes, move the command pointer to QUIT and type [R] to clear the prompt area.

QUIT YES
/→→→→→→→→→[R]→[R]

Ends a spreadsheet session.

RANGE ERASE
/→[R]→→[R]cell coordinate or cell range[R]

Erases or wipes out the content of a cell or a range of cells.

RANGE LABEL—PREFIX RIGHT
/→[R]→[R]→[R]from-to cell range[R]

Right-justifies all labels in the specified cell range.

RANGE FORMAT CURRENCY
/→[R][R]→→[R][R]cell coordinate or cell range[R]

Displays numbers in the specified cell or range of cells in a dollar-and-cents format. (Note: If the column width is too small, cells will print with asterisks instead of numbers.)

WORKSHEET COLUMN WIDTH-SET
/[R]→→→[R][R]value[R]

Changes the width of the column that the cell pointer is in. The new width is any specified value between 1 and 72.

WORKSHEET ERASE YES
/[R]→→→→[R]→[R]

Erases or wipes out an entire worksheet.

WORKSHEET GLOBAL FORMAT FIXED 0
/[R][R][R][R]0[R]

Removes decimal digits in numbers throughout the spreadsheet. It makes all numbers integer values.

Built-In Functions

Lotus built-in functions are invoked by typing the "@" key. There are more than 40 built-in functions. Only two, the @SUM and @AVG are described here.

For example, assume coordinate K8 is to hold the sum of K1, K2, K3...K7. Instead of typing at cell K8 the long formula +K1+K2+K3... +K7, simply type @SUM(K1.K7). Similarly, to get an average of all the numbers, the more efficient formula would be @AVG(K1.K7).

Two useful function keys (see Fig. 2-5) are:

F1 Help key—displays help screens for additional assistance. When through using the help screens, type the ESC escape key to return to continue spreadsheet work.

F5 GO TO key—moves the cell pointer to the cell specified. This often is faster than moving the cell pointer over wide distances on a spreadsheet.

The *Lotus 1-2-3 User's Manual* should be consulted for complete user instructions.

Exercises

Exercises do not require restoring the original spreadsheet to answer each question. Let one answer build on the next one.

1. *Apple Core Company Case.* The following table shows employee payroll information for the Apple Core Company.

Name	*Monthly Hours Worked*	*Hourly Salary*
A. Smith	125	$ 7.00
J. Greene	168	$10.25
K. Louis	160	$12.50

Use an electronic spreadsheet to build a model to find:

a. What is the company's total gross salary a month?

b. What if J. Greene becomes a part-time employee and works only 84 hours a month. How much will that change the total gross salary?

c. What if the hourly salary of A. Smith is raised to $8.00. How much will that affect the total gross salary? (*Hint:* This problem parallels the SGD Inc. case.)

2. *Merrill Cynch Company Case.* The following table shows the price per share for five different stocks sold by the Merrill Cynch Company.

Stock	*Price*
A	$ 4.75
B	$10.25
C	$32.00
D	$ 7.50
E	$12.25

Use the electronic spreadsheet to build a model to answer the following questions:

a. What will total sales be if 2,000 shares of each stock are sold?

b. What if the price of stock C dropped to $30, and 2,500 shares are sold. How will that affect sales?

c. What if the price of stock B goes up to $11 and only 1,600 shares are sold. How will this affect total sales?

3. *Fox Film Company Case.* The following table results from using an electronic spreadsheet program to calculate variable cost and profit for the Fox Film Company:

Cost Variable	55%
Sales	$12,000
Cost-Fixed	$ 1,750
Cost-Variable	$ 6,600
Profit	$ 3,650

Three spreadsheet items come directly from the Fox Film Company records. They indicate that variable costs are 55% of sales, sales are $12,000, and fixed costs are $1,750. The profit is the result of sales minus all costs. (*Hint:* Variable Costs = Sales × (55/100). Use variable cost as a "parameter" or "factor" similar to that on rows 14–17 of the Phoenix District spreadsheet in Figure 6–4.)

Modify the electronic spreadsheet to display answers to the following what-if questions:

a. What if sales increase to $15,200. How much profit can be expected?

b. What if fixed costs increase to $2,000. How much profit can be expected?

c. What if the percentage of the variable costs over sales becomes 62 percent. How much profit can be expected?

d. What if the percentage of variable costs over sales becomes 60 percent. What amount of sales is necessary to make $5,000 in profit? (*Hint:* Use either a trial-and-error technique to solve this or a formula.)

4. *Create a Spreadsheet.* Develop a spreadsheet that would be useful at work, school, or home. Create three what-if questions that would be appropriate to test the usefulness of the spreadsheet. Enter the spreadsheet, and test the three questions. Are the results what you expected? List questions, answers, and formulas used on a printed copy of the spreadsheet.

7

GRAPHICS

Business users increasingly turn to bar and pie charts, instead of to columns of numbers, to assess volumes of data. Studies indicate an improved comprehension ability when viewing information presented graphically versus textually.

With the availability of graphics software and hardware, business users do not have to be either graphic artists or computerists to retrieve graphic images of data.

This chapter reviews both analytic and presentation graphics software. It also discusses common graphic output devices, such as color graphic displays, plotters, and printers. Alternate devices to keyboard input, like the digitizer and light pen, are also discussed. The chapter concludes with some guidelines and checklists for computer graphics evaluation.

ANALYTIC

Mr. Williams often creates bar and pie charts out of spreadsheet information to help him understand the tabular figures. People in the graphics industry would distinguish this use as *analytic graphics.* The end purpose of an *analytic graph* is to help the decision maker analyze a problem, discern a trend, assess relationships, or any of many other decision-related possibilities. VisiPlot, BPS Business Graphics, and Business Graphics System are representative analytic graphics packages. Almost all multifunction packages, like Lotus 1-2-3 and Context MBA, include a graphics component.

Using a multifunction graphics and spreadsheet package, Mr. Williams can watch how figures "look." Each time he asks for a bar chart, like the one in Figure 7–1, he readily sees how each sales region is performing in relation to others. The shaded vertical bars instantly highlight proportional differences in regional sales performance for a new product. It is a line of tennis racquets in three qualities: top-of-the-line or premium, midrange, and budget categories.

The spreadsheet in Figure 7–2 produced the bar graph in Figure 7–1. In graphics terminology, each bar represents a series of *data points*. The first data point corresponds

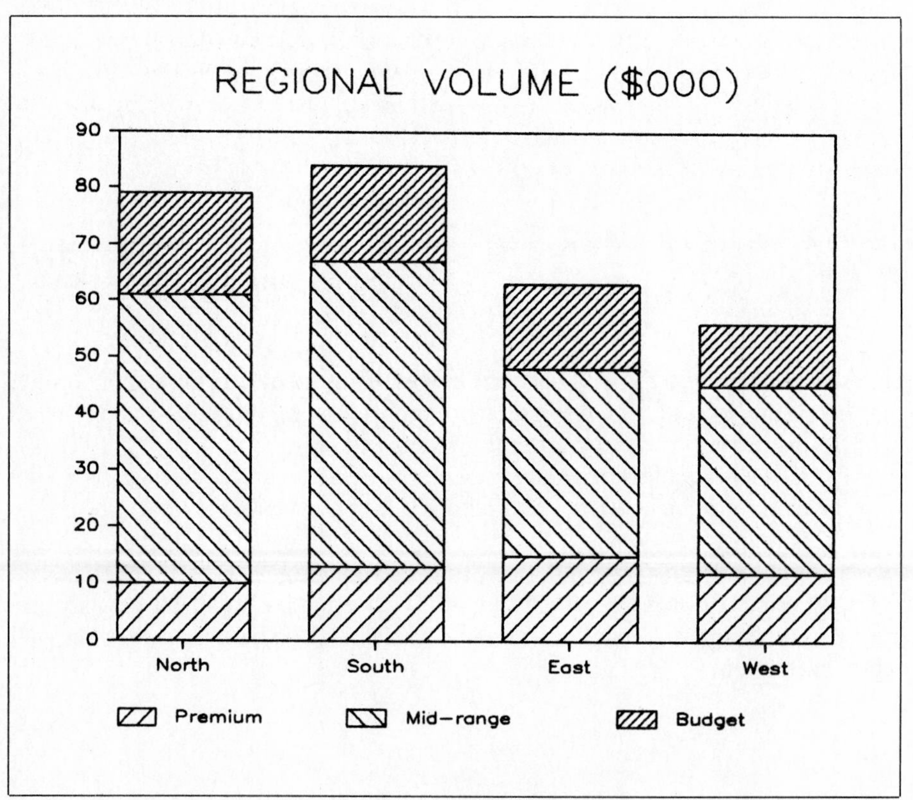

Graphics by Lotus 1-2-3 software, used with permission of Lotus Development Corporation

Figure 7-1 A bar graph printed on a dot-matrix printer from the spreadsheet in Figure 7–2

to sales of the premium racquet, the second to the mid range one, and the third to the budget category.

Many graphics applications accept files of data points created by other applications. Even multifunction packages usually accept input from foreign applications.

One feature of multifunction packages is their ability to easily change data points and instantly have them reflected in a graph without changing programs or disks. By contrast, with stand-alone graphics software, sometimes the time and trouble involved in changing graphs often outweighs the benefit they provide. It involves switching from spreadsheet to graphics package programs.

Standard Charts

Mr. Williams has a friend whose company makes use of standard charts to assess the financial health of the company. The standard charts include an income statement and balance sheet, such as those shown in Figure 7–3.

The intent in presenting common financial forms in graphic form is to help company analysts zero in on a company's strengths and weaknesses at a glance. In each chart, current-year figures appear in solid blocks, and previous-year figures in unshaded blocks. The entire layout of each chart is predefined, from the positioning of totals, subtotals, and titles to other labels on the page.

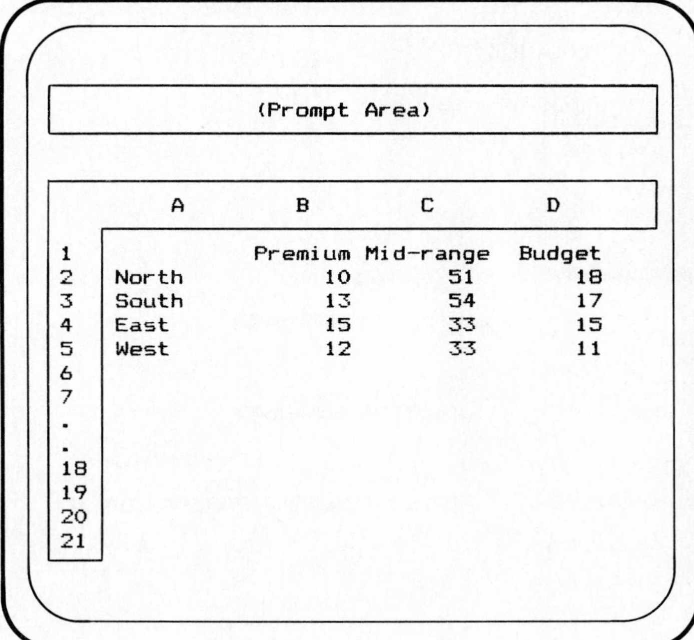

(Prompt Area)

	A	B	C	D
1		Premium	Mid-range	Budget
2	North	10	51	18
3	South	13	54	17
4	East	15	33	15
5	West	12	33	11
6				
7				
.				
.				
18				
19				
20				
21				

Figure 7-2 An electronic spreadsheet of regional sales figures by product category

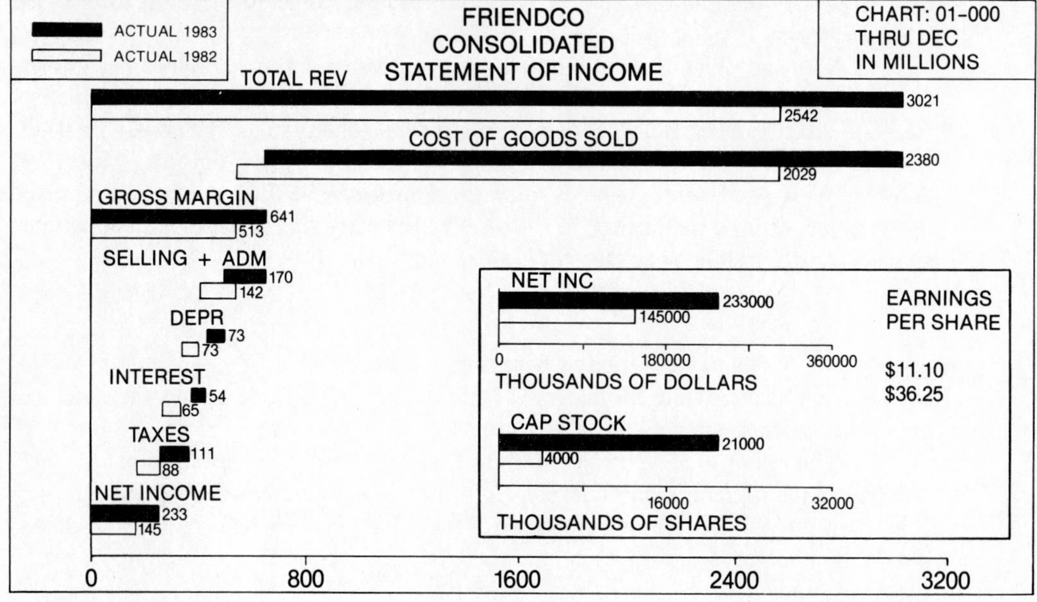

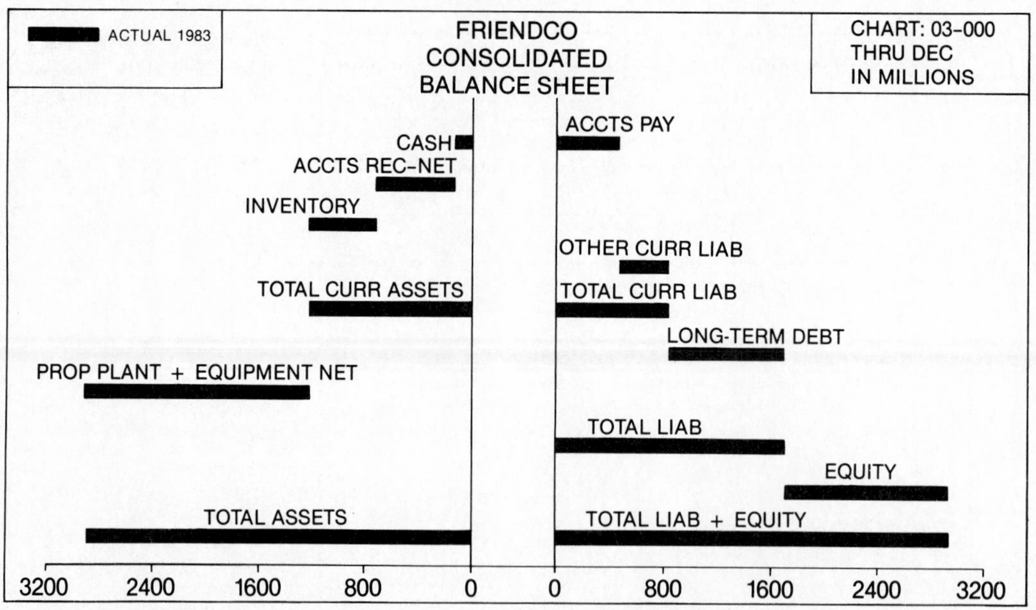

Graphics by Fingraph software, courtesy of Fingraph Corporation

Figure 7-3 Standard graphic charts for financial analysis

While the charts are easy to use, they do limit a user's flexibility. Some would argue that the standardized format lends itself to consistent recognition and interpretation. It eliminates a management concern that graphics can be used to distort or manipulate data.

Studies conducted on the use of color in graphics conclude that color visuals have a persuasive, as opposed to a strictly informational, effect on viewers. The chart manufacturer, for example, advocates the use of one color only.

On the other hand, psychological studies have found that color-coded graphs can be perceived 80 percent more effectively than black-and-white graphs. Understandably, there is some dispute over the propriety, in some applications, of using color graphics.

PRESENTATION

When Mr. Williams makes special presentations to others, in his own or in external organizations, he generally uses graphics to illustrate or emphasize certain points. People in the graphics industry distinguish this use as *presentation* graphics. Representative standalone packages are Graphwriter, Fast Graphs, Chart-Master, GraphPower, and Graftalk.

Since the graphic is for public viewing, he usually wants it more polished than he gets from the analytic graphics package combined with his low-speed black-and-white dot-matric printer.

Presentation graphics packages offer a host of options. They include sending output to a color plotter such as the one shown in Figure 7–4. Some packages accept spreadsheet input, but many do not. If no automatic input is possible, a user must enter data manually. The presentation graphics package Mr. Williams uses offers both options.

Until he got his presentation graphics software and a plotter, Mr. Williams went to an outside art firm. They helped develop charts and overhead transparencies. Overhead *transparencies* are graphics printed on clear plastic sheets. When placed on an overhead projector, the transparency is projected onto a screen or wall for large audience viewing. Sometimes he waited days for graphic orders. But now he produces comparable results himself in a few minutes.

The package he uses comes with over twenty standard graphic formats. The main formats include variations on the standard bar, pie and line graphs, such as those illustrated in Figure 7–5.

Creating Graphs

To learn how to create presentation graphics, Mr. Williams elects to prepare the sample segmented bar chart shown in Figure 7–5. He begins by filling in the input form for segmented bars, provided by the software manufacturer, and given in Figure 7–6. The standard input form simplifies graphic production for the novice user. The form contains answers to prompts from the format program. Once formats became familiar, Mr. Williams found the input form unnecessary. Sometimes he filled out forms when he had clerical help to produce the charts.

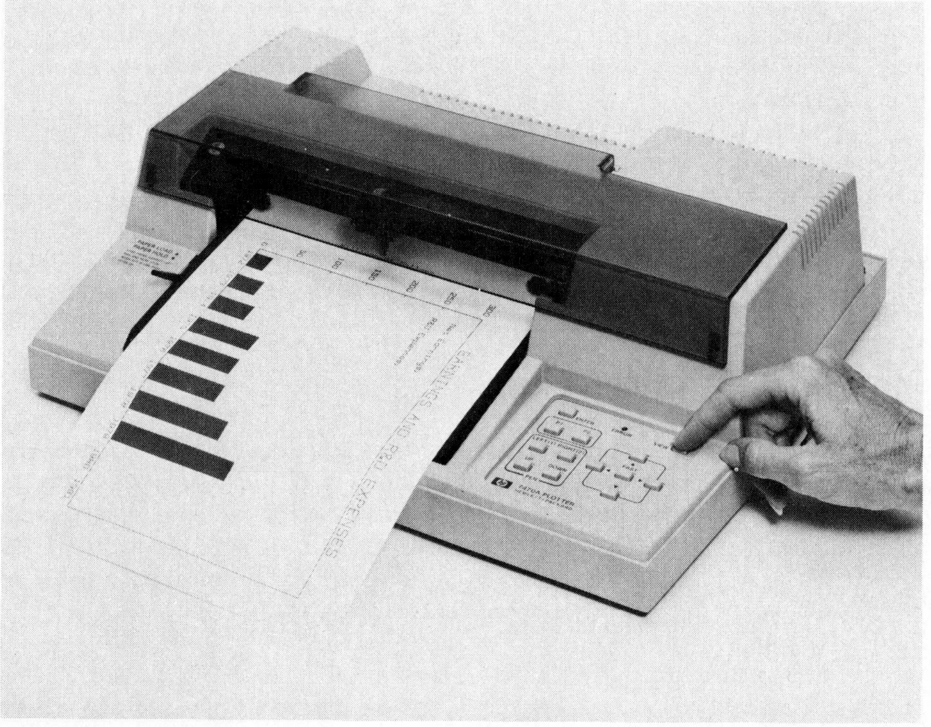

Courtesy of Hewlett-Packard

Figure 7-4 A flatbed plotter

Entering Data

After loading the graphics program, Mr. Williams selects Execute a Format from a main menu. He has a choice of entering all new data from the keyboard, inputting automatic data from an interfaced program, using data from the last segmented bar chart, or retrieving another saved chart. He elects to enter new data.

Because the chart is specific, menu choices and prompts are also specific. The technique eliminates extraneous prompts required by more generalized approaches.

Mr. Williams found the specific chart element guide, like the one in Figure 7–7, helpful. It eliminated references to the User Guide.

The data entry procedure, given in Figure 7–8, follows the input form data sequence. Figure 7–8 shows only selected sample entries. A detailed list of style options chosen in the sample entries is given in Figure 7–9. A list of these options is available at any point in the data entry procedure by pressing the help key.

The data entry procedure and the sample data entries are self-explanatory when Figure 7–5 is compared with Figure 7–6. The bar chart element guide clarifies graphics terminology.

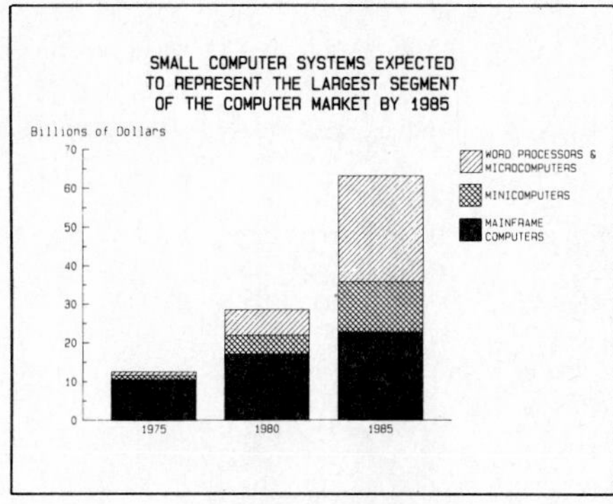

Segmented Bars

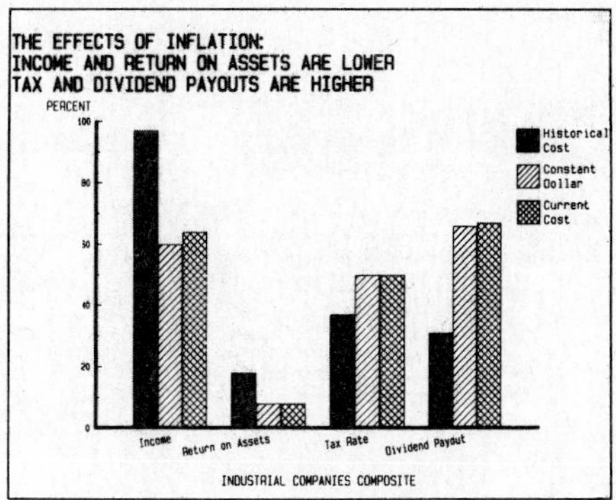

Clustered Bars

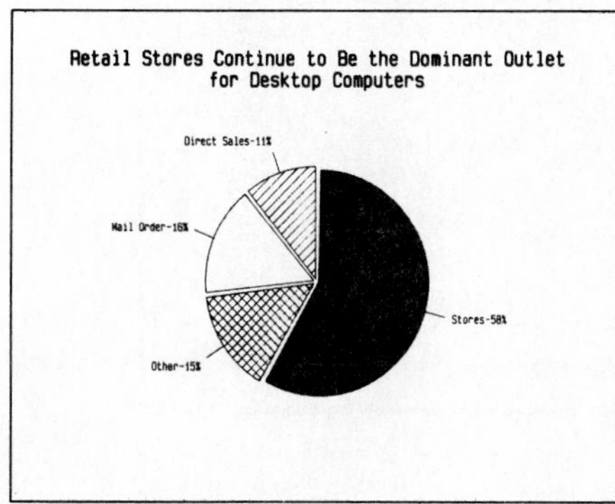

Pie

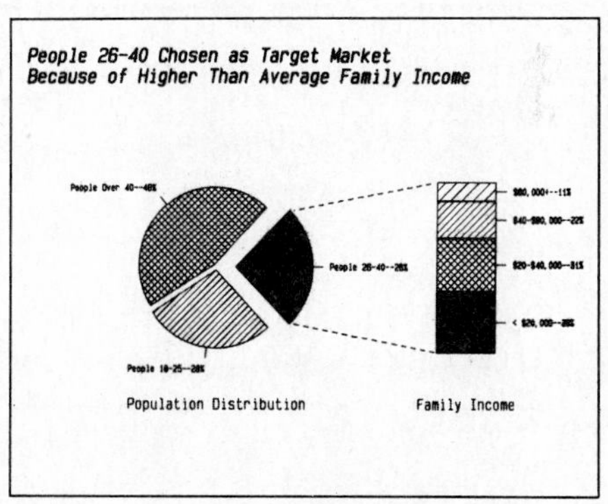

Pie-Bar Combination

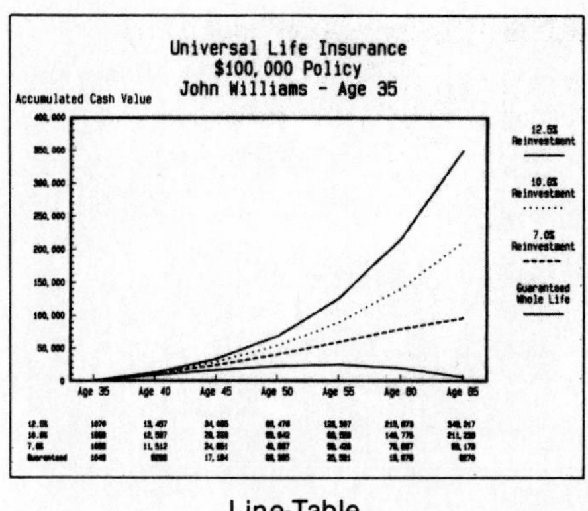

Line-Table

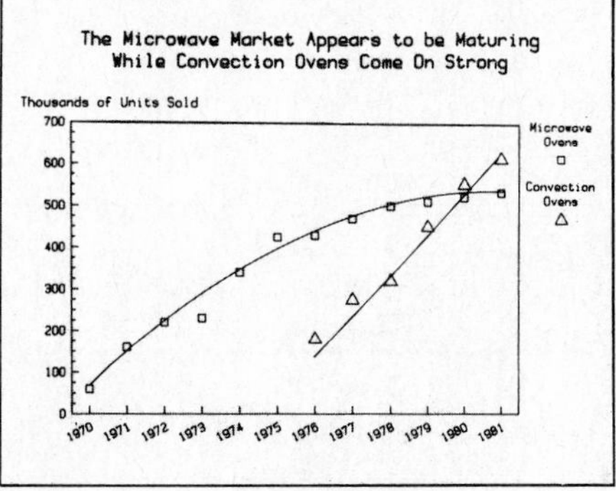

Scatter

Graphics by Graphwriter software, courtesy of Graphic Communications, Inc.

Figure 7-5 Examples of computer-generated presentation graphics printed with a plotter

Segmented Bars

Titles

Print exactly as desired; observe character count maximum.

Field	Entry	Max
Heading 1 ▸	SMALL COMPUTER SYSTEMS EXPECTED	48
Heading 2 ▸	TO REPRESENT THE LARGEST SEGMENT	48
Heading 3 ▸	OF THE COMPUTER MARKET BY 1985	48
Note 1 ▸		48
Note 2 ▸		48
Note 3 ▸		48
X axis ▸		48
Y axis ▸	Billions of Dollars	48

Scales

y axis minimum ▸	0
y axis maximum ▸	70
y label interval ▸	10
y tic interval ▸	5
Number of bars (1–20) ▸	3
Number of segments per bar (1–8) ▸	3

Bar legend

Bar	Line 1 (20)	Line 2 (20)	Color	Pattern
1	MAINFRAME	COMPUTERS	BLACK	SOL
2	MINI COMPUTERS		BLA	2
3	WORD PROCESSORS +	MICROCOMPUTERS	RED	3
4				
5				
6				
7				
8				

Color codes

1 Black	6 Brown
2 Blue	7 Violet
3 Green	8 Turquoise
4 Red	9 Gold
5 Orange	10 Lime green

Pattern codes

1, 2, 3, 4, 5, 6, 7, 8

Data

Use additional forms for bars 13–20.

Bar	Bar label (20)	Segment values 1	2	3	4	5	6	7	8
1	1975	10.6	1.2	.9					
2	1980	17.2	4.9	6.6					
3	1985	22.8	13.3	27.3					
4									
5									
6									
7									
8									
9									
10									
11									
12									

Comments

Comment 1

Comment 2

Comment 3

Location

©

Courtesy of Graphic Communications, Inc.

Figure 7-6 Sample input form for a segmented bar chart

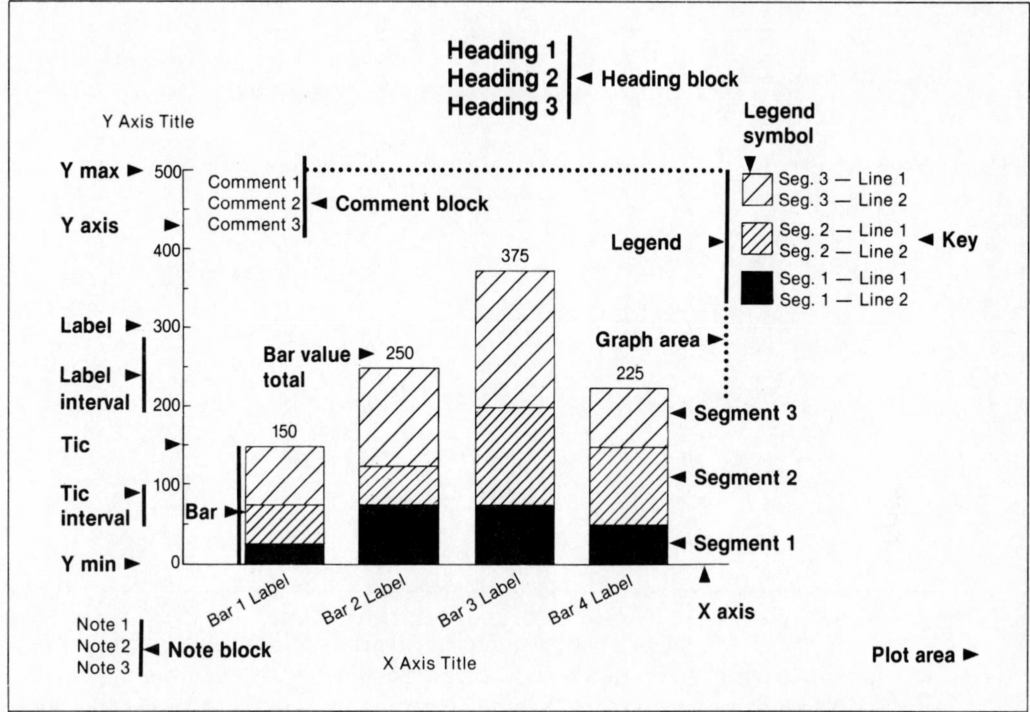

Courtesy of Graphic Communications, Inc.

Figure 7-7 Segmented bar chart elements

Figure 7-8 Production of segmented bar chart from Figure 7-5

Selected Sample Display Prompts	*Selected Sample Data Entry from Standard Input Form in Figure 7-6*
Enter new heading 1	SMALL COMPUTER SYSTEMS EXPECTED
Enter Axis Scales and Titles	
Enter new y axis title	Billions of Dollars
Enter new y axis minimum	0
Enter new y axis maximum	70
Enter y axis labeled interval	10
Enter y axis tic interval	5
Enter new number of bars	3
Enter new number of segments	3
Enter Legend for Segment 1	
Enter new line 1	MAINFRAME
Enter new line 2	COMPUTERS
Segment 1 color is . . . red	
Enter new segment 1 color	BLACK

Figure 7-8 (continued)

Selected Sample Display Prompts	*Selected Sample Data Entry from Standard Input Form in Figure 7-6*
Segment 1 fill is. . . solid fill	
Enter new segment 1 fill	SOLID
Enter Bar Labels	
Enter new bar 1 label	1975
Enter new bar 2 label	1980
Enter new bar 3 label	1985
Enter segment 1 values (MAINFRAME COMPUTERS)	

Bar No.	*Label*	*New Value*
1	1975	10.6
2	1980	17.2
3	1985	22.8

When all format data entry is complete, a menu option enables him to *preview* the chart on the display. *Previewing* is a common and necessary feature with graphics. It allows a user to examine and revise things like color, fill pattern, and other selections. When satisfied with the result, a printer or plotter option is selected to get a hard copy of the color graph.

Options

From a graphic artist, Mr. Williams learned some basic rules of chart creation as outlined in Figure 7-10. Following the guidelines, he kept graphics simple and uncluttered.

Graphic options include superimposing one graph on another. This is an *overlay* and is useful to those who want a company insignia or logo in the background of all graphics. Many packages provide for placing four or more graphics on a single page.

A few packages like Diagram-Master do organizational and programmer flowcharts. Charts are assembled from shapes, like squares and rectangles, stored in a *shape-table* file. Needed shapes can be called up and manipulated by enlargement, reduction, rotation, and the like. For users who want to draw their own shapes, an assortment of packages are available.

Packages like Calligraphy and Character Generator enable a user to design new characters. An empty dot-matrix character grid is presented in enlarged form on the screen. A user can create any character or other image desired.

Still other packages offer typeset letters and sign-making capabilities. Pages of text produced in typeset are ready for presentations, transparency reproduction, or perhaps direct mail promotions. They can enlarge or reduce individual characters. Several large letters could be combined for sign creation.

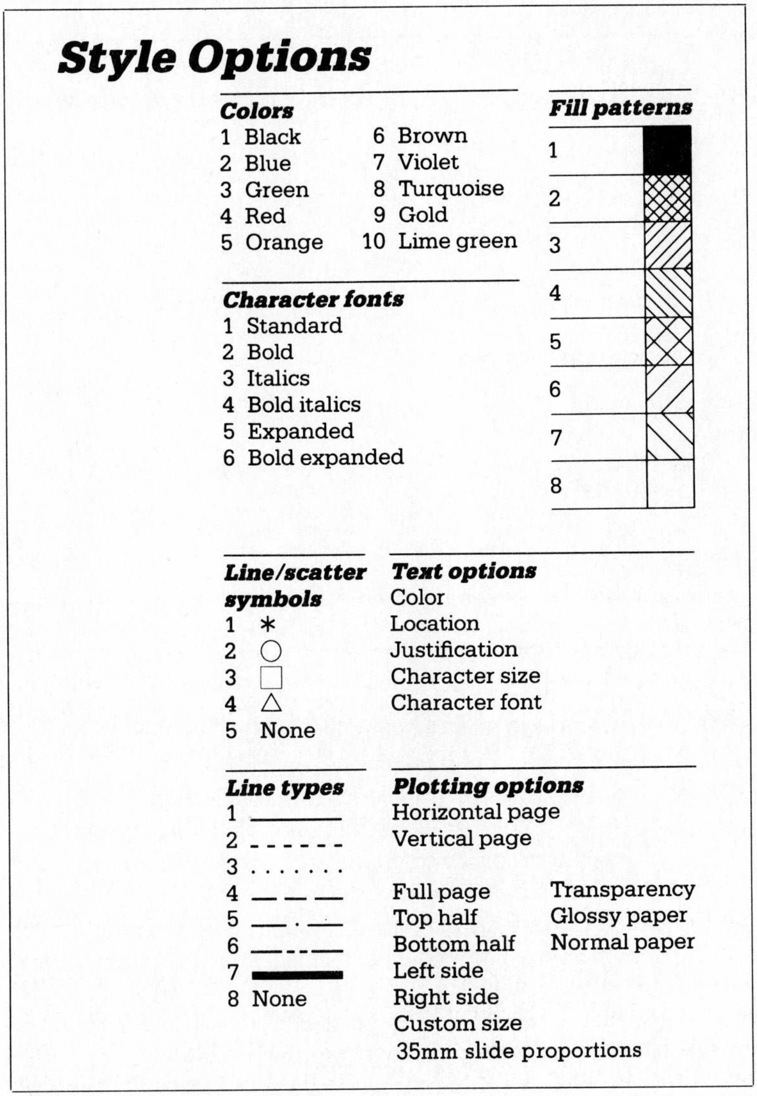

Style Options

Colors

1 Black
2 Blue
3 Green
4 Red
5 Orange
6 Brown
7 Violet
8 Turquoise
9 Gold
10 Lime green

Fill patterns

1
2
3
4
5
6
7
8

Character fonts

1 Standard
2 Bold
3 Italics
4 Bold italics
5 Expanded
6 Bold expanded

Line/scatter symbols

1 *
2 ○
3 □
4 △
5 None

Text options

Color
Location
Justification
Character size
Character font

Line types

1 ———
2 - - - - - -
3 . . . .
4 — — —
5 —— . ——
6 —— - - ——
7 ▬▬▬
8 None

Plotting options

Horizontal page
Vertical page

Full page
Top half
Bottom half
Left side
Right side
Custom size
35mm slide proportions

Transparency
Glossy paper
Normal paper

Courtesy of Graphic Communications, Inc.

Figure 7-9 Style options

COLOR GRAPHIC DISPLAY

Mr. Williams used a color graphics display that his company bought to do in-house graphics. Using presentation graphics software, charts were developed and previewed in color on the screen. Final versions of charts were printed by the plotter on paper or overhead transparencies. Occasionally the display also functioned as a slide-show projection device.

Figure 7-10 Selected presentation graphics guidelines

Keep graphs uncluttered.
Keep them brief.
Make only one point with one graphic.

Pie Charts
Use to emphasize the relationship of the parts to the whole.
Consider pulled-out slices for special emphasis.

Bar Charts
Use for data arranged in segments (by month, year, and so on).
Use vertical or horizontal bars.
Show complex facts clearly by using multiple or segmented bars.

Line Graphs
Use to display trends or continuous data.
Select baseline and scale for maximum effectiveness.

Word Charts
Use key words only.
Use bullets and colors to highlight key points.
Break up information to make a series of graphs (a progressive or "build" series). Use color to show the new line added to each chart.

When evaluating color displays, Mr. Williams found *resolution* was important. *Resolution* refers to the number of distinguishable points or dots on the display: the higher the resolution, the more precise the final graphic image.

One computer divides the screen for graphics use into 240 lines of 960 columns each. This gives the screen 230,400 points, or *pixels. Pixel* is the graphic industry term for one *pic*ture *el*ment. Through appropriate software, each can be turned on or off, as illustrated in Figure 7-11. Each can also be assigned a color.

Each dot is associated with a reserved part of random access memory called the *bit-mapped* or *dot-mapped* memory. The amount of memory reserved restricts display resolution.

Nominal screen graphics resolution breakpoints, given in terms of the number of individual horizontal and vertical picture elements, appear as follows:

Color Display Resolution	*PIXELS*		*Sample Price*
	Horizontal by Vertical		
High	1,280	1,024	$1,700–4,000
Medium	640	480	$600
Low	320	240	$450

After resolution, another major consideration is the color range a display provides. Some offer 16 colors with high resolution. Generally these are the expensive, so-

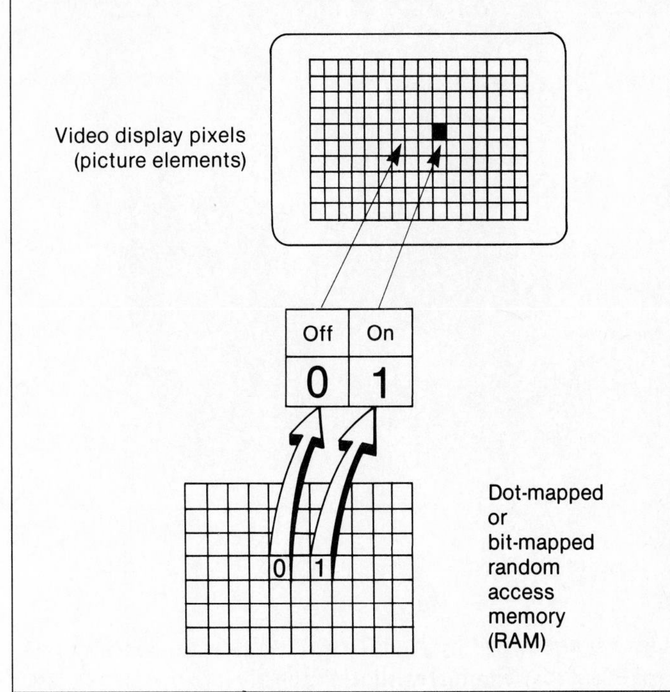

Figure 7-11 A memory-mapped video display

called *RGB monitors. RGB* stands for red, green, blue and identifies a refined color separation and signaling technology.

Lower-resolution and less-expensive displays use a combined or *composite* color signaling scheme. Ordinary televisions use a composite video color signal. Often it is inadequate to display 80 columns of standard text characters. Characters appear smeared. To compensate, text is reduced to 40 columns per line. This makes color displays inadequate for many word processing applications.

Slide Shows

SGD Inc.'s graphics package included a slide show capability. This enabled using the color display as an ordinary 35-mm slide projector. Graphics are prepared in advance and sorted into the desired showing order. During a presentation, pressing a function key retrieves another pseudo-slide on demand.

Such a slide-show is adequate for a small audience. Larger audiences need images projected on a screen larger than an ordinary color video display. Some companies make color projection devices that operate directly off a small computer, such as the one shown in Figure 7-12.

This technique automatically by-passes the need to create 35-mm slides from computer-generated graphics. Without this capability, companies used to send digitized graphics to service bureaus for 35-mm slide production. Graphics were sent using ordinary

Electrohome Projection System, courtesy of Emes Systems

Figure 7-12 Projecting presentation graphics to a large screen

data communications. Slides were returned by mail. Now both time and expenses are saved with an in-house capability that eliminates slides altogether.

PLOTTERS

Mr. Williams purchased an inexpensive (under $2,000) flatbed plotter like the one shown in Figure 7-4. It has two pens attached to arms that move horizontally to draw a graph. Drawing stops for manual color pen changes. Up to ten colors are available. Other plotters are available with more pens. Some require fewer pen changes, and some require no manual intervention for color changes.

The plotter that Mr. Williams uses makes all his presentation graphics and overhead transparencies. He had to learn only how to place paper or transparencies and to change color pens.

The flatbed plotter restricts the size of graphs to the size of the flatbed. But charts could be done in sections and manually attached together for larger plots. Alternately, plotters in many sizes are available to accommodate frequent use of large plots.

Other choices are drum and electrostatic plotters. With drum plotters, such as the one shown in Figure 7-13, paper moves over a rotating cylinder to achieve one direction of movement. The writing instrument moves in the opposite direction. An advantage of drum plotters is that very long designs can be produced by a relatively compact unit. The drawback is that, while many drum widths are available, very wide drawings usually cannot be produced, except in sections.

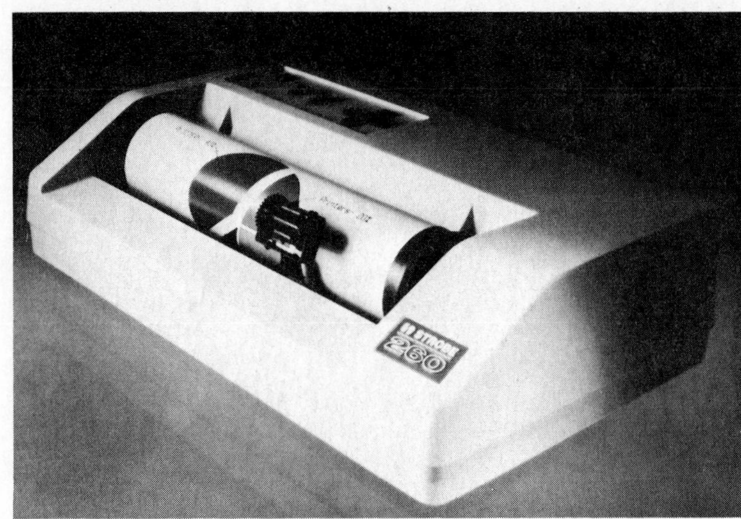

Courtesy of Strobe, Inc.

Figure 7-13 A drum plotter

Electrostatic plotters work like drum plotters. Paper movement provides one direction of drawing. Instead of a pen, a row of *styli* sit across the width of the paper. The styli leave electric charges on special paper to create images. The special paper or other media used to produce images represents a limitation of electrostatic plotters. Producing plots in only one color is another limitation.

An electrostatic plotter's main advantage is speed. It can double as a high-speed printer when equipped with a character generator.

GRAPHICS PRINTERS

For low-cost printed color graphics applications, an alternative to a plotter is a printer that also does plotting. Dot-matrix printers handle *dot-addressable* graphics. Some that do only fixed character printing would be inadequate for graphics.

Mr. Williams' personal dot-matrix printer produces only black-and-white graphs. Other printers, identified in Figure 7–14, offer various color graphic capabilities.

One dot-matrix printer offers a multicolored ribbon to produce hard copies of colored graphics. Some images require repeat print-head passes over the paper to produce the image. For a four-color ribbon, it could require four passes. This delivers slow copy but carbons, in one color, are possible.

Ink jet printers produce good-quality images that depend, in part, on the special paper and ink selected. The technique takes drops of ink and projects them onto the paper's surface. Because dot size can be controlled, an optimum combination of paper and ink can be reached to provide good area filling and good line definition. A signifi-

Figure 7-14 Sampler of color graphic printers

Printers	Time for 8½ × 11 Copy (Minutes)	Material Cost Per Copy	Paper	Example of Equipment Cost	Dots Per Square Inch
Dot-matrix multicolored ribbon	5	$ .15	Plain	$ 2,000	84 × 84
Ink jet	3	$ .20	Special	$ 800	85 × 90
Photographic	3	$6.00	Special	$ 8,000	140 × 150
Xerographic	0.33	$ .05	Plain	$25,000	100 × 100

cant advantage of ink jet copying over other technqiues is speed. Such a printer can simultaneously image all colors to minimize production time.

Photographic prints are copied from the display image to 8 × 10-inch Polaroid color print material. This printing produces superior quality on both paper and transparent film. A significant drawback, however, is the several dollars per copy price of the color print material. The price increases whenever several attempts are required to obtain the correct exposure settings.

Xerographic images are the lowest cost-per-copy price of all at about 5 cents each. Image quality is less satisfactory than with photographic techniques. But the major disadvantages are price (about $25,000), and large equipment size, which dictates a permanent location for the copier.

INPUT DEVICES

Mr. Williams uses an ordinary keyboard to tell the graphics application what kind of an image he wants. More exotic ways to tell an application how to create an image include digitizers and light pens, among other devices.

Digitizers

Digitizer boards, like the one in Figure 7–15, typically resemble a drafting board with a movable cursor. The moveable cursor can be a pen-like device among other options. The board contains an embedded matrix of wires that, in effect, creates pixels similar to those in display devices.

The so-called *graphic tablet* system is used to enter drawings into computer graphic systems. Free-hand drawings are possible, or prepared drawings can be taped to the surface of the digitizing board. Tracing the cursor over the image electronically sends *x-y* coordinate signals to the computer. Each coordinate crossed causes a dot to appear on the display.

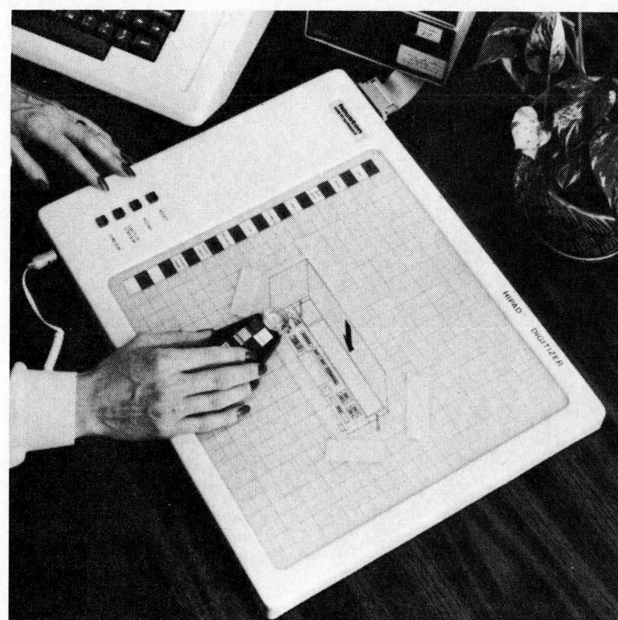

Figure 7-15 Using a digitizer graphics tablet

Courtesy of Houston Instruments, Division of Bausch & Lomb

An architect, office planner, engineer, or anyone who draws or designs three-dimensional plans, models, or simulations finds digitizers useful. Using a digitizer requires specialized application software. Software might cost $500 and the digitizer can cost $65–$20,000. Tablet sizes range from 6 × 8 inches to 48 × 60 inches with backlit translucence.

Light Pen

Light pens, such as the one shown in Figure 7–16, enable a user to touch a point on the screen and have the computer read the location of the point. They offer an alternative input to digitizers in applications for architects, engineers, and others. They have been used for years as input devices for engineers working at the screens of very expensive mainframe-oriented design systems. The systems are usually referred to as *computer-aided design* (CAD) applications.

Some graphic and other applications use the light pen as an alternative way to make menu selections. Simply pointing at a choice activates it.

Some pen-oriented graphics packages offer users the ability to create ordinary business charts and graphs from prestored forms. They often also allow users to do free-form *screen painting* and animation. The light pen is used as an artist's paint brush. Combining the results of all capabilities can result in imaginative graphic presentations.

The screen painting option employs symbols arranged along the bottom or side of the screen. For example, a circle could be drawn by pointing the light pen to the circle symbol. Painting color in the circle requires touching the paint symbol until the desired color appears. The circumference of the painted circle could be increased by touching

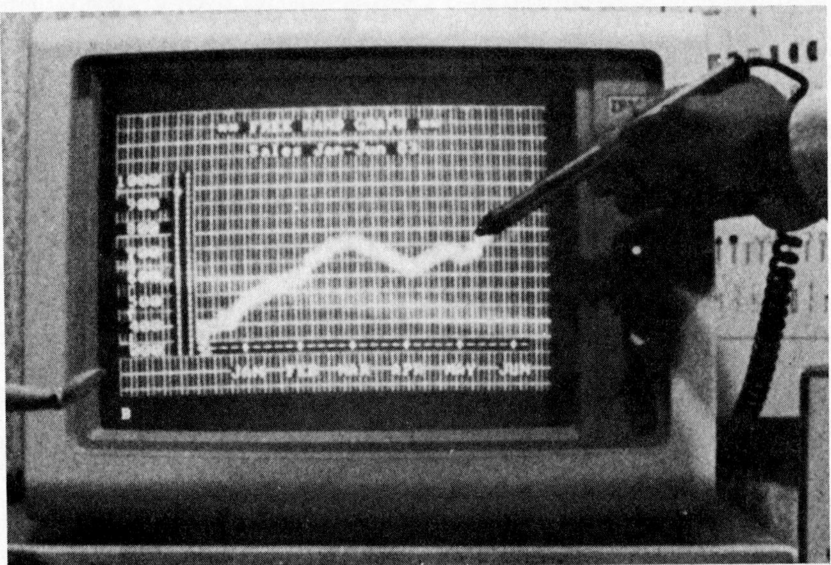

Courtesy of Duncan-Atwell

Figure 7-16 Using a light pen to do screen painting

the increase-scale symbol until the desired size is attained. To chain together a series of similar circles requires touching the chain symbol until satisfied. To use this type of application costs about $200 for the graphics software and $150 for the light pen.

EVALUATION

When he examined graphics software, Mr. Williams decided his main criterion would be ease of use. Many rejected packages required the talents of a professional graphic artist who also had computer experience.

But he found a larger problem was evaluating output devices. In graphic applications, the *soft copy* graphic on the display gets transferred or copied to other media, such as projection screen, plotter, or printer. The primary requirement for any display or *video copier* is image quality. Image quality is a measure different from image resolution.

From experience he determined the best way to judge image quality is by an "eye-ball" examination of the copy. Image quality is reflected in three major areas. First, line and edge definitions should be free of a stair-stepped appearance. Second, area filling should be solidly covered and free of streaks and voids. Shaded areas should be uniform. Third, color accuracy should be reproduced using all the color shades on the video monitor.

After image quality, speed is important. It is especially critical if the computer is unavailable for processing while printing is going on. Delays have cost implications and can lead to user frustration.

Guides like the two checklists in Figure 7-17 and 7-18 helped in the graphics evaluation process.

Figure 7-17 Graphics Checklist

Candidate Packages Names:
A: ______
B: ______
C: ______

Check "must have" items		Rating (Scale: 1 = poor to 10 = excellent) A	B	C
	General			
	Orientation:			
____	Analytic	____	____	____
____	Presentation	____	____	____
____	Automatic input links to relevant data files	____	____	____
____	Manual input	____	____	____
____	Programming knowledge required	____	____	____
____	Graphic artist knowledge required	____	____	____
____	Slide-show capability	____	____	____
	Drawing capability:			
____	Free-form	____	____	____
____	Prepared symbol guides	____	____	____
____	Prepared animation enhancement	____	____	____
____	Prepared audio enhancement	____	____	____
	Compatible hardware:			
	Displays:			
____	Monochrome	____	____	____
____	Color	____	____	____
____	Plotters	____	____	____
____	Printers	____	____	____
____	Large screen projectors	____	____	____
____	Digitizers	____	____	____
____	Light pens	____	____	____
	Hard-copy output capability:			
____	Paper	____	____	____
____	Overhead transparencies	____	____	____
____	Slides	____	____	____
	Formats			
____	Prepared formats	____	____	____
____	Customization possible	____	____	____
____	Input form guide provided	____	____	____
____	Store charts for reuse and updating	____	____	____
____	Preview on display for revision	____	____	____
	Bar charts:			
____	Maximum vertical per chart	____	____	____
____	Maximum horizontal per chart	____	____	____
____	Segmented	____	____	____
____	Clustered	____	____	____
	Pie charts:			
____	Maximum slices	____	____	____

Figure 7-17 (continued)

Check "must have" items	Rating (Scale: 1 = poor to 10 = excellent) A	B	C
Formats			
___ Maximum "pull-outs" per pie	___	___	___
___ Maximum per chart	___	___	___
Line charts:			
___ Maximum lines per chart	___	___	___
___ Area fills between lines	___	___	___
Word charts:			
___ Number of character sets	___	___	___
___ Number of sizes	___	___	___
___Scatter plots	___	___	___
___Gantt chart	___	___	___
___Organization chart	___	___	___
___Tables	___	___	___
___Combination charts	___	___	___
___Maximum charts per page	___	___	___
___Overlays	___	___	___
___Three-dimensional charts	___	___	___
Subtotal	___	___	___
Divide by number of items rated for average rating	___	___	___

Transfer average rating to Selection Summary: Software, Figure 5-3.

Figure 7-18 Hardware: Components Checklist

Items to Check — Rating (Scale: 1 = poor to 10 = excellent) A B C

Graphic Output Devices
(Color displays, plotters, printers)

Product name A: ______________ B: ______________ C: ______________

Items to Check	A	B	C
Ease of use	___	___	___
Image quality	___	___	___
Line and edge definition	___	___	___
Area filling	___	___	___
Color accuracy	___	___	___
Speed	___	___	___
Maximum size output	___	___	___
Maximum number of colors	___	___	___

Figure 7-18 (continued)

Items to Check	*Rating (Scale: 1 = poor to 10 = excellent)* A	B	C
Graphic Output Devices (Color displays, plotters, printers)			
Noise level	______	______	______
Hard copy:			
Paper:			
Plain	______	______	______
Special	______	______	______
Overhead transparencies	______	______	______
Slides	______	______	______
Cost per copy	______	______	______
Interfaces with graphics software	______	______	______
Additional programming required	______	______	______
Subtotal	______	______	______
Divide by number of items rated for average rating	______	______	______

Transfer Average Rating to Selection Summary: Hardware, Figure 5–2.

SELF TEST

1. Identify the difference in purposes between analytic and presentation graphics.
2. What advantage do multifunction packages have over stand-alone packages for analytic graphic use?
3. Using a segmented bar example, explain what executing a format involves when using a standard input form.
4. What is previewing?
5. Describe the following:
   - Overlay
   - Shape table
   - Transparency
   - Resolution
   - Pixel
   - Bit-mapped memory
   - RGB monitor
   - Composite monitor
   - Dot-addressable graphics
6. Identify three types of plotters, and explain some limitations of each.
7. What printer options are available for graphic imaging?
8. Identify two exotic graphic input devices and the potential uses for each.
9. How is a graphic's image quality determined?

EXERCISES

1. *Modify a Graph.* Modify the sample input form for a segmented bar chart in Figure 7–6. Assume:
   - A fourth bar is added for 1990 with the amounts 25.4, 15.7, and 35.2
   - Add a comment line to read "Estimated Figures"
   - Change the *y*-axis to "Billions of $"

   Use the element chart in Figure 7–7 as a guide.
2. *Create a Graph.* Create your own segmented bar chart using pencil and paper. Assume it will be implemented with Mr. Williams' graphics package. Assume that you will use the segmented bar chart input form in Figure 7–6 with the element chart in Figure 7–7 as a guide. Use the style options list in Figure 7–9 to customize your graphic.
3. *Lark Enterprises Case.* Lark Enterprises wants to develop an in-house graphics capability. They needed both appropriate hardware and software.
   a. Evaluate two presentation graphics packages using the Checklist in Figure 7–17 to hands-on test the package. Justify your selection of the best package.
   b. Evaluate two color graphic displays using the checklist in Figure 7–18. Try to do word processing on each, in addition to running the graphics package selected in section a. Justify your selection of the best display.
   c. Evaluate flatbed plotters under $2,000. If possible, use the graphics package selected in section a to hands-on test the output. Use the checklist in Figure 7–18. Justify your selection of the best plotter.

RESOURCES AND REFERENCES

Books

HOUSE, WILLIAM C., ed., *Interactive Computer Graphics Systems,* Petrocelli, 1982.

JARETT, IRWIN M., *Computer Graphics and Reporting Financial Data,* Wiley, 1983.

Periodicals and Directories

Anderson Report

Computer Graphics News

Computer Graphics World

IEEE Computer Graphics and Applications

KLEIN, S., *Directory of Computer Graphic Suppliers,* Technology and Business Communications.

KLEIN, S., *Newsletter on Computer Graphics,* Technology and Business Communications.

Organizations

SIGGraph (Special Interest Group on Graphics), Association for Computing Machinery.

National Computer Graphics Association.

World Computer Graphics Association.

8

WORD PROCESSING

Business professionals seldom buy small computers for word processing alone. But once they have a computer, this function becomes important. Word processing is helpful to store thoughts for the next major report, to embellish spreadsheets, and to prepare correspondence for electronic mail, among a host of other tasks.

This chapter begins with an examination of the difference between word processing and word processors. Then it considers each phase in a word processed document's life cycle. It involves document creation, editing, formatting, and printing.

Word processing features that help to create personalized form letters, and to do fancy formatting, are also discussed. Spelling and style checkers are reviewed before the chapter concludes with word processing evaluation guidelines.

WORD PROCESSING AND WORD PROCESSORS

Word processing application software needs to be distinguished from a *word processor.* To Mr. Williams, word processing is another application, like his electronic spreadsheet. It is used to make his general purpose small computer perform a specific user task. In the case of word processing, the task consists of capturing keystrokes and converting them to printed documents more efficiently than with manual methods. Some of the many word processing applications available include WordStar, Microsoft Word, Volkswriter Deluxe, VisiWord, EasyWriter, Perfect Writer, and many others. Most cost under $500.

At any point Mr. Williams can replace the word processing application with another as different as a graphics application. His computer passively accepts its new role in processing graphics.

By contrast, a *word processor* is a special purpose computer designed to do only word processing tasks. It has been around for over a decade performing typing and editing tasks. Users of these dedicated machines, costing from $6,000 to $25,000, are mostly word processor specialists, typists, and secretaries who produce high volumes of documents.

General purpose small business computers, equipped with word processing software, are eroding the traditional word processor market. But new word processing users with more varied professional needs are entering the market. They are the managers, supervisors, and general business professionals who require more than word processing to support their varied work patterns. The nature of their work requires a single multifunction machine instead of perhaps three separate machines like a word processor, a terminal for data communications, and a computer for calculation and other support tasks.

Some dedicated or stand-alone word processors have been retrofitted with application packages to give them multifunction usefulness.

WORD PROCESSING CHARACTERISTICS

Word processing, as the term implies, concerns the automated processing or manipulation of words. Words of a typed document often need to be inserted, deleted, shifted elsewhere, and the like. This contrasts with data processing, which concerns the computation of numbers. Numbers are multiplied, divided, and so on. Computation is not the primary focus of word processing, although some packages provide this capability.

Like an electronic spreadsheet, a word processing application requires as much up-front work as if the job were done manually. Someone has to create the words to be processed. Whether those words form a letter, contract, or manuscript, typing it into the computer is not much different from typing the same document on a typewriter.

It may require, in fact, learning a new command language. Even if the application is part of a multifunction package with common commands throughout, learning word processing functions and vocabulary is preliminary to use.

Like an electronic spreadsheet application, the payoff comes when document changes are needed. The ability to enter only changes and to print a fresh original document after typing a few keystrokes immesurably reflects on productivity. The time saved from not retyping tedious drafts can be spent on other tasks.

Because of the ease of producing fresh drafts, changes to upgrade any document can be made more freely. Proofreading is reduced to just the changes. This encourages revision to produce even better crafted documents.

Final printing is left to the computer. The document is printed with justified right and left margins, if desired, and without typing errors. The improved visual quality of printed work enhances the professional image of an individual or a company.

Some word processing tasks still remain more appropriate on a typewriter. For example, putting an occasional address on an envelope or filling in random forms are not worth the effort to do on computers with detached printers.

Everything else from a conventional business letter to a full book length manuscript can be done faster and cheaper with a word processing application. It is widely published, for example, that it costs approximately $7 to produce a single spaced, one page letter using a typewriter. The cost includes labor, materials, postage, and overhead. With word processing, however, letter writing costs are estimated to be cut in half.

As cost figures go down, productivity figures go up. At least two vendors claim that word processing increases typing productivity by 50 percent in the secretarial environment. For complex documents, with lengthy, heavily edited text, the productivity increase is from 400 to 500 percent.

Many studies have been done to justify the value of word processing in the traditional secretarial environment. But what about the business professional's own use of word processing? At least one of these studies finds professionals, managers, and supervisors using word processing almost as much as secretaries from 1985 on. This is because professional workstations, equipped with word processing software, will be used for other convenient functions, such as sending electronic mail. It often is easier to type a memo to send electronically than to dictate it to a secretary, wait to examine a final draft, then have the memo distributed.

Also, studies show secretaries are becoming scarce as they move into more professional ranks. This leaves business professionals doing more of their own clerical tasks. With word processing software, the tasks become more manageable.

PACKAGE FUNCTIONS

Standard word processing applications divide into five functions related to a document's life cycle. They are:

Function	*User Action*
1. Create a document	Type text on keyboard
2. Edit a document	Make corrections
3. Format a document	Insert print instructions
4. Print a document	Start printing
5. Document/file handling utilities	Save and copy documents

Many word processing packages are sold with additional functions that enhance their value to professional users. The abilities to automatically check document spelling and syntax for example, is often more effective than when done manually. Other auxiliary software automates mailing lists and personalizes form letters. Such functions help propel office routine into the automated office that is the driving force behind modern computer technology.

DOCUMENT CREATION

Mr. Williams and most staff members at SGD Inc. use word processing software. They create and update documents such as catalogs, contracts, product specifications, order sheets, mailings to prospective customers, and ordinary business correspondence.

When Mr. Williams wants to produce a memo or any typed document, he powers up the word processing software, performs some set-up procedures, then begins to type. During document creation his screen looks like the one in Figure 8–1. He types the text as if using an ordinary typewriter. Text is automatically right justified as he types.

Mr. Williams' typing technique falls into the hunt-and-peck category. Nonetheless, he finds he can produce final draft copy without assistance and with little effort using the computer. He would never have attempted the same thing without the computer.

Previously memos would wait until he could coordinate time to dictate to his secretary. By that time, ideas became stale and memos lost some of their spontaneity and impact. Now he just creates memos whenever convenient and lets his secretary retrieve them to edit, print, and distribute final copy.

When creating text, Mr. Williams never hits a carriage return until the end of a paragraph. The computer automatically performs a *word wrap* at the end of each line. The *word wrap* function moves any word that crosses the right-hand margin to the next line and adjusts all subsequent text. This feature speeds composition because there is no need to watch, or to listen for a bell, to manually control end-of-line word placement.

Document creation is further simplified by built-in *scrolling* and *cursor control* functions. They are activated by keys shown in Figure 8–2. *Scrolling* moves text up and down so that desired portions appear in the display. *Cursor control* keys allow free movement all around the current display.

EDITING

Correcting or editing a document is where word processing software earns its reputation as a productivity enhancer. Whenever Mr. Williams thinks of a better way to phrase something, he simply types over the old text. Sometimes he inserts words, phrases, or paragraphs.

To do inserts, he presses the insert key, which functions as an on-off toggle switch. Once toggled on, he types as long as he pleases. When done inserting, he hits the insert key to toggle it off. He deletes as easily.

Sometimes it becomes necessary to move a paragraph from one place to another. This requires marking the beginning and end of text to be moved. Marking is done with a *function key.*

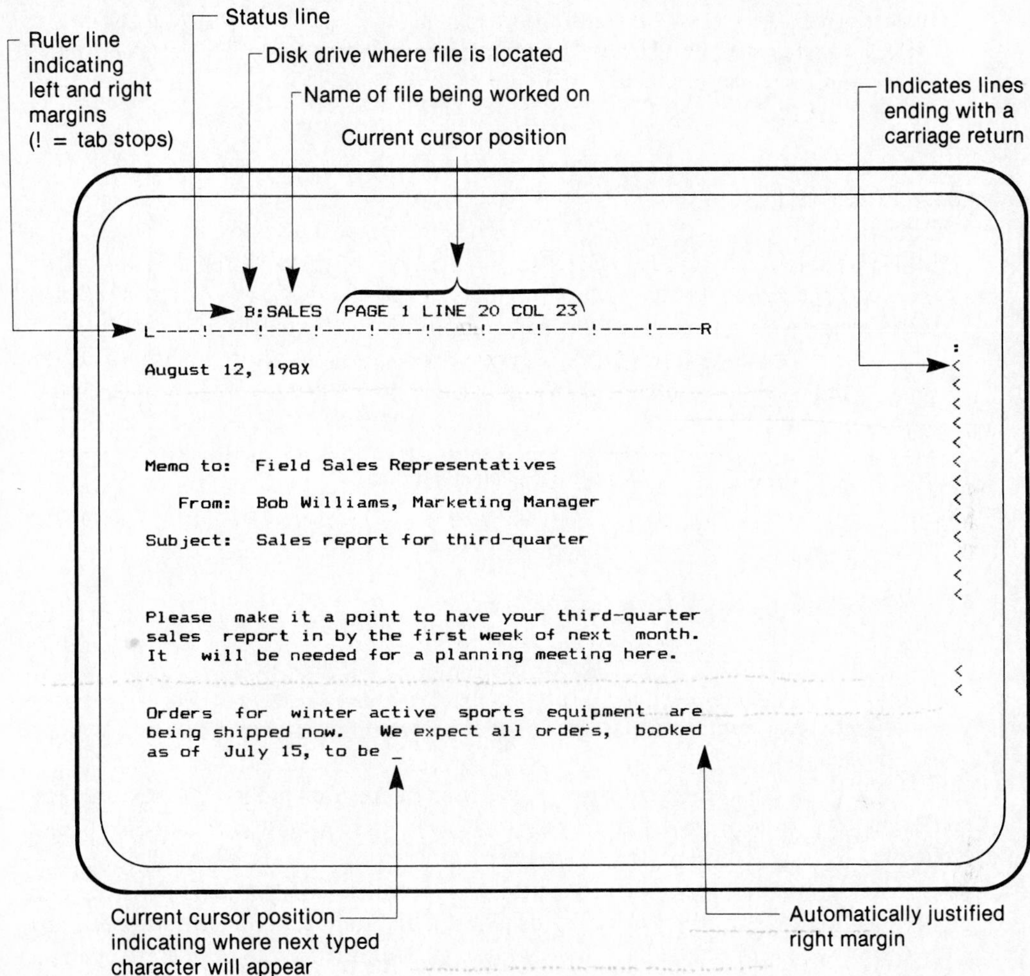

Figure 8-1 Creating a document

As illustrated in Figure 8-3, *function keys* are a separate part of the keyboard. Often they are called *soft keys*. Their function varies according to the software used. Each application software package can program what function keys will do.

Once a block of text is marked, Mr. Williams moves the cursor to the new insert location. By typing three keys in succession, CTRL K and V, the block move occurs instantly on the screen.

Instead of moving the block of text, it could as easily be deleted or duplicated elsewhere, or it could be copied to a separate disk file.

Another editing task that Mr. Williams occasionally uses is called a *find and replace operation*. For example, assume "third-quarter" should be replaced by "fourth-quarter" in the memo that appears in Figure 8-1. It is done by invoking an appropriate function key, then entering the word to be found and the word to replace it with.

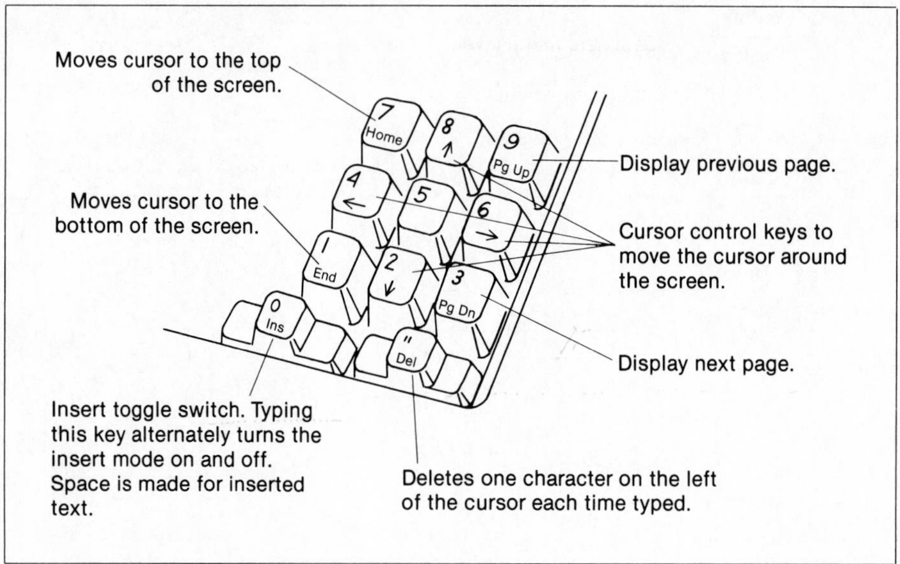

Figure 8-2 Keys that activate cursor control and other functions

If "third-quarter" is replaced by "fourth-quarter" throughout a document, it is referred to as a *global* change. Alternately, it is possible to stop at every occurrence to make whatever individual change is desired before continuing to the next occurrence and so on.

The find and replace feature is well used by the legal industry. A standard last will and testament for John Doe, for example, can be changed to one for Harry Smith effortlessly.

Many word processing applications that perform *find* or *search* operations also provide *wild card* searches. Such a search allows a user to find words without specifying the entire word. For example, if Ms. Malone at SGD Inc. wants to revise a contract and is unsure whether Product-ABC or Product-XYZ is included in it, she could type "Product-*" to search for the *ambiguously* named product. The asterisk signifies the ambiguous, or *wild card* characters. In this case, the *find* operation will stop at every place in the document that has a match on "Product-," regardless of what characters are after the hyphen.

One way writers use the find and replace function is as a kind of shorthand. For example, one writer doing a report on prescription drugs enters only "t" every time tetracycline is used. When the report is done, he finds all occurrences of "t" and replaces them with "tetracycline." The author saves a lot of typing time. This shorthand technique also reduces the possibility of typing errors.

FORMATTING

Formatting concerns preparing a document's appearance for the printed page. It requires setting up the format on the display before actual printing begins.

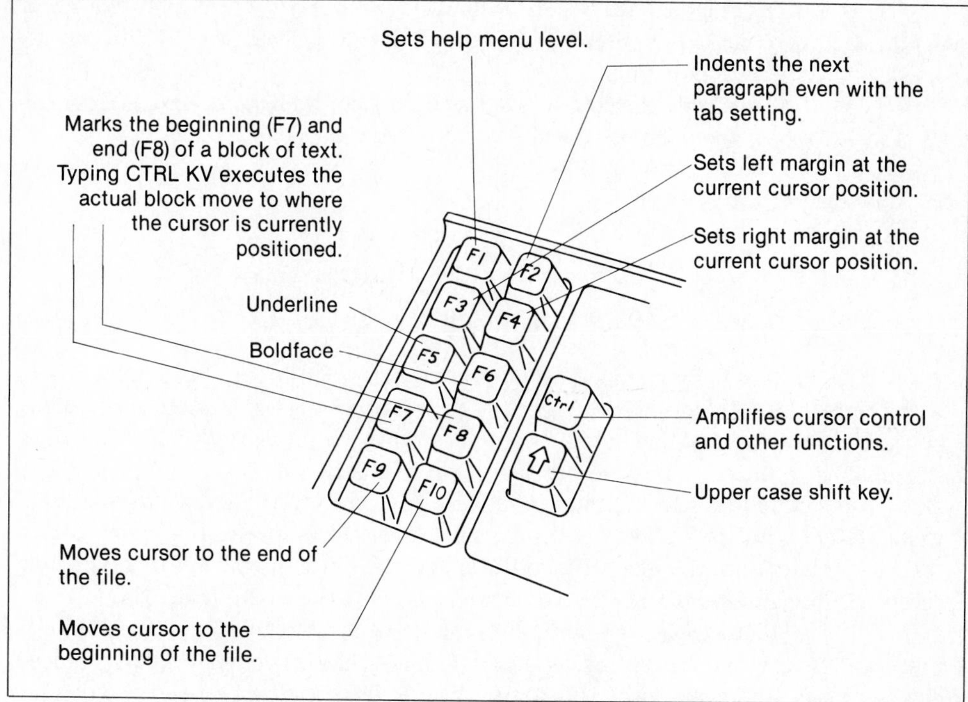

Figure 8-3 Function and other key actions

Mr. Williams sets margins by placing the cursor in an appropriate column under the ruler line. Typing the F4 function key while the cursor is under column 50 sets the right margin to 50. He leaves the left margin alone to have a 50 character line.

Dot Commands

To get the correct left margin on the printed page, Mr. Williams types a special dot command into the text. Dot commands begin with a dot and can be inserted anywhere in a document. They control margin width, line spacing, pagination and other format characteristics.

To set the left margin Mr. Williams uses the dot command .PO14 to get a *p*age *o*ffset. Fourteen offset spaces are added to the left margin on the screen when printing the document. Some experimentation is needed to find the number of offset spaces to correctly center a 50 character line on the printed page. Once found it is noted for future use.

Alternately, Mr. Williams could have set a right margin using the F3 function key. This option also requires experimentation to center text on the printed page. The application provides alternate ways to perform many formatting options.

Mr. Williams frequently uses two other dot commands. One is .MT15 to get a *m*argin on the *t*op of the page 18 lines deep. The margin header is set at a standard default value of three lines. That is not enough for so short a memo.

Another dot command is .OP to *o*mit *p*age numbers. The application has a built-in feature to put page numbers at the bottom of each printed page. A short memo does not need page numbering.

Mr. Williams types dot commands after he finishes typing a document. He places them at the top of the document, which looks somewhat like the following:

.OP
.MT15
.PO14
∧ BAugust 12, 198X

The ∧ B is another embedded or inserted non-printing format command. The ∧ indicates the CTRL key. The ∧ B specifies that all following text is printed in boldface or extra dark type. Boldface typing continues during printing until another ∧ B is encountered in the text. That occurs at the end of the memo.

Inserting these dot commands to format each document is tedious and error prone. Other word processing applications overcome these disadvantages by storing formats for later reuse as needed. Still other applications offer prepared formats or style sheets for paragraphs, memos, letters, articles, or anything else one desires.

Mr. Williams follows a common practice of using regular print intensity for drafts and boldface for final printing. Users with dot-matrix printers regularly achieve close to formed character printer quality with boldface print options.

Most correspondence sent outside the company gets printed on a formed character printer. This printer can do proportional spacing. For example, an upper case "M" takes up more space than a lower case "i." A group of dot commands are available to manipulate the optional features provided on formed character printers. At SGD Inc., Ms. Malone is the resident expert on fancy formatting and printing.

Special Formats

When doing multipage documents, Ms. Malone prints a title and page number at the top of each page. To achieve an automatic page heading, she types a dot command line into the document as shown in Figure 8–4. It produces the result also illustrated in Figure 8–4.

A page footing is handled in much the same way. If desired, Ms. Malone could print in what publishers call *book style.* In book style, headings or footings alternate flush right and flush left depending on whether the page is odd or even numbered.

Ms. Malone likes another feature called an *intelligent page break.* It prevents a single line, sometimes called a *widow* or *orphan,* from being left all by itself on a separate page.

Other formatting features Ms. Malone uses include printing only one page of a longer document and mixing several formats in one document. Other features, some of which are never used and others which are used occasionally, are also available.

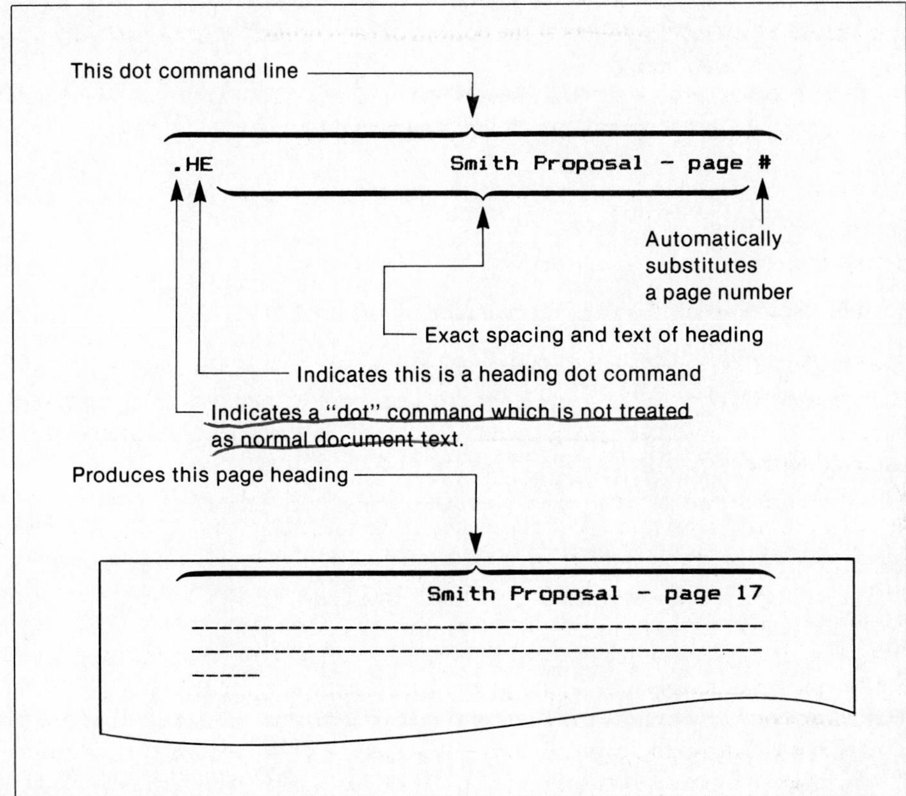

Figure 8-4 A command line used to generate an automatic heading

PRINT A DOCUMENT

To get a printed copy, Mr. Williams first saves the document complete with embedded dot commands. Then he types P for print. The application asks for the name of the file. He types SALES, the name used to save the document file. Within minutes his memo is printed.

The printed memo looks very professional with its justified right margin as shown in Figure 8-5. Right margin justification is a built-in standard format option that Mr. Williams likes and leaves turned on.

UTILITIES

Saving a document is part of the application's file handling utilities. Utilities are accessed in Mr. Williams' application through an unfortunately named No-File Menu as shown in Figure 8-6.

```
August 12, 198X


Memo to:  Field Sales Representatives

   From:  Bob Williams, Marketing Manager

Subject:  Sales report for third-quarter


Please  make it a point to have your third-quarter
sales  report in by the first week of next  month.
It   will be needed for a planning meeting here.

Orders  for  winter active  sports  equipment  are
being shipped now.   We expect all orders,  booked
as  of   July  15,  to be shipped by  the  end  of
August.

The  new  spring catalog is being  mailed  to  all
customers.   It  is  attached for your  reference.
You can book orders immediately from this catalog.

Best regards,


Bob Williams
```

Figure 8-5 A word processed document with a justified right margin

The menu is called No-File because no document file is active when it is displayed. It is the first menu used to open a new document file. It is also the last menu to appear after a file is saved.

As apparent from Figure 8-6, document files can be copied, renamed, deleted, and printed. Appropriate prompts display to guide Mr. Williams through these functions.

When he powers up the word processing application, he types the L command to change the logged disk drive from A to B. Drive A contains the word processing program while drive B contains his own created files. Making B the logged or default drive simplifies file handling tasks.

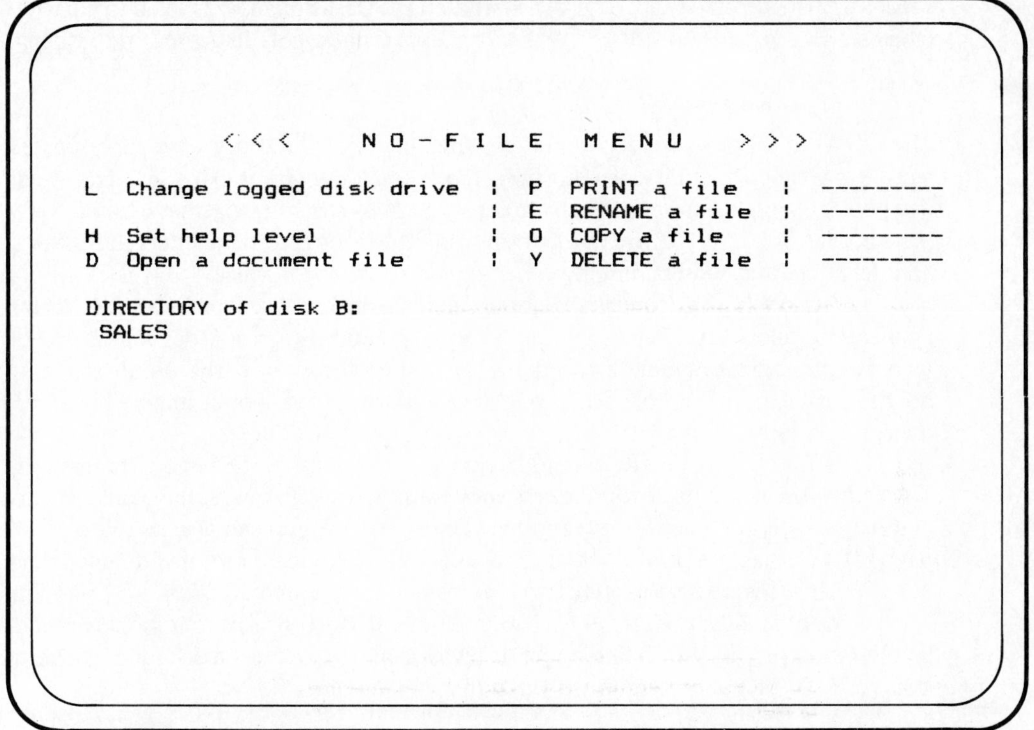

Figure 8-6 A portion of a utility menu

The menu lists the directory of disk B. It shows SALES is stored there. Another menu command invoked on power-up is the H command to set help level. Help levels from zero to three provide varying degrees of menu displays. Zero indicates none and three displays all menus. Usually Mr. Williams selects level two which gives the status and ruler line display evident in Figure 8-1. It also provides full displays of support menus for things like formatting, block moves, and other options.

Mr. Williams' application contains five sub-menus filled with word processing jargon that overwhelmed him as a novice. Once the application became familiar, he found the menu detail helpful. All sub-menus are accessed with a control key plus another key combination. A third key must to be typed to invoke a specific menu option.

OTHER CAPABILITIES

Word processing software that offers more than basic features provides capabilities like automatically creating a second or back up copy when a file is saved. While some packages retain one backup copy others save a separate backup copy each time a file is resaved. This is often referred to as *one* versus *multiple generation backups.*

Still other applications backup files without user intervention at timed intervals. This provides insurance against a system crash. Occasionally this can be a nuisance when saving long files on floppy disks. It causes a noticeable interruption in typing.

Document Assembly

Assembling documents from prestored material is another more sophisticated word processing capability. An attorney, for example, might prepare wills and deeds or a politician might answer letters from constituents by stringing together selected *boiler plate* paragraphs. At SGD Inc., document assembly is used to send letters to potential and delinquent customers, among other standard correspondence.

Assembling a document requires an ability to include text from other files. Many applications allow this, but they require using an entire file, not a portion of it. For a name and address mailing list, one file is required for every name. While this may not be a problem with a short list, it could be a major problem—or be impossible—with a large mailing list.

Some applications accommodate document assembly with elaborate features. They allow the creation of form letters with blank spaces. Filling in the blanks occurs automatically, using values from another file. Inserted values can also be typed by an operator as letters are printed. Some packages let a user create prompts to guide data entry. Such software also captures and stores manually entered values.

Another advanced feature of document assembly concerns conditional branching. For example, an application might be set to print one phrase if a delinquent balance is under $200 and another if it is over $200.

User Convenience

Word processing enhancements increase user convenience. Function keys, for example, can be given user specified meanings. As many as forty key combinations can be specified with some applications. Forty is the number that comes from taking ten function keys and assigning them other meanings if used in combination with the (1) control key, (2) shift key, and (3) a special *alternate* key, which is available on some keyboards.

Another user-definable feature concerns a *phrase library.* This involves substituting shorthand notation for commonly used lengthy phrases and storing both. Afterward, every time the shorthand is typed, the full phrase from the stored phrase library is retrieved.

Some applications also offer functions that support more efficient personal time management. They include an appointment calendar, as well as phone and card file indexing.

Special Features

Users doing academic and scientific manuscripts require special features. These include an automatic table of contents, indexing, and footnote numbering. Special symbols are also needed for formula notation, which often requires *superscripts* and *subscripts.*

Writers who store notes in one file and create reports from the notes in another find simultaneous split screen viewing of multiple documents useful. As many as eight windows may be available at once to examine footnotes, bibliographies and other references as the need arises. Often more advanced features require more skill to use.

SPELLING AND STYLE CHECKERS

Some word processing applications come with a built-in *spelling checker.* For those that do not, a spelling checker can be separately purchased. Some *spelling checkers* are SpellStar, The Benchmark Spelling Checker, EasySpeller, Proofreader, and Perfect Speller. A spelling checker proofreads documents for spelling and typographical errors by comparing text to words contained in a built-in dictionary. It requires a good deal of human intervention to correct errors.

Proofreading

When Ms. Malone uses her spelling checker, which she purchased as a stand-alone package, she must type the name of the file to be proofread. The program temporarily takes over. It assumes that every series of letters between spaces, numbers, or special characters is a word and compares it to the dictionary file. Each word is then determined to be a match or a mismatch.

After the proofreading, which takes about ten seconds for one-and-a-half double-spaced pages, Ms. Malone reviews the list of mismatches on the display. She can make changes immediately, or mark selected mismatches for later correction. To correct later requires reactivating the word processing application to make changes. Some checkers allow only this delayed correction option.

With immediate correction, the document scrolls to a mismatch, pauses and displays options on a menu. A question mark appears at the problem such as:

This proposal is vallid until May 15

?

Unknown word is: vallid

Ms. Malone can accept or correct the word. Correction involves entering a replacement word and another dictionary check of the new word. If no match is found for the new word, the application asks for another replacement. In such a case, Ms. Malone selects an option for dictionary help.

Dictionary Help

When requesting dictionary help, three rows of words that approximate the spelling of the checked word are displayed. Generally the list includes the right word and eliminates more dictionary checks.

If desired, she can add a word to the dictionary. Beside the main dictionary, some applications provide user created dictionaries or *lexicons*. One allows up to five lexicons that can be tailored according to document needs, such as one for sales proposals. A doctor might have a medical lexicon and a lawyer a legal one.

Grammatical Help

Ms. Malone's stand-alone package also contains a *style checker.* It picks out errors that a spelling checker would ignore. For example, it correctly detects "can not" as an error that would pass through a spelling checker.

It catches style errors, such as archaic usages (using "upon" instead of "on"), awkward usages ("and/or"), redundant phrases ("join together"), and wordy phrases. Her application dislikes, for example, "a number of" and gives the message illustrated in Figure 8-7 if it finds the phrase in the text.

Punctuation errors located include inconsistent capitalization and unbalanced parentheses, brackets, or quotes. Frequent errors, such as double punctuation ("??"), double words ("the the"), and inappropriate capitalization ("THe"), are also caught.

After running documents through the style checker, Ms. Malone gets summary statistics. They include average word and sentence length, number of questions and imperatives, number of "to be's" and propositions, and others. A separate option reports on the occurrence frequency of each word used.

Professional writers find the statistics helpful. Such style checkers have been used in studies that attempt to develop indices of readability.

Ms. Malone uses hers to help polish documents that go outside the company. She uses the spelling checker, though, to verify all internal and external documents.

Neither package substitutes for her own careful proofreading. The spelling checker, for example, does not detect errors that are also real words, like the use of "too" instead of "to." The style checker does not detect split infinitives.

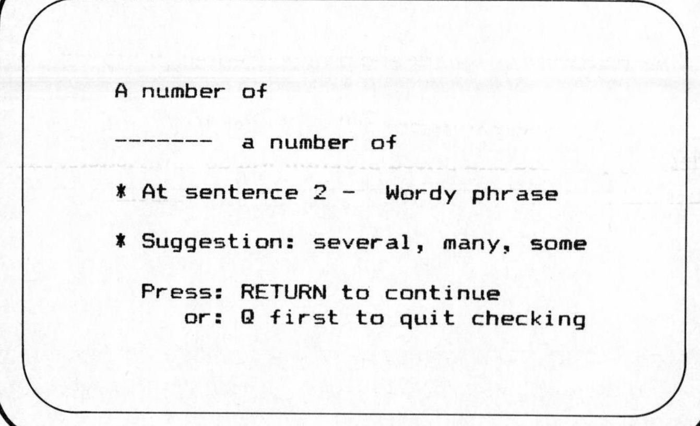

Figure 8-7 A style checker correction routine

Root Word vs. Literal Dictionary

If she had been using a so-called *root word* dictionary, the spelling checker would not have found "disfunction" as a misspelling of the word "dysfunction."

A *root word* dictionary strips off the prefix from the root word. It would consider *dis* and *function* both spelled correctly. It would fail, therefore, to bring the correct spelling of *dysfunction* to a user's attention.

Root word dictionaries tend naturally to be smaller than *literal dictionaries. Literal dictionaries* store words according to their exact spelling. Both function and dysfunction would be separate entries. So would all verb conjugations such as use, uses, used, using. This accounts for why spelling checker dictionaries can range from 7,000 to 100,000 words.

There is always the possibility that a dictionary does not contain a valid word. The custom dictionaries solve that, but they require word entry.

Some applications use software versions of hardcover dictionaries like the *Random House Dictionary of the English Language.* Others create dictionaries using sources that may be less reliable but more attuned to a user's needs. An intensive hands-on test with representative documents can verify the value of either approach for a user's needs.

EVALUATION

A systematic evaluation is important with a word processing application to get the right package the first time. Studies show that users usually do not switch after learning to use a word processing package. This remains true even though they clearly bought the wrong package or a demonstrably better package for their needs is readily available.

Word processing applications are printer dependent. More than one user has been disappointed with a word processing package that did not support the printer owned.

Users become easily dazzled by all the fancy capabilities of new word processing packages. But everyone who wants to process words has different requirements. A good way to begin is to work backwards from the end product desired. What will word processing be used for?

The simplest and least expensive software will easily handle short letters and be easy to learn. A moderately powered and priced program will do form letters, short papers, and articles, and it will be more difficult to learn than the least expensive system. The elaborate packages will do the most complex word processing tasks and provide special features like automatic table of contents, index, footnotes, spelling and grammar checks.

Users occasionally make the mistake of buying a package so powerful and complex to learn that they never use it. On the other hand, buying a package with so little power that it cannot grow as needs and skill levels increase is also a problem. To avoid either extreme, a careful evaluation process is critical.

Consistency of the command structure is also important. For example, if the control key amplifies a command, like turning a *word deletion* into a *line deletion,* it should similarly amplify other commands.

Word processing software that features a "what you see is what you get" display is more desirable than alternate choices. Alternates may not, for example, display justified, proportionally spaced, enhanced characters in finished page formats complete with heading, footing, and page number. With such software, a user has no idea of what a page will look like until a trial print is made.

Because most word processing time is spent entering and revising documents, the speed and convenience of basic editing is critical. Comparative testing reveals such glaring differences between packages as 22 seconds versus 4 seconds to scroll through a seven page double spaced document. When combined with the fact that seven keystrokes are required to do a search, versus two keystrokes, software choices narrow quickly.

In general, simple things should be simple to do and complex things should be possible to do. Advanced features like footnoting, indexing, and subscripting, nonetheless, should have a command format consistent with normal simple functions.

Some word processing packages restrict document size to available memory size. One allows documents up to only ten double-spaced pages. Size restrictions require dividing longer documents into smaller segments or files. Editing may be inconvenient, but generally files can be linked for continuous printing.

Some word processing software can handle documents larger than memory. To do so, it *swaps* text to and from the disk. The technique is also called *virtual memory* or *disk buffering.* Swaps theoretically are invisible to a user. Floppy disk swaps, however, are often noticeably sluggish. With such software, document size limit becomes the total available disk capacity. Performance, such as when scrolling from the beginning to the end of a long document, can be much slower than with applications that work only with documents already in memory.

Like document length, document width may be a limitation with some word processing software. Eighty column wide document processing is standard. One goes to 240 columns wide. If wide documents are to be processed, the horizontal scrolling feature should be examined.

For a hands-on test, Ms. Malone used the longest and most complex representative document possible. Nearly all systems seem easy when working on a single paragraph. It takes a more demanding test to see where the frustrations are hidden.

Figure 8-8 Word Processing Checklist

Candidate Packages Names:

A: ____________________

B: ____________________

C: ____________________

	Rating (Scale: 1 = poor to 10 = excellent)		
Check "must have" items	*A*	*B*	*C*
Document Creation			
Cursor movement:			
___ Right and left by character/word/line	___	___	___

Figure 8-8 (continued)

Check "must have" items		Rating (Scale: 1 = poor to 10 = excellent) A	B	C
	Document Creation			
	Cursor movement:			
___	Top of screen	___	___	___
___	Bottom of screen	___	___	___
___	Beginning/end of document	___	___	___
___	Specified page	___	___	___
	Scroll text:			
___	Previous screen	___	___	___
___	Next screen	___	___	___
___	Continuously	___	___	___
	Screen formatting:			
___	Set/clear right and left margins	___	___	___
___	Set/clear tabs	___	___	___
___	Word wrap	___	___	___
	Automatic:			
___	Paragraph reformat after change	___	___	___
___	Hyphenation	___	___	___
___	Page breaks	___	___	___
	Multiple documents available simultaneously:			
___	Number of document files	___	___	___
___	Number of windows	___	___	___
___	Status line always displayed	___	___	___
___	Help key/menus available	___	___	___
	Editing			
	Delete:			
___	Current/next/preceding character	___	___	___
___	Next word	___	___	___
___	Preceding part/remainder of line	___	___	___
___	Entire line	___	___	___
___	To end of document	___	___	___
___	Through specified character	___	___	___
___	Paragraph	___	___	___
___	Pull back deleted text	___	___	___
	Block operations:			
___	Move text to another location	___	___	___
___	Copy same text again in another location	___	___	___
___	Delete text block	___	___	___
___	Print block	___	___	___
___	Hide/display block	___	___	___
___	Write block to file	___	___	___
	Find and replace operations:			
___	Find a string of characters	___	___	___
___	Find string that includes ambiguous *wild card* characters	___	___	___

Figure 8-8 (continued)

Check "must have" items	Rating (Scale: 1 = poor to 10 = excellent) A	B	C
Editing			
Find and replace operations:			
___ Find string and replace with new text	___	___	___
___ Find and replace a specified number of times	___	___	___
___ Find and delete	___	___	___
___ Match whole words only	___	___	___
___ Global find, replace, delete	___	___	___
Formatting			
Justification:			
___ Right/center	___	___	___
___ Retain typed spaces and hyphens	___	___	___
___ Automatically align decimal data	___	___	___
Page layout:			
___ Standard style sheets provided	___	___	___
___ Save formats for reuse	___	___	___
___ Set margin top, bottom, left, right	___	___	___
___ Set temporary left margin	___	___	___
___ Indent first line of paragraphs	___	___	___
___ Outdent first line of paragraphs	___	___	___
___ Number paragraphs	___	___	___
___ Set page length	___	___	___
___ Set number of characters/lines per inch	___	___	___
___ Set space between lines	___	___	___
___ Change space between lines in same document	___	___	___
___ Intelligent page breaks	___	___	___
___ Force new page	___	___	___
___ Number of header lines	___	___	___
___ Number of footer lines	___	___	___
___ Automatic page numbers	___	___	___
___ Page number suppression	___	___	___
___ Book style page numbering	___	___	___
Character attributes:			
___ Underline	___	___	___
___ Boldface	___	___	___
___ Combined attributes (like underline and boldface)	___	___	___
___ Superscript	___	___	___
___ Subscript	___	___	___
___ Multilevel super- and subscripts	___	___	___
___ Overprint one character on another	___	___	___
___ Proportional spacing	___	___	___
Printing			
___ One specific page	___	___	___

Figure 8-8 (continued)

Check "must have" items	Rating (Scale: 1 = poor to 10 = excellent) A	B	C
Printing			
____Start from a specific page	____	____	____
____Through a specific page	____	____	____
____Start from cursor position	____	____	____
____Several linked/chained documents	____	____	____
____Several paper copies	____	____	____
____Interrupt/restart printing	____	____	____
____Pause to display a message	____	____	____
Utilities			
Document/file operations:			
____ Display file directory	____	____	____
____ Exit without saving file	____	____	____
____ Save and continue editing file	____	____	____
____ Save from cursor to end of file	____	____	____
Automatic backup:			
____ One generation	____	____	____
____ Multiple generations	____	____	____
____ Delete file	____	____	____
____ Rename file	____	____	____
____ Copy file	____	____	____
Document assembly:			
____ Create fill-in-the-blank areas in a form letter	____	____	____
____ Input from keyboard	____	____	____
____ Prompt operator for input	____	____	____
____ Capture keyboard input on disk	____	____	____
____ Conditional branching	____	____	____
Spelling and Style Checkers			
____Interactive correction without going through word processing application	____	____	____
____Dictionary help	____	____	____
____Root word dictionary	____	____	____
____Literal word dictionary	____	____	____
Dictionary source:			
____ Established hardcover dictionary	____	____	____
____ Other: ________________________	____	____	____
Miscellaneous			
____Integrated mailing list program	____	____	____
____Move rows/columns	____	____	____
____Calculator capability	____	____	____
____Scientific notation	____	____	____

Figure 8-8 (continued)

Check "must have" items	Rating (Scale: 1 = poor to 10 = excellent) A	B	C
Miscellaneous			
Automatic:			
____ Table of contents	______	______	______
____ Index	______	______	______
____ Footnote numbering	______	______	______
____Security passwords by document, by library	______	______	______
____User definable phrase library	______	______	______
____User definable function keys	______	______	______
____Phone index	______	______	______
____Appointment calendar	______	______	______
____Card file index	______	______	______
____Horizontal/vertical border lines	______	______	______
Interfaces			
With products from:			
____ Same publisher	______	______	______
____ Other publishers	______	______	______
____Database management	______	______	______
____Electronic worksheet	______	______	______
____Data communications	______	______	______
____Electronic mail	______	______	______
____Graphics	______	______	______
____Mailing lists	______	______	______
User Friendliness			
____"What you see is what you get" orientation	______	______	______
____Command letters reflect meaning (such as, P for print)	______	______	______
____Menu bypass for experienced user	______	______	______
____Rapid editing, searching and retrieving functions	______	______	______
____Text movement with minimum keystrokes	______	______	______
____Compatible and uncomplicated advanced features	______	______	______
____Short learning curve (supported with good manuals and tutorials)	______	______	______
Limitations			
____Document length	______	______	______
____Document width	______	______	______
Subtotal	______	______	______
Divide by number of items rated for average rating	______	______	______

Transfer Average Rating to Selection Summary: Software, Figure 5-3.

The Word Processing Checklist given in Figure 8–8 provides guidance in systematically evaluating word processing software. It should to be supplemented with other checklists, which are summarized in Figure 5–3. Together these tools provide a comprehensive approach to word processing software acquisition.

SELF TEST

1. What is the difference between word processing and a word processor?
2. What ways are word processing and electronic spreadsheet applications similar?
3. List and briefly describe the functions related to a word processing document's life cycle.
4. What functions help speed document creation?
5. Justify the statement that "correcting text is where word processing software earns its reputation as a productivity enhancer."
6. What are book style headings and footings?
7. Describe how a lawyer might use document assembly.
8. What is the difference between a spelling and a style checker? Give specific examples.
9. List four items to check during a word processing evaluation.

EXERCISES

1. *Brighton Company Case.* Assume you have been asked by the Brighton Company Marketing Manger to select a word processing application for general department use. All except one in the department are hunt-and-peck typists. They will need to produce:
   a. Company memos
   b. Customer correspondence
   c. Marketing reports (five pages maximum)

   Budget is no problem. Prepare a report comparing three word processing applications. Justify why the one you select is better than others for Brighton's marketing department personnel.
2. *Brighton Company Case.* For a full evaluation of the Brighton Company project, do a hands-on test of two word processing applications. Use the memo in Figure 8–5 as the first benchmark test document. Then use the Word Processing Checklist itself, in Figure 8–8, for the second benchmark test document. Write a report on the best and worst feature of each word processing application tested.
3. *Brighton Company Case.* To support the Brighton Company project, find three periodical articles on word processing applications that appeared in the last two months. They should be on products other than those hands-on tested. Identify features in the articles that are not implemented in the software tested. Identify features described in the article that are handled differently from those tested.

   If a hands-on test is not conducted, identify features unique to each product described. Identify features that are in some way similar in all products.
4. An acquaintance who uses word processing decides that a grammar checker will improve his prose and eliminate misspellings forever. What information would you offer to enlighten this person?

RESOURCES AND REFERENCES

Books

BERGERUND, MARLY AND JEAN GONZALEZ, *Word/Information Processing Concepts: Careers, Technology and Applications,* Wiley, 1978.
BOYER, R. DEAN, *Computer Word Processing,* Que, 1983.
CASADY, MONA, *Word Processing Concepts,* South-Western, 1980.
ETTLIN, WALTER A., *WordStar Made Easy,* Osborne/McGraw-Hill, 1982.
GLATZER, HAL, *Introduction to Word Processing,* Sybex, 1981.
GOOD, PHILLIP, *Choosing a Word Processor,* Reston, 1983.
MCWILLIAMS, PETER A., *Word Processing Book,* Prelude, 1982.
NAIMAN, ARTHUR, *Introduction to WordStar,* Sybex, 1983.
NAIMAN, ARTHUR, *Word Processing Buyer's Guide,* Sybex, 1983.
A Practical Guide to Word Processing and Office Management Systems, Digital, 1983.
POYNTER, DEAN, *Word Processors and Information Processing,* Para, 1982.
SCRIVEN, MICHAEL, *Wordmagic: Evaluating and Selecting Word Processing,* Lifetime Learning, Inc., 1983.
VisiWord, VisiCorp, 1983.
WAITE, MICHAEL AND JULIE ARCA, *Word Processing Primer,* McGraw-Hill, 1983.

Periodicals

Word Processing and Information Systems, Geyer-McAllister Publications.
Words, International Information/Word Processing Association.
ACU Newsletter (Word Processing Section), Association of Computer Users.

Tutorials

ATI Training Power—WordStar, disk-based tutorial, ATI.
How to Use WordStar, audio cassette course, Fliptrack Learning Systems.
VisiTutor for VisiWord, VisiCorp.

Word Processing Associations

International Information/Word Processing Association.
Canadian Information Processing Society.

Supplement: WORDSTAR TUTORIAL

This Supplement is a keystroke-by-keystroke tutorial on how to use the word processing software WordStar, by MicroPro International Corporation. It is written to be used as a guide while sitting at a computer. If a computer is not available, reading the tutorial can serve as a simulation of the actual session.

WordStar works on many brands of small computers. The IBM Personal Computer WordStar version 3.2 is used in the tutorial. It requires the PC-DOS operating system, a minimum of 64 Kybtes of memory, two floppy disk drives, and a printer. It assumes the WordStar install program has been used as needed to activate the printer in use.

The tutorial aims to create the memo in Figure 8-5. While the memo is being created, several changes are introduced to explore the editing capabilities of word processing. The memo is then printed, saved and later modified in additional exercises.

SET-UP PROCEDURE

1. Open the left disk drive unit door (or latch) by pulling up at its bottom edge. The left drive will be known as drive A throughout this tutorial.
2. Carefully insert the PC-DOS program disk, with its label up, into the drive. The oval cutout in the square disk jacket should enter the drive first. The label should enter the drive last. Gently push the disk all the way in and close the drive door.
3. Place a blank formatted disk in the right disk drive unit. The right drive will be known as drive B throughout this tutorial. It will be for user created document files.
4. Turn the computer's power switch on. The A disk drive begins to whir and click, and the red "in use" light on the drive comes on. When asked for the date and time, type information or carriage return through the prompts. This information will not be used.

   When A> comes on the screen remove the PC-DOS disk. Replace it with the WordStar disk in drive A. Type WS and a carriage return to begin the application. A carriage return after typed entries is indicated by a [R] in the rest of this tutorial.

   All typed commands in the tutorial are indicated in upper case capital letters. They can be typed more easily, however, in lower case letters.
5. A display called the No-File Menu, similar to the one in Figure 8-6 appears. No-File relates to the fact that no document file is active anytime this menu is accessed. The menu contains many options. Only three command options are used for start-up tasks. Type the following while observing the screen changes:

Type	*Action*
L	Option to change the logged or default disk drive. Options choices and function keys execute without a carriage return.
B[R]	Make B the default drive.
H or F1	Option to set the level of help menu displays.
2	Make 2 the level of help menus displayed. This frees more screen space for

Type	*Action*
	document creation. It also eliminates a screenful of options that appear confusing to a beginner.
D	Option to open a document file. A prompt appears: NAME OF FILE TO EDIT?
SALES[R]	Name the file SALES that will contain the typed document.

CREATE A DOCUMENT

A document can be created after a file has been named or activated for it. First a screen, similar to the one in Figure 8–1, but without the text, automatically appears. It has status and ruler lines with a cursor in the upper left corner of the document creation area.

In addition, it has an INSERT ON message on the status line. Remove the INSERT ON message by typing the INS insert key once. The insert key, as shown in Figure 8–2, functions as a toggle switch. Typing it once turns the insert function off.

Set Margins

To set the right margin, type the space bar to move the cursor to column 50. The status line will indicate when the cursor is at column 50. Once there, type function key F4 to set the margin. The left margin should remain as is.

Use a carriage return to return the cursor to the left margin. Notice that a < symbol appears at the right margin. Every time a carriage return is typed during document creation, the right margin will indicate this with a < symbol.

Now experiment using the arrow keys to move the cursor. The cursor seems frozen except for line 1 (check the status line) and one character space in line 2. This experiment illustrates that the cursor will only move over display area that has already been activated by space or characters. Type another row of spaces to activate line 2, then try again to move the cursor using the arrow keys.

Start Over

At any time it is possible to abandon work to restart from scratch. This requires typing a control key command to abandon the file. In this tutorial, the control key will be indicated by a ∧ symbol.

Type ∧ K and observe the ∧ K in the left corner of the menu that appears, called the Block Menu. It is one of five control character support menus. The letter Q appears as the command to abandon a file, so type Q. A prompt may ask for a Yes/No confirmation to abandon the file. Type Y for yes. This returns the display to the familiar No-File Menu where is it possible to start over.

Type Document

Begin typing the memo in Figure 8–5 as if using an ordinary typewriter. First return the cursor to line 1 column 1. Type the date, then carriage return five times. Type the "Memo to:" line and another carriage return. The same general steps should be used to get the other two header lines typed. Four more carriage returns gets the cursor to the body of the memo which begins on line 14.

No carriage returns are needed in the body of the memo except to indicate the end of a paragraph. Text automatically is wrapped around to the next line without user intervention. Type the rest of the memo using the same general typing pattern. Observe how text is automatically right justified.

Correct Mistakes

Any time a correction or revision is desired, move the cursor to the position to be changed. Cursor movement keys are illustrated in Figures 8–2 and 8–3. Try them all to explore faster ways to navigate through the text.

Once at an editing location, type over text or insert and delete text. The insert and delete key actions are described below:

Type	*Action*
INS	This key acts like an ON/OFF toggle switch. Hit it once to turn the insert function on. INSERT ON appears on the status line. While INSERT is on, each character typed moves existing text to the right one character. When done typing the insert, hit the INS key again to turn the function off.
DEL	This key deletes one character each time it is typed. It deletes characters to the left of the cursor.
∧G	Holding down the control key and typing a G deletes one character at the cursor position. Repeatedly typing G, while the control key is still depressed, deletes characters to the right of the cursor.

To experiment with these capabilities, try the following editing tasks:

- Change "as of" in paragraph two to "before." The change requires typing over five characters then inserting one. Remember to toggle the INS insert key on and off for the single character insert.
- Delete the word "active" in paragraph two. It requires use of ∧ G.
- Change Bob Williams to your own name in two places.

Inserting and deleting entire lines is another common editing task. The control key must be held down while another key is typed to perform actions as follows:

Type	*Action*
∧N	Creates a new line where the cursor is positioned by pushing the text down one line. Repeated ∧ Ns create several lines.
∧Y	Deletes a line where the cursor is positioned.

To experiment with these capabilities, execute the following editing tasks:

- Delete one blank line between the heading and the first paragraph.
- Insert one extra blank line between the last paragraph and "Best regards."

Paragraph two will now need reformatting. To reformat type ∧ B at the beginning of the paragraph. The cursor may suddenly stop at the right margin, and the line may extend beyond the margin in an awkward way. Just type ∧ B again to release the cursor. Automatic formatting will occur instantly. (As a later exercise, explore the hyphenation option that is possible during reformatting.)

Two other commands that are helpful when editing text are described below.

Type	*Action*
∧QS	Moves the cursor to the beginning of the line.
∧QD	Moves the cursor to the end of the line.

FORMAT A DOCUMENT

Before printing the memo, it is necessary to format it. This requires typing some dot commands. First type F10 to move the cursor to the beginning of the document.

Make some room for the commands by creating three blank lines above the date. To recall, ∧N creates blank lines in the document.

The dot commands to insert are:

Type	*Action*
.OP	*O*mits *p*age numbers at the foot of the document.
.MT15	Inserts 18 blank lines in the *m*argin at the *t*op of the page (three lines are standard).
.PO14	Adds 14 spaces to the left margin as a *p*age *o*ffset in the printed version of the document.

In addition, have the document print in darkened boldface type. To do this, turn INSERT ON by typing the INS key. Place the cursor at the A in August of the date line. Type function key F6 to indicate boldfacing. The date shifts two spaces to the right to make room for the ∧B symbols. The shifted spacing is not reflected in the printed document. The symbols indicate the beginning of boldface text.

Type function key F9 to get the cursor to the end of the document. When there, type F6 again to enclose the full text within a pair of boldface symbols. Type the INS insert key to turn insert off.

Now that the memo is formatted, save the document. Type ∧ K then D to save the file and return to the No-File Menu.

PRINT A DOCUMENT

The No-File Menu contains a P option to print the document. The document file name should be listed at the bottom of the screen, indicating that it exists in disk B's directory. Before printing it, set the top of the paper in the printer even with the print head. Turn the printer on.

Type P to print the file. The application asks for the name of the file to print.

Type SALES and the ESC escape key. Typing the escape key avoids a series of questions that are not necessary to print the memo.

OTHER EDITING FEATURES

Two of many unexplored editing features include block moves and find and replace text. They can be executed using a copy of the memo already prepared.

Retrieve the stored memo from disk by typing D to open a document file at the No-File Menu. The program asks for the name of the file desired. Type SALES. Immediately the screen displays the text of the retrieved file.

Block Move

To explore moving text from one place in a document to another, set the cursor under the P of Please in the first paragraph. The objective will be to move the first paragraph to be the last one in the memo.

Type	*Action*
F7	Mark the begining of the text block to be moved. A <B> appears at the cursor position and shifts the text line to the right. Move the cursor to the blank line after the first paragraph.
F8	Mark the end of the text block to be moved. The marked text displays in a dim intensity. Move the cursor under the B of Best regards.
∧KV	Execute the block move.
∧KH	Restore the intensity of the moved text. Move the cursor under B of Best regards.
∧N	Restore one blank line between the last paragraph and Best regards.
∧QV	Return to the place where the block came from.
∧T	Delete one blank line to restore the space between the heading and body of the memo.

Practice the steps in the block move procedure by moving the current first paragraph under the current last paragraph. The procedure will be the same as that outlined above.

Find and Replace

Assume that the memo should read "fourth-quarter" instead of "third-quarter." To execute this change:

Type	*Action*
∧QA	Command the application to execute a find and replace operation. It responds with: FIND?
third-quarter	Type the characters to be found, for example, third-quarter. REPLACE WITH?
fourth-quarter	Type the characters that will replace the found characters. OPTIONS?
GN[R]	Select the global option to find and change every occurrence in the document.

Observe how the text is immediately changed throughout. The change throws the first paragraph out of alignment. Move the cursor to the P in Please and reformat by typing ∧B.

There is no need to save the revised document when through. Exit by typing ∧KQ, or *quit* without saving.

The WordStar *General Information Manual* and *Reference Manual* should be consulted for complete user instructions.

EXERCISES

1. *Sporting Goods Distributors Case.* Assume that Mr. Williams sends individual letters to people on the sales staff. Instead of the memo header he wants a specific name and address. Delete the memo heading and in its place type at the left margin:

   Mr. B. Lawrence
   255 Jay Place
   Columbus, OH 22222

   Dear Bill:

   Print a copy of the letter. Then type your own name and address and print another copy of the letter.
2. *Waterford Paper Products Case.* As the Customer Relations Manager of Waterford Paper Products Company, Harold Weaver tries to promote the company's products whenever he can. He prepared a standard letter, as shown in Figure 8S–1, to send to all sales prospects. Type the letter using the word processing software. Use a 60 character line in the body of the letter. The command to center text is∧OC. Print two copies of the letter, each having a different "send to" address. Make up the second address. Save the letter for reuse in the next exercise. (Note: Type the INS key to turn the INSERT ON before typing∧OC. Type the INS key again when done with centering to return to regular document creation.)
3. *Waterford Paper Products Case.* Mr. Weaver decided to revise the standard letter. In the second paragraph, between "ideas" and "There" insert the following:

   Many of the items, like the Executive Desk Notepad on page 47, can be imprinted with your corporate seal or "logo."

   Print one copy of the revised letter.
4. *Drake Employment Agency Case.* The Drake Employment Agency wants resumes for job placement purposes. To practice how to prepare your own resume to submit to Drake, try one that is already done. One appears in Figure 8S–2 that is from the College Placement Annual. For practice, type the sample resume with the word processing application. The objective is to have a perfectly aligned and spelled final copy. Print one copy with your own name and address on it. It might be more convenient to have only one centered address.
5. *Create a Resume.* Now type your own resume. It should follow the model in alignment and grammar. It uses verb action words to describe experience and avoids use of personal pronouns. Print one copy of the resume and save it as a disk file to update as needed.

WATERFORD PAPER PRODUCTS
P.O. BOX 417
ESTILL SPRINGS, TN 37330
(205)837-7777

February 21, 198X

Mr. James Miller, Vice President
The Hartford Corporation
2011 State Street
Boise, ID 83704

Dear Mr. Miller:

Thank you for your interest in Waterford Paper Products. The enclosed brochure describes our product line and our current prices.

You will notice that brochure pages 45-55 contain corporate gift ideas. There is no charge for gold-letter imprinting, up to four lines, on orders of 25 gifts or more.

If I can be of further help, please let me know.

Sincerely,

Harold Weaver
Customer Relations Manager

HW:ik
Enclosure

Figure 8S-1 A standard letter used by Waterford Paper Products company

NAME

Permanent Address	Temporary Address
4922 Clover Ave. Westburg, NY 32786 Tel. (422) 356-3245	Room 312, Smith Hall Alumni University Sunnydale, NY 64234 Tel. (381) 879-3425

Professional Objective	Retail Sales Management.
Education	Alumni University, Sunnydale, NY, BA Marketing, 1984. Special emphasis on retail sales and merchandising; considerable work in consumer economics and accounting.
Experience Summer 1983	Sales Clerk, Housewares Department. Arranged merchandise displays, assisted buyer, handled consumer relations. Also assisted department manager in training new sales personnel, sold successfully on commission basis.
1980 to 1983	Sales Clerk. Worked part-time in specialty clothing store. Assumed increased responsibility during time of employment. Sold merchandise, arranged window displays, assisted with inventory and ordering, assisted with advertising and copy layout.
Summer 1979 to 1980	Lifeguard. Performed general pool maintenance and gave swimming instructions to children and young adults.
Extracurricular Activities	Program Chairperson for American Marketing Association. Planned programs, contacted speakers from area business community, and coordinated programs. Corresponding Secretary for National Sorority. Handled all correspondence to national headquarters, alumnae, and others. Maintained files and records for group. Ordered materials.
References	Furnished upon request.

Courtesy of the College Placement Council

Figure 8S-2 Sample resume

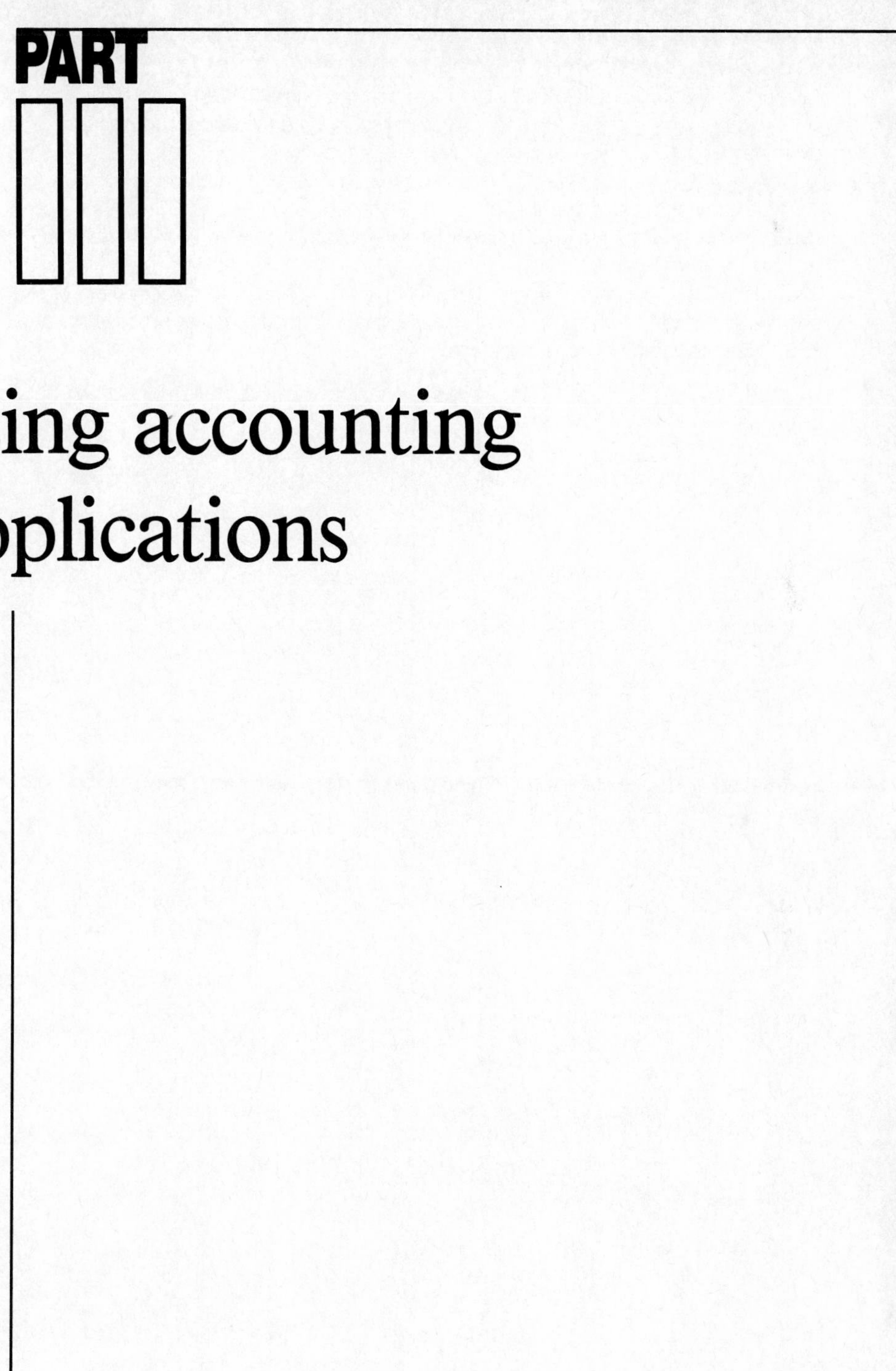

PART III

using accounting applications

Accounting applications represent the most common type of packaged business programs in use. They usually are combined in a so-called *integrated accounting package.* Part III examines how accounting and integrated packages work.

A single case study followed throughout unifies work flow concepts. Because a distributor usually implements all integrated accounting functions, it is used as the case study subject.

Chapter 9 is an overview of applications included in an integrated accounting package. Chapters 10 and 11 examine representative applications, the order processing, and accounts receivable packages, in detail.

9

INTEGRATED ACCOUNTING

Accounting applications represent the most common type of packaged business programs in use. They are used singly, as is an accounts receivable package, or in combinations, as is an integrated set of order processing, accounts receivable, and general ledger packages.

This chapter is an overview of integrated accounting packages. It begins with a discussion of accounting and general integrated package characteristics. Then it uses Sporting Goods Distributors, Inc. (SGD Inc.) as a case study to explore individual application functions within an integrated package. It concludes with some evaluation guidelines.

This chapter also serves as an introduction to the next two chapters. Each takes one of the many applications in an integrated package and examines how it works in more detail. Since both applications belong to the same revenue accounting cycle, it represents a comprehensive view of how this business activity is automated.

BUSINESS ACTIVITY CYCLES

Business activities in any profit-oriented organization typically fall into two broad cycles, as shown in Figure 9–1. Operating cycle activities produce and sell an organization's

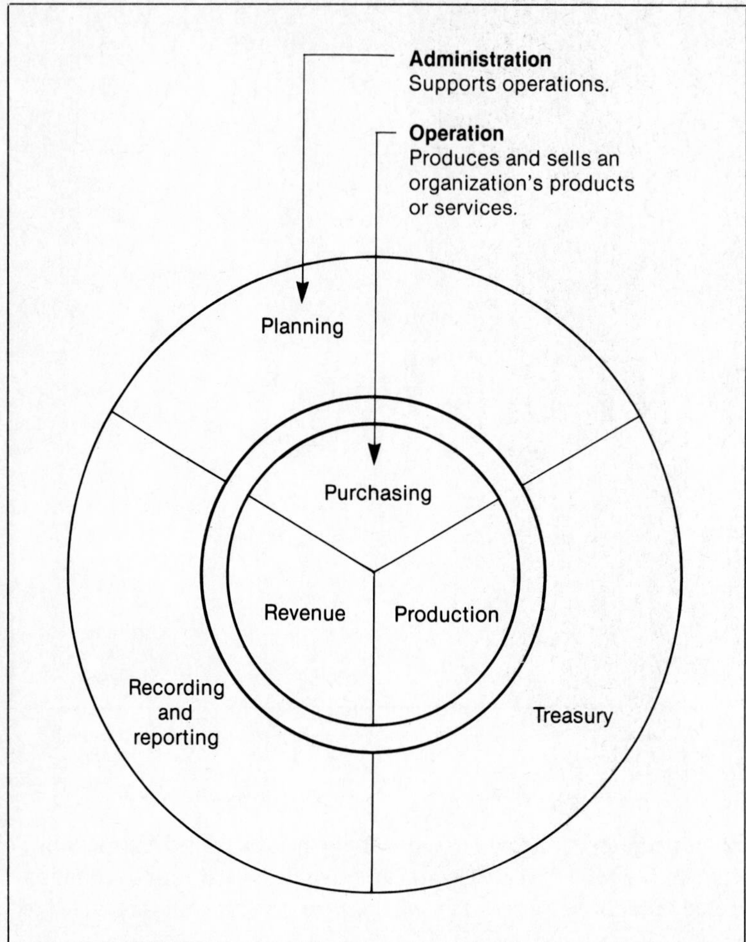

Figure 9-1 Business activity cycles

products or services. Administrative cycle activities support operations. Some specific activities that occur within these functions are listed in Figure 9–2. The same figure also identifies computer applications associated with activities.

INTEGRATED PACKAGES

Integrated accounting packages mainly support operating cycle activities. Applications in an integrated package may include:

OPERATION

- Order processing
- Accounts receivable

- Inventory
- Purchasing
- Accounts payable
- Payroll

ADMINISTRATION

- General ledger

As Figure 9–3 demonstrates, all operating applications pass information to the general ledger administrative application.

Figure 9-2 Computer applications identified with business activity cycles

	Selected Business Activities	*Computer Applications*
Administration Cycle		
Planning	Strategic long-range planning Economic and sales forecasting Research and development planning Sales and production planning Budgeting	Electronic spreadsheet On-line database retrieval (private and public)
Treasury	Capital funds received from investors Dividends and interest returned to investors Investments and loans arranged Employee benefit plans administered	Investment/stockholder accounting Employee benefits accounting
Recording and reporting	Routine accounting performed Accounting records adjusted and closed Financial reports prepared	General ledger
Operation Cycle		
Revenue	Sales orders processed Customers billed Cash received from customers Returns and allowances processed Potential customers cultivated	Order processing Accounts receivable
Production	Sales orders filled and shipped Inventory management coordinated with sales and production Products produced and routed to finished goods inventory	Inventory Manufacturing
Purchasing	Inventory and other supplies purchased Inventory received Vendors and employees paid for goods and services	Purchasing Accounts payable Payroll

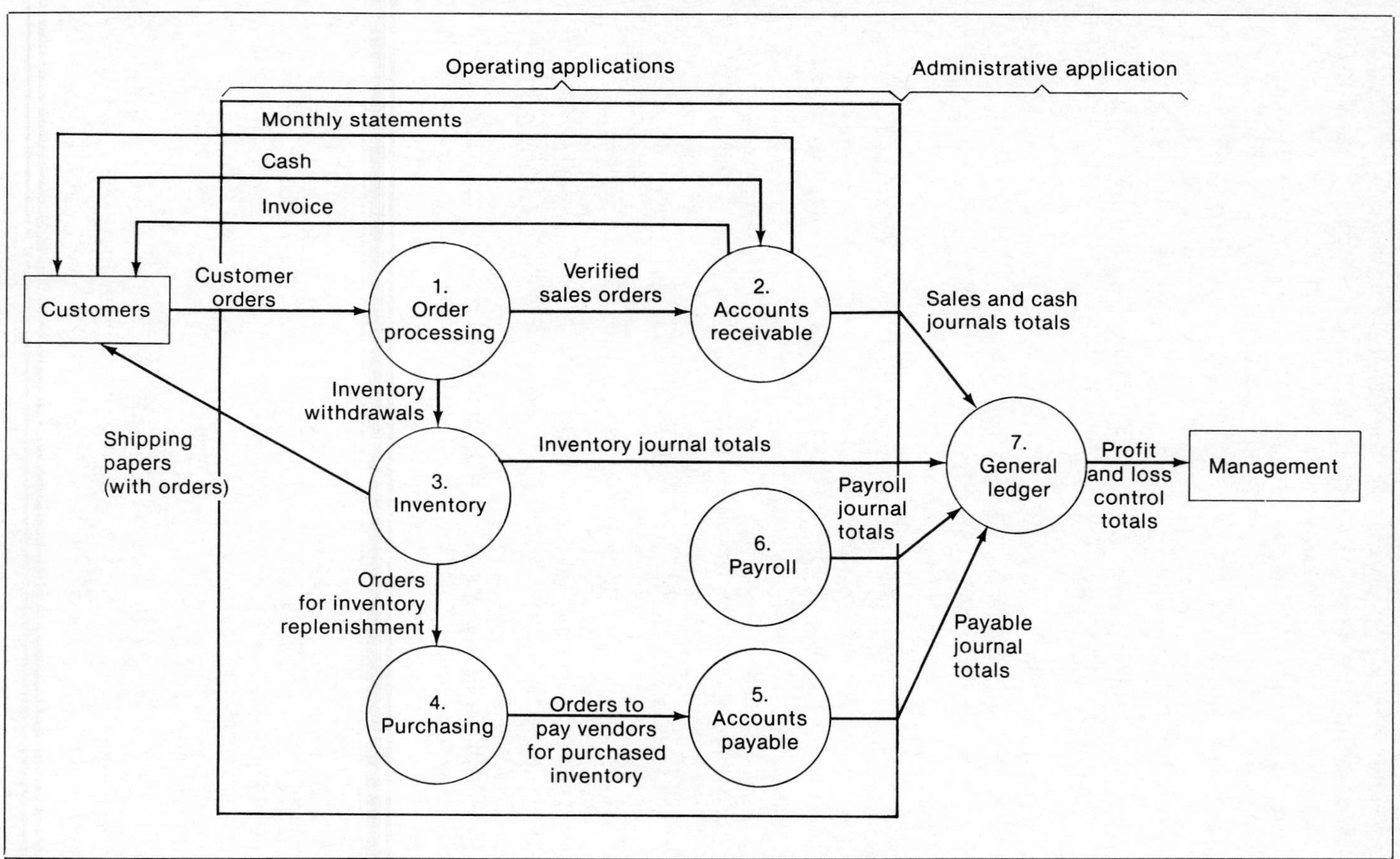

Figure 9-3 Overview of information flow in an integrated accounting system

Sporting Goods Distributors, Inc., where Mr. Williams works as Marketing Manager, uses an integrated accounting package. SGD Inc. so far has implemented all the applications just listed, except purchasing, which is planned to be added later.

Because SGD Inc. is in the distribution business, they provide a warehousing service for goods produced by others. They are part of a distribution channel for delivering goods from manufacturers to users. They concentrate on distributing active sporting goods for such things as outdoor camping, scouting, tennis, skiing, and other sports.

Nonservice-oriented companies often manufacture goods from scratch. These companies use additional application software. Material requirements planning (MRP) application packages help to automate production planning from raw materials to finished goods.

Whether a company has a service or nonservice orientation, business activities usually divide into operating and administrative cycles. The general ledger application acts as the integrating force for all other computer applications.

Databased

In an integrated accounting package, all applications feed the general ledger file. Files and their interrelationships are shown in Chapter 4, Figure 4–1. Because files interrelate with one another, they collectively make up a company's database of information.

In databased accounting, several files are in use at the same time. In the SGD Inc. case, for example, when a sales order is entered, the customer file is checked to be sure a customer's credit is in order. The inventory file is checked to be sure goods are available to fill the order. The sales transaction itself creates a new record in the order file.

The processing demands of files interacting with each other often requires the increased speed and mass storage capacity offered by a hard disk. Floppy disks can do the job, in many cases, but processing is noticeably slower and often requires many disk swaps.

Many integrated accounting applications claim they are databased. Many of these applications, however, do not offer the file manipulation capability associated with a package called a database management system (DBMS). A DBMS allows a user to ask random questions of a database and get instant answers. Chapter 16 covers such DBMS capabilities in more detail.

SGD Inc.'s integrated accounting package offers a random inquiry feature. It does so through an application called a report writer. The report writer allows SGD Inc. to manipulate their database and receive instant responses very similar to the report writer feature in most DBMSs.

Stand-Alone Capability

Even though SGD Inc.'s integrated package links all applications together, each application can work alone. Each application can function independently as a so-called *stand-alone package*. SGD Inc. needed the stand-alone capability when first installing the system. They brought up one application at a time. It is equivalent to building one major file at a time.

Each new computer accounting application changed business procedures. Employees learned the new procedures before adding more. They heard disaster stories about companies that tried to put everything on the computer at once. The last thing they wanted was to disrupt the entire business all at once.

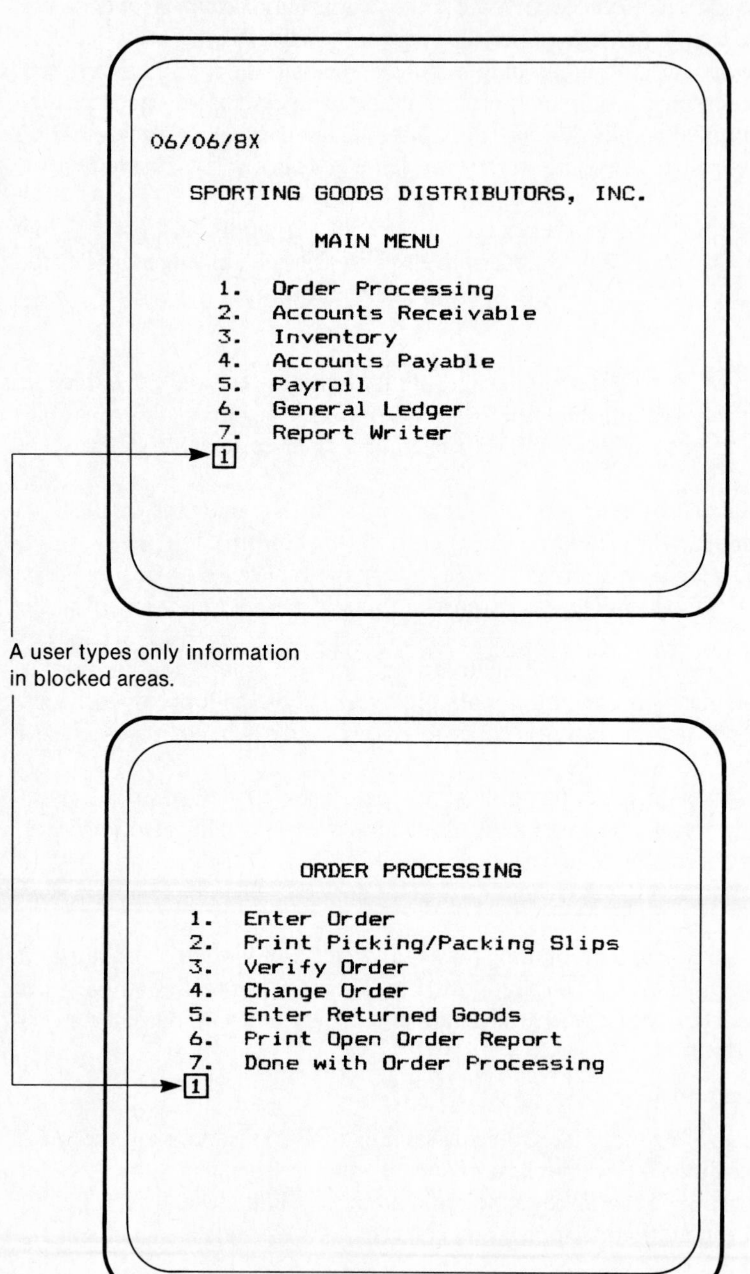

Figure 9-4 The main and order processing menus of a menu-driven integrated accounting application

Menu-Driven

SGD Inc.'s integrated accounting package begins with a main menu that retrieves a submenu, such as the one shown in Figure 9–4. This selection technique identifies the integrated accounting application as a menu-driven package.

Preceding the main menu is a request for a password as a security clearance. Since several SGD Inc. employees have access to the applications, security is important. In some systems, each individual application can be further protected with a second level of passwords.

Industry-Specific Packages

The integrated accounting package SGD Inc. uses is not oriented towards any specific industry. But many users find their automation needs met by highly specialized industry specific packages. Physicians, for example, keep patient history profiles, and contractors keep labor and material costs by job. Each requires a different type of application.

Regardless of industry orientation, companies often find only the accounts receivable, accounts payable, and general ledger portions of any integrated package of interest. These three applications make up the core of most integrated accounting packages.

GENERAL LEDGER

The general ledger application is the heart of SGD Inc.'s—or any other company's—integrated accounting package. It is responsible for producing a company's two important financial reports, the balance sheet and the income statement. As the abbreviated samples in Figure 9–5 show, these documents contain summary totals of all business activity.

Other applications feed summary totals to the general ledger file whenever a batch of transactions is summarized. For example, when a batch of invoices are printed, the batch total gets "posted," to use the accountant's term, to the sales and accounts receivable records in the general ledger file. Often several general ledger account records are posted for a more refined total distribution.

Because totals are automatically updated as activity requires, SGD Inc.'s financial statements are always up-to-date and available on demand. A menu selection retrieves the document desired. Without automation, SGD Inc. depended on professional accounting assistance to prepare financial statements once a month by hand.

The balance sheet is a snapshot view of a company at a fixed moment in time. It shows the net position of the company's assets and liabilities. When SGD Inc. negotiates capital loans from a bank, the balance sheet is examined by bank officers. It lets them see at a glance what financial shape the company is in.

The income statement, on the other hand, is a more dynamic document. It shows SGD Inc.'s income and expenses over a period of time. It is a record of the company's performance during the period covered by the report. Changes in this document trigger management policy changes that reinforce positive trends and try to reverse negative ones.

1/31/8X

SAMPLE BALANCE SHEET

ACCT. NO.		AMOUNT
	Assets	
1000	Cash	$ 500
1010	Accounts Receivable	1,000
1500	Equipment	2,000
1510	Less Depreciation	500
	Total Assets	3,000
	Liabilities	
2000	Accounts Payable	750
2500	Bank Loan	800
	Total Liabilities	1,550
	Equity	
3000	Stock	1,000
	Net Income	450
	Total Equity	1,450
	Total Liab & Equity	3,000

1/31/8X

SAMPLE INCOME STATEMENT

ACCT.		CURRENT MONTH		YEAR TO DATE	
NO.	DESCRIPTION	AMOUNT	% OF SALES	AMOUNT	% OF SALES
4000	Sales	$10,000	100	$10,000	100
5000	Cost of Sales	7,000	70	7,000	70
	Gross Income	3,000	30	3,000	30
	Expenses				
6000	Salaries	$ 1,500	15	$ 1,500	15
6010	Rent	750	8	750	8
6020	Depreciation	300	3	300	3
	Total Expenses	2,550	26	2,500	26
	Net Income	450	5	450	5

Figure 9-5 Abbreviated samples of the balance sheet and income statement produced by general ledger applications

Chart of Accounts

In order for the general ledger application to produce the balance sheet and income statement, SGD Inc. had to set up a chart of accounts. This procedure assigns account numbers to account names. The account number system that SGD Inc. uses is apparent from Figure 9-5. It follows the commonly accepted numbering practice, as follows:

Account Number Range	*Account Type*
1000–1499	Current assets
1500–1999	Fixed assets
2000–2499	Current liabilities
2500–2999	Long-term liabilities
3000–3999	Equity
4000–4499	Sales and other income
4500–4999	Sales returns and allowances
5000–5999	Cost of sales
6000–6999	Expenses

All general ledger accounts are named as desired.

Other integrated applications deposit amounts through automatic transfers to appropriate records. For accounts that have no automatic deposits, a separate program is provided for manual postings.

SGD Inc. had to tell the application during setup how many accounting and history totals to carry for each account. Often totals are retained one or two years for comparative reporting.

REVENUE CYCLE APPLICATIONS

The main revenue cycle computer applications are order processing and accounts receivable. SGD Inc. uses both applications to record sales transactions as well as cash received from customers. As Marketing Manager, Mr. Williams gets directly involved with SGD Inc.'s revenue-producing transactions.

His main concern is with sales orders. Once a sale is made, it is entered into the computer application called order processing. The application tracks an order from the moment it enters the company.

When the order is shipped and becomes billable, the accounts receivable application takes over. It prints an invoice prepared from previously saved order information. When customers send cash to SGD Inc. for received goods, the cash collected is recorded. The accounts receivable application knows which payments are due because it checks which invoices are still unpaid in the open invoice file.

Some benefits of computerized revenue operations include *automatic*:

- Order tracking
- Invoice printing
- Customer statement printing
- Accounts receivable posting
- General ledger posting
- Management reporting about revenue status

Efficiencies realized from this automation include *better control of:*

- Revenue-producing transactions
- Customer credit
- Service to customers

PRODUCTION CYCLE APPLICATIONS

The main production cycle computer applications are inventory and manufacturing control. SGD Inc.'s inventory application manages the inventory item file. Efficient sales order processing depends on accurate item file information, such as price, description, and quantity available.

Some benefits of computerized inventory management include *automatic reports of:*

- Trends in inventory item demand
- Inventory turnover problems and opportunities
- Item profitability problems and opportunities
- Stock replenishment requirements

This information enables SGD Inc.'s management to do better inventory and sales planning.

Since SGD Inc. does not manufacture goods, it does not have any manufacturing-oriented production cycle applications.

PURCHASING CYCLE APPLICATIONS

The main purchasing cycle applications are purchasing, accounts payable, and payroll. At companies that already have automated purchasing, when inventory items go below normal stock levels, a purchase order is printed. Usually this applies only to selected high turnover items. Other items are manually verified before the computer is signaled to print purchase orders.

The same application enables users to compare goods received with the original purchase order. If acceptable, the goods are received and stock-on-hand is automatically incremented in the item file.

Part of the purchasing cycle requires paying vendors for goods purchased. The accounts payable application automatically generates checks for approved purchases.

SGD Inc.'s employees represent labor purchased to execute the company's operations. Their checks are cut through the payroll computer application.

Some benefits of these computerized applications include *automatic generation of:*

- Purchase orders
- Vendor checks
- Employee paychecks
- Government-required payroll documents, like an employee's W-2 form

Even though SGD Inc. has its payroll done on their in-house computer, many companies prefer to have payroll done by an outside bank or computer service bureau. They do not want sensitive salary information processed internally for security reasons. Also, every time there is a tax change, the payroll program needs modification by an experienced programmer. This practice of keeping payroll off the company computer is common.

EVALUATION

Implementing an integrated accounting package can be frought with installation and financial surprises. To avoid both requires a systematic approach to package evaluation, selection, and implementation.

The benefits of selecting a satisfactory package are many. Some companies that acquire a satisfactory package claim a 50-percent increase in productivity over manual methods. Their invoices and statements contain far fewer errors, resulting in better customer service. In addition, they receive management decision-making reports that they never had before.

Accounting software usually requires that a person setting up the system have a good working familiarity with computers and accounting. The company's accountant may have the competencies needed.

Companies without internal support can hire a consultant. A consultant can help choose an appropriate package, as well as handle all the technical and administrative details of installation. They can also provide advice about whether a hard disk is needed.

Some integrated accounting package suppliers are Open Systems, Douthett Enterprises, TLB, Inc., IBM, TCS Software, Micro Business Software, and Peachtree Software among a host of others.

The way SGD Inc. narrowed package choices was to quantify requirements by application. They used a form like the one given in Figure 9–6. The numbers filled out on this form helped to find only packages that could handle their volumes.

Detailed application checklists, similar to the examples in Chapters 10 and 11, were prepared for each accounting package evaluated. In addition, the supporting software checklists given in Chapter 4 were also prepared for each application. They are the General Software Checklist and the Hands-On Test Checklist.

If hardware, software, and service are provided by a single turnkey vendor, the Turnkey Checklist and the Reference Questionnaire, also given in Chapter 4, are supportive.

Figure 9-6 Integrated Accounting Requirements Specification Form

	Specification	
General Ledger		
# General ledger accounts		_____
# Digits in largest balance		_____
# Accounting periods		_____
# Periods history retained (12, 24)		_____
# Companies		_____
Order Processing		
# Orders/day	Average _____	Peak _____
# Line-items/order	Average _____	Peak _____
# Days until order filled	Average _____	Peak _____
% Line-items backordered	Average _____	Peak _____
# Days on backorder	Average _____	Peak _____
# Prices for all items		_____
# Quantity breaks for all items		_____
# Price contracts		_____
# Sales history periods retained (12, 24)		_____
Accounts Receivable		
# Customers		_____
# New customers added/year		_____
# Customer ship-to addresses		_____
# Invoices/day	Average _____	Peak _____
# Cash receipts/month	Average _____	Peak _____
# Days invoices unpaid	Average _____	Peak _____
Inventory and Purchasing		
# Items		_____
# New items added/year		_____
# Product classes		_____
# Issues/month	Average _____	Peak _____
# Receipts/month	Average _____	Peak _____
# Adjustment/month	Average _____	Peak _____
# Purchase orders/month	Average _____	Peak _____
# Lines/purchase order	Average _____	Peak _____
# Warehouses		_____
# Warehouse transfers/month	Average _____	Peak _____
Accounts Payable		
# Vendors		_____
# New vendors added/year		_____
# Invoices/month	Average _____	Peak _____
# Days invoices unpaid	Average _____	Peak _____
# Checks/month	Average _____	Peak _____
# General distributions/invoice		_____
Payroll		
# Employees		_____
# Departments		_____

Figure 9-6 (continued)

	Specification
Payroll	
# Pay periods/year	_____
# States	_____
# Special deductions/employee	_____
# Unions	_____

SELF TEST

1. What computer applications may be included in an integrated accounting package?
2. What is an integrated accounting package?
3. What is a company database?
4. Use an example to describe how a databased integrated accounting system works.
5. Why is stand-alone capability important in an accounting package?
6. Use an example to describe how a menu-driven integrated accounting package works.
7. What is an industry-specific package? Give examples.
8. Why is the general ledger package important in an integrated accounting package?
9. What is the chart of accounts in a general ledger package?
10. List the benefits of automated:
    - Revenue cycle applications
    - Production cycle applications
    - Purchasing cycle applications
11. What is one way to narrow candidates when evaluating an integrated accounting package?

EXERCISES

1. *WMK Associates Case.* Mr. Kennedy, president of WMK Associates, a distributing company, wants to automate the company's accounting procedures. Do some preliminary investigatory work by finding three reviews of integrated accounting packages in recent periodical articles. Using the specifications form in Figure 9–6 as a guide, list how each package addresses the capacities, capabilities, and features identified for each application.
2. *WMK Associates Case.* Write to the companies identified in exercise 1. Ask for literature that describes their integrated package. Ask especially for detailed information on the general ledger, order processing, and accounts receivable packages.

   When literature is available, prepare a written or oral report on the following differences in the general ledger packages:

   - Chart of accounts numbering scheme
   - Chart of accounts setup procedure to define the balance sheet and income statement
   - Balance sheet print options
   - Income statement print options

3. *WMK Associates Case.* Research application availability in software or periodical directories of computer applications. Look for integrated accounting applications for the distribution industry. Write to four of five companies for more detailed information. Follow the requirements of exercise 2 for executing this exercise.
4. Arrange to have a demonstration of a general ledger package. Before the demonstration, read the User's Guide to learn about:
   a. Setup tasks
   b. Operating procedures
   c. Printed and displayed output

   After the demonstration, make an oral or written report about how the first two items were executed. Use the outputs to explain how they compare to other packages you have investigated.

RESOURCES AND REFERENCES

DAVIDSON, SIDNEY, CLYDE B. STICKNEY, AND ROMAN L. WEIL, *Financial Accounting: An Introduction to Concepts, Methods, and Uses,* Dryden, 1982.

ELIASON, ALAN L., *Online Business Computer Applications,* SRA, 1983.

HAUEISER, WILLIAM D., AND JAMES L. CAMP, *Business Systems for Microcomputers,* Prentice-Hall, 1982.

NEEDLEMAN, THEODORE, *Microcomputers for Accountants,* Prentice-Hall, 1983.

PAGE AND HOOPER, *Accounting and Information Systems,* 2nd ed., Reston, 1982.

ROBERTS, MARTIN B., *EDP Controls: A Guide for Auditors and Accountants,* Wiley, 1983.

10

ORDER PROCESSING

The order processing computer application initiates the main accounting cycle at Sporting Goods Distributors, Inc. Orders are revenue-producing transactions, which drive most other production transaction cycles.

The focus of the order processing application is to get a sales order into the computer and track it until it becomes a sale. The application functions as a front end to the accounts receivable application, which takes over the information flow once an order becomes a sale.

This chapter examines SGD Inc.'s order entry method and procedures. It follows the user tasks required to get orders into the computer, make modifications if needed, and print shipping documents. It then reviews the Open Order Report that is automatically generated as a by-product of processing. It concludes with a checklist for application evaluation.

METHODS OF ORDER ENTRY

SGD Inc. uses what is referred to by the distributing industry as "prebilling" or "two-pass billing."

Prebilling

As diagrammed in Figure 10–1, prebill orders are entered as the first process step when an order is received from a customer. Since SGD Inc.'s application is integrated, several things occur automatically. Among them are:

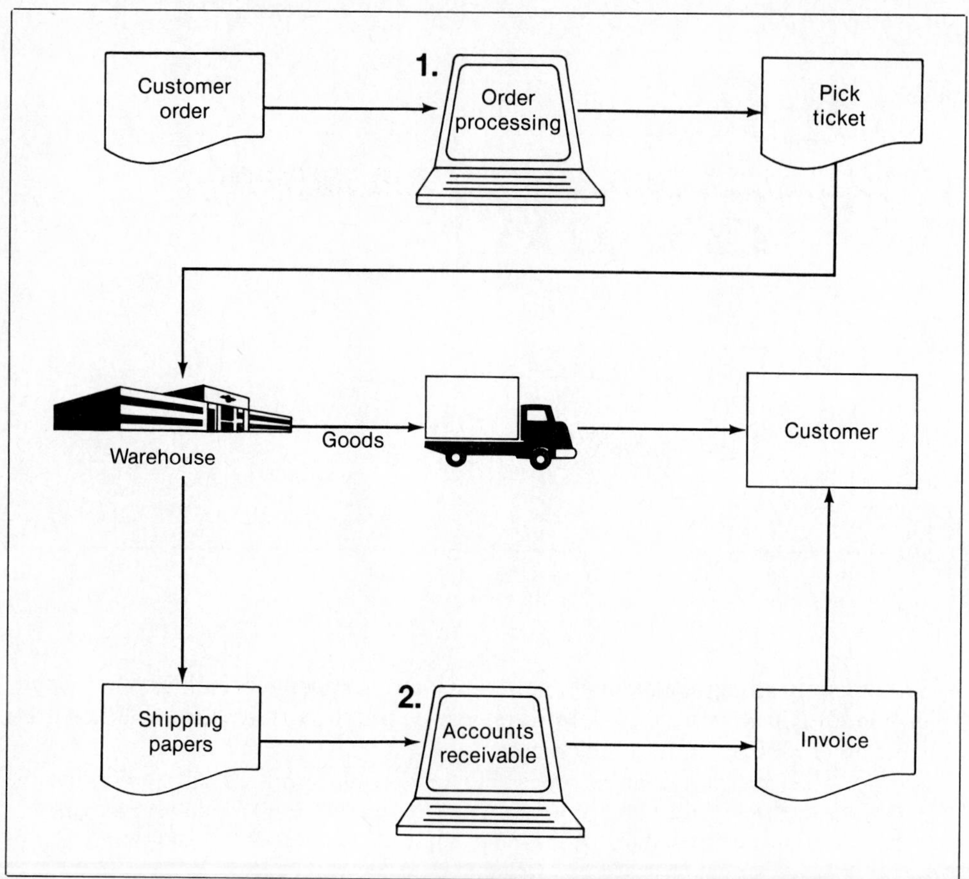

Figure 10–1 Two-pass billing, or prebilling—a common method used in the distribution industry

- A check for inventory item availability and a reservation of the quantity ordered
- A check that the order does not exceed the customer's credit limit
- The printing of a dual-function picking/packing slip as shown in Figure 10–2. The warehouse uses it to gather or pick items, pack, and ship them.

Postbilling

In "postbilling," or "single-pass billing," the system is not notified of an order until it has been shipped. This is the method used in many stand-alone accounts receivable applications.

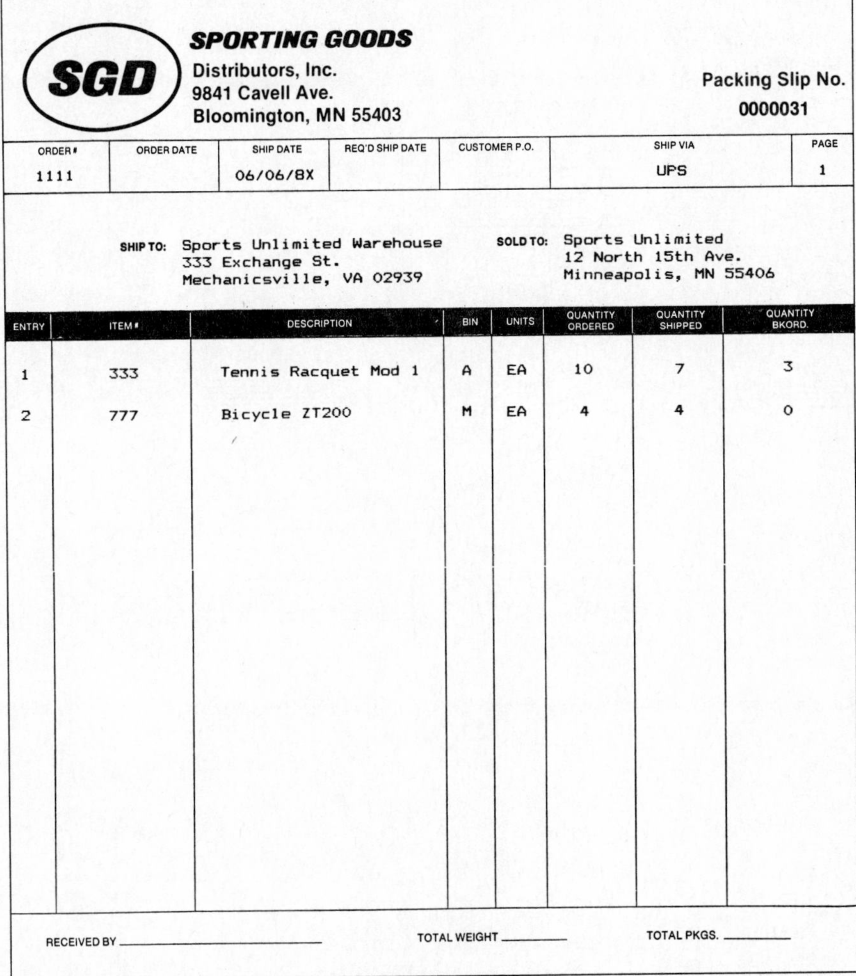

SPORTING GOODS
SGD Distributors, Inc.
9841 Cavell Ave.
Bloomington, MN 55403

Packing Slip No.
0000031

ORDER #	ORDER DATE	SHIP DATE	REQ'D SHIP DATE	CUSTOMER P.O.	SHIP VIA	PAGE
1111		06/06/8X			UPS	1

SHIP TO: Sports Unlimited Warehouse
333 Exchange St.
Mechanicsville, VA 02939

SOLD TO: Sports Unlimited
12 North 15th Ave.
Minneapolis, MN 55406

ENTRY	ITEM #	DESCRIPTION	BIN	UNITS	QUANTITY ORDERED	QUANTITY SHIPPED	QUANTITY BKORD.
1	333	Tennis Racquet Mod 1	A	EA	10	7	3
2	777	Bicycle ZT200	M	EA	4	4	0

RECEIVED BY ________ TOTAL WEIGHT ________ TOTAL PKGS. ________

Figure 10-2 A computer-generated packing slip using a preprinted form

Prebilling is more sophisticated than postbilling. But computerized accounting helps simplify prebilling procedures. Both methods are used by companies receiving telephone and mail orders, like SGD Inc.

Counter Sales

Companies that sell items over-the-counter usually bill customers on the spot. These companies use retail management packages linking point-of-sale terminals or cash registers to a centralized computer. Such systems have different characteristics from those described in this and the next chapter. Other integrated functions, like accounts payable, inventory, and general ledger, however, are similar.

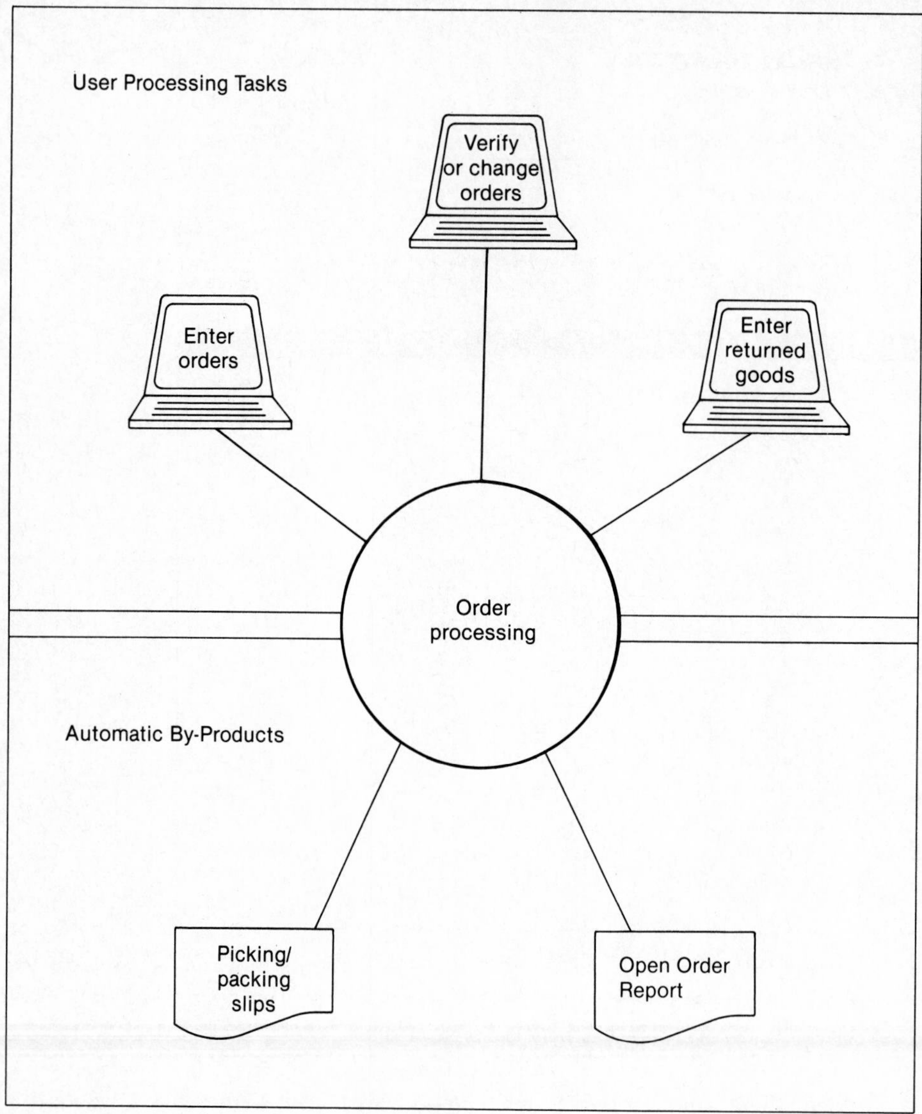

Figure 10-3 User processing tasks and the automatic by-products of the order processing application

PROCESSING OVERVIEW

It is important to SGD Inc. to receive, process, and bill orders rapidly and accurately. To make order entry as efficient as possible, the process works with minimal user intervention.

SGD Inc.'s prebilling package requires three user processing tasks:

- Enter orders
- Verify or change orders
- Enter returned goods

From these processing tasks, the package automatically generates the picking/packing slip and the Open Order Report. Figure 10–3 illustrates the division between interactive user processing tasks and the automatic by-products of these tasks.

SETUP TASKS

Before SGD Inc. could use the order processing application, they created the customer file as described in the next chapter. They also set up tables in the computer as follows:

- *Sales tax table* to store nine sales tax percentages, referenced by codes 1–9.
- *Terms table* to store up to nine different discount percentages and the number of days the discount is allowed. For example, an order sold with terms of "1%/10" means that a 1-percent discount off the bill can be taken up to ten days after the date of the bill. The nine different sets of terms stored are referenced by codes 1–9.
- *General ledger table* to store up to eighteen general ledger account numbers, which are used when posting sales to the general ledger file.

Other similar tables are initialized to support the accounts receivable function.

ORDER ENTRY

When an order comes in to SGD Inc., Ms. Fenton types a minimal amount of information to record the order. From the order processing menu shown in Figure 9–4, she selects the option to enter an order. This produces the screen shown in Figure 10–4.

Before the order header screen appears, Ms. Fenton makes another menu selection to tell the computer if the order is a:

1. New order
2. Shipped order
3. Cash order

She selects the new order option for the Sports Unlimited order.

Order Header

The display in Figure 10–4 is known as the *order header* data entry screen. It accepts all order information except lines of item detail. The detail is held for a second screen.

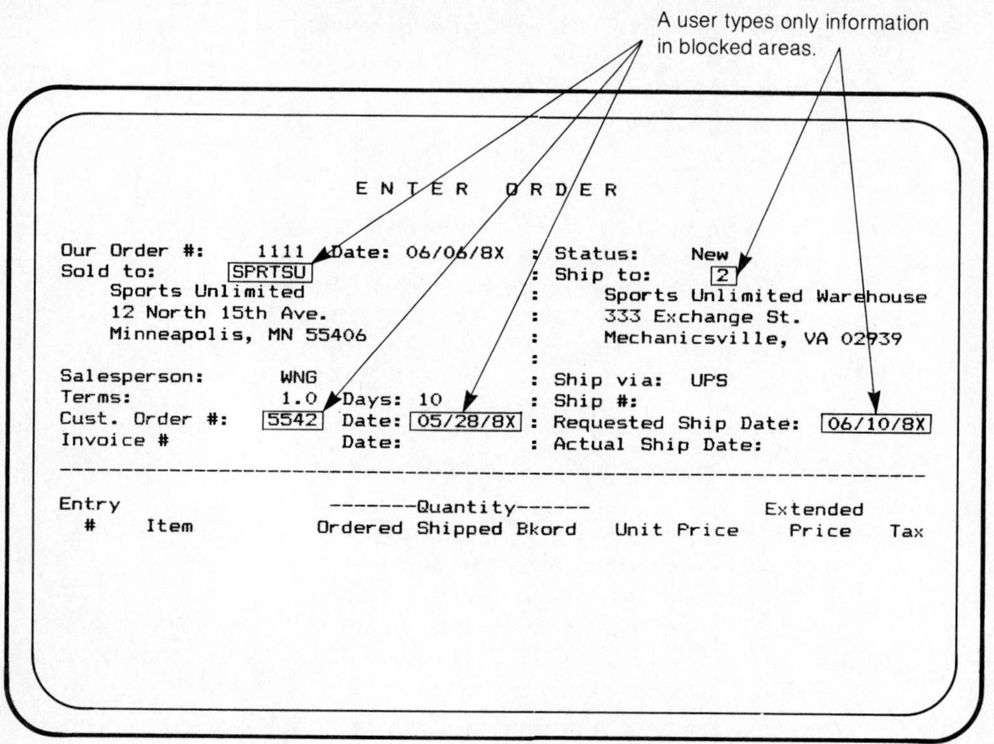

Figure 10–4 A data entry screen to enter order header information

As Figure 10–4 indicates, a minimum amount of order header information needs entering. Much of the information that automatically fills itself in on the form comes from the customer file. The entry of SPRTSU identifies and retrieves the Sports Unlimited customer record. Then the screen fills with the stored information.

Alphabetic customer account identifiers are used because they are easier to recall than numeric identifiers. Usually numeric identifiers require an extra manual step to find the customer number from a printed list. Some systems provide only numeric identifiers.

The customer record automatically supplies the following information:

- Sold to name and address
- Salesperson identifier
- Terms of sale

A numeric entry is required to identify which one of a possible 99 ship-to addresses is used for this order. The ship-to name and address are retrieved from a separate ship-to address file. Ship via carrier information also comes from the ship-to addresses file.

Information unique to the order that needs typing is:

- Customer order number and date
- Requested ship date

Since this is a new order, other items are not applicable, like the invoice number or shipping document number and actual ship date.

SGD Inc.'s order entry date is automatic. It fills in with the date generated by the computer as today's date. The order number is also computer-generated as the next sequential new order number.

An override of any displayed information is possible. For example, assume this order is for "Net 30," or no discount. Ms. Fenton can enter the current terms as a so-called *override* to the one displayed. This does not change the term coded as file information. It affects only the current order record.

The way Ms. Fenton does an override is to type a C when the cursor arrives at the place to be changed. She then types the new information.

As the cursor moves from data element to data element, Ms. Fenton can enter any of the following codes:

Code	*Action*
C	Change the data already displayed.
D	Delete the entire record from the file. A prompt at the bottom of the screen asks for another D to be typed to confirm this action.
L	Print or list a copy of the display on the printer.
M	Return to the application menu.
P	Go to the next page or next data element, whichever is first.
S	Start over at the beginning of the screen or line item.
X	Start over from the beginning of the entire order.

These same rules apply to everything entered. Once Ms. Fenton learned these rules, she was able to use them for all data entry screens throughout the entire package.

Line Items

After header information is completed, Ms. Fenton enters line items using the screen shown in Figure 10–5. Each line item is automatically given an entry number. Generally all Ms. Fenton enters are the item number and the quantity ordered and shipped for each item. Information, such as description and unit price is pulled from the inventory item record and automatically displayed. Extended line amount is automatically calculated and displayed.

If a customer tax code exists, the tax percentage related to the code is calculated for the line item. This amount is added to the tax total shown in the total area at the bottom of the screen.

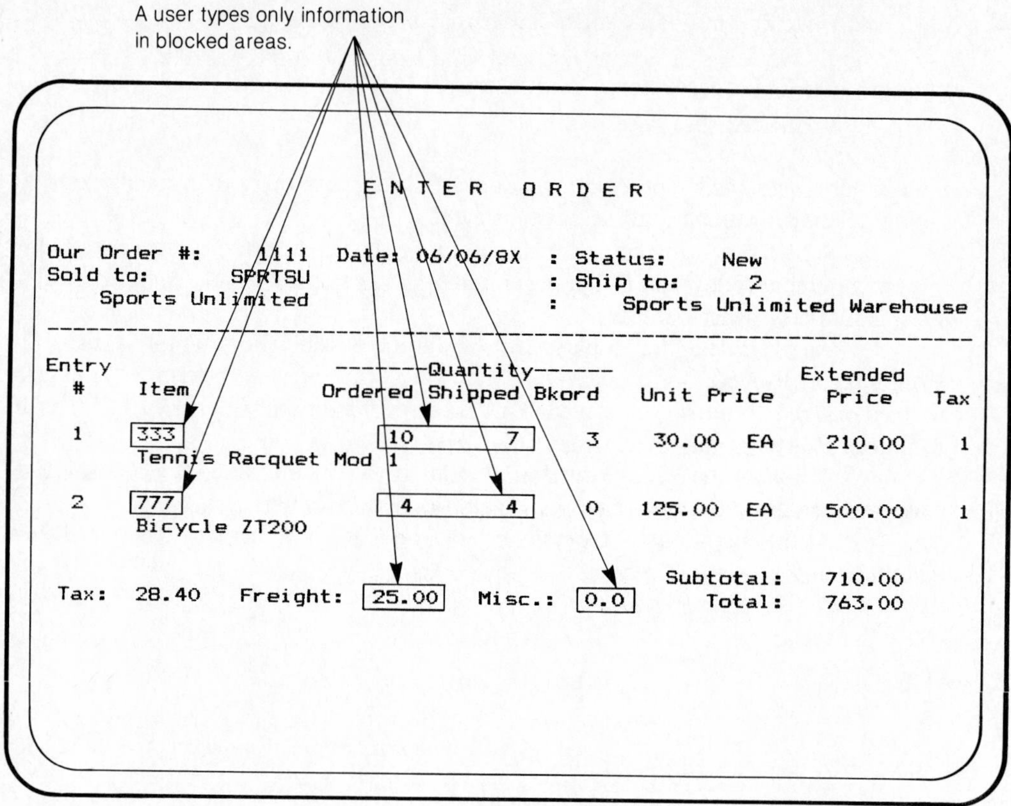

Figure 10-5 A data entry screen to enter, verify, or change order line items

Inventory Item Check

At each line, the quantity ordered is checked in the item record to see if enough stock is on hand and available for shipping. If enough is available, it is entered as the shipped quantity.

If there is not enough of an item to fill an order, a displayed prompt tells Ms. Fenton how much is available. Alternate items are also displayed. Ms. Fenton only adds alternate items to orders that indicate substitutes are permissible.

If alternate items are not desirable, Ms. Fenton types the quantity available as the shipped quantity. A backorder quantity is then automatically calculated as the difference between ordered and shipped quantities.

Each line item entry updates the appropriate inventory item record. For example, all ordered quantities increase the "committed" amount and reduce the "available" amount in the inventory item record.

SGD Inc.'s application provides for price breaks based on quantity ordered. Other applications provide for special promotional prices. In the latter case, the computer checks to see if the order date is within the start and end dates for the special price offer.

When done entering line items, Ms. Fenton types END for item number. The totals are already displayed for verification. She types P to page to the beginning of a new order entry.

Credit Check

After line items are complete, SGD Inc.'s application does a credit limit check. If the order total is under the credit limit, the order becomes a record in the open order file. If not, the order transaction is aborted, and Ms. Fenton is notified with a displayed prompt. She places such orders aside for further manual processing by the credit manager.

PRINT PICKING/PACKING SLIPS

After orders are entered, a multipart form, called a picking/packing slip, is printed for each new order. One copy of the form, called the picking slip, is used in the warehouse to gather, or pick, items from storage bins. Another copy of the form, called the packing slip, is packaged with the order and sent to the customer.

When Ms. Fenton selects the menu option to print picking/packing slips, she is asked to indicate if they will be for:

1. New orders
2. Backorders
3. Lost orders
4. A list of orders

Her daily routine is to print slips for orders with a NEW order status. As slips are printed, the order status is changed to PICKED.

She prints slips for backorders after new inventory stock replenishments are received.

Occasionally she prints slips for lost orders. These are orders with a PICKED status whose picking slips are misplaced. Sometime she will type a list of specific orders for which SGD Inc. wants picking slips prepared.

SGD Inc. uses preprinted forms with preprinted sequence numbers. Ms. Fenton enters the first slip number that will be used. Alternately, if preprinted numbers are not used, any starting number entered is used for sequentially numbering slips.

If some slips are misprinted, it is possible to reprint them. If restarting, a prompt asks for the last good slip number used. The computer begins printing using the next sequential number.

VERIFY OR CHANGE ORDERS

After the picking slip copy is returned from the warehouse, Ms. Fenton verifies orders. To do this she uses the same data entry screens she used to enter order header and line items.

Verifying orders consists mainly of being sure that the quantities actually sent match the quantities listed as shipped in the computer order file. In case of a difference, an adjustment is entered to a line item as needed.

The actual ship date and freight charge are entered at this time. So is any miscellaneous charge assessed.

Selecting the verify orders option from the order processing menu automatically changes any order retrieved from PICKED to VERIFY status. Invoices later get printed for every order with a VERIFY status.

The change option from the application menu similarly allows adjustments to any order. The difference is that an order's status is left alone. Also, in the change function, new line items can be added to orders.

ENTER RETURNED GOODS

Occasionally merchandise is returned to SGD Inc. This results from goods being damaged during shipment or from customer dissatisfaction with an item. Returned goods result in a credit memo.

The screens to enter returned goods look like the order header and line item screens. The only difference is the screen title change to ENTER RETURNED GOODS.

When the returned goods option is selected from the application menu, it automatically causes the data entry to be a credit memo with a RETURNED status. Credit memos are later printed for all items in the order file with a RETURNED status.

Undamaged goods that are being returned to stock are entered as ordinary line items. Goods not being returned to stock are manually entered.

OPEN ORDER REPORT

In addition to the picking/packing slip, another automatic by-product of the order processing application is the Open Order Report. The report, shown in Figure 10–6, allows SGD Inc.'s management to review the status of all ordered items that have not been invoiced.

The option menu for this report is given in Figure 10–7. It shows the variations possible when producing this report. If Ms. Fenton wants a list of all customers with open orders on file, for example, she skips through the pick customers option. But if she wants only a range of customer orders, she enters the first and last customer identifiers in the range. Selecting open orders by inventory item numbers works the same way as selecting customers.

Usually Ms. Fenton produces this report sorted by customer identifier. This gives Mr. Williams and other managers a profile of all unbilled orders by customers. It is examined to see where potential customer problems exist that could be averted.

06/08/8X | Sporting Goods Distributors, Inc. | Page 1

OPEN ORDER REPORT

ORDER	ENTRY	STATUS	CUST ID	DATE ORDER	DATE REQ'D	DATE SHIP	DESCRIPTION ITEM NO.	DESCRIPTION PRICE	QTY AVAIL	QTY/$ ORIG	QUANTITY/DOLLAR ORDERED	QUANTITY/DOLLAR SHIPPED	QUANTITY/DOLLAR BACKORDER
214	1	PICKED	ABLE	05/24		05/26	Ski-Rosner 190		510	8	8	8	0
							420	200.00		1600.00	1600.00	1600.00	.00
1114	1	BKORD	ABLE	06/06	06/15		Ski-Water Adult			10	0	0	10
							666	50.00	2	500.00	1600.00	1600.00	500.00
							TOTAL			2100.00	1600.00	1600.00	500.00
1111	1	BKORD	SPRTSU	06/06	06/10	06/08	Tennis Racquet Mod 1		0	10	0	0	3
							333	30.00		300.00	.00	.00	90.00
							TOTAL			300.00	.00	.00	90.00

Figure 10-6 A daily report of unbilled orders

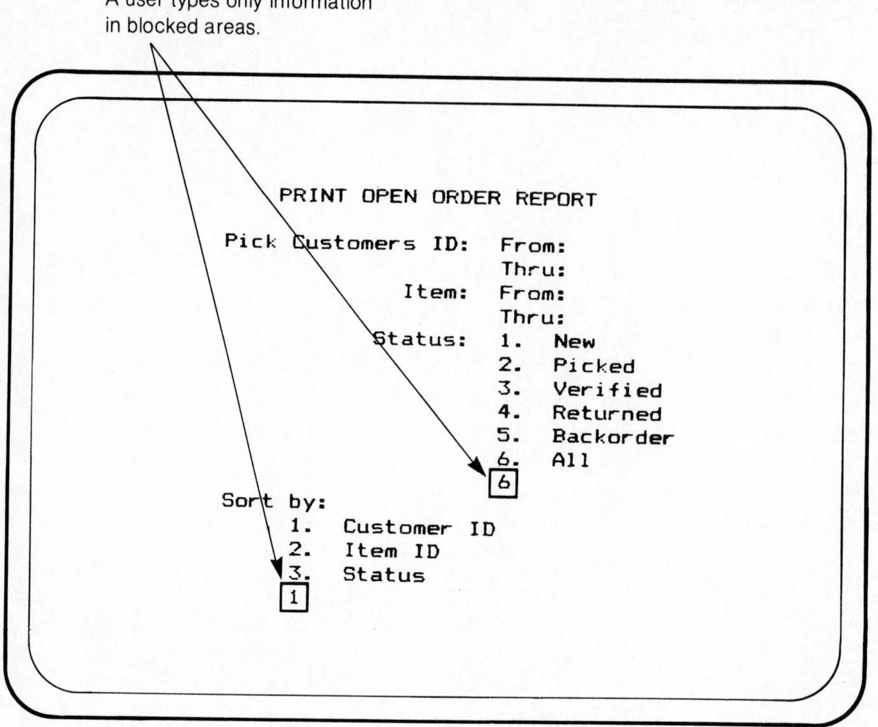

Figure 10-7 A completed menu of options to print the Open Order Report in Figure 10-6

EVALUATION

The checklist in Figure 10-8 is an aid to evaluate an order processing application. It is also an aid to help specify requirements. The list of what a package must do to fulfill requirements helps to narrow candidate packages.

Some capabilities available in SGD Inc.'s package do not exist in all packages. SGD Inc.'s application includes provisions for handling multicompanies and multiusers. It also allows the entry of a hold order status and the entry of noninventoried items.

On the other hand, some users require other types of orders not specifically identified in SGD Inc.'s application. A direct order, for example, is one that is to be delivered directly from a manufacturer to the customer. It is also called a drop shipment order. Blanket orders, another type, are orders placed for shipment in partial quantities at prearranged future dates. Another type is a quotation, which is not really an order at all. A quotation simulates an order so that prices can be developed and quoted to a prospect or customer for a possible sale. Some users also require an ability to print formal order acknowledgements.

Order pricing, as well as variations in discounting terms, cover a range of application possibilities. Packages vary widely in how they handle these and other functions that need close evaluation.

Figure 10-8 Order Processing Checklist

Candidate Packages Names:
A: ____________________
B: ____________________
C: ____________________

Check "must have" items	Rating (Scale: 1 = poor to 10 = excellent) A	B	C
Type			
____Prebilling	____	____	____
____Postbilling	____	____	____
____Cash/counter sales	____	____	____
____Multiuser	____	____	____
Capacities			
____# Customers	____	____	____
____# Ship-to addresses/customers	____	____	____
____# Items	____	____	____
____# Branches	____	____	____
____# Warehouses	____	____	____
____# Companies	____	____	____
____# Orders	____	____	____
____# Line-items/order	____	____	____
____# Prices for all items	____	____	____
____# Quantity breaks for all items	____	____	____
____# Price contracts	____	____	____
Interfaces			
____Accounts receivable	____	____	____
____Inventory	____	____	____
____General ledger	____	____	____
____Report writer	____	____	____
____Other ____________________	____	____	____
Displays Provided			
____Open order inquiry	____	____	____
____Backorder inquiry	____	____	____
____Other ____________________	____	____	____
Order Entry			
____Check credit before accepting customer order	____	____	____
____Hold order status	____	____	____
____Ship-to multiple addresses	____	____	____
Accept:			
____ Noninventoried items	____	____	____
____ Returned goods/credit memo	____	____	____
____ Debit memo	____	____	____
____ Direct shipped order	____	____	____
____ Future orders	____	____	____
____Suggest substitute for out-of-stock items	____	____	____
____Add special charges to order	____	____	____
____Modify or cancel order	____	____	____
____Enter shipped quantities	____	____	____

Figure 10-8 (continued)

Check "must have" items	Rating (Scale: 1 = poor to 10 = excellent) A	B	C
Item Pricing Options			
Item identification:			
____ Numeric only	____	____	____
____ Any characters or numbers	____	____	____
____Automatic by customer type	____	____	____
____Automatic based on quantity ordered	____	____	____
____Entered item price override	____	____	____
____Base unit cost plus mark-up percent pricing	____	____	____
____Contract pricing	____	____	____
____Other ____	____	____	____
Discounting Options			
____Base unit-price minus discount depending on customer and/or item type	____	____	____
____Line item discounts	____	____	____
____Trade discount for entire order	____	____	____
____Other ____	____	____	____
Backorders			
Automatically filled when inventory is received by:			
____ Customer type priority	____	____	____
____ Other ____	____	____	____
____Manually filled by operator who releases selected backorders (system maintains and lists backorders)	____	____	____
____Original order price retained to avoid customer penalty	____	____	____
____Other ____	____	____	____
Printed Output Provided			
____Picking/packing slips	____	____	____
____Preprinted forms	____	____	____
____Prenumbered forms	____	____	____
____Window envelope style	____	____	____
____Open Order Report	____	____	____
Options: ____	____	____	____
____Order acknowledgement	____	____	____
____Shipping labels	____	____	____
Subtotal	____	____	____
Divide by number of items rated for average rating	____	____	____

Transfer Average Rating to Selection Summary: Software, Figure 5-3.

SELF TEST

1. Describe the difference between prebilling and postbiling.
2. Use examples to explain what setup tasks might be needed before using an ordering processing application.
3. What is an order header in a computerized order processing application? What order header information is automatically filled in?
4. What are line items? What information is manually entered in a computerized order processing application?
5. Explain what automated inventory item and credit limit checks are.
6. What is a picking/packing slip used for?
7. What is the purpose of SGD Inc.'s verify orders task?
8. Use an example to explain what a credit memo is.
9. Explain the purpose of the Open Order Report.
10. Identify two areas that need close attention when evaluating order processing applications.

EXERCISES

1. *WMK Associates Case.* Mr. Kennedy wants to continue to automate the company's accounting procedures by adding the sales order processing application. Do some preliminary investigatory work by finding three reviews of sales order processing packages in recent periodical articles. Write an analysis of the packages that compares capacities, capabilities, and features offered. Use the Checklist in Figure 10–8 as a guide.
2. *WMK Associates Case.* Write to the companies identified in exercise 1. Ask for detailed information on their order processing packages (unless information is already available from Chapter 9, exercises 2 and 3).

   When literature is available, prepare a written or oral report on the differences in package:

   - Order entry types accepted
   - Backorder handling
   - Information displays provided
   - Printed output provided
3. *WMK Associates Case.* Research the availability of sales order entry applications in software or periodical directories of computer applications. Write to four or five companies for more detailed information. Follow the requirements of exercise 2 for executing this exercise.
4. Arrange to have a demonstration of a sales order processing package. Before the demonstration, read the User's Guide to learn about:

   - Setup tasks
   - Operating procedures
   - Printed and displayed output

   After the demonstration, make an oral or written report about how the first two items were executed. Use the outputs to explain how they compare to other packages you have investigated.

ACCOUNTS RECEIVABLE

The accounts receivable computer application closes the revenue-producing transaction that begins as a sales order. Most of SGD Inc.'s sales are to companies who maintain approved credit "accounts" with them. Once a sale is made "on account," the transaction is called a "receivable." Their accounts receivable application maintains records of both customer sales and payments on account.

This chapter examines SGD Inc.'s computerized accounts receivable procedures. The first one is to print customer invoices for verified orders. Then other daily work procedures, such as adding customers to the file and entering cash received from customers, are examined.

SGD Inc.'s method of maintaining accounts receivable is also examined in relation to producing monthly customer statements. The chapter concludes with a checklist for evaluating accounts receivable applications.

PROCESSING OVERVIEW

SGD Inc.'s accounts receivable package prints invoices, as shown in Figure 11–1, for all orders with a VERIFY status. The procedure requires no user intervention other than starting the print process.

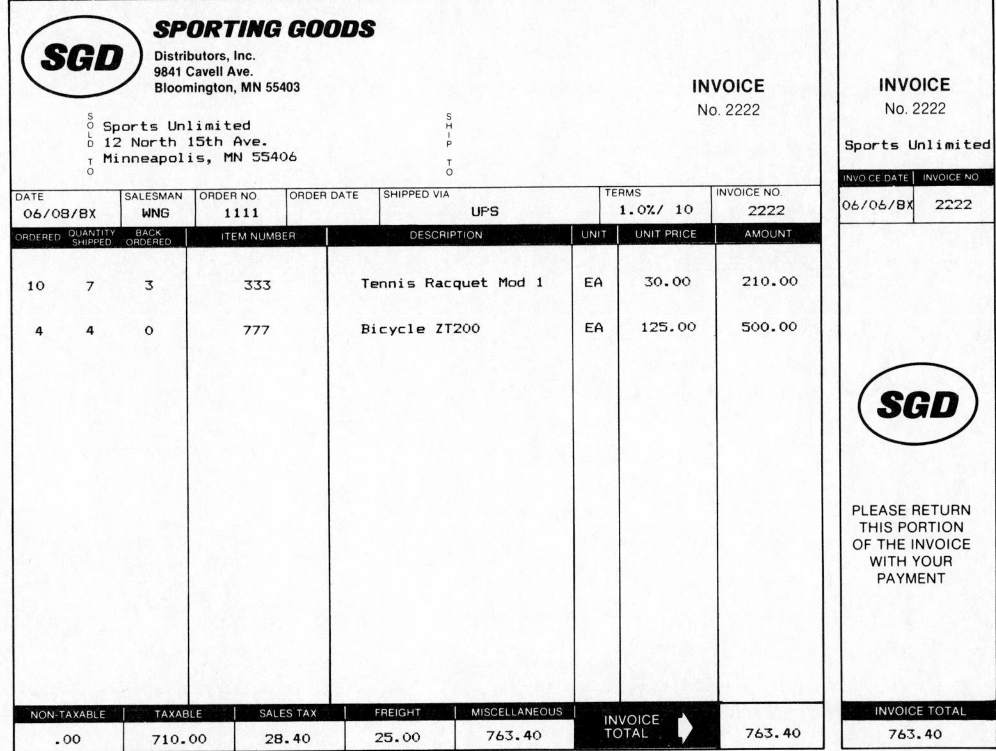

SPORTING GOODS
SGD
Distributors, Inc.
9841 Cavell Ave.
Bloomington, MN 55403

INVOICE
No. 2222

SOLD TO: Sports Unlimited
12 North 15th Ave.
Minneapolis, MN 55406

SHIP TO:

DATE	SALESMAN	ORDER NO.	ORDER DATE	SHIPPED VIA	TERMS	INVOICE NO.
06/08/8X	WNG	1111		UPS	1.0%/ 10	2222

ORDERED	QUANTITY SHIPPED	BACK ORDERED	ITEM NUMBER	DESCRIPTION	UNIT	UNIT PRICE	AMOUNT
10	7	3	333	Tennis Racquet Mod 1	EA	30.00	210.00
4	4	0	777	Bicycle ZT200	EA	125.00	500.00

NON-TAXABLE	TAXABLE	SALES TAX	FREIGHT	MISCELLANEOUS	INVOICE TOTAL
.00	710.00	28.40	25.00	763.40	763.40

INVOICE
No. 2222
Sports Unlimited

INVOICE DATE	INVOICE NO.
06/06/8X	2222

SGD

PLEASE RETURN THIS PORTION OF THE INVOICE WITH YOUR PAYMENT

INVOICE TOTAL
763.40

Figure 11-1 A computer-generated invoice using a preprinted form

The main accounts receivable daily processing activities that do require user intervention are:

- Add customers to the file
- Enter cash receipts

From these activities the package is capable of generating a host of user audit and control reports. Most control reports are printed on demand as needed.

Figure 11-2 illustrates the division between interactive user processing tasks and the automatic by-products of these tasks.

Figure 11-2 highlights the customer statement as an automatic by-product. Statements are sent to customers once a month. They summarize for the month all activity that transpired between SGD Inc. and a customer. An example of a statement appears in Figure 11-3.

PRINT INVOICES

Ms. Fenton does not handle SGD Inc.'s accounts receivable functions. Ms. Malone is responsible for generating invoices every day. The separation of duties is a common

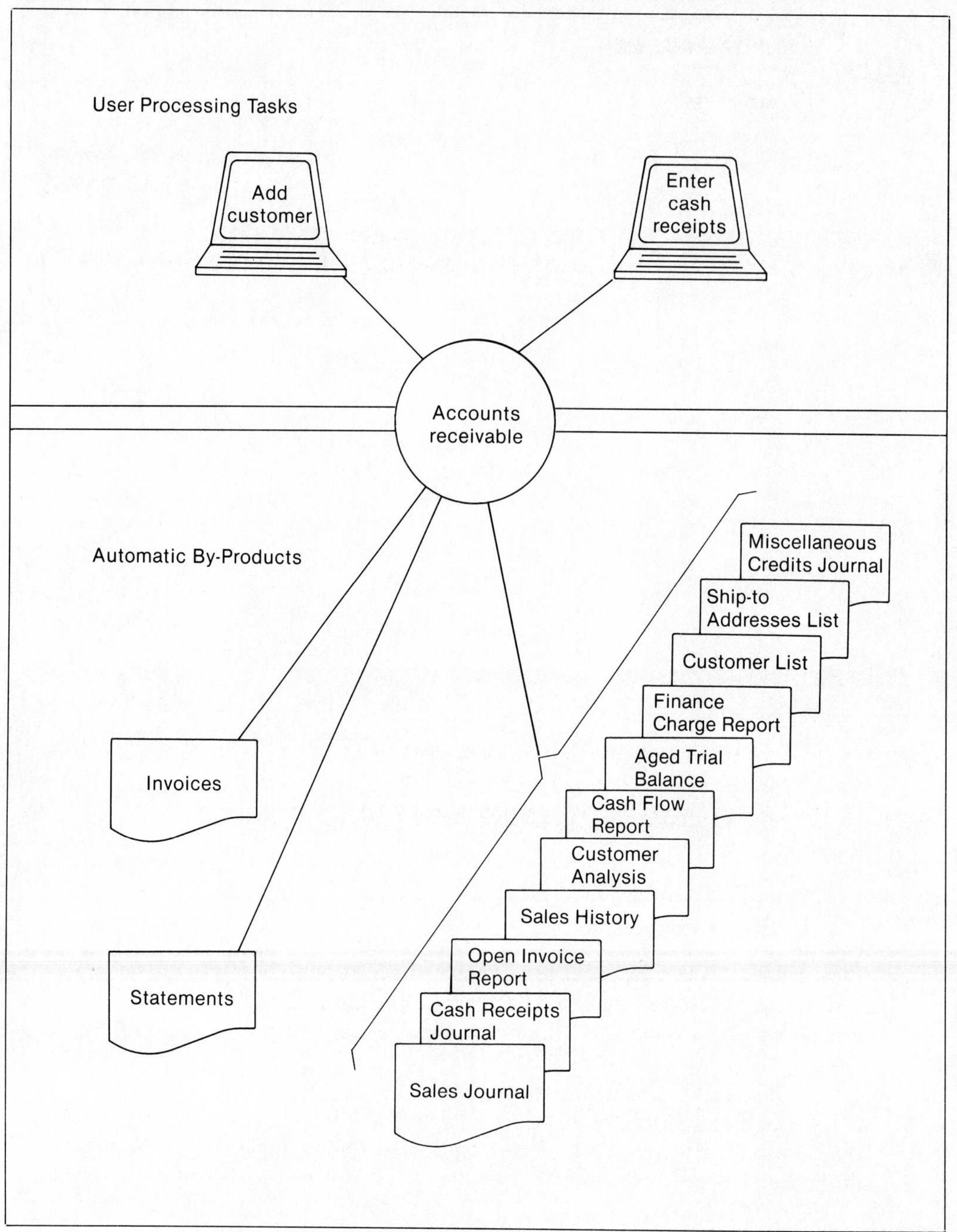

Figure 11-2 User processing tasks and the automatic by-products of the accounts receivable application

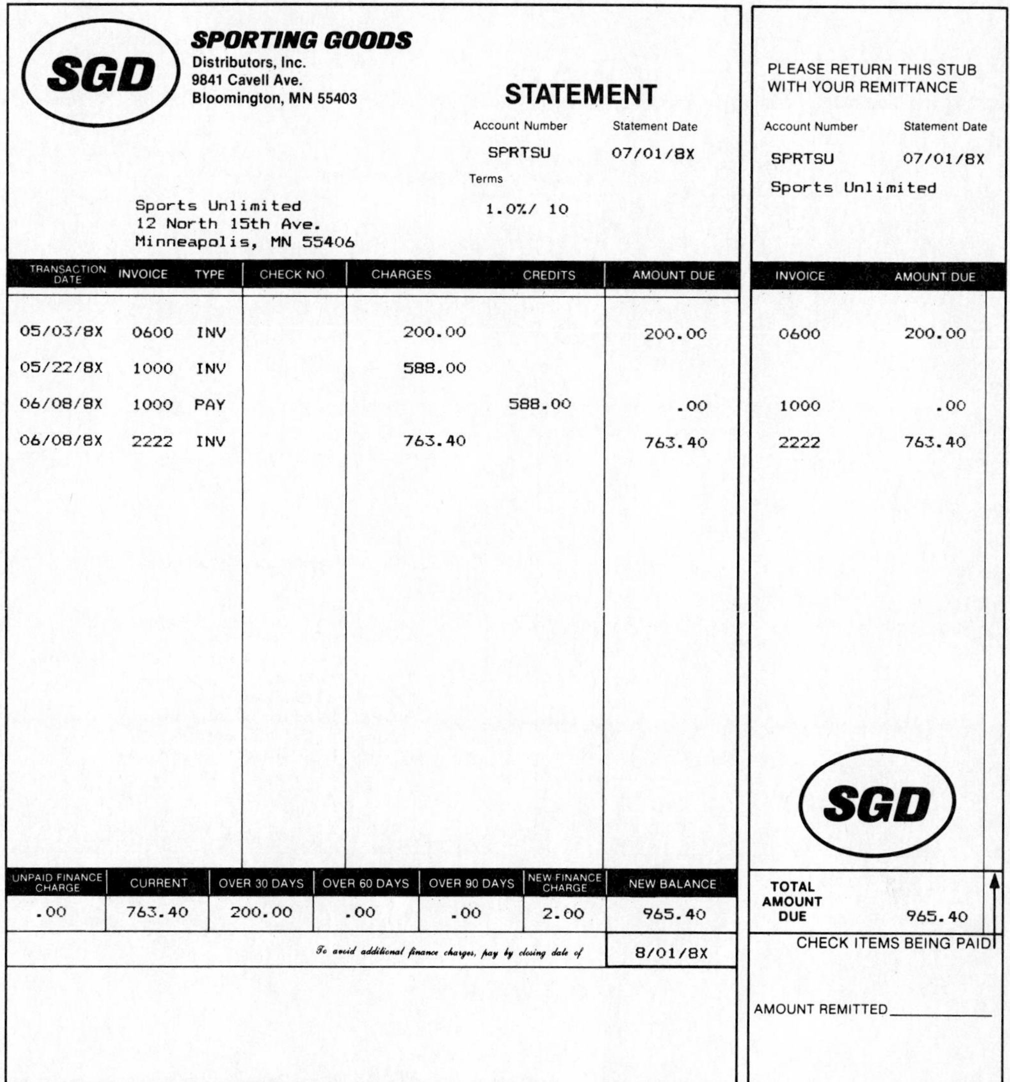

SGD SPORTING GOODS Distributors, Inc.
9841 Cavell Ave.
Bloomington, MN 55403

STATEMENT

Account Number: SPRTSU
Statement Date: 07/01/8X
Terms: 1.0%/ 10

Sports Unlimited
12 North 15th Ave.
Minneapolis, MN 55406

TRANSACTION DATE	INVOICE	TYPE	CHECK NO	CHARGES	CREDITS	AMOUNT DUE
05/03/8X	0600	INV		200.00		200.00
05/22/8X	1000	INV		588.00		
06/08/8X	1000	PAY			588.00	.00
06/08/8X	2222	INV		763.40		763.40

UNPAID FINANCE CHARGE	CURRENT	OVER 30 DAYS	OVER 60 DAYS	OVER 90 DAYS	NEW FINANCE CHARGE	NEW BALANCE
.00	763.40	200.00	.00	.00	2.00	965.40

To avoid additional finance charges, pay by closing date of 8/01/8X

PLEASE RETURN THIS STUB WITH YOUR REMITTANCE

Account Number: SPRTSU
Statement Date: 07/01/8X
Sports Unlimited

INVOICE	AMOUNT DUE
0600	200.00
1000	.00
2222	763.40

SGD

TOTAL AMOUNT DUE 965.40

CHECK ITEMS BEING PAID

AMOUNT REMITTED____________

Figure 11-3 A computer-generated customer statement using a preprinted form

accounting practice for security and control purposes.

To print invoices Ms. Malone selects the daily work option from the accounts receivable menu, as shown in Figure 11-4. Another menu appears and she selects the print invoices option.

She is then given a choice to accept today's date to print on all invoices or to enter another date. She normally uses today's date. She often uses another option to include a short message on all invoices. Usually it is "Thank you for your order."

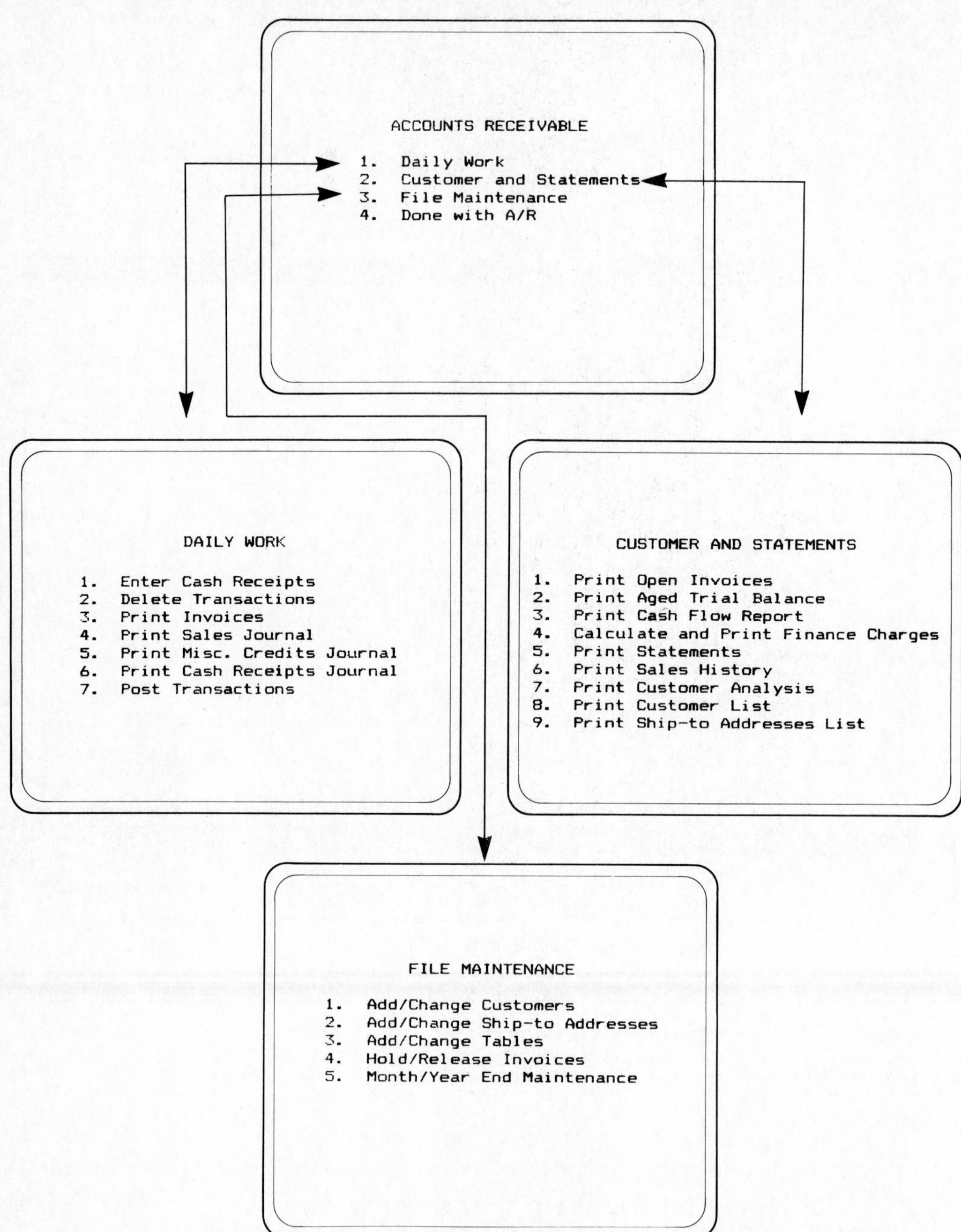

Figure 11-4 The main accounts receivable application menu and submenus

Since SGD Inc. uses preprinted invoice forms, Ms. Malone indicates the first invoice number to use. Should some invoices misprint, she can restart and enter the last good invoice number so that printing begins with the next sequential number.

A test pattern prints to achieve proper forms alignment and is normal when using preprinted forms or labels. The test pattern repeats as often as needed. When forms are properly aligned actual invoice printing begins.

Credit memos print at the same time as invoices. A credit memo is an invoice that has CREDIT MEMO typed across the header.

Everything printed has a status change from either VERIFIED or RETURNED to INVOICED.

Print Journals

After invoicing, Ms. Malone prints the Sales Journal, as shown in Figure 11-5, and the Miscellaneous Credits Journal. The Sales Journal in Figure 11-5 contains full detail, whereas a summary version prints only the total line for each invoice. The journals are permanent audit trails of all invoice and credit memo activity for the day.

The menu of options to print the Sales Journal appears in Figure 11-6. SGD Inc.'s accountants want the report to list all customers with full invoice detail. They also like the report printed in invoice number order.

A similar menu of options appears for all reports throughout SGD Inc.'s integrated accounting package.

Post Transactions

After journals are printed, Ms. Malone posts transactions. This is a separate procedure that uses the open order file to update four other files in SGD Inc.'s database. It is an unattended operation once initiated.

The first file updated is the open invoice file. A new open invoice record is created in the file for each invoice printed. The record is a summary of the invoice. Its content resembles an INV or invoice line on the customer statement. The open invoice file is the main file used to print the customer statement.

The second file updated is the sales history file. It retains a copy of the detailed invoice lines for use in sales analysis.

These two file updates eliminate a need to carry INVOICED status orders on the open order file. They are therefore deleted and the open order file is compressed. It is ready to be refilled with the next day's orders.

The third file updated is the customer file. Balance due amounts in the customer file are updated to reflect new invoiced amounts.

The last update is the general ledger file. Summarized amounts are posted to general ledger accounts as set up in the application's general ledger table. The table is created when the application is initialized.

An audit trail listing prints to trace totals of all general ledger postings. Ms. Malone compares the totals to journal totals to cross-check processing accuracy.

```
06/08/8X                                   Sporting Goods Distributors, Inc.                                   Page   1
                                   S A L E S   J O U R N A L  -  F U L L   D E T A I L


TRANSACTION     CUST   ORDER   --INVOICE---   ----QUANTITY----   ------------ITEM-----------   -----UNIT-----            T
 NO.  ENTRY      ID     NO.     NO.   DATE    ORDER SHIP BKORD   NUMBER     DESCRIPTION        PRICE    COST    AMOUNT   X

0008   001     SPRTSU  1111    2222   06/08     10    7    3       333  Tennis Racquet Mod 1    30.00   15.00   210.00   1
       002                                       4    4    0       777  Bicycle ZT200          125.00   65.00   500.00   1
                                  T O T A L   NON-TAX         TAXABLE        SALES TAX      FREIGHT    MISC.     CREDIT
                                                  .00          710.00            28.40        25.00      .00     763.40

0009   001     ABLE    1114    2223   06/08     10    0   10       666  Ski-Water Adult         50.00   25.00      .00   1
                                                 8    8    0       777  Bicycle ZT200          125.00   65.00  1000.00   1
                                              NON-TAX         TAXABLE        SALES TAX      FREIGHT    MISC.     CREDIT
                                  T O T A L       .00         1000.00            40.00          .00      .00    1040.81

                                              NON-TAX         TAXABLE        SALES TAX      FREIGHT    MISC.     CREDIT
                       G R A N D   T O T A L S    .00         1710.00            68.40        25.00      .00    1804.21


                                      T A X   S U M M A R Y

                                           SALES    TAX     TAX
                                  TYPE    AMOUNT     %    AMOUNT          SALES TOTAL    1710.00
                                    0        .00    .00      .00          COST TOTAL      885.00
                                    1    1710.00   4.00    68.40
                                    2        .00    .00      .00
```

Figure 11-5 A daily Sales Journal with full detail

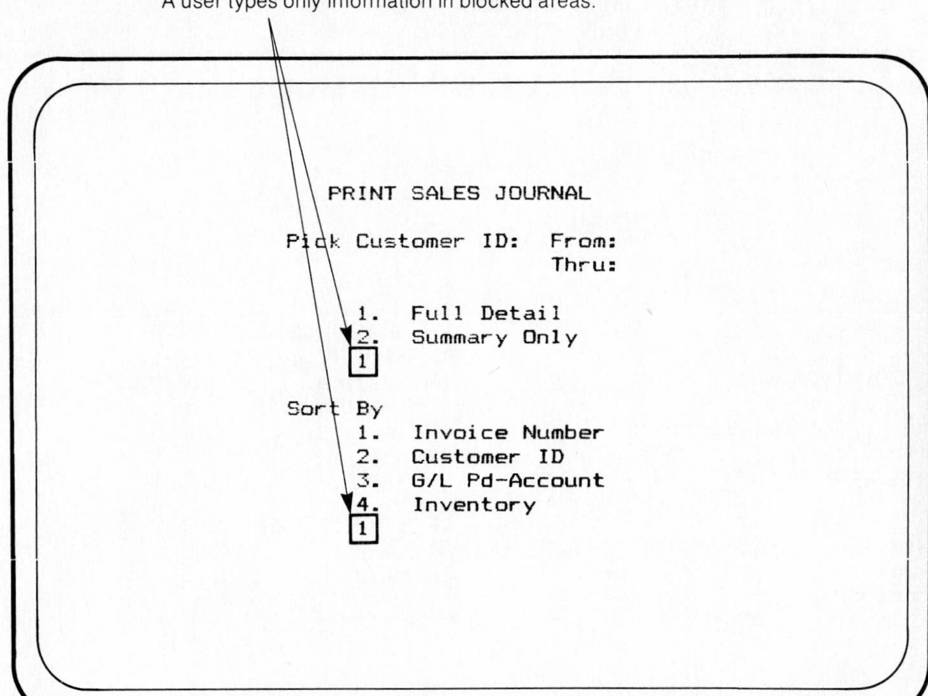

Figure 11-6 A completed menu of options to print the Sales Journal in Figure 11–5

Some applications do not need a separate post transactions procedure. These applications post every time a transaction is entered. They offer instantly updated files versus daily or periodically updated files. Sometime these packages require a user to accept trade-offs like slower processing, fewer audit trails, or more complex data entry session controls.

ADD CUSTOMERS

While printing invoices and posting transactions are considered automatic functions, adding customers to the customer file is not. It requires user entry of information as identified in Figure 11-7.

The same data entry editing commands are used to enter customer information that are used to enter orders.

To add the Sports Unlimited account to SGD Inc.'s customer file, Ms. Malone types the alphabetic customer ID. The credit manager assigns an ID to all new accounts. She also types static information like name, address, phone number, and the code of the salesperson assigned to the account. The credit limit is authorized by the credit manager and represents the maximum amount the customer can owe at one time.

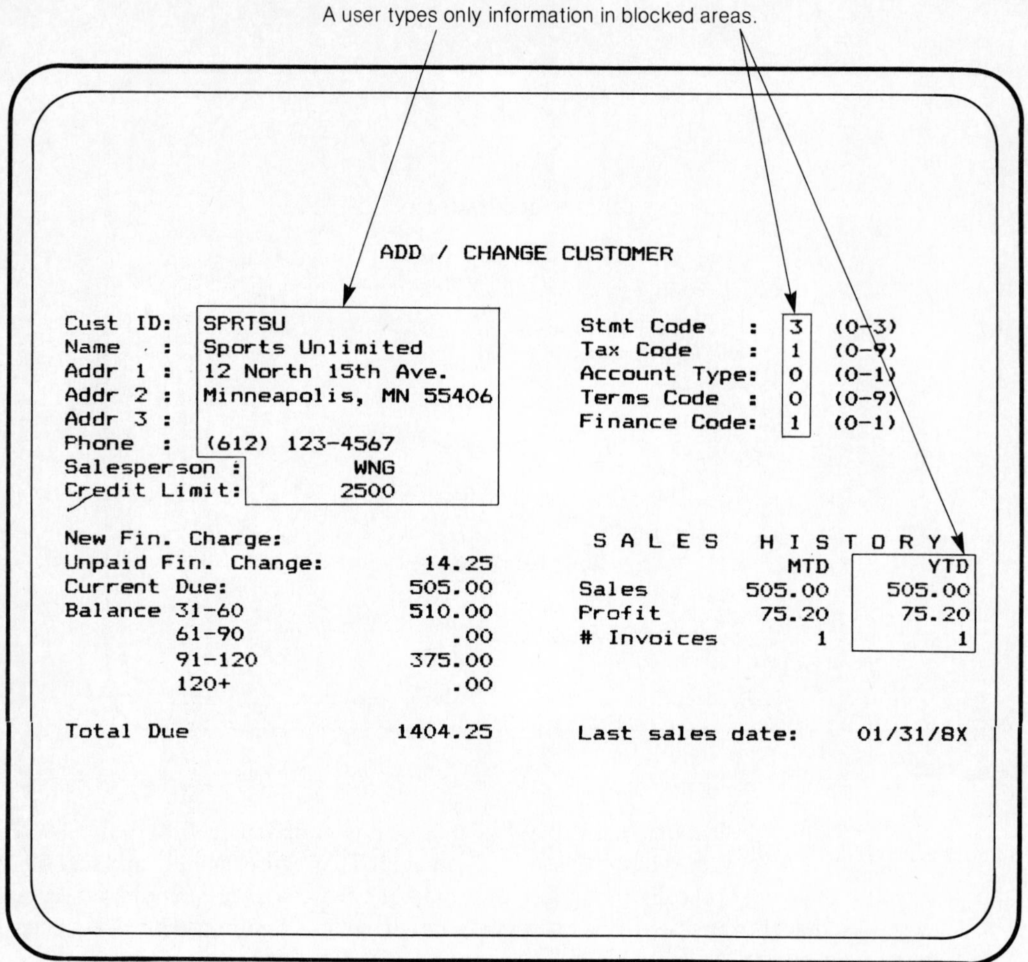

Figure 11-7 A data entry screen to add a customer to the customer file

The coded area relates to tables created when the accounting system was initially installed. At that time the tax codes and terms codes were established and set up as tables that are described in Chapter 10.

Other tables established at the same time provide codes for:

Code	*Meaning*
Statement Code:	
0	Send no invoices or statements
1	Send statements only
2	Send invoices only
3	Send both statements and invoices

Code	*Meaning*
Account Type Code:	
0	Open invoice account
1	Balance forward account
Finance Code:	
0	Finance charges are not assessed
1	Finance charges are assessed

As Figure 11–7 reveals, Sports Unlimited is to receive both statements and invoices. They are to be assessed finance charges for overdue amounts. They will be maintained on the computer as an open invoice account.

Account Types

There are two conventional ways to maintain a receivables account, whether computerized or not. One is the open item method. Another is the balance forward method. Some companies like SGD Inc. have both open item and balance forward customers on the same system.

The *balance forward* is the simpler of the two methods. It keeps one balance-forward total of all unpaid invoices. Payments are subtracted from one lump sum.

Accounts of this type get monthly statements that list all transactions for only the current month. Transactions are new invoices, credit memos, and payments. Unpaid invoices from previous months are summarized into the one-line balance forward amount. The balance due on a statement becomes the balance forward on next month's statement.

The *open item method* is more detailed. A customer's monthly statement, when using this method, lists each invoice that remains unpaid or "open." Even a three-month-old unpaid invoice is listed. This is the kind of statement shown in Figure 11–3.

Account Activity

After the static information, sales history detail is added to the customer record. Other information, like balances due and finance charges, comes from the post transactions update. This requires first creating invoices in the open invoice file. Then the posting function is used to update balances automatically.

A change routine is used as needed to change static information in a customer record. Deleting a customer record from the file is allowed only if all account balances are zero.

Ship-To Addresses

SGD Inc.'s application provides for a separate ship-to address file. Up to 99 ship-to addresses can be stored for each customer. The data entry screen to add ship-to addresses is given in Figure 11–8. The same data entry rules are in effect that are used in order entry.

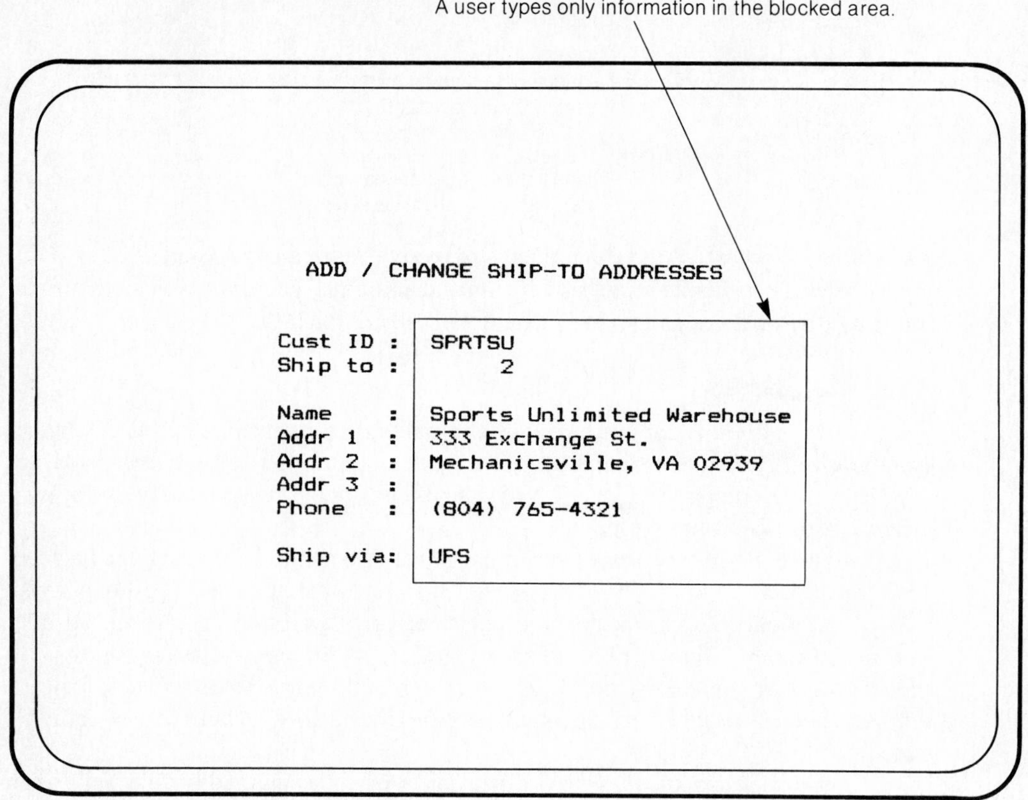

Figure 11-8 A data entry screen for entering customer ship-to addresses

ENTER CASH RECEIPTS

Entering cash received from customers to pay off open invoices is the main user-intensive accounts receivable task. The data entry screen to enter cash receipts is given in Figure 11-9.

The same data entry rules apply as used earlier. For example, the entry of a C in any supplied field will blank it out and allow a change entry. Two fields are immediately supplied. The date is today's date. The general ledger period always corresponds to the month in today's date, unless Ms. Malone changes it.

When Ms. Malone enters SPRTSU for the customer identifier, the name, and the account type of the customer display. She then enters the customer's check number and an invoice number to which payment will be applied. The number and name of the general ledger account appear. It is usually 1010 accounts receivable for a normal cash receipts entry. This information comes from the accounts receivable table of general ledger accounts. All she does is approve the account number displayed.

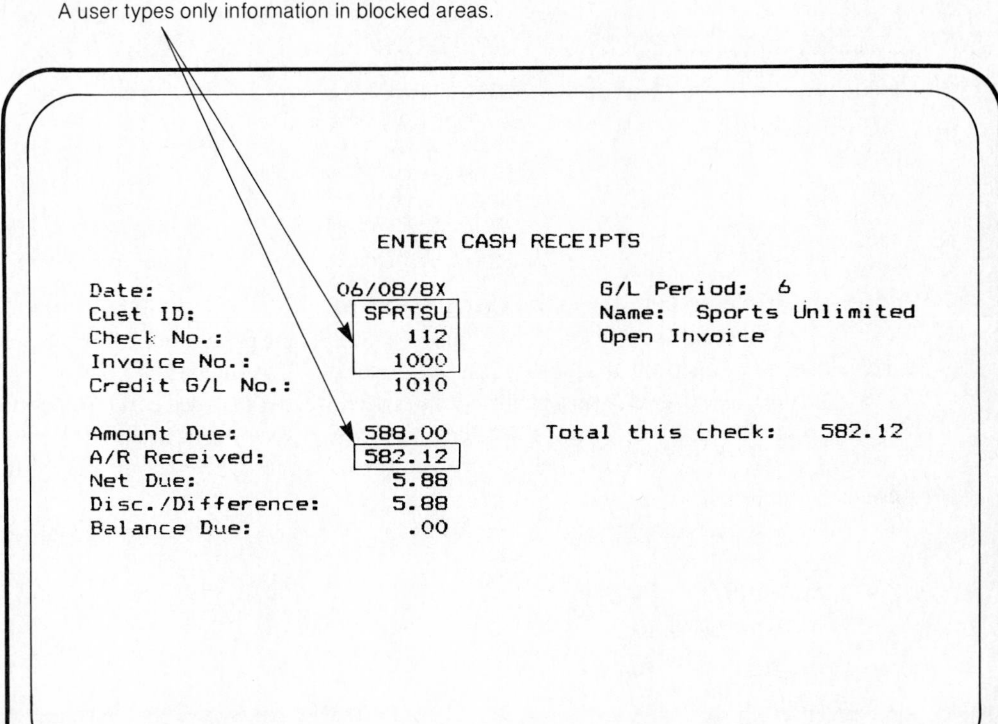

Figure 11-9 A data entry screen to record cash receipts

The invoice amount due also displays. Ms. Malone enters the amount of the payment to apply. In the example case it is the full amount. The payment is within the allowable ten-day discount period, so the discount amount automatically appears on the discount line. Since the Sports Unlimited discount matches the net due, the balance due is zero.

If the same check is to be applied to several invoices, another screen repeats repetitive information from the previous entry. New information to enter includes a new invoice number and the information on the lower left of the screen. With each invoice entry in the A/R Received field, the amount in "Total this check" keeps incrementing to show the total balance entered.

Sometime customers do not specify invoices against which payment is to be applied. Should this happen, Ms. Malone has the option to view all open invoices, one at a time, to determine check allocation.

The cash receipts entry procedure varies for a balance forward customer. An aging period code needs to be entered, instead of invoice numbers. The code, as follows, indicates which period to apply a payment:

Aging Code	*Apply Payment to*
0	Oldest balance first
1	Any unpaid finance charge
2	Balance: 120+ days
3	Balance: 91–120 days
4	Balance: 61–90 days
5	Balance: 31–60 days
6	Current balance

Periods can be chosen until the entire check is applied.

When Ms. Malone is through entering cash receipts she prints the Cash Receipts Journal. It is an audit trail of all cash transaction activity for the day.

During the end-of-day post transactions procedure, as described earlier, all cash receipt transactions also get posted to the open invoice file. Every transaction becomes one record in the file. The record gets printed on the customer statement as a PAY or payment line.

The post transactions procedure updates the following general ledger accounts:

- Cash sales
- Accounts receivable
- Sales tax
- Freight
- Miscellaneous
- Cash receipts
- Discounts
- Inventory
- Finance charge

Posted amounts are printed as an audit trail after the procedure is executed.

PRINT REPORTS

Throughout the month SGD Inc. depends on reports generated by the accounts receivable application. These reports include one listing critical to daily operations, the Open Invoice Report. This report lists all invoices, credits, and payments in the open invoice file. It is a constant reference list for sales and accounts receivable personnel.

In addition to this report, some packages provide a display of a customer's account. This includes a one-line listing of all open invoice activity. Such a display is a convenience when answering telephone customer inquiries.

Automatically generated lists and mailing labels of customer and ship-to addresses are other daily print needs met by the package. Labels are used for shipping goods and promotions in addition to other uses.

Some other more important reports, from SGD Inc.'s management perspective, are described below.

Aged Trial Balance

The Aged Trial Balance report lists customer balances aged into periods from current to over 120 days. An example of the report, printed in summary style, is given in Figure 11–10. A full-detail version, listing and aging every customer open invoice, is also available.

SGD Inc. uses this report to see who owes them money and who is paying late. The report is an indicator of collection performance, and its status foreshadows cash flow profits.

This report generates corrective action that includes everything from a gentle phone reminder to customers to pay through placing a bad debt with a credit service for collection.

Open items on the summary and full detail reports are aged by current, 30-, 60-, 90-, and 120-day periods. They are the periods most commonly used.

The credit manager uses the Aged Trial Balance to guard against unfavorable trends. Measures to reverse a trend, such as an increase in 60- and 90-day accounts, can be instituted once such information is known.

Cash Flow Report

A companion to the Aged Trial Balance report is the Cash Flow Report. It is printed in the exact same format. The only difference is that the Cash Flow Report lets a manager specify any four dates. It provides SGD Inc.'s managers with an approximate idea of how much cash is due to be received within any of the four dates specified.

Sales History

SGD Inc. can produce the Sales History report in one-line summary form, as shown in Figure 11–11. The report can also be printed with full line item detail for any range of dates up to one year. When full detail is requested, additional information is provided, such as listing profit by invoice.

The Sales History report can be sequenced any of four ways, as follows:

- *Item number* identifies products that are the most and least profitable. On examining this report, SGD Inc.'s management asks, "Is the sales effort directed towards the most profitable products?"
- *Product category* identifies groups of products that are the most and least profitable lines for SGD Inc. to carry.
- *Customer* identifies which customers are the most profitable. From this summary, management asks, "Does the sales staff presently spend the most time with these customers?"
- *Salesperson* identifies which salespeople are the most profitable. The report answers the question, "Are the leading volume salespeople also the most profitable?"

06/30/8X Sporting Goods Distributors, Inc. Page 1

A G E D   T R I A L   B A L A N C E - S U M M A R Y

CUSTOMER			AGED BALANCE				
ID	NAME	AMOUNT	CURRENT	OVER 30	OVER 60	OVER 90	OVER 120
ABLE	Able Active Sports	5400.11	.00	.00	5400.11	.00	.00
SPRTSU	Sports Unlimited	963.40	763.40	200.00	.00	.00	.00
G R A N D T O T A L S		6363.51	763.40	200.00	5400.11	.00	.00

Figure 11-10 An on-demand summary version of the Aged Trial Balance

06/08/8X Sporting Goods Distributors, Inc. Page 1

S A L E S   H I S T O R Y - S U M M A R Y

CUSTOMER					
ID	NAME	COST	SALES	PROFIT	%
ABLE	Able Active Sports	26,120.25	37,252.80	11,132.55	29.9
SPRTSU	Sports Unlimited	3,805.21	5,535.40	1,729.83	31.3
G R A N D T O T A L S		29,925.46	42,788.20	12,862.38	30.1

Figure 11-11 An on-demand report of profit by customer

The consequences of these sales reports are considerable. SGD Inc. adjusts its marketing strategies based on answers that the reports provide.

Customer Analysis

The Customer Analysis report gives management a detailed profile about credit and sales activity. It includes the average invoice amount for both month- and year-to-date. It is used for further analysis of customer account status, activity, and profitability.

PRINT STATEMENTS

One of the most important by-products of accounts receivable processing is the automatic generation of monthly customer statements. The statement is the second document sent to remind a customer of an obligation to pay. With timely statement mailing, SGD Inc. improved its cash flow and reduced its need to borrow operating cash.

There is no user intervention to print statements except to set up preprinted forms and start the process. An example of the SGD Inc. statement for an open item customer is given in Figure 11–3.

Before statements are printed, Ms. Malone runs a separate program that calculates finance charges. The program uses a table to calculate assessments. A Finance Charge Report prints as an audit trail. The program updates the finance charge in a customer's record.

A prepared return stub appears on the right of the statement. It helps Ms. Malone to apply cash to specific invoices when checks are received.

Dunning Messages

SGD Inc.'s application allows dunning messages to be printed on statements. Messages can correspond to statements that have balances overdue by 90, 60, or 30 days. A 35-character message, such as "Your payment is overdue," could be set for over 60-day-old balances. A more severe message could appear for older balances.

If an account does not receive a dunning message, it gets a general message. The usual one is, "Thank you for your business." Sometime Ms. Malone changes the general message to a holiday greeting. Some companies use the general message feature to announce sales or promotions.

END OF MONTH

Each month- and year-end special procedures are followed. Primarily they are file maintenance tasks that execute without user intervention after started. Often they are time-consuming and all other processing comes to a halt until they are completed.

Some tasks that execute include:

- Delete paid invoices from the open invoice file and compress the file.
- Shift the aging in the customer file.

- Verify balances in the customer file against the balances in the open invoice file.
- Delete sales history records for selected periods.

EVALUATION

Evaluating an accounts receivable package is relatively straightforward if requirements are specified. The checklist in Figure 11-12 serves as a guide to help specify requirements and to help evaluate candidate packages.

Some integrated accounting packages include the invoicing function with the order entry application. Other packages provide no invoicing function at all. In such a case, summary invoice information is manually entered to generate statements.

Some packages offer separate add-on features like a sales analysis application. Another might include a salesperson commission accounting application.

Most packages offer a wide variety of reports. With the added capability of a report writer, a company like SGD Inc. can generate any report desired based on the availability of the data.

The data contained in the customer, order, and sales history files are especially important if a report writer capability is provided. SGD Inc. did a detailed check of file content that paid off with every random report requested. As long as the data existed, they could generate any report desired.

Since some packages have highly restrictive file capacities, SGD carefully planned file needs. They did not want to outgrow file capacity in six months. These and other considerations guided their systematic package evaluation.

Figure 11-12 Accounts Receivable Checklist

Candidate Packages Names:
A: ______________________
B: ______________________
C: ______________________

Check "must have" items	*Rating (Scale: 1 = poor to 10 = excellent)* A	B	C
Type			
___Balance forward	___	___	___
___Open item	___	___	___
___Multiuser	___	___	___
Interfaces			
___Order processing	___	___	___
___Sales analysis	___	___	___
___Sales commission accounting	___	___	___
___General ledger	___	___	___
___Inventory	___	___	___
___Report writer	___	___	___
___Others ______________	___	___	___

Figure 11-12 (continued)

Check "must have" items	Rating (Scale: 1 = poor to 10 = excellent) A	B	C
Capacities			
____# Customers	____	____	____
____# Open items	____	____	____
____# Balance forward customers	____	____	____
____# Open item customers	____	____	____
____# Ship-to addresses/customer	____	____	____
____# Sales history periods	____	____	____
____# Branches	____	____	____
____# Companies	____	____	____
Customer Information			
____Customer name	____	____	____
Customer identification:			
____ Numeric only	____	____	____
____ Any characters or numbers	____	____	____
____Sold-to address	____	____	____
____Telephone	____	____	____
____Contact name	____	____	____
____Open item/balance forward type code	____	____	____
____Send invoices/statement code	____	____	____
____Tax code	____	____	____
____Resale number	____	____	____
____Credit limit	____	____	____
____Terms code	____	____	____
____Finance code	____	____	____
____Customer category	____	____	____
____Customer price category	____	____	____
____Sales contract number	____	____	____
Salesperson identification:			
____ Numeric only	____	____	____
____ Any characters or numbers	____	____	____
Date of:			
____ First sale	____	____	____
____ Last sale	____	____	____
____Largest balance	____	____	____
____Date of largest balance	____	____	____
Month-to-date:			
____ Sales	____	____	____
____ Profit	____	____	____
____ Number of invoices	____	____	____
Year-to-date:			
____ Sales	____	____	____
____ Profit	____	____	____
____ Number of invoices	____	____	____
____Average number of days to pay	____	____	____
____Total due	____	____	____
____Current due	____	____	____

2. *WMK Associates Case.* Write to the companies identified in exercise 1. Ask for detailed information on their accounts receivable package (unless information is already available from exercises 2 and 3 in Chapter 9).

   When literature is available, prepare a written or oral report on the differences in package:

   - Customer file or data content
   - Ability to carry both open items and balance forward customers at the same time
   - Invoice and statement format variations
   - Ability to send dunning messages or notices

3. *WMK Associates Case.* Research the application availability in software or periodical directories of computer applications. Look for accounts receivable applications for the distribution industry. Write to four or five companies for more detailed information. Follow the requirements of exercise 2 for executing this exercise.

4. Arrange to have a demonstration of an accounts receivable package. Before the demonstration, read the User's Guide to learn about:

   - Setup tasks
   - Operating procedures
   - Printed and displayed output

   After the demonstration, make an oral or written report about how the first two items were executed. Use the outputs to explain how they compare to other packages you have investigated.

PART IV

using data communications

From the corporate manager, who wants to link a small business computer with a corporate mainframe computer, to the self-employed professional, who wants to send a manuscript by electronic mail for typesetting, data communications are an indispensable professional tool.

Equipping a small business computer for data communications usually requires specialized hardware and software. Data communication hardware varies depending on where the data communication is going. Chapter 12 discusses the hardware required for long-distance data communication. Such communication is known as wide area networking because of the long-distance connections possible through the public telephone network. Alternately, Chapter 13 discusses local area networking for data communication that occurs within one building or a complex of buildings.

With all the appropriate hardware in place, Chapter 14 discusses data communication applications. The new ways of doing business through data communications include electronic mail, electronic conferencing, and other applications. Both data communication software and services are covered.

12

WIDE AREA NETWORKS

A commonplace forecast is that the availability of inexpensive data communications will make as large an impact on our culture as the printing press did in the fifteenth century. With a properly equipped small business computer, any user can feel that impact first hand. It may be to send a business letter electronically across town or across the globe whenever desired.

Wide area data communications characteristically use the telephone network as the medium to carry the communicated message. The telephone network's design goal is to carry analog voice messages, not computer messages, which are digital. So the technology is suboptimal in this oldest form of data communications.

The purpose of this chapter is to provide an orientation to the use of wide area networks. It focuses on the special hardware needed, like a modem and an RS-232-C interface. Concepts like asynchronous versus synchronous transmission, full- and half-duplex directional capability, baud, and protocols are also reviewed.

The chapter concludes with a discussion of newer all-digital wide area networks called packet switched networks.

MODEMS

In order to communicate with public information utilities located hundreds of miles away, Mr. Williams needed a *modem*. He bought a *direct-connect modem,* similar to the one shown in Figure 12–1. The device allows a computer to use an ordinary telephone line for data communications. Because it plugs into an ordinary telephone jack, it is called a direct-connect modem.

Modem is a short form for *mo*dulate and *dem*odulate. Modulation is a process that takes discrete digital computer signals of 1's and 0's and endows them with sound to go through the telephone network in wave-like analog form, as shown in Figure 12–2. Signals are modulated on the transmitting end, then demodulated back to computer signals on the receiving end of a data communications exchange.

In addition to the modem, which cost from $150 to $600, Mr. Williams had to buy a cable for about $40 to connect the modem to the computer. He also had to buy an interface board, for about $500 to make the computer into a communicating device. Then he had to buy an over-the-counter asynchronous communications software package. The package cost can range from $35 to $200. Sometimes communication software and a cable are sold with the modem.

Mr. Williams' modem is called a *smart modem*. To reach the outside telephone network, for example, he does not physically have to dial. He can use the keyboard to type the telephone number instead, or he can type a single number to have his software do the dialing. He also can reconfigure the modem to match various remote computer communication parameters. If necessary, he can set the modem to dial remote computers, exchange files with them, and hang up the connection, all without operator intervention. To do so, the system requires sophisticated communication software (discussed in Chapter 14).

Courtesy of Hayes Microcomputer Products, Inc.

Figure 12–1 A direct connect smart modem (approx. size: 1½ inches × 5½ inches by 9½ inches) that attaches directly to a telephone line

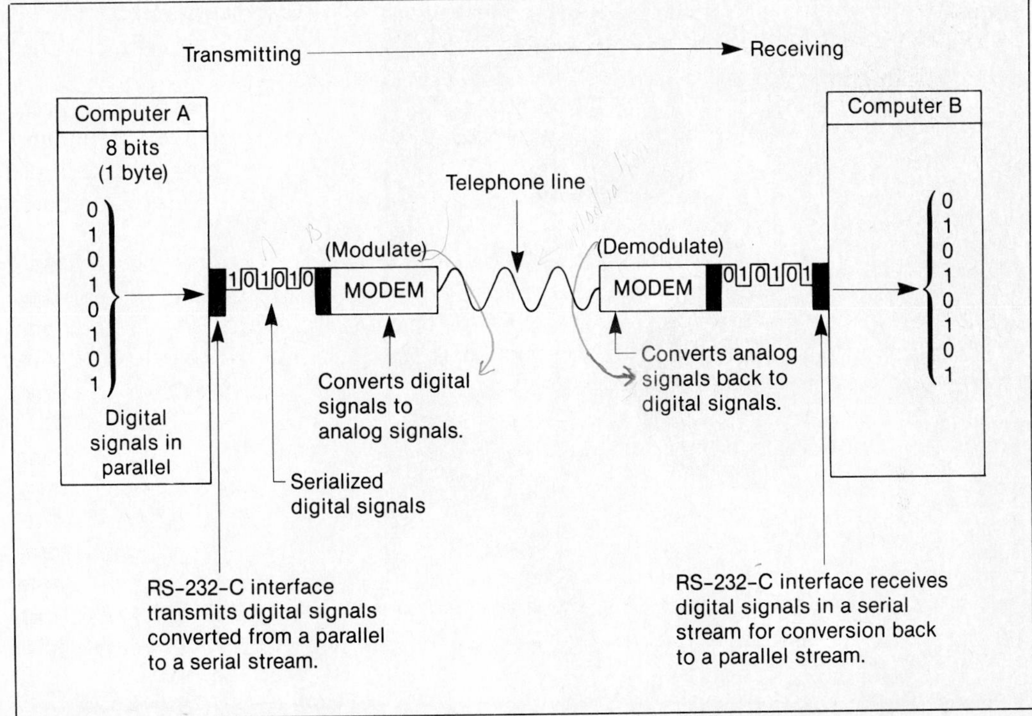

Figure 12-2 Two data communicating computers linked by modems through the public telephone network

Although Mr. Williams chose a direct-connect smart modem, he could have bought an *acoustic coupler,* as shown in Figure 12-3. This device has receptacles into which a telephone handset can be inserted. It usually requires manual dialing of the number of the receiving computer. However dialing access is achieved, it gives the common name of *dial-up network* to wide area data communications.

An acoustic coupler functions like a modem although it is more prone to poor transmission. Because peripheral noise can get through an acoustically coupled connection, there is a greater chance for transmission error than with a direct-connect modem. Couplers are widely used with portable small computers.

Some modems are sold functionally integrated on the data communications interface board. It eliminates an extra piece of hardware in the workplace.

The modem function is necessary for any computer device to connect to the public telephone network. The device could be Mr. Williams' stand-alone computer, a communication gateway server from a local area network, a terminal, or other devices. All need digital computer signals converted to analog telephone signals.

RS-232-C INTERFACE

Because telephone lines do not have the capacity to carry all bits of one byte or character at a time, bits must be passed out of the computer one bit at a time. The data com-

Courtesy of Datec, Inc.

Figure 12-3 An acoustically coupled modem with receptacles into which a telephone handset can be inserted

munications interface board has a special microprocessor chip on it that does the parallel to serial conversion. A special plug, called the EIA (Electronic Industries of America) standard *RS-232-C serial interface* carries the serialized bits to the modem.

The communications interface board fits into one of the system units expansion slots. Its RS-232-C serial socket sticks out the rear of the board and system unit, as shown in Figure 12–4. It has little signaling pins that couple with the modem cable's RS-232-C plug. Although 25 signaling pins are available, only a half-dozen or fewer are used in ordinary asynchronous transmission.

ASYNCHRONOUS TRANSMISSION

In data communications, asynchronous means sending data over a telephone line one character at a time, with random timing between characters. This accommodates interactive use where typing is slow compared to data communication speeds.

Mr. Williams' modem is capable of sending either 30 or 120 characters-per-second. With human typing speeds ranging from about one to five characters-per-second, either capacity is more than adequate for interactive use. But many users, like Mr. Williams, prefer the 120-character modems. When receiving computer data, a screen

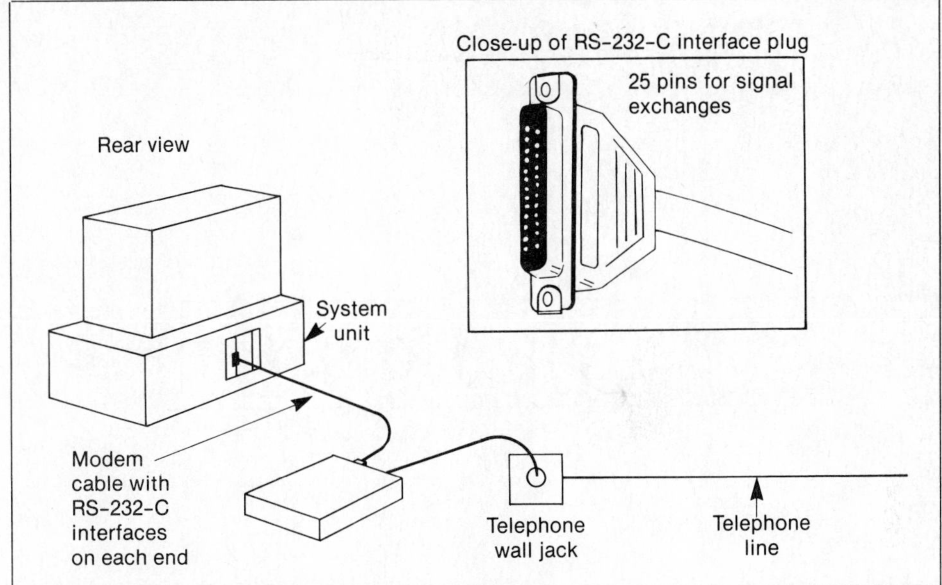

Figure 12-4 Direct-connect modem installation

fills faster. In addition, entire files can be transferred faster. Increased speed reduces the total telephone connect time, and on a long-distance toll call, it could make a cost difference.

The data communication industry often lists modem information handling capacity as either *bits-per-second* or *baud* (pronounced bawd). Mr. Williams' modem would be referred to as a 1,200-baud or 1,200-bits-per-second modem. Baud rate is normally ten times the character rate in asynchronous communication. Each asynchronous character is 10 bits, as illustrated in Figure 12-5.

Each ASCII character has 7 bits, plus a parity bit. Added to this is a start and a stop bit to signal the beginning and end of each character.

The combination of 7 data bits, a start and a stop bit, plus a parity bit is the most common asynchronous *protocol* used. *Protocol* is the data communication industry's term for a set of rules or procedures established and followed by cooperating devices. To successfully communicate, transmitting and receiving computers need to follow the same procedure.

SYNCHRONOUS TRANSMISSION

The procedures commonly used in private large computer networks are often faster synchronous transmission protocols. Two are *Bisynchronous (Bisync)* and *Synchronous Data Link Control* (SDLC). Both are IBM mainframe protocols. Another synchronous

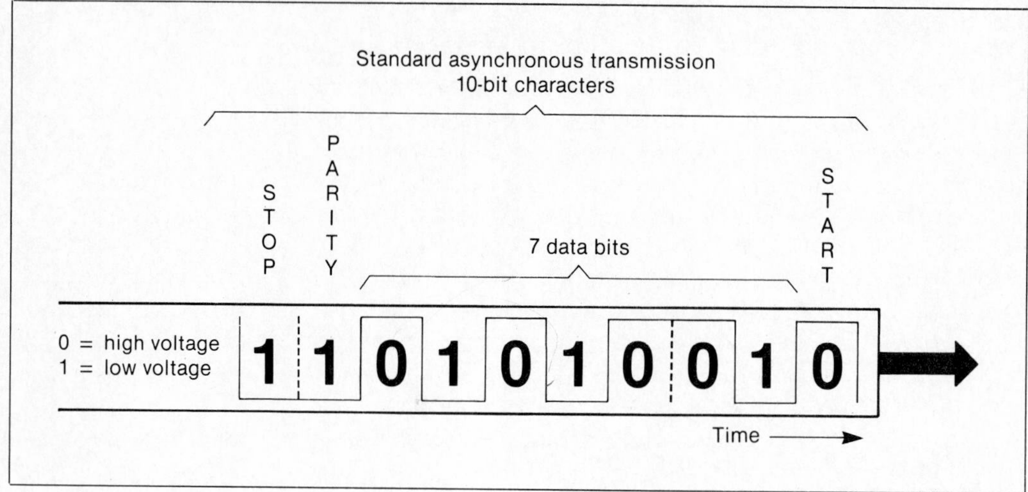

Figure 12-5 Serialized asynchronous ASCII character "J" with even parity

protocol similar to SDLC is *High-Level Data Link Control* (HDLC), a recommended standard of the International Standards Organization.

Synchronous protocols send groups of characters instead of a single character at a time. Bits are precisely timed by the host mainframe computer, unlike in asynchronous transmission. In the Bisynchronous protocol, characters are stored and sent one *block* at a time. The SDLC and HDLC protocols refer to blocks as *frames* or *packets*. Elaborate control schemes to detect and correct errors are part of the transmission procedure. Such schemes do not exist in the simpler asynchronous procedure.

These synchronous protocols operate at faster baud rates and usually travel over private lines leased from the telephone company. Established intracompany computer networks, driven by large host computers, use these protocols to link user terminals or other computers.

Many hardware/software packages are available to make small business computers *emulate,* for example, an IBM 3270 Bisynchronous terminal. Such a package is required by many large company users of small computers who also want to communicate with their mainframe computer.

The hardware to emulate a synchronous terminal, versus an asynchronous one, is similar. It usually requires an interface board that fits into a slot in the system unit, along with a cable that connects to a terminal cluster controller. A cluster controller acts as a focal point for linking many similar terminals. All communication is consolidated there in such a way that it requires only one modem and one physical leased line to send the data communication traffic for many terminals to a host computer.

While the small computer is emulating a terminal, it is participating in a wide area computer network. This does not, however, preclude its functioning in a local area network. In many large company cases, a user in a local area network indicates to the local network software a desire to dial out to a wide area network. The local network provides the wide area communication hardware and software to enable the connection.

DIRECTIONAL CAPABILITY

Asynchronous data communications can travel in either a full- or half-duplex direction. *Full duplex* means that data can be transmitted and received simultaneously. For normal full-duplex transmission, a single telephone wire is split into two sound frequencies, one to transmit data and the other to receive it. A full-duplex modem handles this automatically. It is the normal operating mode for asynchronous transmission.

Half-duplex transmission means that the single telephone line is used either to send or to receive data communications. Half-duplex is normal for Bisynchronous transmission. Because of the faster baud rates, the full capacity or width of the telephone line is needed for one-way transmission. Often, however, two private leased lines are used with Bisynchronous transmission. One line permanently transmits, under such an arrangement, while the other permanently receives.

Asynchronous transmission may also be sent half-duplex, where either the sender or the receiver has charge of the line, but not both at one time. Should Mr. Williams need it to communicate with a service, he can direct his modem, through a menu change in the software, to function in a half-duplex fashion.

PACKET SWITCHED NETWORKS

To avoid long-distance telephone connect charges when communicating with a public information utility, Mr. Williams depends on the services of large established data communication networks like Telenet, Tymnet, or Uninet. They charge between $6 and $10 an hour. They are often called *public packet switched networks,* and are designed specifically to carry digital data communications. They have local access points in most major cities.

Calling a utility many miles away is still a local telephone call, as indicated in Figure 12–6. The charges for network use is often part of the monthly bill from the information utility. Since packet switched networks charge for data carried, not for connect time, monthly bills are considerably less than if a long-distance toll call is made to use an information utility.

Packet switched networks charge only for packets sent because the physical transmission line is time-shared by many packets. It is unlike voice transmission, which dedicates a line or communication channel for the duration of a call or session, as illustrated in Figure 12–7.

Since data messages tend to occur in isolated bursts rather than in one continuous stream like a telephone conversation, the bursts often require the entire capacity, or *bandwith,* of the communication channel for short periods of time. In relation to a two-second or shorter burst of data that may be required to fill a display with information, the 17 seconds or so it takes to dial and establish a telephone connection is long. The amount of time between data transmissions is commonly much longer than the transmission time itself.

When data is transmitted over the public telephone network, a maximum of about 2,400 bits-per-second of data can be sent if the line is a dial-up one. If the line

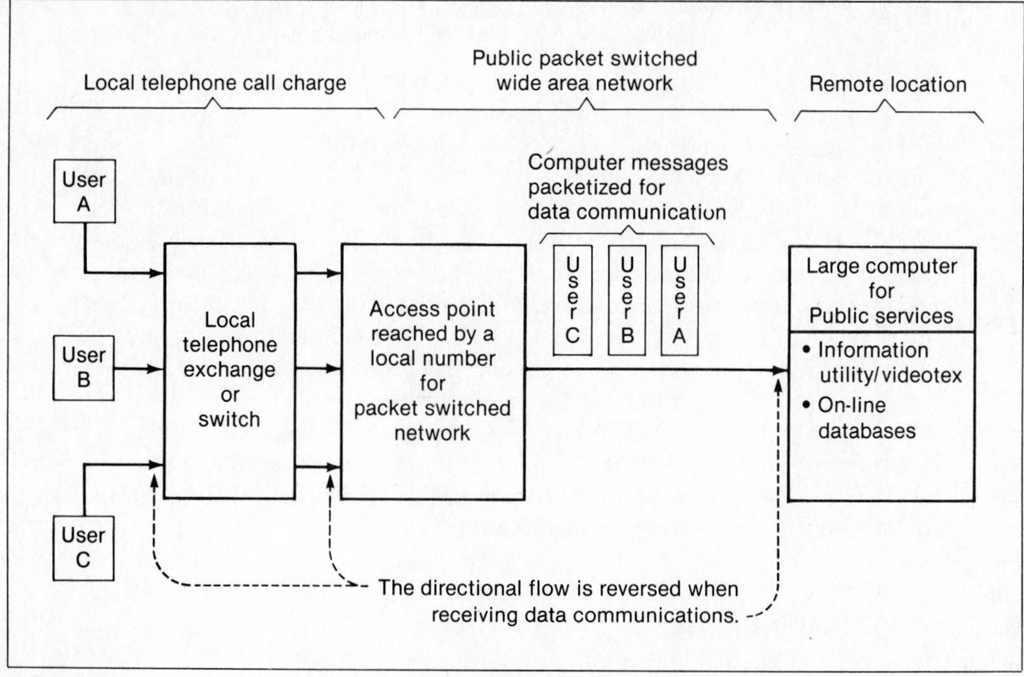

Figure 12-6 Transmitting data communications to an information utility using a public packet switched network

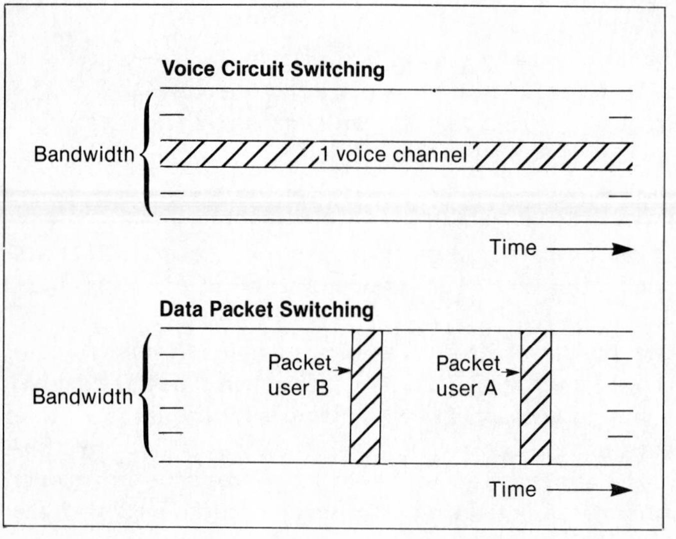

Figure 12-7 Voice circuit versus data packet switching

is a private one with special conditioning, as used in Bisynchronous transmission, it can carry up to 9,600 bits-per-second. Packet switched networks, on the other hand, transmit data in millions of bits-per-second.

Packets sent over wide area networks are similar to packets sent over local area networks. Packets are whole messages divided into discrete units such as 128 bytes. Constructed by the network communication software, they can contain bits for network use like destination and source address, message number, current and last packet number, in addition to user data. The layout of a typical packet is given in Figure 12–8.

OPEN SYSTEMS INTERCONNECTION

The packet conforms to the standards established by the International Standards Organization (ISO) whose aim is universal connectivity between networks. To achieve free data exchange and transfer, this organization recommends a model for open systems interconnection that defines seven standard communication functions, as shown in Figure 12–9.

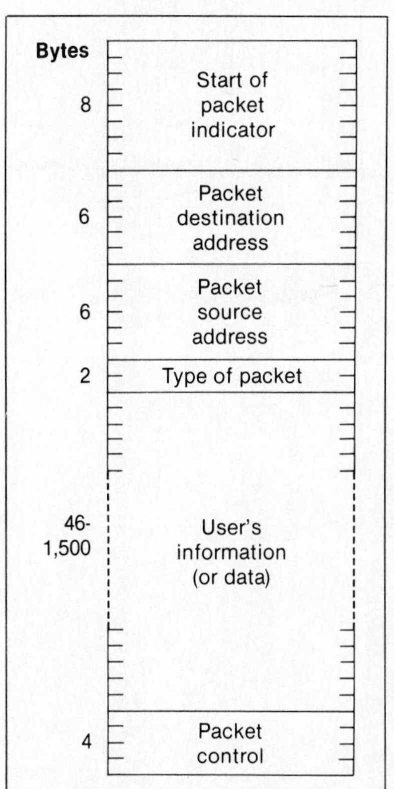

Figure 12-8 A packet format

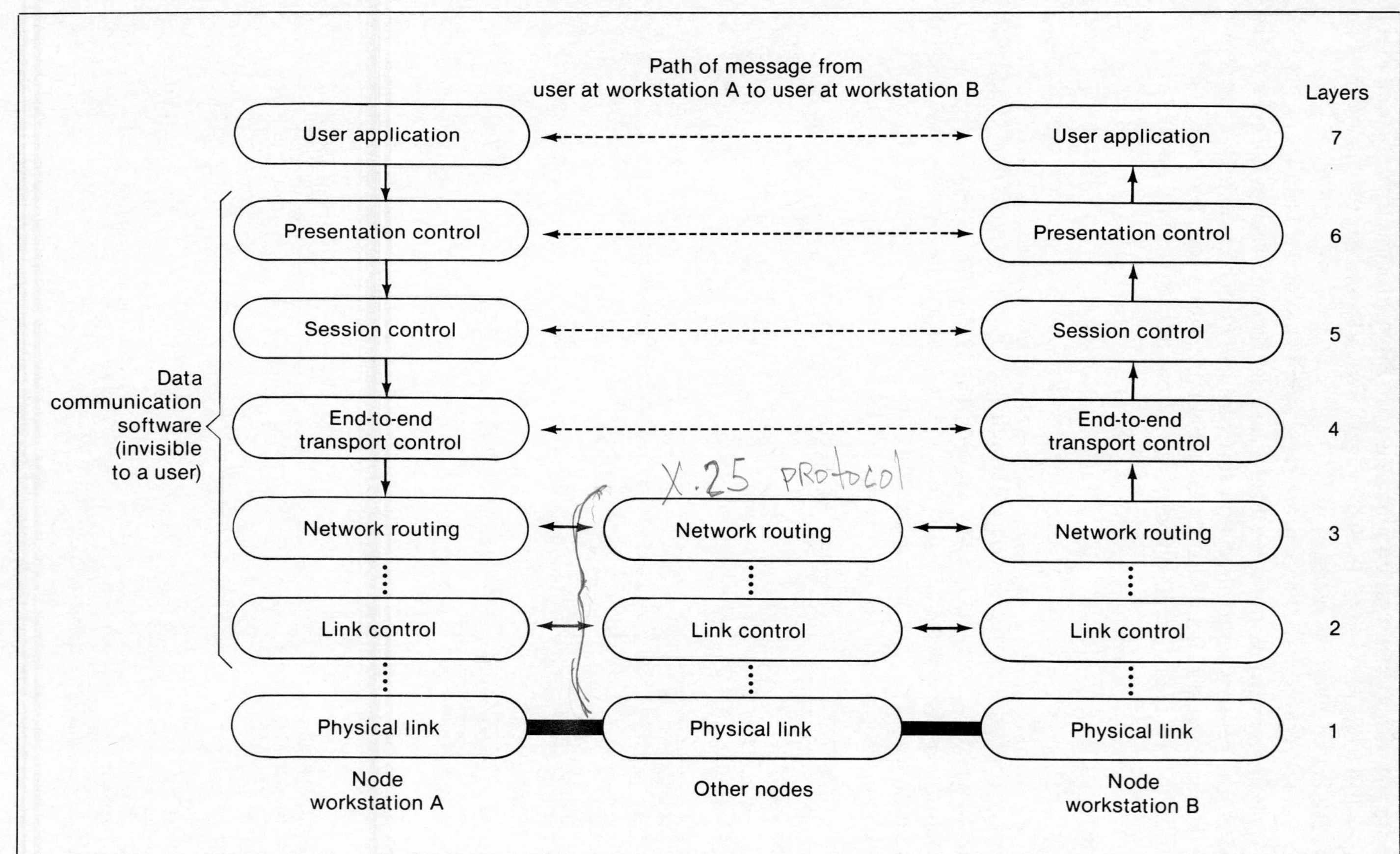

Figure 12-9 The ISO seven-layer model for open systems interconnection

The layered software to perform these functions is much like system software layers. Although all layers works as a unit, each function can be separately extracted for change, modification, or upgrade without affecting the software layers above or below it. This flexibility and uniformity is a goal to be achieved rather than a given fact. Most wide area and local area network vendors follow the first three layers, collectively called the *X.25 protocol.* Other layers are less rigidly defined and followed. It presents an unresolved problem for users wanting to interconnect applications.

EVALUATION

To use wide area data communications requires mainly a modem and some software. A checklist to guide the evaluation of a modem is given in Figure 12–10.

Mr. Williams found that the modem and data communications software evaluations resemble each other. One serves as a cross-check on the other. It is especially important to insure that a modem can execute all the features data communication software can provide.

Figure 12–10 Hardware: Component Checklist

Items to Check	*Rating (Scale: 1 = poor to 10 = excellent)* A	B	C
Modem			
Product name A: ________ B: ________ C: ________			
Asynchronous:			
0–300-baud (Bell 103/113 compatible)	____	____	____
0–300/1,200-baud (Bell 212-A compatible)	____	____	____
Synchronous:			
1,200–9,600 baud	____	____	____
Other ________	____	____	____
RS-232-C serial interface	____	____	____
Full-/half-duplex transmission	____	____	____
Software selectable communication parameters	____	____	____
Automatic selection of pulse or tone dialing	____	____	____
Automatic dial/answer	____	____	____
Automatic repeat dial	____	____	____
Telephone number storage	____	____	____
Set sign-on message	____	____	____
Executes and responds to:			
User commands	____	____	____
Special parameter settings	____	____	____
Indicator lights for visual status check	____	____	____
Self-test	____	____	____
FCC approved	____	____	____
Subtotal	____	____	____
Divide by number of items rated for average rating	____	____	____

Transfer Average Rating to Selection Summary: Hardware, Figure 5–2.

Users who purchase a combination modem and data communication software package, created by a single manufacturer, only need to do the software evaluation. It helps determine whether or not all desired data communication features are available.

SELF TEST

1. What function does a modem serve in data communications?
2. How is an acoustic coupler different from a direct-connect modem?
3. What hardware components are typically interfaced using an RS-232-C cable?
4. How is asynchronous communication different from synchronous communication?
5. What are communication industry terms for the information handling capacity of a modem or communication channel?
6. What is a protocol?
7. Identify the bit pattern in the asynchronous protocol.
8. What are three synchronous protocol names?
9. How is full-duplex different from half-duplex?
10. What function do packet switched networks serve?
11. Describe what a packet contains.
12. What is the purpose of the open systems interconnection model? What is X.25?

EXERCISES

1. Examine the rear side of a small business computer. Examine the sockets to determine which is the RS-232-C serial interface. Answer the following questions about the hardware:
   a. How many pins are used of the possible 25?
   b. Describe what the plug (versus the socket) looks like.
   c. Are there any other sockets or ports extending out the rear of the system unit?
   d. Is one a parallel port? What does it interface? Describe what the socket and plug look like.
2. Modems usually come with blinking lights on the front to identify the action in process or the active state. These are the symbols on the front panel of one smart modem:

MR	OH	SD
TR	CD	RD
AA		

   Identify the symbols with the help of a User Guide or manual supplied with any modem. If there are different symbols, identify them also. Each modem symbol is activated by an assigned pin on the RS-232-C interface.

RESOURCES AND REFERENCES

Books

GLOSSBRENNER, ALFRED, *The Complete Handbook of Personal Computer Communications,* St. Martin's, 1983.

JORDAN, LARRY E. AND BRUCE CHURCHILL, *Communincations and Networking,* Brady, 1983.
LOOMIS, MARY E. S., *Data Communications,* Prentice-Hall, 1983.
SHAPIRO, NEIL L., *The Small Computer Connection,* McGraw-Hill, 1983.
SIPPL, CHARLES J., *Data Communications Dictionary,* Van Nostrand, 1976.
TUROFF, MURRAY AND ROXANNE HILTZ, *Network Nation,* Addison-Wesley, 1978.

Periodicals

Telecommunications
Data Communications

Loose-Leaf References

Communications Solutions, Datapro.
Data Communications Reports, Auerbach.
Data World, Vol. IV, Auerbach.
Reports on Data Communications, Datapro.

13

LOCAL AREA NETWORKS

Small business computer users throughout organizations have an increasing need to share information and communicate. One generally accepted premise is that 80 percent of the information generated within a local organizational environment is used only within the environment. The other 20 percent of the information flow comes from outside the organization and is sent outside.

These figures suggest the reason progressive organizations install *local area networks* (LANs). Their people need to communicate and exchange local information quickly, easily, and reliably. They also need to share application programs and output devices, such as expensive printers and graphic plotters.

This chapter examines how a typical local area network operates and what to consider when specifying requirements for one. It then considers the main implementation choices: twisted-pair wire, baseband, and broadband cabled systems.

TYPICAL OPERATION

Figure 13–1 shows typical local area networks cabled throughout office buildings to enable the exchange of information. The most common environment is a single building, but local area networks can also extend to other office buildings, such as those in a university or other campus-like environment.

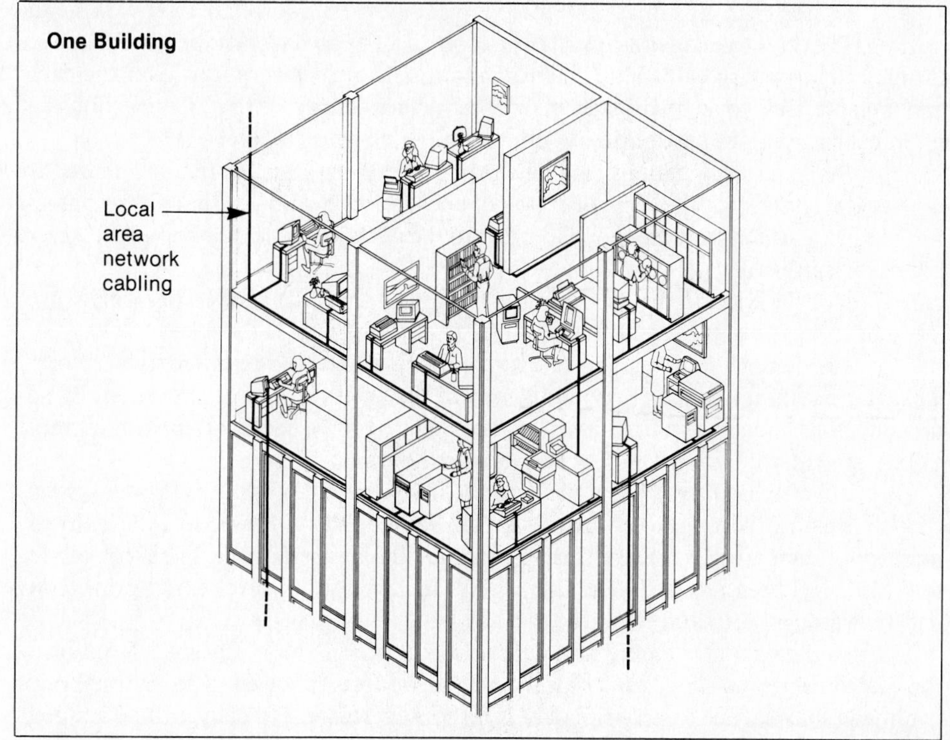

Courtesy of Xerox Corporation

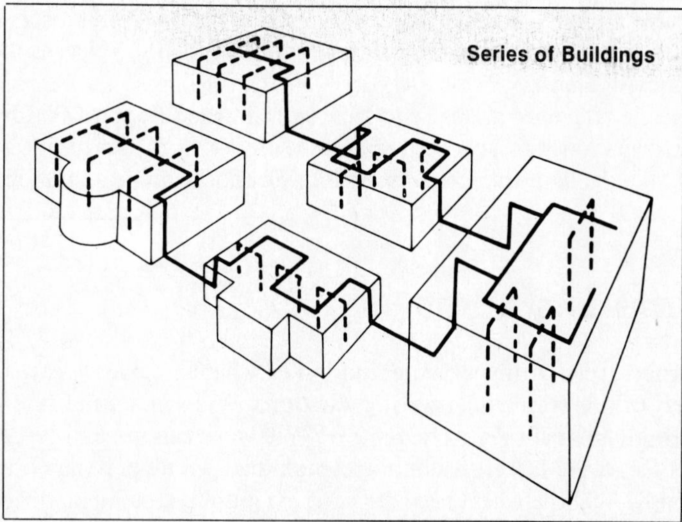

Courtesy of Digital Equipment Corporation

Figure 13-1 Local area networks cabled throughout an office building and through a series of buildings in a campus-like setting

Figure 13–2 illustrates how three typical users on a local area network might operate. The physical network consists of a cable that ties each workstation to each other through the common cable attachment. Data traffic or messages flow over the cable and are accessible to any workstation or other device connected to it. Connections are often called *nodes* in networking terminology.

Personal workstations can have printers or disks attached that are shared by others. But some local area networks do not allow a workstation to share its resources. Instead, they attach separate shared devices to the network cable that are called *servers* or *shared resources.*

Every device on the network has a unique address. It enables personal workstations to send messages and file transfers to users or attached devices.

In Figure 13–2, user 3 creates a word processed letter file and stores it on a floppy disk. It is essential that user 1 reviews a copy of the letter before it is circulated. By addressing user 1's workstation, the letter file is sent over the cable, often with a simple COPY statement. Network software executes the transfer.

User 1 can interact with the letter as if it were created locally. Some systems copy the sending file to the receiving user's disk. Some do this only if permission is already granted for such privileges. Some treat the transfer like electronic mail. The user is alerted that a file has been received. The user directs its disposition: save, erase, print, copy and forward, modify and forward, and the like.

In the second example of a typical logical process, user 1 prints a letter using the shared printer attached to workstation 3. An address followed by the normal print command may suffice to accomplish this on some systems. Typically, printer requests are queued and printed in sequence. Sophisticated software allows modification of the queue or the print files.

In the third example user 2 stores a file on the shared hard disk. Every network user might have a private area, or *volume,* on the hard disk. Other users may access private areas according to the access privileges granted them. Privileges include read, write, and update, among others.

Working off a hard disk is faster than working off a floppy disk. Ideally, a local network's information transfer speed should be as fast as the hard disk access speed in order to make the data transfer *transparent,* or unobservable and unobtrusive, for the user.

SPECIFYING REQUIREMENTS

Planning started at SGD Inc. with a definition of what employees needed to do on a local area network. It required answering questions: Will communications occur often or only intermittently between workstations? Will workstations transfer large files or 300-character messages? Is there a month-end peak-load period, or is the workload spread out each month? Will there be a need for carrying graphics, audio, and video applications? Will they need to be carried simultaneously? And so on.

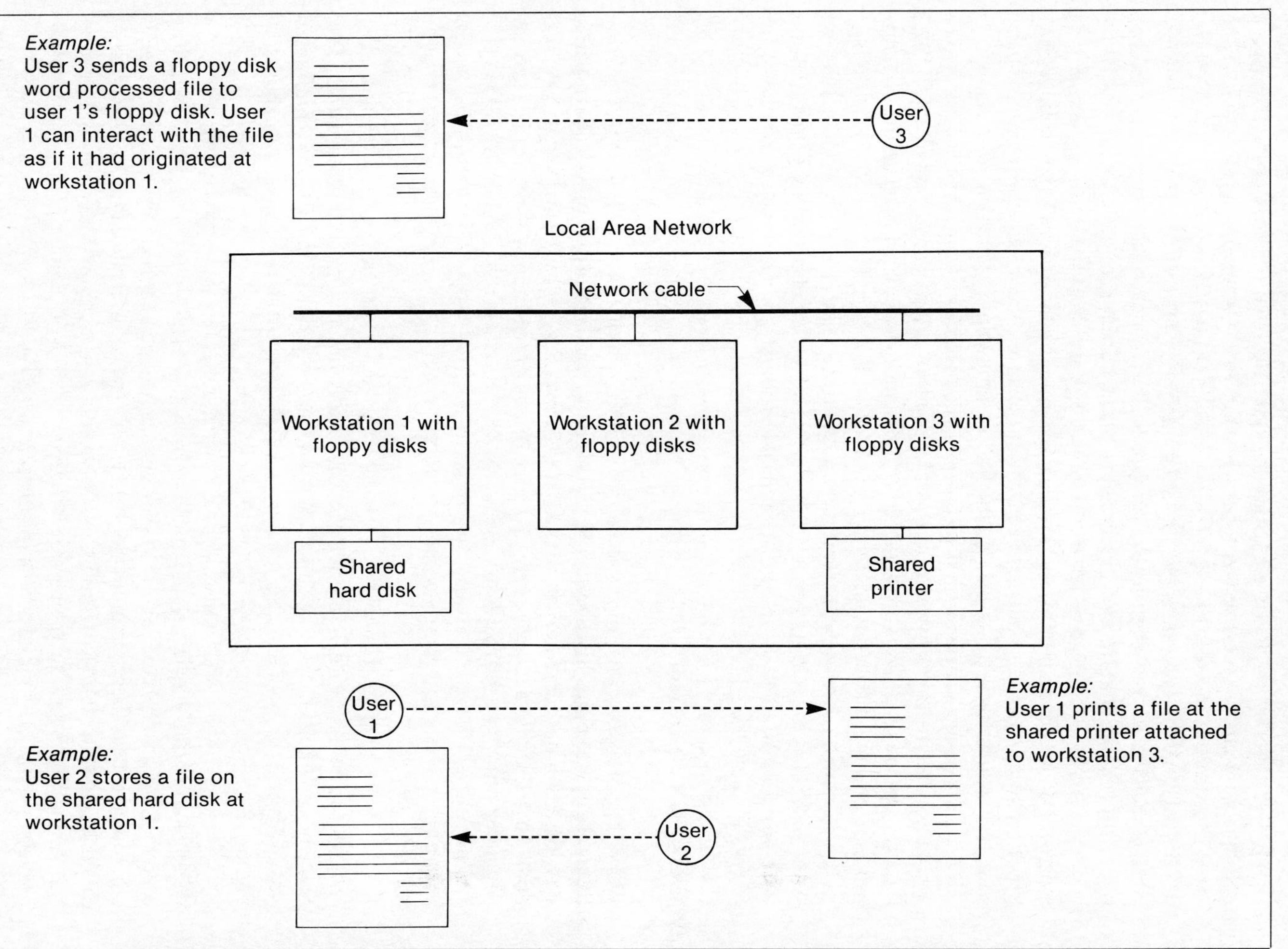

Figure 13-2 Examples of how a local area network is used

The management team at SGD Inc. specified that the network is to be used mainly for executive access to the company database. It also will enable sharing each other's ideas through electronic mail and messages, as well as personal work files and programs. Longer-range plans will put other burdens on the network's shared resources.

SGD Inc. hired a consultant who specialized in local area network installations to assist in the evaluation and implementation of a local area network.

A strategy evolved to set up a pilot test of a few workstations. The networking scheme used had to be modularly expandable without a lot of *downtime,* or idle time, to make alterations. It also had to have software that was uncomplicated and unintrusive so users could resume being productive almost immediately after installation.

Since several brands of workstations were already in use, the network had to accommodate their *multivendor* hardware situation. This might prove even more necessary in the long run when planned equipment is introduced that almost certainly will be from multiple vendors.

Finally, the new local area network had to be reliable and affordable. Because of the wide differences in system capability, prices varied widely. It appeared that systems were available from $400 to several thousand dollars per connection.

IMPLEMENTATION CHOICES

When they shopped, SGD Inc. had a choice of three popular local area network cabling technologies: telephone twisted-pair wire, baseband coaxial and broadband coaxial cable systems. Each has a unique set of characteristics and is optimized for certain applications. In order to make an informed choice, members of the LAN project learned the advantages and disadvantages of each.

TWISTED-PAIR WIRE

Ordinary telephone wire is referred to as *twisted-pairs* in data communications. Two thin wires are braided or twisted around each other. Often local area networks configured with twisted-pair wiring have a star topology or geometric pattern as shown in Figure 13–3.

At the time they researched local area networks, the star with the switched center was the most widely installed system. It resembled a telephone central office switching center. When a telephone call arrives at the local public telephone branch exchange, it is rerouted on another available line, if available, to connect the call. The circuit from the sender to the receiver is temporarily one continuous *point-to-point* line for the duration of the call. These switching stations are called *P*ublic *B*ranch E*x*changes (PBXs). The connection they make are called *circuit switched* calls.

To retain the similarity, the ones SGD Inc. examined were called *P*rivate *B*ranch E*x*changes (PBXs), or *P*rivate *A*utomated *B*ranch E*x*changes (PABXs). These required a modem for every workstation because the PBX transmitted analog signals.

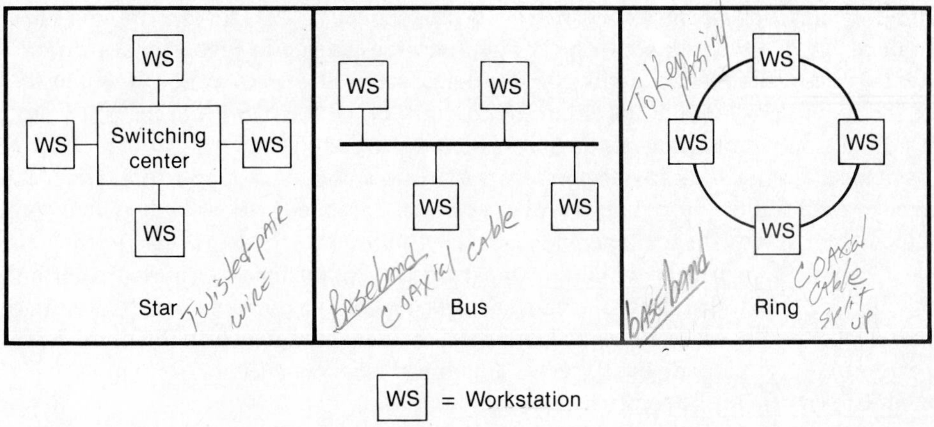

Figure 13-3 Three local area network topologies

An upgraded switching center system also considered is a *D*igital *B*ranch E*x*change (DBX). Because it carries all-digital information, modems are not needed for workstation connections. Voice and electronic mail are offered as options. Voice messages are digitized and stored, and they can be played back on demand.

One limitation of all centralized exchange systems is that the central control switch is a single point of system failure. If it goes down, so does the entire network. To insulate against system failure, redundant parts are built into the switch to reduce the chance of system failure.

Twisted-pair wire systems have inherent limitations that prevent large-volume data transfers. In local area networks, the information carrying capacity of various cabling tends to be distinguished as follows:

Cable Used	*Information carrying characteristics*
Twisted-pair wire	Entry-level, low-speed, economical
Baseband coaxial cable	Medium-speed
Broadband coaxial cable	High-volume, high-speed, expensive

Twisted-pair wires often carry up to 9,600 bits-per-second for analog transmission and 56,000 for digital transmission. It is a well established technology that is widely used and appropriate for many organizations. Local area networks in this category are manufactured by Rolm, Northern Telecom, and Datapoint, among others.

BASEBAND

Almost all other local area networks SGD Inc. examined were baseband-oriented. Some baseband systems among many are Ethernet, PC Net and Ether Series. They are medium-speed systems that use cable TV wiring, called *coaxial cable.* Workstations are connected to the cable in either a bus or ring configuration, as shown in Figure 13–3.

Baseband systems, unlike PBX systems, are optimized to work as an extension of the computer system unit's electronic circuitry called the *input/output (I/O) bus.* The input/output bus transfers data from peripherals to and from the central processor. For a local area network to operate transparently to a user, it must make data transfers as close to the input/output bus speed as possible. Baseband coaxial cable systems can match these speeds, as the table in Figure 13–4 indicates.

Baseband signals are unmodulated signals. An ordinary telephone call is unmodulated. The electrical signal created by the telephone to represent voice travels into the telephone network at its original unmodulated signal frequency. In this sense, baseband differs from broadband systems. Broadband local area networks use modems to modulate signals to different frequencies.

Baseband systems share one physical channel with all users attached to it. All users have equal access to the single channel. Only one user at a time can transmit data. The entire capacity of the channel or cable is occupied by each transmission.

Since one user fully occupies a baseband system when on the cable, some access control is necessary. As the SGD Inc. team viewed it, the two different access techniques used, *CSMA/CD* and *token-passing,* each had a number of advantages and disadvantages.

CSMA/CD

The Carrier Sense Multiple Access/Collision Detect (CSMA/CD) access technique functions like a party-line telephone. This access protocol checks to see if a line is busy with someone else transmitting data. If no traffic is sensed, it is free to broadcast data. The workstation, in effect, seizes the line. All workstations hear the message as it passes by, and each checks to see if it is addressed to itself. Observation of cable traffic by workstations, however, is *passive.* Workstations do not have to handle passing messages addressed to other nodes.

Figure 13-4 Data transfer rate comparison

Operation	*Representative Data Transfer Rates or Information Carrying Capacity in Bits-per-Second*
Baseband coaxial cable	1,000,000–50,000,000
Random access memory	9,500,000
Central processor initiated input/output	7,600,000
Hard disk input/output	6,500,000–8,000,000
Floppy disk input/output	250,000
Modem at 1200 baud	1,200

The ability to *broadcast* messages, to a select group of workstations or all workstations, eliminates redundant message traffic.

But collisions can occur with two workstations trying to transmit simultaneously. If a collision is detected, this protocol waits for a random period before retransmitting the data. On a well configured system, collisions cause no performance degradation.

Ethernet

The SGD Inc. team was made aware of a performance study that suggested collisions did not affect system performance. The test was of *Ethernet,* the local area network system that pioneered the CSMA/CD protocol. The Ethernet system was specifically designed to optimize digital data transfer over limited distances. The data is transferred in *packets* like those used by public packet switched networks. The Ethernet packet follows the X.25 standard for open systems interconnection, or data transfer between networks.

On the test of CSMA/CD packets over the Ethernet network, a 3-Mbit cable was used. It was an experimental version of the 10-Mbit cable that is commercially available. Over 120 devices were connected to the Ethernet and observed under normal, high, and overhead conditions. Under normal conditions, the user load on the test was 300 million bytes, (or 300 million bytes × 8 bits per byte = 2,400 million bits) in a 24-hour period, with most occurring during the normal workday. The system reportedly was less than 1-percent utilized. During the busiest hour it was 17-percent utilized.

Under controlled experiments for high and overload conditions, the cable matched a 90-percent load with an equal amount of service. At stressful overloads of 150 percent, the cable offered 96 percent service.

Bus Topology

The CSMA/CD protocol is typically identified with a bus topology, as shown in Figure 13–3. Because control is distributed to each node on the network, there is no central controller presenting a single point of total network failure. If any device fails, it cannot bring down the entire network because of its passive role on the cable. Workstations and other devices can be added to the network without complication for the same reason. The passive role of the cable and devices attached to it make this networking scheme flexible for expansion or reconfiguration. Up to 1,024 nodes can be attached over 1.5 miles on the Ethernet system.

The hardware components needed for an Ethernet baseband bus configuration include:

- Coaxial cable
- Transceiver and coaxial cable tap to connect a workstation to the cable
- Transceiver cable to connect the workstation to the tap
- An interface board for each workstation that fits into an expansion slot in the system unit (serving as the communications control interface and functionally connecting the network to the system unit's input/output bus)

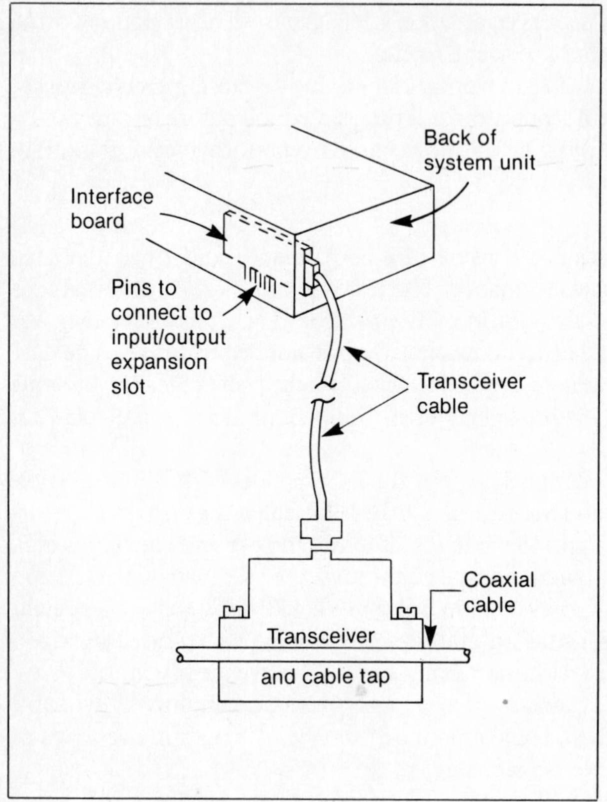

Adapted with permission of Digital Equipment Corporation

Figure 13–5 Ethernet hardware components

A diagram of hardware components is given in Figure 13–5. Other optional components include the following:

- *Print and file servers* allow sharing of storage and printers and eliminate the need for individual workstations to have their own set of storage devices and printers.
- *Terminal servers* allow low-speed dumb asynchronous terminals access to any computing or information processing resource on the network.
- *Routing servers* interconnect local area network segments of similar architecture.
- *Gateway servers* interconnect networks of different architecture requiring protocol conversion.

Figure 13–6 diagrams a hypothetical network using all optional components.

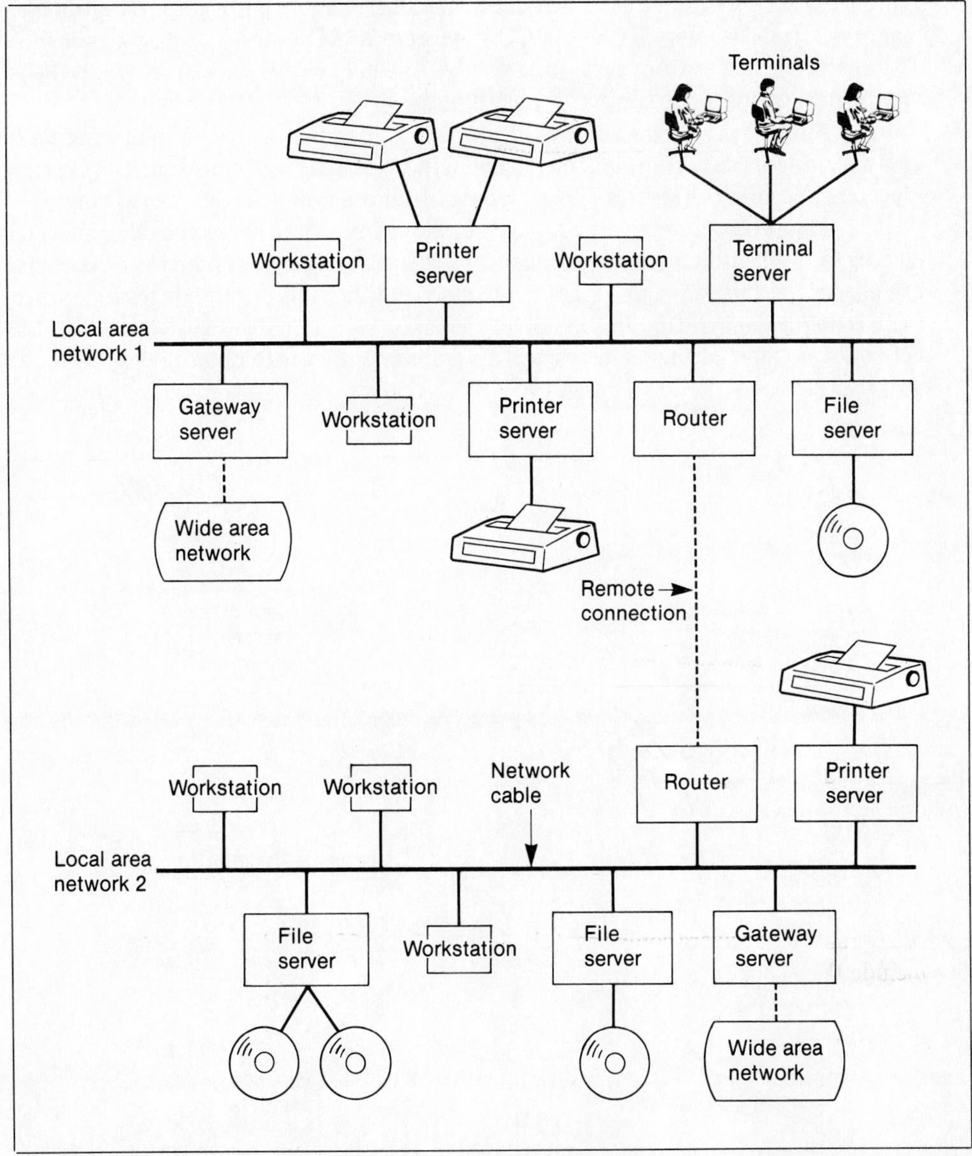

Adapted with permission of Digital Equipment Corporation

Figure 13-6 An Ethernet network with optional hardware components

Token Passing

The SGD Inc. team considered the token passing protocol as an alternate baseband scheme to CSMA/CD. Token passing is usually implemented in a ring topology, as shown in Figure 13-7, and avoids collisions entirely. Everyone on the network is guaranteed access within a predetermined time slot. The price for this is data transfer that drops from 10 Mbits in CSMA/CD systems to 2.5 Mbits in token passing systems. The difference comes from each node's active role in checking data to see if it is theirs and, if not, acting as a repeater to pass it along.

Another price is the vulnerability to failure. Because each node on the ring plays an active role in data transmission, if one node fails the ring is broken. Duplicating repeaters and other measures allow by-pass of failure points in distributed rings.

This protocol employs electronic tokens to allow workstations and other attached devices to transmit in an orderly sequence. Tokens are special bit patterns or packets, usually several bits in length, that circulate around the ring from node to node when there is no message traffic. Possession of the token gives a node exclusive access to the network for transmitting its message. This avoids conflict with other nodes that want to transmit.

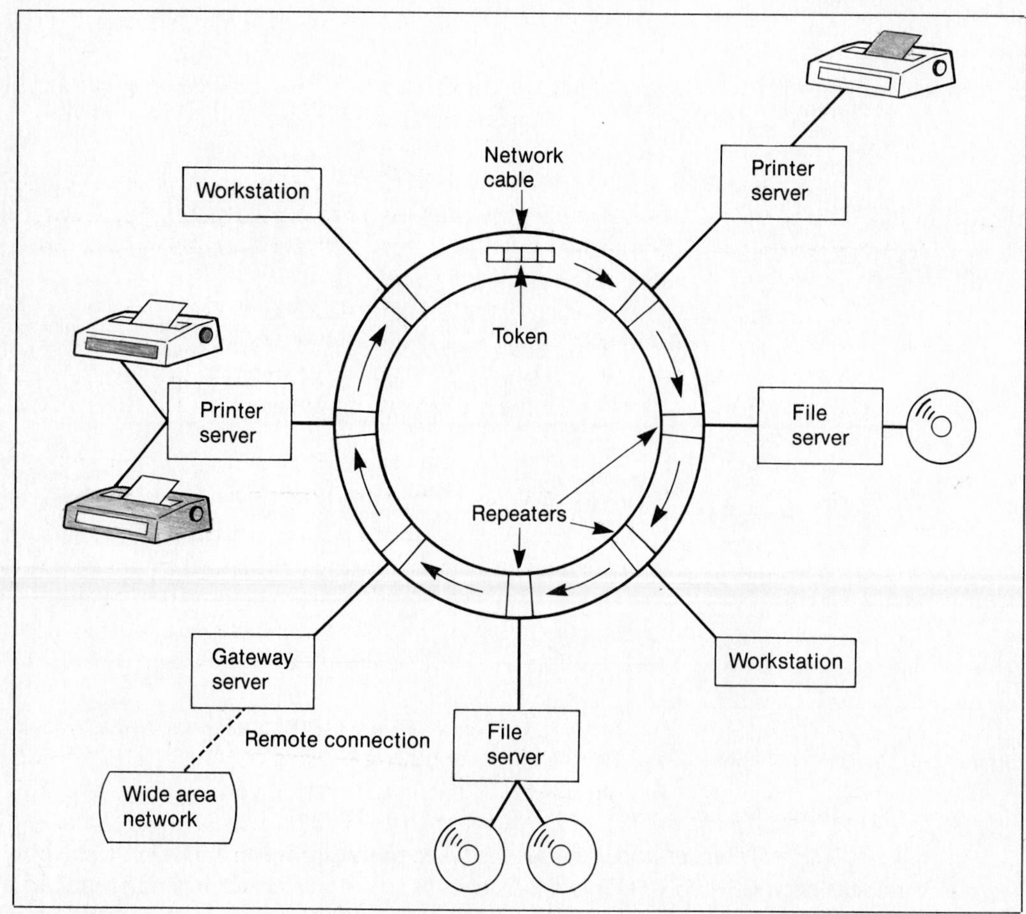

Figure 13-7 Token passing in a local area network with a ring topology

If a node wants to transmit a message, it holds the token and sends the with an appropriate address. Nodes on the ring check the message as it passes by. They must be able to identify messages, accept them, or act as a repeater to pass them along.

Messages usually must circulate back to the sender to confirm receipt by the destination node. This causes a delay that prevents the cable from being used by other nodes. After confirmation is received, the node puts the token back into circulation. It cannot use the token twice in a row to prevent unfair use of the cable.

BROADBAND

Broadband local area networks were also examined by the SGD Inc. team. While they were far too expensive and elaborate for their needs, they felt broadband would become cost-effective in time. In theory it is what the hypothetical automated office requires to be fully integrated and automated. Some commercially available broadband local area networks include DAX (Data Exchange) and Advanced Local Area Network among others.

Broadband cable carries large volumes of audio, video, and data simultaneously. It also carries *facsimile* or *fax* page images. Fax machines transmit image patterns of light and dark, rather than specific characters.

Broadband systems use coaxial cable, but, instead of using it as one channel, they divide cable capacity into many smaller channels, as shown in Figure 13–8. In effect, each channel becomes a private network. Every device attached needs a modem tuned to the *frequency* of the specific channel being used.

Hertz is a measure of a channel's frequency, or the number of electromagnetic waves that oscillate up and down. One wave passing in one second equals one hertz (Hz). Kilohertz (KHz, thousands of hertz), megahertz (MHz, millions of hertz), and gigahertz (GHz, billions of hertz) are the units most frequently encountered in data communications.

The sample cable frequency allocation scheme given in Figure 13–8 is divided by a technique called *frequency division multiplexing* (FDM). The coaxial cable's 300-Megahertz (300-MHz) *bandwidth* is divided according to a combination of the user's needs and a vendor's offering options. *Bandwidth,* expressed in hertz, indicates the number of cycles that can be sent through a transmission channel in one second.

In the sample case, frequencies are allocated to dedicated and switched data channels as well as video channels. Some could be allocated to voice as well. Unused allocations are available for future expansion.

The first dedicated data channels might be used with a large centralized multiuser computer system. Terminals using assigned frequencies have direct permanent access to computer use. It assumes the multiuser computer's communication controller has 48 input/output ports, each tuned to the same frequency as that of each user. Only one device can transmit at an assigned frequency, so there are no conflicting demands for the channel.

The next 32 dedicated channels function the same way, only at higher speed. They might be links to sensitive factory floor robots, instruments, or control devices.

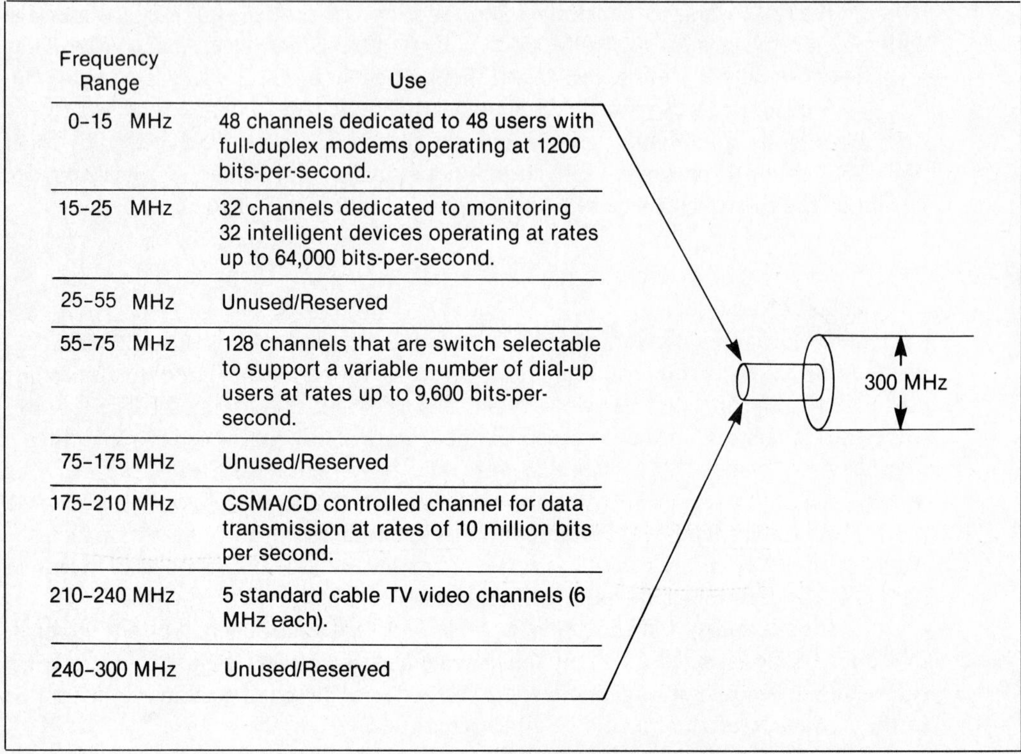

Frequency Range	Use
0–15 MHz	48 channels dedicated to 48 users with full-duplex modems operating at 1200 bits-per-second.
15–25 MHz	32 channels dedicated to monitoring 32 intelligent devices operating at rates up to 64,000 bits-per-second.
25–55 MHz	Unused/Reserved
55–75 MHz	128 channels that are switch selectable to support a variable number of dial-up users at rates up to 9,600 bits-per-second.
75–175 MHz	Unused/Reserved
175–210 MHz	CSMA/CD controlled channel for data transmission at rates of 10 million bits per second.
210–240 MHz	5 standard cable TV video channels (6 MHz each).
240–300 MHz	Unused/Reserved

Adapted with permission of Digital Equipment Corporation

Figure 13-8 Sample frequency allocation scheme for a 300-MHz broadband local area network

The next group of switched channels work like the PBX system already described. Users contend for an available channel and need *frequency agile* modems to manually or automatically adjust to the one that is assigned, if available.

Using a switch on a local area network gives the switched channel the characteristics of a star configuration. The switching software and physical cable become the central point of control, or failure, for this portion of the network.

The next band functions like the CSMA/CD baseband local area network already described. Connection and data conversion are, however, more complex. First the CSMA/CD protocol acts on the data in the workstation. Then data must be converted from digital to analog form. Once in analog form, they must be tuned to the CSMA/CD channel frequency. The reverse order gets data off the channel at a receiving node.

Other factors in implementing the CSMA/CD contention protocol on broadband networks must be considered. They concern the fact that data travel in only one direction in a broadband channel. If the *central retransmission facility* (CRF) that controls all traffic is not optimally located, response time could double.

Broadband local area networks hold a great deal of promise as high-performance, multiuse, local area networks. While they allow a great variety of equipment to operate on separate networks, the real gain made is a simplification of the wiring problem—one coaxial cable instead of many. The need for communication between the large number of participating nodes still must be resolved.

By putting everything on one cable, network control and maintenance become a more complex function. The commercial availability and the cost of required equipment need to be assessed. Finally, the software needed to make all the hardware work in harmony is, in some cases, still in development stages.

EVALUATION

Evaluation of candidate products begins after specifying requirements and a budget. The main requirements, as previously mentioned, are the number of users along with the type and volume of traffic. These figures need to consider peak loads as well as long-range plans.

Some advocate that local area networks are not for users with under five workstations. They believe a multiuser system is best. A multiuser system has one central processor where users with dumb terminals share a centralized computer.

Some powerful new multiuser microcomputer-based systems are satisfying many company needs. In addition, clusters can be local area networked if needs expand. The arrangement resembles the terminal server in Figure 13–6.

With frequent computer, performance, and price option changes, users like SGD Inc. find that they have more than one viable local area networking alternative to select from.

When evaluating alternatives, SGD Inc. found many hybrid alternative systems. Having a professional consultant helped sort out the more complex data communication differences among alternatives.

When determining the traffic load a network must carry, some rule-of-thumb guidelines are used for rough estimating. For a ring or bus network, one guide is ten times the required capacity. If all peak throughput requirements from all devices add up to 100,000 bits-per-second, then the cable should be able to carry data at the rate of 1,000,000 bits-per-second.

For PBX-oriented systems, the main criteria is the *blocking factor.* The term refers to the number of devices that can be simultaneously active on a network. If all devices can be active the PBX is nonblocking. Generally the factor should at least equal the peak load and be upgradable as growth occurs. In a case where 100 workstations are connected, but only 50 are in use at peak periods, a desirable blocking factor would be at least 50. Usually PBX units are readily expandable, once installed.

Local area networks typically involve vendor-supported installations. They involve hardware, software, and service like a turnkey installation. The Local Area Network Checklist, given in Figure 13–9, therefore needs to be supported with other turnkey system checklists. They are identified on the Selection Summary: Turnkey System, Figure 5–3.

Figure 13-9 Local Area Networking Checklist

	Name	Vendor	Type	Cost per Workstation Min. vs. Max.	
A:	______	______	______	___	___
B:	______	______	______	___	___
C:	______	______	______	___	___

Check "must have" items	Rating (Scale: 1 = poor to 10 = excellent) A	B	C
General			
Simultaneous user workstation connections:			
___ Minimum	___	___	___
___ Maximum	___	___	___
___ Average cost per workstation	___	___	___
Traffic supported:			
___ Text/data	___	___	___
___ Graphics	___	___	___
___ Audio	___	___	___
___ Video	___	___	___
___ Noninterfering with normal user operations	___	___	___
___ Uses familiar operating system commands for operation and error handling	___	___	___
___ Time from installation to functional use	___	___	___
___ Off-the-shelf single-user applications executed over network	___	___	___
Workstations			
___ Multivendor products	___	___	___
___ Single-vendor products	___	___	___
___ Local floppy disk required	___	___	___
Minimum memory required as:			
___ User	___	___	___
___ Server	___	___	___
Interface board slots needed as:			
___ User	___	___	___
___ Server	___	___	___
Operating systems supported:			
___ Multivendor products	___	___	___
___ Single-vendor products	___	___	___
Sharable Resources			
___ Multivendor products	___	___	___
___ Single-vendor products	___	___	___
___ Server can also simultaneously function as a workstation	___	___	___
Server connections:			
___ Minimum	___	___	___
___ Maximum	___	___	___

Figure 13-9 (continued)

Check "must have" items		Rating (Scale: 1 = poor to 10 = excellent) A	B	C
	Disks:			
____	Minimum servers	____	____	____
____	Maximum servers	____	____	____
____	Maximum users per server	____	____	____
	Size:			
____	Minimum	____	____	____
____	Maximum	____	____	____
____	Supports public and private directories and files	____	____	____
____	Record locking	____	____	____
____	Date and time stamps files	____	____	____
____	Backup hardware required	____	____	____
____	Backup transfer time	____	____	____
	Printers and plotters:			
____	Minimum servers	____	____	____
____	Maximum servers	____	____	____
____	Maximum users per server	____	____	____
____	Print-spooling	____	____	____
____	Special software required	____	____	____
	Gateway to wide area networks:			
____	Minimum servers	____	____	____
____	Maximum servers	____	____	____
____	Maximum users per server	____	____	____
	Protocols supported:			
____	Asynchronous	____	____	____
____	Synchronous	____	____	____
____	Specific protocols preset	____	____	____
____	Router to other similar protocol networks	____	____	____
	Value-Added Applications			
____	Database management system	____	____	____
____	Electronic mail	____	____	____
____	Community bulletin board	____	____	____
____	Station-to-station chat	____	____	____
____	Reminder function	____	____	____
____	Other ____________________	____	____	____
	Environment Restrictions			
____	Workstation location	____	____	____
____	One building	____	____	____
	Multibuilding:			
____	Connected	____	____	____
____	Detached	____	____	____
____	Space required for network components	____	____	____
	Cable housings:			
____	False ceilings	____	____	____
____	Conduits	____	____	____
____	Buried	____	____	____

Figure 13-9 (continued)

Check "must have" items		Rating (Scale: 1 = poor to 10 = excellent) A	B	C
	Security			
____	User passwords	____	____	____
____	Directory access privileges by user/group	____	____	____
____	File permissions	____	____	____
	Network Control			
	Statistics for:			
____	Users connected	____	____	____
____	Amount of traffic	____	____	____
____	Type of traffic	____	____	____
____	Error rates	____	____	____
____	Hardware status	____	____	____
____	Fault isolation	____	____	____
	Ability to:			
____	Connect workstations	____	____	____
____	Disconnect workstations	____	____	____
____	Self-diagnosis	____	____	____
	Characteristics			
	Distance between any two nodes:			
____	Minimum	____	____	____
____	Maximum	____	____	____
____	Total network length	____	____	____
____	Information carrying capacity	____	____	____
	Data path:			
	Coaxial cable:			
____	Broadband	____	____	____
____	Baseband	____	____	____
____	Twisted-pair wire	____	____	____
____	Fiber optic cable	____	____	____
____	Microwave	____	____	____
____	Other ________________	____	____	____
	Topology:			
____	Star	____	____	____
____	Ring	____	____	____
____	Distributed bus	____	____	____
	Access rules:			
____	Token passing	____	____	____
____	Polling	____	____	____
____	CSMA	____	____	____
____	CSMA/CD	____	____	____
	Token passing:			
____	Time for node-to-node token pass	____	____	____
____	Message cycle time	____	____	____
	Message size:			
____	Minimum	____	____	____
____	Maximum	____	____	____

Figure 13-9 (continued)

Check "must have" items	Characteristics	Rating (Scale: 1 = poor to 10 = excellent) A	B	C
	PABX:			
____	Blocking factor	____	____	____
____	Analog	____	____	____
____	Digital	____	____	____
	Subtotal	____	____	____
	Divide by number of items rated for average rating	____	____	____

Transfer Average Rating to Selection Summary: Turnkey System, Figure 5-4.

SELF TEST

1. Offer an argument for why an organization might consider local area networking.
2. Identify two common local area network environments.
3. Give examples of how users with access to a local area network's facilities might operate.
4. What is user transparency?
5. What kind of questions must be answered in order to specify requirements?
6. Identify three local area network cabling technologies.
7. What is the difference between a PABX and a PBX?
8. Identify the limitations of a centrally switched system.
9. Describe the design goal of baseband systems.
10. What are common baseband topologies?
11. What does CSMA/CD mean and how does it work?
12. List optional hardware components that often are attached as servers to local area networks.
13. Explain how token passing works.
14. Describe how a broadband cable can carry data, video, and audio simultaneously.
15. What do megahertz and frequency division multiplexing mean?
16. Identify rule-of-thumb guidelines for estimating network capacity.

EXERCISES

1. Locate three recent articles on local area networking. Prepare an oral or written report on the products described and the advantages and disadvantages of each.
2. Write for product literature to two companies that sell broadband local area networks. Make a report comparing bandwidth options among the products reviewed.

3. *Walsh Company Case.* Most Walsh Company professional employees use small computers. They have an increasing need to share computer-stored information and applications. They find trading disks too time-consuming. They have to wait for printed listings to see what the company database of interest looks like. If the listing is out-of-date, planning assumptions are likewise out-of-date. Additionally, they find traditional ways of phoning messages and delivering notes to be bottlenecks on a day-to-day basis.

   You have been asked to research the possibility of using local area networking to help to solve the Walsh Company data communication problem.

   a. Write to companies for literature about their local area network offerings. Use periodical advertisements and directories for vendor name and address information. Concentrate on only PABX and baseband systems.
   b. When literature arrives, make a list of features and functions for each product. The Local Area Network Checklist could be used as a guide to what to look for.
   c. Assume Walsh has a long-range peak traffic load of 20,000 bits-per-second. It is all data traffic generated by 35 workstations. What products would you recommend be further researched and why?

RESOURCES AND REFERENCES

DERFLER, FRANK, JR. AND WILLIAM STALLINGS, *A Manager's Guide to Local Networks,* Prentice-Hall, 1983.

Guidelines for the Selection of Local Area Computer Networks, U.S. Government Printing Office, 1981.

Introduction to Local Area Networks, Digital, 1982.

Multi-Vendor Data Communication Networks, QED, 1982.

14

DATA COMMUNICATION SOFTWARE AND SERVICES

This chapter concerns the data communication software and services that business professionals use. It provides the justification for buying a modem or installing a local area network.

It begins with a look at services that a public information utility offers and the software needed to communicate with one. Once their systems are connected to a utility, users can avail themselves of electronic mail, message or bulletin board services, computer conferencing, and on-line database capabilities. Services described are available for all small computer single-user, multiuser, and local area networked environments.

INFORMATION UTILITIES

Information utilities achieve a good part of their success with the business community by offering a solution to the telephone tag syndrome. Telephone tag results when one party calls another who is not available and leaves a message to please return the call. The returned call finds no one in and results in leaving another message. And so it goes—wasting time, money, and effort.

To eliminate telephone tag with his field sales representatives, Mr. Williams uses the services of a public *information utility* to send electronic mail instead. Public information utilities make such services available to registered users or subscribers for a fee. Sample fee schedules are given in Figure 14–1 for two utilities, The Source and CompuServe. Registration includes a User Guide, and it is available through local computer stores or directly from the information utility.

Information utilities, sometimes also called *videotex* services, also offer information databases. They either develop the information themselves or get it from *information providers*. United Press International (UPI) is a provider who makes its national, state, and regional news stories available to at least one utility.

One accountant with a large firm uses the UPI database to find articles about his clients. He also uses the business news service to locate other articles about computer auditing. He even books airline and hotel reservations through a travel agency service offered on the utility.

Many other public utilities exist and offer a host of services, including electronic banking, shopping, entertainment, education, and career-oriented services. Many also offer computer languages for software development.

Figure 14–1 Sample fees for public information utilities

Fees Charged	*The Source*	*CompuServe*
One-time registration	$100.00	$30.00 (includes one free hour of evening use)
Connect cost per hour:		
300-Baud		
Day use	$ 20.75	$22.50
Evening use	$ 7.75	$ 5.00
1,200-Baud		
Day use	$ 25.75	$35.00
Evening use	$ 10.75	$17.50
Communication line surcharge to connect through a packet switched network	Included in rates above	$2–$20 per hour, depending on time and place of connection
Minimum monthly usage fee	$ 10.00	None
Monthly data storage	4,000 bytes free $.25 per 1,000 bytes for next 20,000 bytes Mass storage discounts offered after 20,000 bytes	128,000 bytes free $17 per 64,000-byte increment

IBM sells software that enables corporations to turn their large centralized computers into private information utilities. The software product, called Videotex, can be accessed by small computer workstations.

Using a private videotex service is very similar to using the public one. The difference is in how a user accesses service. With the private videotex, a user's workstation often is permanently linked to the corporate computer. This is done through a data communication interface board that makes the workstation appear as a terminal to the centralized corporate computer. All a user has to do is access the videotex program for service.

On the other hand, to use a public videotex, Mr. Williams first has to establish a temporary data link between his computer and the public utility's computer.

LINKING COMPUTERS

Before data communication can take place, compatibility must exist between the communicating computers. Data communication software enables Mr. Williams to configure his transmitting small computer to make it compatible with almost any receiving computer.

He uses the most fundamental kind of data communication software sold over-the-counter at retail computer stores. It is called an *asynchronous communication* package. Packages sold include Asynchronous Communication Software, PC-TALK, ASCOM, Crosstalk, and many others.

To access the public utility's remote computer, the data communication software disk is loaded. Then two keystrokes retrieve a menu where commonly called computer phone numbers are stored.

Because Mr. Williams has a smart modem connected, it can do the dialing task automatically. He enters a single number from the phone dialing directory, as shown in Figure 14–2. Typing "3" results in the modem automatically dialing the phone number associated with the entry for The Source information utility. Familiar dialing sounds and the remote telephone ringing sounds are audible through the modem. When the phone is answered at the host end, a high-pitched tone is audible. It is the familiar host modem frequency *carrier* sound. Typing two carriage returns in response to the carrier sound establishes a link between the two computers. Once the carrier sound is gone, the link is established.

The very first time Mr. Williams used the data communication software, no dialing directory numbers existed. He had to set them up.

He also had to verify that the communication parameters listed in the dialing directory were appropriate. They generally were good because they are the standard parameters used by asynchronously communicating devices. The only item he had to change was the baud rate, from 300 bits-per-second to 1,200 bits-per-second. His modem provided both. He chose to communicate with the utility at the faster speed. It helped reduce overall connect charges for some uses.

To change the baud rate required typing a "y" to indicate the need to revise. He typed a carriage return through all acceptable *default*, or prestored, parameters.

```
===DIALING DIRECTORY ===

                                              Communication
     Name                         Phone #      Parameters         Echo
                                            Baud        Data Stop
                                            Rate-Parity-Bits-Bit
  1 -Dataservice                  876-7170      1200-E-7-1          Y
  2 -CompuServe                   346-7330      1200-E-7-1          N
  3 -Source                       361-4005      1200-E-7-1          N
  4 -Express 57th St.             372-2141      1200-E-7-1          Y
  5 ______________________        ___ ____      1200-E-7-1          N
  6 ______________________        ___ ____      1200-E-7-1          N
  7 ______________________        ___ ____      1200-E-7-1          N
  8 ______________________        ___ ____      1200-E-7-1          N
  9 ______________________        ___ ____      1200-E-7-1          N
 10 ______________________        ___ ____      1200-E-7-1          N

                                   Type     __________To______________
Dial Entry #:             or...      y      Revise or add to directory
                                     x      Exit from directory
                                    f/b     Forward/backward paging
                                              through the directory
                                     L      Long distance dialing
```

Figure 14-2 Dialing directory

Adaptation of PC-TALK software, with permission of the Headlands Press, Inc.

The communication parameters E-7-1 refer to how the characters are transmitted. Figure 12-5 showed this standard asynchronous method of transmitting characters:

E = Even parity

7 = Number of data bits

1 = Number of stop bits

They were compatible with the service with which he planned to communicate.

Even the "N" for no *echo* was appropriate. *Echo* in Mr. Williams' package refers to sending each keyboard character to both the remote host and the display, as illustrated in Figure 14-3. For public networks, such as the one providing SGD Inc.'s electronic mail service, local echoing is not needed. The remote end returns all keyboarded characters. It happens so quickly, it is as if characters typed locally go right to the screen. This distant end echoing of characters acts as a positive and constant check on the quality of the transmission path.

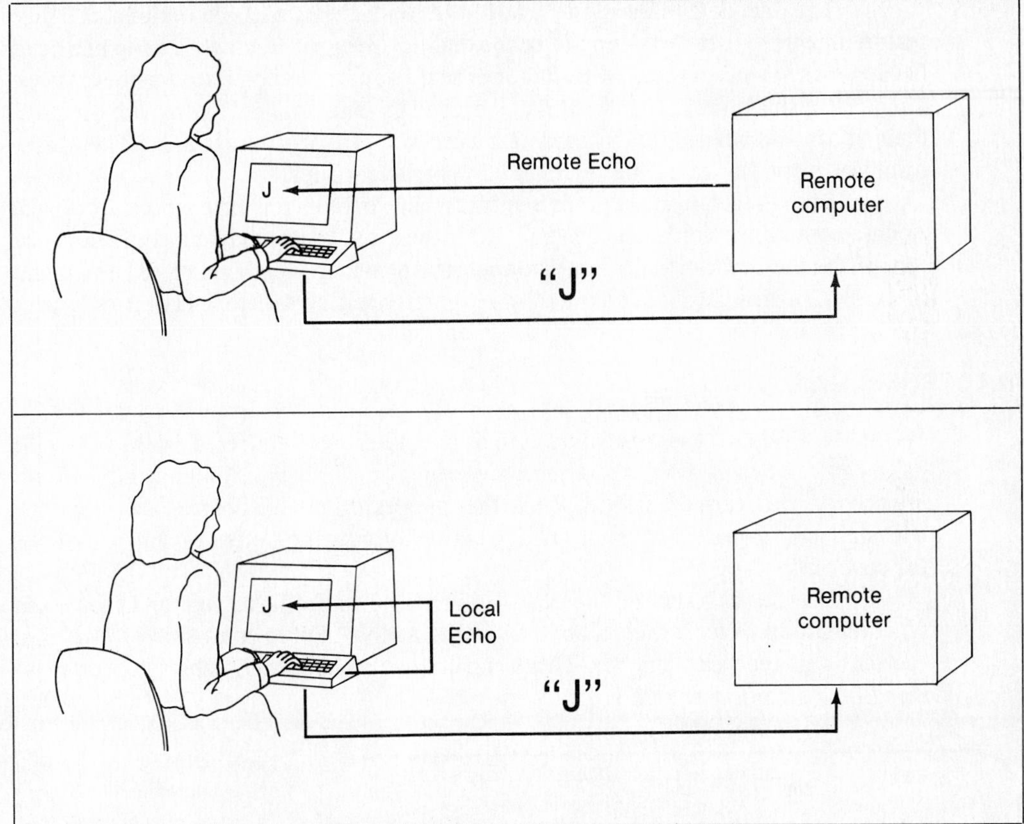

Figure 14-3 Remote and local echoing of keyboarded characters

The appearance of garbage characters on the screen means trouble on the telephone line. It is up to the user to detect problems and retype entries to correct them.

Had Mr. Williams chosen to enter a "yes" for the echo parameter, he would have two characters on his screen for every one keyboarded. This is because he would get both the local and remote end echoes.

All communication parameters could have been changed. Fortunately they didn't have to be, because they made Mr. Williams, as they do most users, very uneasy. For the majority of cases, preset defaults usually work as is.

LOG-ON

Once the data communication link is established, the host computer takes control and requires Mr. Williams to *log on* to the host system. Multiuser computers usually require a *log-on*, or sign-on, sequence to validate their data communicators. Generally it includes a request for an ID or account number and password. Both are registered when originally contracting to use the service.

The data communication package Mr. Williams uses has an optional message feature directory that works similar to the dialing directory. It allows storing messages like log-on sequence responses. By loading the ID number and password in the message directory, a single keystroke is all that is needed to send answers to host log-on questions. It can also be used for any other text a user wants to condense to a single keystroke response entry. Messages can be up to 126 characters long.

Both the setup and log-on procedures that Mr. Williams experienced are typical of data communication use in general. After these two steps, the data communicator connects to the application desired. The application might be anything offered on a menu of services, such as the one in Figure 14–4. He selects menu item six to send electronic mail.

ELECTRONIC MAIL

When Mr. Williams uses electronic mail or any other service offered by the utility, he has a choice of using a series of interactive menus or simply typing commands. Menus are necessary to learn the system. While they are easy to use for novices, they are time-consuming for experienced users. This is a major consideration when paying by the hour for service.

Now an experienced user, Mr. Williams works from the command level and types MAILCK to see if there is any mail in his mailbox. When contracting for service, each subscriber gets a "mailbox." Mail can only be exchanged by subscribers or sponsors of subscription accounts.

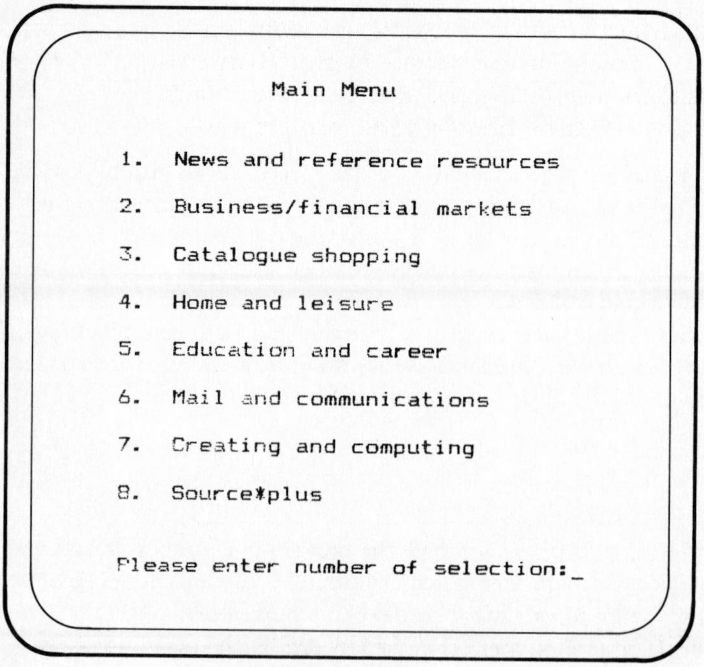

```
              Main Menu

    1.  News and reference resources

    2.  Business/financial markets

    3.  Catalogue shopping

    4.  Home and leisure

    5.  Education and career

    6.  Mail and communications

    7.  Creating and computing

    8.  Source*plus

    Please enter number of selection:_
```

Figure 14-4 A main menu from an information facility

Courtesy of Source Telecomputing Corporation

Typing another command generates a report of letters already read as well as those unread. It also indicates letters marked "Express" by the sender. By typing MAIL R he can read his mail. After reading a displayed piece of mail, he is asked for its disposition. He can file, delete, or reply to the letter, forward it to another subscriber, or do any combination of these. To answer, he types REPLY and enters the text. The rest of the reply procedure is similar to sending mail.

To send mail Mr. Williams types MAIL S and specifies the recipient's account number. He is prompted for a brief subject line then types the text. The finished letter is sent with a dot command, .S for send. Other dot commands, like .CC, sends a carbon copy to someone else, and .EX sends it express. A copy can also be saved in his own mailbox. He can also request an acknowledgement that the letter was received.

When Mr. Williams began to use electronic mail, he, like many others, felt there was something magical about this instant communication—receiving a letter, typing a reply, and knowing it is instantly in another person's mailbox. There are drawbacks, though. Unsolicited junk mail pops up as it does in conventional mail. Also, when a reply is typed, the sender's mail is not visible. This causes some inconvenience when wanting to make direct reference to received mail. A solution often requires first printing out the received mail. Doing this efficiently requires transferring the received letter as a file into the personal workstation disk, then printing the disk file.

Electronic mail also involves a number of legal and other issues that have to be resolved. For example, one of the critical legal and business functions served by the U.S. Postal Service is certified and registered mail. If electronic mail is to reach full utility, there must be a way for two companies or individuals to sign and witness receipt of mail and approval of contracts.

Besides public information utilities, one can subscribe to specialized electronic mail networks, such as Ontyme Electronic Message Network Service. The U.S. Postal Service offers microcomputer owners access to E-COM, an electronic mail service aimed at large-volume mail shippers. Packages like E-COM Connection and ECOMNET provide access directly to the Postal Service's network. Small computer packages like E-Mail come with an electronic mail facility, a bulletin board service, and other features.

UPLOADING AND DOWNLOADING

Bringing any file from a remote host computer into one's own computer is called *downloading* a file. Conversely, sending a file to the host is called *uploading* a file. Mr. Williams' data communication software requires two keystrokes to transfer files.

He had to be sure when he bought his data communication software that it allowed file transfers. In the data communication industry, his package is called an *intelligent* or *smart terminal emulation* package. A *dumb terminal emulation* package would not permit file transfers.

Many large companies are no longer acquiring dumb terminals. Instead, dumb terminals are being replaced by more capable workstation computers. Some, in fact, are less expensive than terminals.

Any participant can track conference activity by displaying or printing the conference notebook file, like the one listed in Figure 14–5. This tracking feature gives computer conferencing a significant advantage over telephone conferencing, as well as over face-to-face conferencing.

Tracking the decision-making process is perhaps the most powerful argument for using computer conferencing. One major bank using it found it indispensable when a key member of a project management conference was transferred. The new replacement was able to get into the conference file and search, using key words such as the former member's name, everything that was said about her area of responsibility.

She was also able to check why certain things were suggested and why they were accepted or rejected. Based on her research, she avoided putting together a proposal similar to one that was dropped over six months ago.

The Electronic Information Exchange System (EIES, pronounced eyes), has conducted controlled experiments dealing with computer conferencing. One finding suggests that conferencing results in at least as good a solution to a problem or task as could be expected from a group of people in one room. More often than not, the quality of the solution is far better.

Figure 14–5 Printout of a sample computer conference notebook file

```
Now joining: Randall (Tom)

114 Perez (Gil) 7-Oct-8X 10:21AM-PDT
Good morning Tom! Have you had a chance
to read my analysis of the company's
long-range plan yet? The section on the
profit-sharing proposal needs
improvement. Any ideas?

115 Randall (Tom) 7-Oct-8X 10:25AM-PDT
Hi Gil. Yes I read it and have some
ideas you might be interested in. I
need more time to work on them, but I
shall post them before seven tonight.
Are we still all planning to conference
on Friday morning?

Now joining: Stein (Sandra)

116 Perez (Gil) 7-Oct-8X 10:27AM-PDT
Hello Sandra. Have you heard whether or
not the Friday morning meeting is on.
Tom and I would like confirmation.

117 Stein (Sandra) 7-Oct-8X 10:29AM-PDT
Hello Gil and Tom. Yes, the meeting is
confirmed for 9:30 a.m. Gil, will your
rewrite of the plan be ready by then?
Tom, can you have some figures ...
```

Organizations use computer conferencing for many purposes. One government agency uses it to coordinate its efforts with geographically dispersed members. The bank just mentioned uses it for its four-year ongoing conference on project management. Several professional organizations use it to keep their members abreast of new information.

Through one conference on office automation that has been running continuously since 1981 on the Notepad conferencing system, subscribers trade current information on the use of office automation technology. Subscribers are office automation consultants and corporate long-range planners in the United States, Australia, and other foreign countries. By swapping information on good and bad hardware, software, and services, members contribute to saving their companies and clients substantial time and money.

Computer conferencing is less expensive than a telephone conference call. Unlike telephone conferencing, users can get printed copies of discussions if needed. Unlike video conferencing, it does not require participants to be in designated places at predetermined times.

To participate in a computer conference, a user needs to log on to the conference computer, get clearance from the computer, then proceed to type messages to other logged-on participants, if desired. Password codes insure that users access only conferences in which they are registered.

When someone joins a conference, all logged-on participants are notified with a message. Figure 14–5 gives an idea of how logged-on participants can instantly interact.

One Notepad conference is used nationwide by the nuclear power industry. The information swapping is designed to prevent nuclear plant accidents and to provide a forum for experts should a crisis occur. Another ongoing conference concerns environmental regulatory issues.

ON-LINE DATABASES

Many external databases exist to provide information to users for a fee. The Dow Jones News and Information Retrieval Service interests corporate financial managers and anyone else who follows the stocks, bonds, and commodities markets. This database is provided directly by Dow Jones who includes in the subscription price a software package for small computer access.

A bibliographic database is provided by DIALOG Information Services. It is the largest database service with over four million summaries of articles, reports, and books in the following general categories:

- Corporate news
- Business information
- Government publications
- Computers and electronics
- Engineering

- Medicine
- Agriculture
- Education
- Magazines

Summary descriptions of all entries in the database include the author, title, publisher, and keywords for topical searches. All elements of the description are searchable. Sometimes a brief summary is available.

Figure 14–6 gives an example of a typical DIALOG database search. It is typical of bibliographic database searches in general. The search given in Figure 14–6 took about two minutes and cost under $1 during nonprime time. Fees can mount rapidly, however, until search techniques are perfected. Both user guides and seminars help to perfect search strategies and techniques.

The advent of on-line database searching has spawned a new profession of *information brokers,* who perform client searches for a fee. Using search techniques and bibliographic searching experience, they provide the infrequent user with a valuable service.

The search illustrated processed over a half-million citations drawn from 2,300 journals and magazines. It found two articles on the specific topic. These statistics make the time and cost seem insignificant by comparison.

A search result sometimes is less ideal than desired. Citations, for example, may be less up-to-date than preferred. Desirable research sources may be excluded from database citations. Such drawbacks, however, may be irrelevant to some searches.

A search through DIALOG's corporate news database, updated by Standard and Poors, provides business financial researchers with information on more than 9,000 publicly held U.S. companies. Descriptive information covers earnings, management changes, contract awards, mergers, acquisitions, bond descriptions, and corporate activities.

To get a full copy, rather than just a summary, of citations requires an on-line request for print service. DIALOG supplies fulfillment vendors with a user's bibliographic information and the mailing instructions. The vendor sends copied material and directly bills clients for services. Prices vary by vendor and document. One example case charges a flat fee of $4.50 for an article, plus 20 cents per page for photocopying.

Attorneys may prefer to do bibliographic searches through the LEXIS database. The specialized legal database is a full text service, rather than summaries. Westlaw is a case research aid for attorneys often offered through law school libraries and large metropolitan libraries.

Medical professionals have the National Library of Medicine's database named MEDLARS for research purposes.

Some banks offer on-line database access to customers for searches in their own accounts. Users can inquire about bank balances and electronically transfer money between accounts. Large companies use the service to check target balances and obtain investment advice.

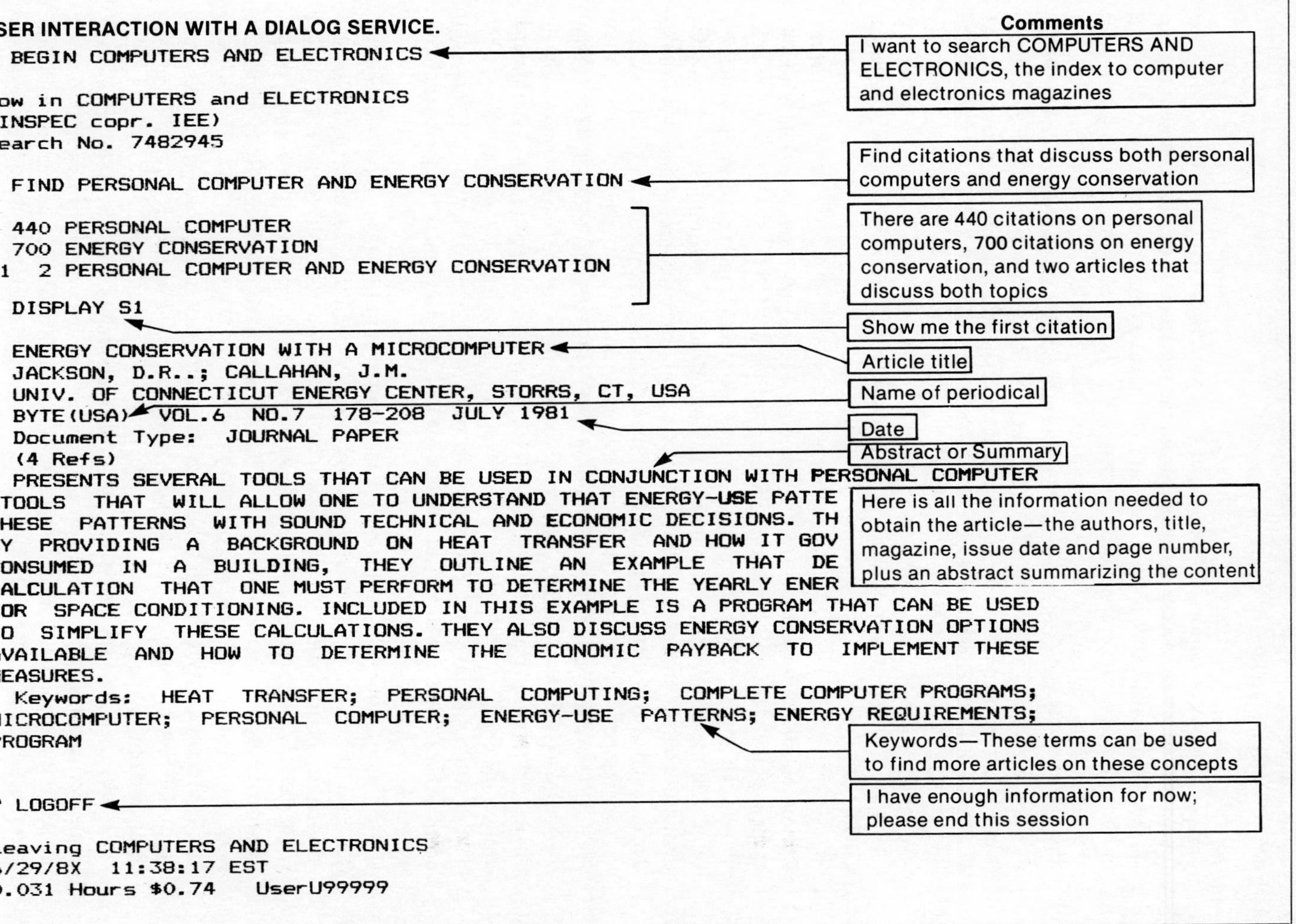

Courtesy of INSPEC and DIALOG Information Systems

Figure 14-6 Example of an on-line bibliographic database search using one of the DIALOG services

TRADE-OFFS AND OPTIONS

Basic data communication software that allows two computers to communicate is the fundamental element needed to benefit from the services and databases described. Using data communications has its pitfalls as well. Additional hardware and software costs more, and time must be expended to learn new procedures. Connect time and service charges need to be figured into any payback calculation.

Maintaining a system that uses data communications is more complex. When a failure occurs while the computer is on-line, the trouble can be in the line, modem, telephone, remote computer, or elsewhere. Troubleshooting the problem can be tedious and may require technical help.

EVALUATION

The checklist that concludes this chapter in Figure 14–7 helps evaluate mainly asynchronous-oriented data communication software.

The optional features not yet discussed concern, among others, *handshaking* details. In the data communication industry, *handshaking* generally refers to any exchange of predetermined signals between two computers or a computer and a peripheral device, such as a modem or printer. Handshaking allows the computer to tell whether another device is present and ready to receive or transmit.

The most common way for one computer to tell another that it is busy is called the X-ON/X-OFF convention. An X-OFF is sent, for example, when a printer buffer fills up. Once the buffer is empty, an X-ON is sent to the remote computer and transmission resumes.

Unfortunately, not every package uses the same conventions. Some send break/return signals or other alternatives. Most data communication packages allow setting handshaking alternative parameters.

In a similar vein, a user may want to interrupt the transmission or receipt of data only temporarily, without otherwise affecting procedures. Some database services and utilities allow this with the transmissionof a BREAK key. But the BREAK key, which is standard on dumb terminals, is not an ASCII character. It consists of sending steady zeros on the line for about 0.1 second. If a desired service requires BREAK, it is necessary to be sure a communication package can send it.

In many cases it is necessary to determine how end-of-line transmission is handled. Some computers send both carriage return and line feed signals. Others require inserting the line feed.

Most small computers use 7-bit ASCII characters, but often 8-bit characters are needed to transfer machine language programs or documents produced by a word processor that uses the eighth bit for control information. Some data communication packages can be reconfigured either to handle 8-bit characters or to provide a means of converting them to two 4-bit characters if the remote system cannot process 8-bit characters.

Sometimes a user dials remote computers through a switchboard or uses an alternative carrier, such as MCI or Sprint. To do this requires that extra numbers be allowed in the dialing directory.

Finally, some users do not know what the communication parameters are for a remote computer. In such a case, an ability to reconfigure a system without disconnecting it from the remote computer is desirable. When the protocol of a remote system is not known, it often must be determined by trial and error.

Figure 14-7 Data Communications Software Checklist

Candidate Packages Names:
A: ______________________
B: ______________________
C: ______________________

Check "must have" items	Rating (Scale: 1 = poor to 10 = excellent) A	B	C
Type			
____Menu-driven	____	____	____
____Command-driven	____	____	____
Terminal Emulations			
____Asynchronous	____	____	____
____Synchronous: ______________	____	____	____
Compatibility with			
____Variety of standard modems	____	____	____
____Variety of communication interface boards	____	____	____
Communication Parameters			
____User-definable	____	____	____
Compatible with sending and receiving computers in terms of:			
____ Transmission rate	____	____	____
____ Parity bit	____	____	____
____ Number of data bits	____	____	____
____ Number of stop bits	____	____	____
____ Interrupt signaling	____	____	____
____ Remote echoing	____	____	____
____ Handling of carriage returns and line feeds	____	____	____
____Defaults provided	____	____	____
____Easy to change	____	____	____
____Changes possible while on-line	____	____	____
Dialing			
____Phone number directory	____	____	____
____Handles expanded phone numbers for alternative communication carriers	____	____	____
____Single keystroke dialing	____	____	____
____Automatic redialing on busy signal	____	____	____

Figure 14-7 (continued)

Check "must have" items	Rating (Scale: 1 = poor to 10 = excellent) A	B	C
Logging-on			
____Save multiple log-on and other repetitive keyboard sequences	____	____	____
____Single keystroke to respond to log-on requests	____	____	____
File Transfers			
File types:			
____ ASCII	____	____	____
____ Other: ____________	____	____	____
____Upload	____	____	____
____Download	____	____	____
____Simple keystroke activation	____	____	____
____Memory buffer adequate to prevent downloaded file overflow	____	____	____
____Automatic file transfer to disk	____	____	____
Printing			
____For transmit, receive, or both	____	____	____
____Easy on-off switching	____	____	____
Unattended operation			
____Control for autoanswer-type modem	____	____	____
____Executes a series of commands	____	____	____
____Automatic hangup on broken connection	____	____	____
____Password security	____	____	____
____Operating system security	____	____	____
____File transfers	____	____	____
Other Features			
____Status Indicators	____	____	____
____Operating system commands accessible while on-line	____	____	____
____Define keys to match control keys required by outside databases and services	____	____	____
____Video screen reformatting to variable column width	____	____	____
____Code conversion table to translate ASCII to, for example, EBCDIC	____	____	____
Subtotal	____	____	____
Divide by number of items rated for average rating	____	____	____

Transfer Average Rating to Selection Summary: Software, Figure 5-3.

SELF TEST

1. What is a public information utility?
2. Compare the difference in fee schedules between The Source and CompuServe.
3. Give an example of an information provider.

4. Describe the following:
   - Dialing directory
   - Carrier
   - Defaults
   - E–7–1
   - Echo
5. What is the purpose of the log-on? How is it accomplished?
6. Explain how electronic mail works.
7. What is the difference between uploading and downloading? Give an example of use.
8. Identify the difference between electronic mail and a bulletin board system. Give two examples of use.
9. Using an example, describe how computer conferencing works.
10. What is the advantage of computer conferencing over other forms of conferencing?
11. Give examples of on-line databases.
12. Describe how an on-line database search proceeds?
13. What is an information broker?

EXERCISES

1. Examine changes that have occurred to the fee schedules of CompuServe and The Source. Update the chart in Figure 14–1.
2. Compare the services available from CompuServe, the Source, Dow Jones, and DIALOG. The companies provide free literature about their services.
3. Locate a source to get a demonstration of an asynchronous communication package using a smart modem. Examine how the communication parameters are set. Listen for the dialing, carrier, and connect sounds. Identify the steps in the log-on sequence.

RESOURCES AND REFERENCES

DERFLER, FRANK J., *Microcomputer Data Communication Systems,* Prentice-Hall, 1982.

Directory of On-Line Services, Datapro.

Directory of Online Databases, New York Zoetrope.

Information Industry Association, for more information on on-line databases.

The NewsNet Action Letter, NewsNet.

creating custom applications

Using a small computer enhances an awareness of its unexploited potential in any given business environment. The desire often emerges to design a custom program or application. An application usually requires an interrelated suite of programs.

Part V demonstrates, through a small worked example, how this desire can be translated into reality.

The example is a simplified real estate tenant billing case study. It begins in Chapter 15 with a methodology to help specify requirements. Chapter 16 then implements the requirements using an off-the-shelf database management system.

Alternately, Chapter 17 examines the additional program design steps needed to implement the billing system from scratch. The assumption is made in Chapter 18 that programs are developed from scratch using BASIC program coding.

15

PHASE ONE: SPECIFYING REQUIREMENTS

Having decided to develop a custom application, a user chooses mainly between purchasing a packaged database management system (DBMS) or programming the application from scratch. Whichever alternative is chosen, phase one involves specifying requirements that the application must fulfill. Requirements for a tenant billing application, for example, could be the production of monthly rent statements and a rent roll report.

Specifying requirements is the concern of this chapter and involves two steps. The first is defining how outputs, such as the actual Rent Statement or Rent Roll Report, will look. Outputs could be displays as well as printed reports. Step two is defining the database.

No program coding is involved in phase one while specifying requirements. It is a mistaken notion that coding an application is the same as specifying or designing it. They are not the same, as later chapters will clarify.

After the steps of phase one are complete, sufficient detail is in place to implement an application with a database management system package. So this chapter becomes the logical introduction to Chapter 16, "Phase Two: Database Management System Implementation."

If no packaged software is used, the custom project assumes that programs will be coded from scratch. So Chapter 17 presents an "Alternate Phase Two: Program Design."

Only when the program design is known is it appropriate to begin coding a custom application developed from scratch.

PREPARATION

Although Mr. Williams of SGD Inc. never planned to get involved with custom applications, one of his relatives did. His sister-in-law, Ms. Irene Jones, owned and managed a modest-sized rental property.

Ms. Jones became intrigued with the possibility of creating a custom application. She once studied programming while in school. Among the books she read since then, one called *Program Design and Construction,* by David A. Higgins (Prentice-Hall, 1979), seemed appropriate for a small computer application project. She used its methodology, with some modification, to create a simple, one-building tenant billing application.

Her tenant billing application prints monthly rental bills for tenants. It also prints a Rent Roll Report that she uses as a control sheet. When rent checks arrive, she manually checks them off on her Rent Roll Report.

Following the prescribed methodology requires that she begin by defining the application outputs and the database.

STEP 1: OUTPUT DEFINITION

The first step in specifying requirements involves drawing a picture of application outputs. Generally outputs include one or more reports, bills, lists, or other kinds of printed documents or displays.

Computer professionals often use printer spacing layout sheets, like that used in Figure 15–1, to design forms. Every rectangle matches a printer position. Bills frequently are designed, as the one illustrated, to fit into a so-called #10 business envelope, which is 85 columns wide. Ms. Jones' design uses plain computer stock 8½ × 11-inch paper.

Having preprinted forms designed requires working with an experienced printing firm to get proper computer spacing alignment on forms. Firms with computer forms experience can provide valuable assistance in specifying printed output.

Using standard preprinted computer forms, such as those offered by large mail order supply houses, is a design aid. Mail order houses also offer to customize preprinted standard forms.

Ms. Jones decided not to use preprinted forms. Figure 15–2 illustrates the bill she had been preparing manually. Each month she filled in the blanks by hand for each tenant's bill. She planned to retain the simplicity of this form while adding the conven-

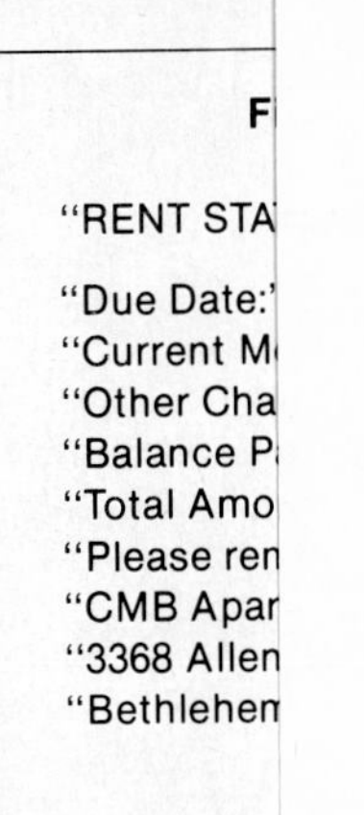

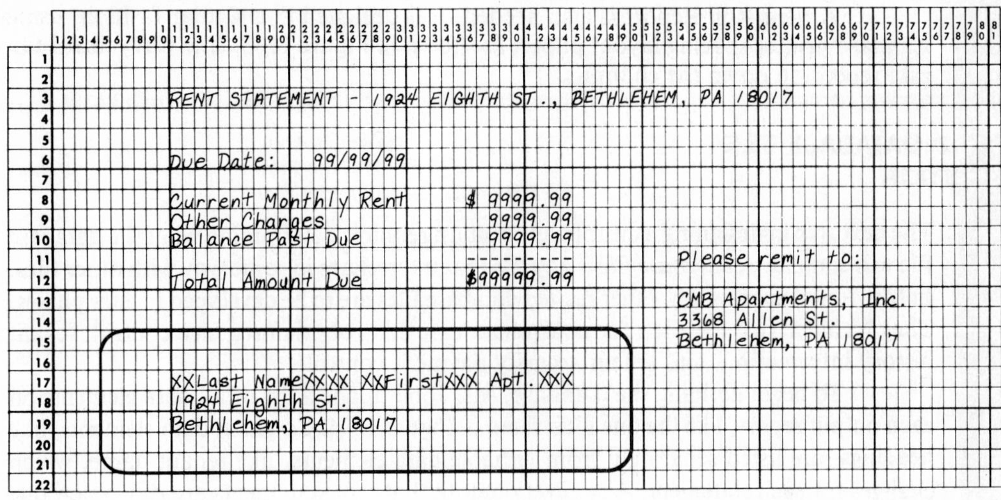

Figure 15-1 The rent statement design prepared on a printer spacing layout sheet

```
Rent Statement - 1924 Eighth St., Bethlehem, PA 18017

Tenant: ______________________________ Apt.:_______

Current month's rent: _________________
Other charges:_________________________
Amount past due:_______________________
Total due:_____________________________

Please remit to: CMB Apartments, Inc.
                 3368 Allen Street
                 Bethlehem, PA 18017

Date:_________
```

Figure 15-2 The old manually typed and photo-copied rent statement form used to send tenant bills. Each month the blanks were filled in by hand for each tenant bill.

ience of window envelope mailing. A window envelope lets the address show through a see-through cutout to eliminate the need for a separate mailing label. It also eliminates a separate program to print mailing labels.

Following report design conventions, Ms. Jones uses 9's to indicate numeric prints on the rent statement in Figure 15-1. The data actually printed will vary with each statement. She uses X's for variable alphabetic or character prints. She writes fixed items, like the "remit-to" address, exactly as it will appear. Her company is called CMB Apartments, Inc., which reflects the names of her three sons Chris, Matt, and Brad.

end of Chapters 15 and 17 should be consulted for a variety of approaches to the analysis and design of custom applications.

DATA DICTIONARY

It is customary to document an application's file characteristics in a data dictionary. Each data element is considered a field in a database record. Figure 15-5 shows the relationship of fields and records to a database file.

Some of the records Ms. Jones uses to test her application are given in Figure 15-6. It is common to view this data as a table with rows and columns. Each row represents another record. Columns represent fields common to all records.

The test data in Figure 15-6 reveal certain characteristics about each field. These record characteristics must be precisely defined for any database.

The data dictionary Ms. Jones manually developed for her system appears in Figure 15-7. Commercial database management systems automate the preparation of the data dictionary.

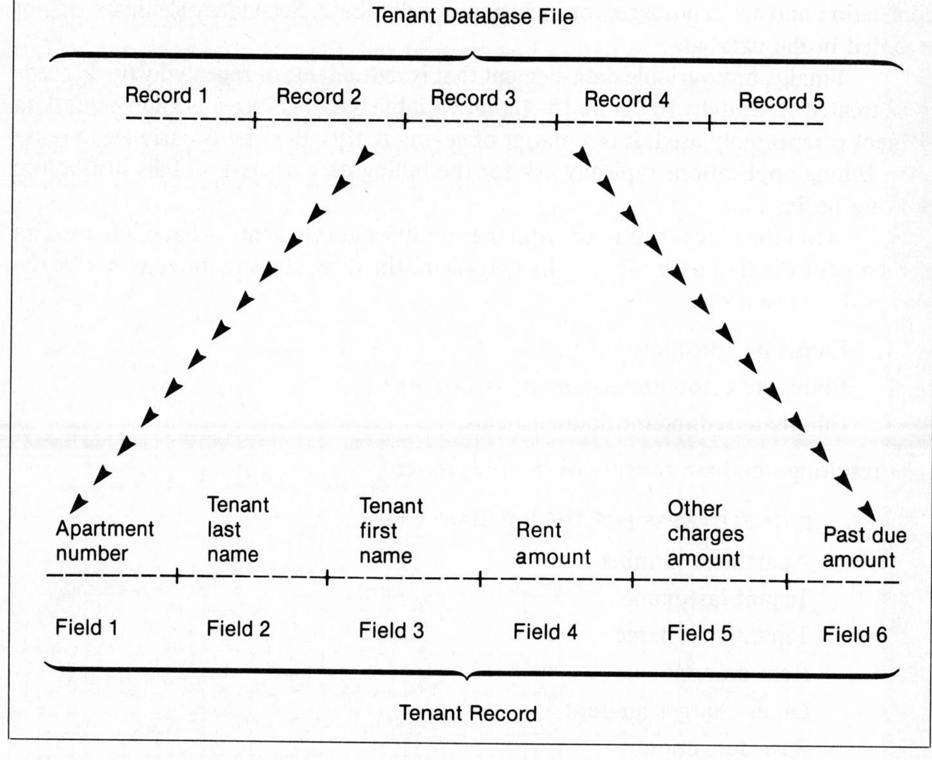

Figure 15-5 Relationship of fields and records to a database file

Figure 15-6 Tenant records used to test the custom-designed application

	FIELD 1	FIELD 2	FIELD 3	FIELD 4	FIELD 5	FIELD 6
	Apartment Number	*Tenant Last Name*	*Tenant First Name*	*Rent Amount*	*Other Charges Amount*	*Past Due Amount*
Record 1	1A	Phillips	Nancy	300.00	16.00	100.00
Record 2	1B	Franklin	Michael	370.00	25.00	370.00
Record 3	2A	Martin	Roger	305.00	15.00	—
Record 4	2B	Dietz	Elizabeth	325.00	—	—
Record 5	3A	Ashley	John	350.00	5.00	—

Figure 15-7 Data dictionary: tenant database file record structure

Field Number	*Field Description*	*Width in Characters*	*Data Type*
1	Apartment number	3	Character
2	Tenant last name	15	Character
3	Tenant first name	10	Character
4	Rent amount	6	Numeric
5	Other charges amount	6	Numeric
6	Past due amount	6	Numeric

When Figure 15–7 is compared with Figures 15–1 and 15–3, a similarity emerges. Every time a tenant's last name is used on a report, 15 character spaces are provided. Every time amount fields appear, they have 4 integer and 2 decimal positions for a total of 6 numeric positions. This consistency is important to good application design.

A database management system maintains data consistency throughout an application with automated controls. In a system programmed from scratch, it is up to the application designer and programmer to maintain uniformity. Inconsistency shows up as confusing reports, displays, and usually program problems.

SELF TEST

1. What steps are required to specify requirements for a custom application?
2. What are outputs? How are they specified?
3. What is a database file?
4. What is the first step to specify a database?
5. Describe the difference between a primary and secondary data element.
6. List the three steps to derive the logical database from a data elements list.
7. Define the following:
   - Data dictionary
   - Record
   - Field

EXERCISES

1. *CMB Apartments, Inc. Case.* The data elements list for the Rent Roll Report has to be created. Prepare the data elements list using Figure 15–4 as a guide.
2. *CMB Apartments, Inc. Case.* Assume Ms. Jones hires a new superintendent for her building. The new super needs a list of tenants by apartment number.
   a. Design the report using the printer spacing layout sheet provided at the end of the chapter in Figure 15–8.
   b. Prepare a data elements list for the report.
3. *Warehouse Company Case.* Assume you are the owner and manager of (your name) Warehouse Company. Customers rent warehouse floor space for which you bill monthly. You decide to design your own custom billing application. Sample customer billing data appear below:

	Customer 1	Customer 2
Number	11000	5000
Name	John Doe	Mary Smith
Address Line 1	123 Union Blvd	444 Fourth Avenue
Address Line 2	Forest Hills	New York
Address Line 3	New York 11385	New York 10020
Account Opened	01/01/83	10/12/79
Telephone #	212-666-7777	212-555-6666
Current Due	$1,000.00	$2,000.00
Past Due	$200.00	$150.00

	Customer 3	Customer 4
Number	16000	30000
Name	Paul Jones	Anna Frost
Address Line 1	888 Jarvis Blvd	555 Main Street
Address Line 2	New Rochelle	Greenlawn
Address Line 3	New York 10804	New York 11740
Account Opened	04/10/81	09/17/82

	Customer 3 (cont.)	Customer 4 (cont.)
Telephone #	914–111–2222	516–777–8888
Current Due	$3,000.00	$500.00
Past Due	—	—

	Customer 5	Customer 6
Number	20000	12345
Name	Jimmy Benson	George Anderson
Address Line 1	222 Dover Court	666 Fifth Avenue
Address Line 2	West Hurley	New York
Address Line 3	New York 12491	New York 10020
Account Opened	08/15/80	03/25/83
Telephone #	914–222–3333	212–999–5555
Current Due	$2,500.00	$1,200.00
Past Due	$100.00	—

a. Design a Customer Report showing customer number, last name, telephone number, current, past due and total amounts. A grand total for current and past due amounts should appear at the end of the report. Use the Rent Roll Report in Figure 15–3 as a guide for the design.

b. Design a customer monthly billing statement using a window envelope.

4. *Warehouse Company Case.* To further specify requirements for (your name) Warehouse Company, prepare a data elements list for the:

   a. Customer Report

   b. Customer statements

   Use Figure 15–4 as a guide for preparing the lists.

5. *Warehouse Company Case.* Prepare a data dictionary for the customer database file record, similar to the one in Figure 15–7.

RESOURCES AND REFERENCES

See also other chapters of Part V, Resources and References.

HIGGINS, DAVID A., *Program Design and Construction,* Prentice-Hall, 1979.

ORR, KEN, *Structured Requirements Definition,* Orr, 1981.

COLUMNS

ROWS	1	2	3	4	5	6	7	8	9	10	11	12	13	14	15	16	17	18	19	20	21	22	23	24	25	26	27	28	29	30	31	32	33	34	35	36	37	38	39	40	41	42	43	44	45	46	47	48	49	50	51	52	53	54	55	56	57	58	59	60	61	62	63	64	65	66	67	68	69	70	71	72	73	74	75	76	77	78	79	80	81	82	83	84	85
1																																																																																					
2																																																																																					
3																																																																																					
4																																																																																					
5																																																																																					
6																																																																																					
7																																																																																					
8																																																																																					
9																																																																																					
10																																																																																					
11																																																																																					
12																																																																																					
13																																																																																					
14																																																																																					
15																																																																																					
16																																																																																					
17																																																																																					
18																																																																																					
19																																																																																					
20																																																																																					
21																																																																																					
22																																																																																					
23																																																																																					
24																																																																																					
25																																																																																					
26																																																																																					
27																																																																																					
28																																																																																					
29																																																																																					
30																																																																																					
31																																																																																					
32																																																																																					
33																																																																																					
34																																																																																					
35																																																																																					

Figure 15-8A Printer spacing layout sheet

COLUMNS

ROWS	1	2	3	4	5	6	7	8	9	10	11	12	13	14	15	16	17	18	19	20	21	22	23	24	25	26	27	28	29	30	31	32	33	34	35	36	37	38	39	40	41	42	43	44	45	46	47	48	49	50	51	52	53	54	55	56	57	58	59	60	61	62	63	64	65	66	67	68	69	70	71	72	73	74	75	76	77	78	79	80	81	82	83	84	85
1																																																																																							
2																																																																																								
3																																																																																								
4																																																																																								
5																																																																																								
6																																																																																								
7																																																																																							
8																																																																																								
9																																																																																								
10																																																																																								
11																																																																																								
12																																																																																								
13																																																																																								
14																																																																																								
15																																																																																									
16																																																																																									
17																																																																																									
18																																																																																									
19																																																																																									
20																																																																																									
21																																																																																									
22																																																																																									
23																																																																																								
24																																																																																									
25																																																																																									
26																																																																																									
27																																																																																									
28																																																																																									
29																																																																																									
30																																																																																									
31																																																																																									
32																																																																																									
33																																																																																									
34																																																																																									
35																																																																																									

Figure 15-8B Printer spacing layout sheet

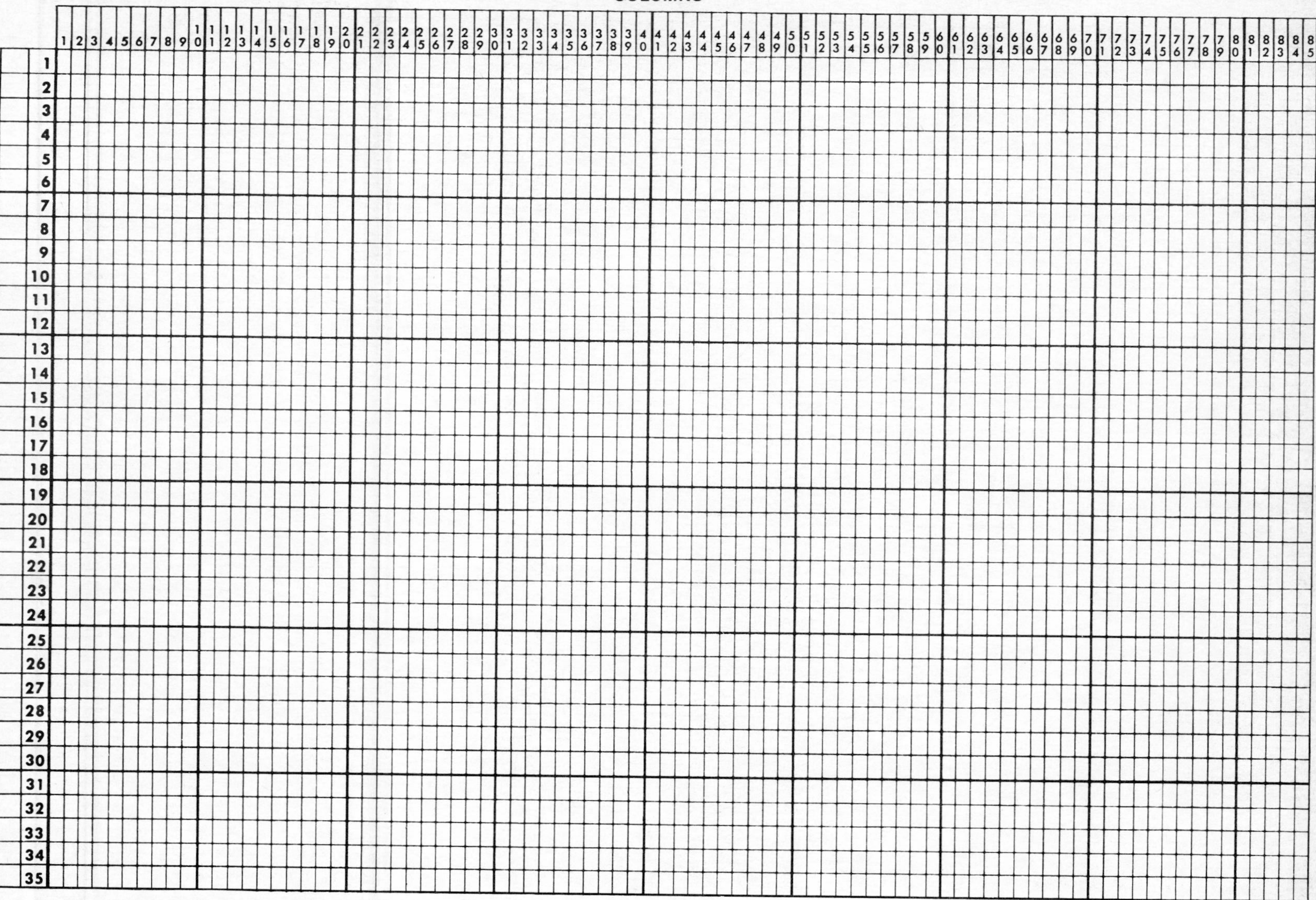

Figure 15-8C Printer spacing layout sheet

16

PHASE TWO: DATABASE MANAGEMENT SYSTEM IMPLEMENTATION

This chapter continues the custom work begun in Chapter 15. It follows the tenant billing application's step-by-step implementation on a database management system (DBMS). Although a specific DBMS is used, it is meant to be representative of DBMSs in general.

This chapter attempts to describes what a DBMS is and examines its parts. Basically a DBMS is a package of programs that enables users to develop and use a database. Among the tasks it helps a user accomplish are: create a database, query or ask questions of the database, generate reports and forms, interface with other non-database applications, build new files from old ones, and update data.

This chapter covers each of these tasks. It concludes with a discussion about relational DBMS concepts, large company trends, and package evaluation.

WHAT IS A DATABASE MANAGEMENT SYSTEM?

A database management system is a package of programs that helps a user establish and use a database. Its components are symbolically illustrated in Figure 16–1. As this

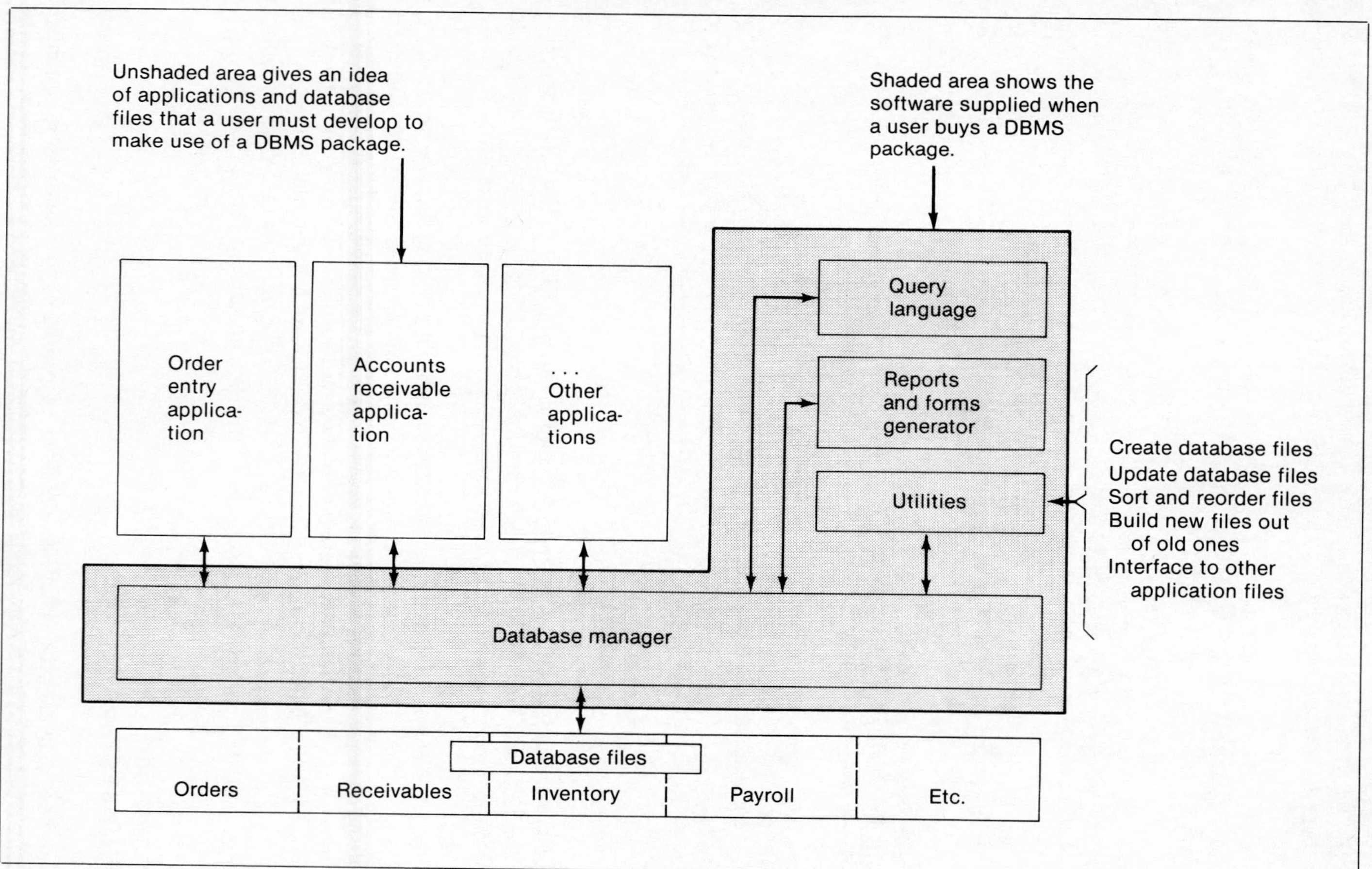

Figure 16-1 Software typically provided in a database management system (DBMS) package

figure shows, the software that actually manages database files is the database manager. Other software comes bundled with it, and the entire collection is referred to as a database management system.

As Figure 16–1 also shows, a user has the biggest burden to make a DBMS productive. By itself, a DBMS is useless. All of Ms. Jones' design work is needed to fill in the unshaded areas on Figure 16–1.

The file defined so far is a tenant file of billing information. Also defined are the rent statement and a Rent Roll Report. With output and database definitions, Ms. Jones is prepared to use the DBMS as a tool to create her custom application.

Why did Ms. Jones decide to use a DBMS? It enabled her to have a custom application in days instead of weeks or months, as programming from scratch typically requires.

Using a DBMS in most cases eliminates the need to hire expensive computer programming experts. In addition, a DBMS generally provides more file manipulation functions than are normally programmed from scratch.

The following discussion progresses in a step-by-step fashion to demonstrate how Ms. Jones uses a DBMS to create her custom application.

Create the Database

Ms. Jones types a function key to generate the word CREATE which tells the DBMS that she is ready to establish a new database file. She is asked to name the new

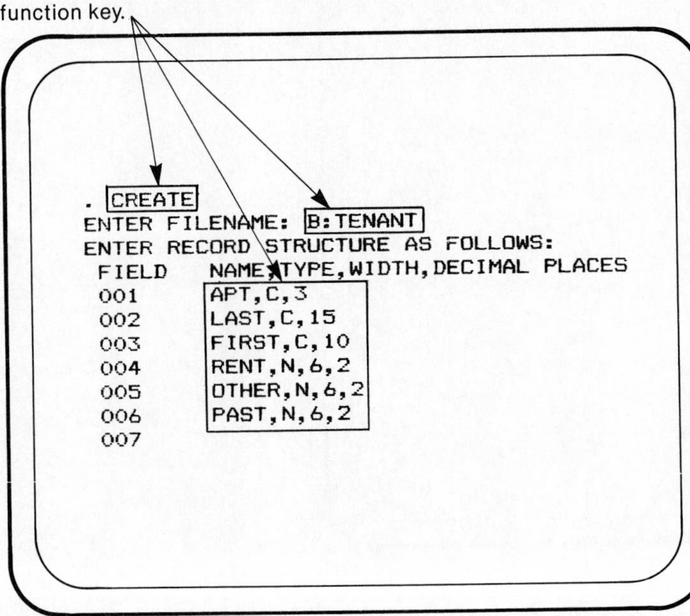

Figure 16–2 Creating the database record structure involves defining each field

file and define its record characteristics as shown in Figure 16–2. The B: in B:TENANT refers to the disk drive where the file will be located. It is not part of the file name.

The DBMS allows her to have many files. She eventually will have other files for apartment lease control, maintenance control, tenant history information, and tenant security payment control.

Once the record structure is declared, an automatic data entry form, like the one in Figure 16–3, appears. Ms. Jones types tenant data, one after another, into the blanks provided. This data entry process is often called building or loading the database file.

If desired, she can create a custom display form for data entry. Companies with many records to enter often create custom forms. They also hire data entry operators to load and maintain files. Once loaded, files can be *queried* or *searched.*

Query the Database

Asking the database questions and getting an immediate response on the display is another reason why users buy a DBMS. The ability to query the database makes any DBMS a powerful information retrieval tool.

When she has a request, Ms. Jones types a direct command, like those illustrated in Figure 16–4. All records that meet query conditions are immediately displayed.

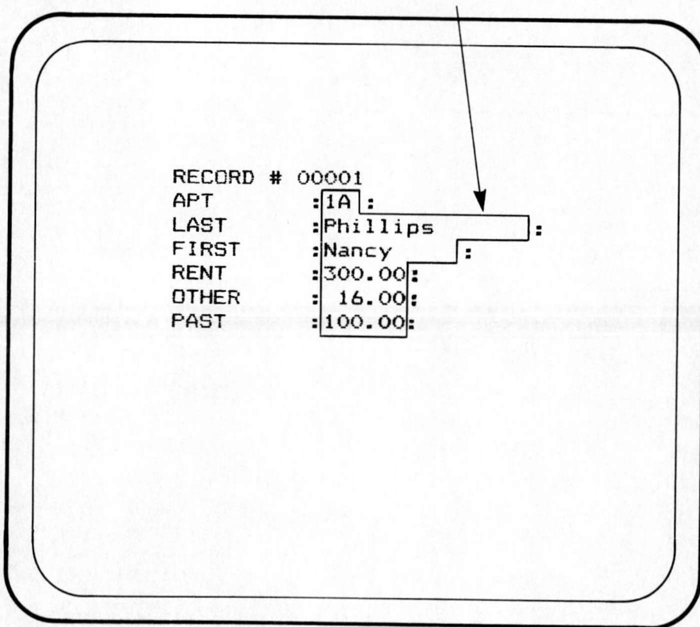

Figure 16-3 A data entry screen that is automatically generated to simplify entering record information

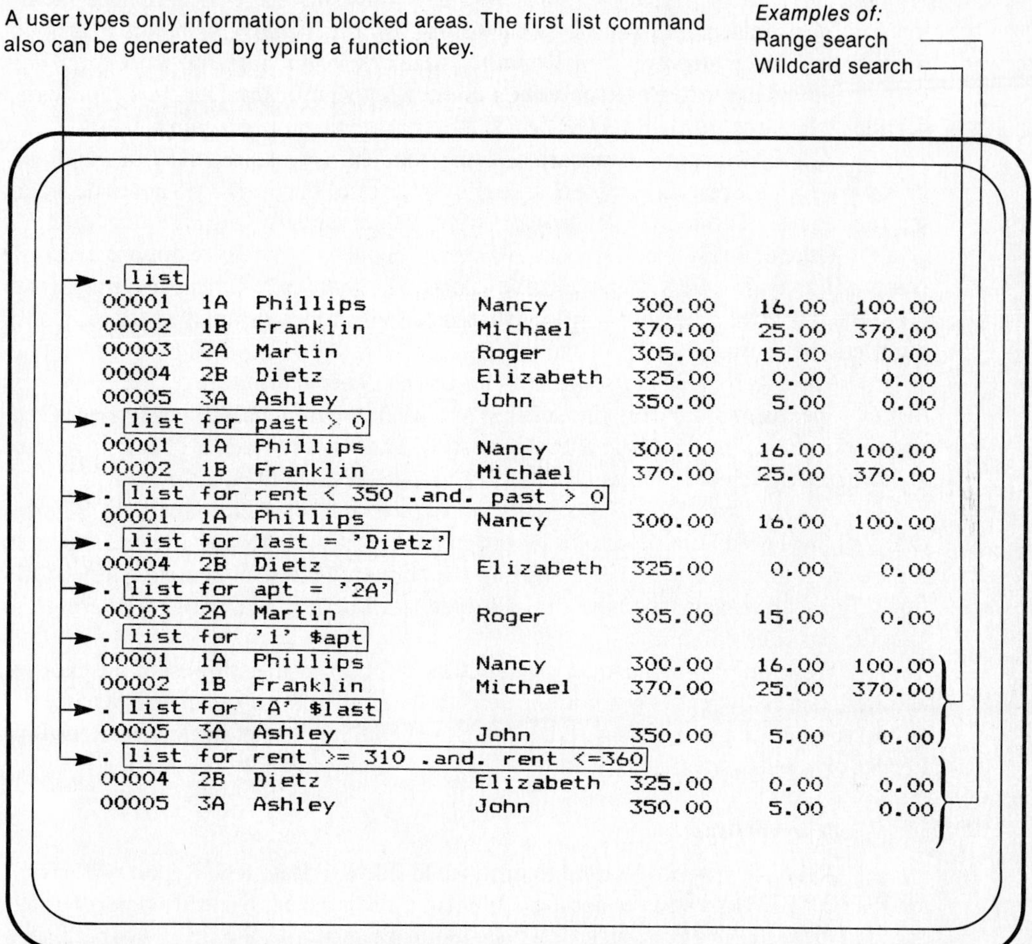

Figure 16-4 Commands, with responses, used to query the database

The examples in Figure 16–4 give an idea of the built-in flexibility to query or search a database. "Greater than" and "less than" searches are possible by entering appropriate ">" and "<" symbols. The last search illustrates a *range* search for all tenants whose rent is greater than or equal to $310 and less than or equal to $360.

Specific searches require identifying a unique record item. Examples are searches for apartment "2A" and the "Dietz" records.

If a search condition is not fully known, Ms. Jones does a so-called *wildcard* search. Assume she wants to find the names of all tenants in first-floor apartments. By typing LIST FOR '1' $APT she indicates that as long as '1' exists as data in the apartment number field, it meets the search criterion. All other characters in the apartment number field are treated as *wildcard* or *ambiguous characters.* If she does not recall how to spell a tenant name, she need only enter one or a few significant characters. The search for the Ashley record, LIST FOR 'A' $LAST, is an example of such a search.

All DBMSs provide wildcard or ambiguous character searches. With command-driven systems, misplacing a single character or space results in the DBMS not understanding the request. The request language is often called a *query language.*

Other DBMSs handle queries differently. Some offer menus of options to choose from until an entire query statement is developed. They are called *menu-driven systems.* On some, the large number of options that need to be cycled through to establish a request can be tiresome.

For experienced users, some menu-driven systems offer the option to by-pass menus. The query statement gets entered just as in a command-driven system. Once one works at the direct command level, one should not have to trade off flexibility. Some menu-based systems offer less flexibility than pure command-based systems.

Another type DBMS is called a *query by example* system. One DBMS in this category displays all the fields of a record in a table format, such as the one shown in Figure 16–5. A user moves the cursor into the column desired and enters query conditions. To list all tenants who have past due balances, for example, requires entering >0 into the past due column.

While one or another query technique may be preferable, the rest of the package features, especially report generation, need to be examined. In one package case, for example, while all query tests worked, Ms. Jones could not generate either a Rent Roll Report or a rent statement.

Generate Reports

A *report generator* is used to produce Ms. Jones' Rent Roll Report. After typing REPORT FORM and the database filename, she is asked to specify report format and data desired. The process follows the sequence shown in Figure 16–6 and results in the report shown in the same figure. It takes only a few minutes to specify report parameters. The format is automatically saved for reuse.

Her DBMS and a few other commercial packages do not allow report revision. But her package supplier announced a future upgrade that will allow revising stored report formats. In the meanwhile she has to re-enter report specifications from scratch each time she wants a column title change. It is inconvenient.

As is apparent in Figure 16–6, page numbering, date, and spacing are automatically provided by the report generator. In some systems these characteristics are determined by the user.

Some DBMSs provide an array of report options. They include automatic calculation of, for example, column or row average, standard deviation, minimum, maximum, and the like.

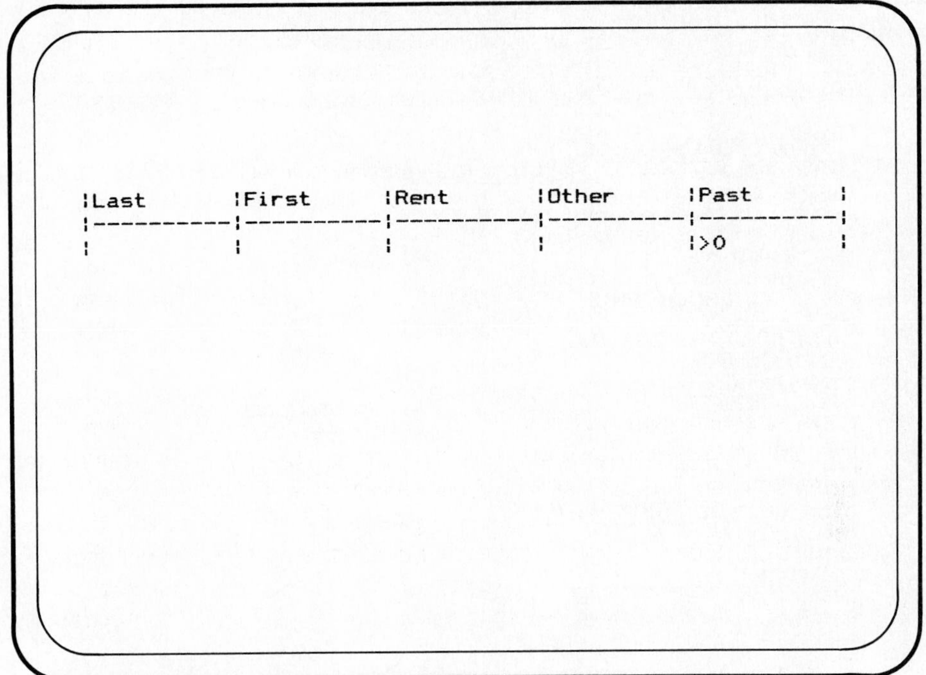

Figure 16-5 A query by example DBMS search technique

Generate Forms

To generate rent statement forms requires writing the program shown in Figure 16–7. As is apparent, it requires study to learn how to write executable programs. Programs are saved as a disk file and can be run later with a single command.

Repetitive or loop processing occurs inside a so-called DO WHILE to ENDDO loop. These statements cause the program to repeat the processing logic contained in them. Three loops are needed. One processes each record until an EOF, or end-of-file, condition is reached. Another creates extra blank lines so that the window envelope address placement is exact. Another creates extra blank lines to position the start of each statement at the top of a new page. The ? symbol alone on a program line causes a blank line to print.

Conditions applied to each record are indicated by an IF and ENDIF structure. For example, the presence of other charges causes a unique line to print. An absence of this amount causes the program to skip the print. The second DO loop compensates for fewer printed lines by creating extra blank lines.

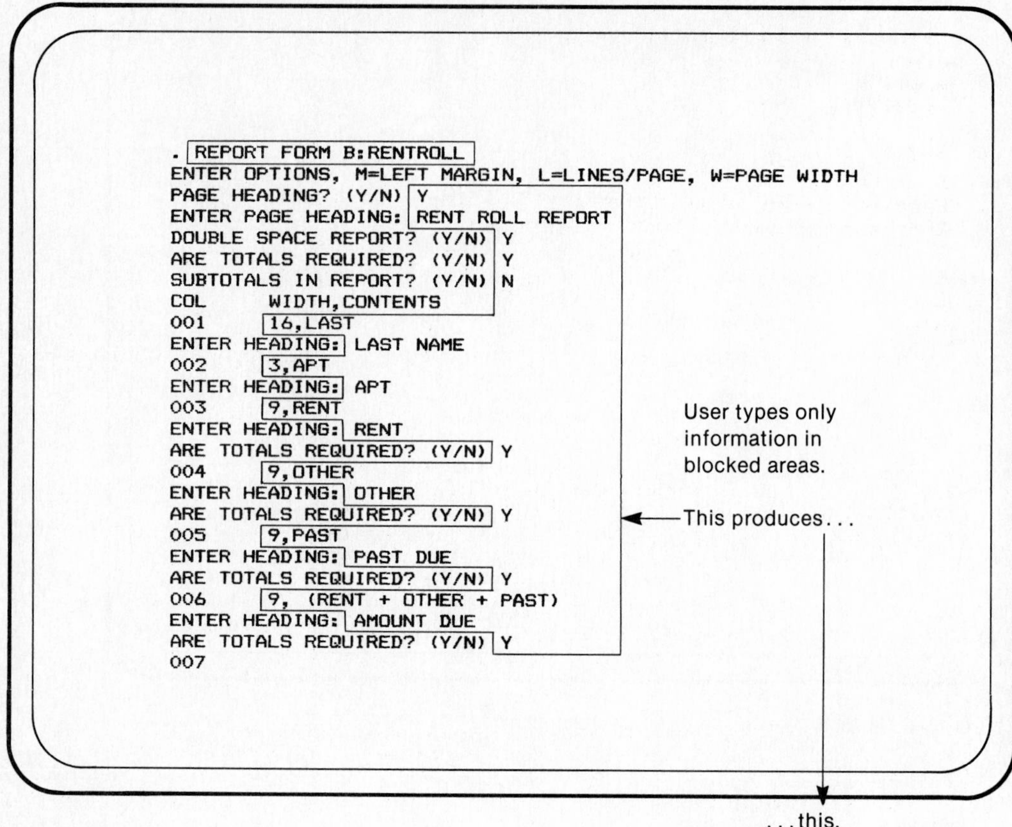

```
. REPORT FORM B:RENTROLL
ENTER OPTIONS, M=LEFT MARGIN, L=LINES/PAGE, W=PAGE WIDTH
PAGE HEADING? (Y/N) Y
ENTER PAGE HEADING: RENT ROLL REPORT
DOUBLE SPACE REPORT? (Y/N) Y
ARE TOTALS REQUIRED? (Y/N) Y
SUBTOTALS IN REPORT? (Y/N) N
COL     WIDTH,CONTENTS
001     16,LAST
ENTER HEADING: LAST NAME
002     3,APT
ENTER HEADING: APT
003     9,RENT
ENTER HEADING: RENT
ARE TOTALS REQUIRED? (Y/N) Y
004     9,OTHER
ENTER HEADING: OTHER
ARE TOTALS REQUIRED? (Y/N) Y
005     9,PAST
ENTER HEADING: PAST DUE
ARE TOTALS REQUIRED? (Y/N) Y
006     9, (RENT + OTHER + PAST)
ENTER HEADING: AMOUNT DUE
ARE TOTALS REQUIRED? (Y/N) Y
007
```


PAGE NO. 00001
09/28/8X

RENT ROLL REPORT

LAST NAME	APT	RENT	OTHER	PAST DUE	AMOUNT DUE
Phillips	1A	300.00	16.00	100.00	416.00
Franklin	1B	370.00	25.00	370.00	765.00
Martin	2A	305.00	15.00	0.00	320.00
Dietz	2B	325.00	0.00	0.00	325.00
Ashley	3A	350.00	5.00	0.00	355.00
** TOTAL **					
		1650.00	61.00	470.00	2181.00

Figure 16-6 Generating a report

```
*******************************
*  Print Statements Program    *
*  Saved as B:BILLS.PRG        *
*******************************
SET TALK OFF
SET PRINT ON
USE B:TENANT
STORE 'Please remit to:' TO REMIT
STORE 'CMB Apartments, Inc.' TO ADDR1
STORE '3368 Allen St.' TO ADDR2
STORE 'Bethlehem, PA 18017' TO ADDR3
STORE 0 TO LINES
DO WHILE .NOT. EOF
  ?
  ? '          RENT STATEMENT - 1924 EIGHTH ST., BETHLEHEM, PA 18017'
  ?
  ?
  ? '          Due Date:  ', DATE()
  ?
  ? '          Current Monthly Rent          $', RENT
  IF OTHER > 0
  ? '          Other Charges                  ', OTHER
             STORE LINES + 1 TO LINES
  ENDIF
  IF PAST > 0
  ? '          Balance Past Due               ', PAST
             STORE LINES + 1 TO LINES
  ENDIF
  ? '                                ---------          ', REMIT
  ? '          Total Amount Due      ', (RENT + OTHER + PAST)
  ? '                                                   ', ADDR1
  ? '                                                   ', ADDR2
  ? '                                                   ', ADDR3
  DO WHILE LINES < 2
             ?
             STORE LINES + 1 TO LINES
  ENDDO
  ?
  ?
  ? '       ',TRIM (FIRST), TRIM (LAST), 'Apt', APT
  ? '          1924 Eighth St.'
  ? '          Bethlehem, PA 18017'
  ?
  ?
  ?
  ? '-------------------------------------------------------------'
  ?
  STORE 0 TO LINES
  DO WHILE LINES < 42
             ?
             STORE LINES + 1 TO LINES
  ENDDO
  STORE 0 TO LINES
  SKIP
ENDDO
```

Figure 16-7 The program code to produce rent statements

Both WHILE loop and IF conditional structures are familiar to Ms. Jones. She learned them when she studied programming. With a few exceptions, much of the other DBMS program contains familiar coding techniques.

To a former programmer, therefore, the coding is simple. To a nonprogrammer, however, it is less so. Nonprogrammers have, nonetheless, found the coding managable after some study.

The rent statement produced by the command DO B:BILLS is given in Figure 16–8. The command first retrieves the program saved as BILLS then executes it.

Having a DBMS programming language enables Ms. Jones to have a good deal of design flexibility. She is virtually unrestricted in the kinds of forms and reports she chooses to generate.

The price for this flexibility is to learn a programming language. It is often called a very high-level language (VHLL) because it is so much like natural English compared to other programming languages. Some label it a *fourth-generation language.* The other three generations progress from machine language, to assembler language, to ordinary high-level languages (HLL) like BASIC and COBOL.

A comparison between third- and fourth-generation languages can be drawn by comparing the program in Figure 16–7 with the BASIC program to print rent statements given in Figure 18–13.

One DBMS has a report generator that does double duty by providing for forms as well. With it a user types an image, like the rent statement, on the screen. Curly brackets indicate where tenant record information should be inserted into the form. Still another similar system uses function keys to distinguish variable inserts from fixed form information.

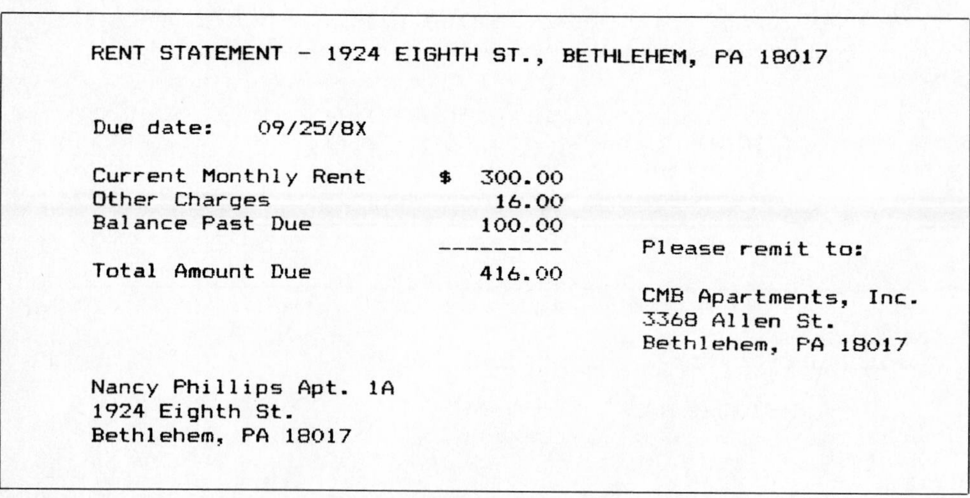

```
RENT STATEMENT - 1924 EIGHTH ST., BETHLEHEM, PA 18017

Due date:    09/25/8X

Current Monthly Rent      $  300.00
Other Charges                 16.00
Balance Past Due             100.00
                          ---------      Please remit to:
Total Amount Due             416.00
                                         CMB Apartments, Inc.
                                         3368 Allen St.
                                         Bethlehem, PA 18017


Nancy Phillips Apt. 1A
1924 Eighth St.
Bethlehem, PA 18017
```

Figure 16-8 The rent statement produced by the program code in Figure 16–7

Interface with Other Application Files

Ms. Jones' DBMS provides commands to transfer files between databases as well as to other nondatabase applications. She uses this interface function to transfer control files into the electronic spreadsheet and word processing applications.

Users with established nondatabase applications find file transfer important. Ms. Jones' husband occasionally has to interrogate his accounts receivable or patient profile records in ways that are not preprogrammed. His medical records and billing application is not built on a DBMS. So whenever he has a so-called *ad hoc,* or unplanned, inquiry, he cannot get it from his packaged application. By transferring files into a DBMS, he can query them just like Ms. Jones queries the tenant database.

Sort and Reorder Files

Having the ability to sort and reorder files in new and different ways is impossible in Dr. Jones' non-DBMS application. By contrast, Ms. Jones can use the SORT command to put records in any alphabetic or numeric order she chooses. Figure 16–9 shows the request for a numeric sort by rent amount in descending order. It involves entering the file and field to be used as well as the name of a new file to hold the sorted result file. When a sort is complete, the sorted file must be invoked with a USE command before it can be interrogated.

Build New Files from Old Ones

Ms. Jones' DBMS enables her to create new files from old ones. When she created her lease control files, for example, she reused information already entered for the tenant file. She had to type only new information or the expiration date, into each record. Lease file records consist of only apartment number and lease expiration date.

By joining the lease file with the tenant file, she could create a useful list for planning apartment turnover. Ideally she wants a listing of lease expiration date in ascending order with apartment number, tenant name, rent, and balance past due. Although in theory her system could produce the joined file for the list, it creates many unnecessary duplicate records. She decided to write a program to get the desired list.

Other DBMSs provide a JOIN command that produces the desired file. Unfortunately, they are less able to provide other things. Before selecting her DBMS, Ms. Jones studied the compromises to be made with any DBMS she selected. All had limitations in one or another area. Usually ones with good file manipulation capabilities had poor report capabilities. The reverse was also true.

Most DBMSs provide a PROJECT command that allows creating a new file using only selected fields from an established file. Ms. Jones' system provides a similar feature.

Besides PROJECT and JOIN, some DBMSs provide other file manipulation options, among which are:

A user types only information in blocked areas. The first list command also can be generated by typing a function key.

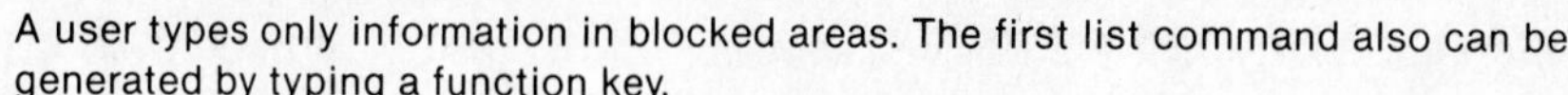

. use b:tenant
. sort on rent to b:rentlist descending
SORT COMPLETE
. use b:rentlist
. list
00001 1B Franklin Michael 370.00 25.00 370.00
00002 3A Ashley John 350.00 5.00 0.00
00003 2B Dietz Elizabeth 325.00 0.00 0.00
00004 2A Martin Roger 305.00 15.00 0.00
00005 1A Phillips Nancy 300.00 16.00 100.00
. use b:tenant
. sort on last to b:namelist
SORT COMPLETE
. use b:namelist
. list last, first, apt
00001 Ashley John 3A
00002 Dietz Elizabeth 2B
00003 Franklin Michael 1B
00004 Martin Roger 2A
00005 Phillips Nancy 1A

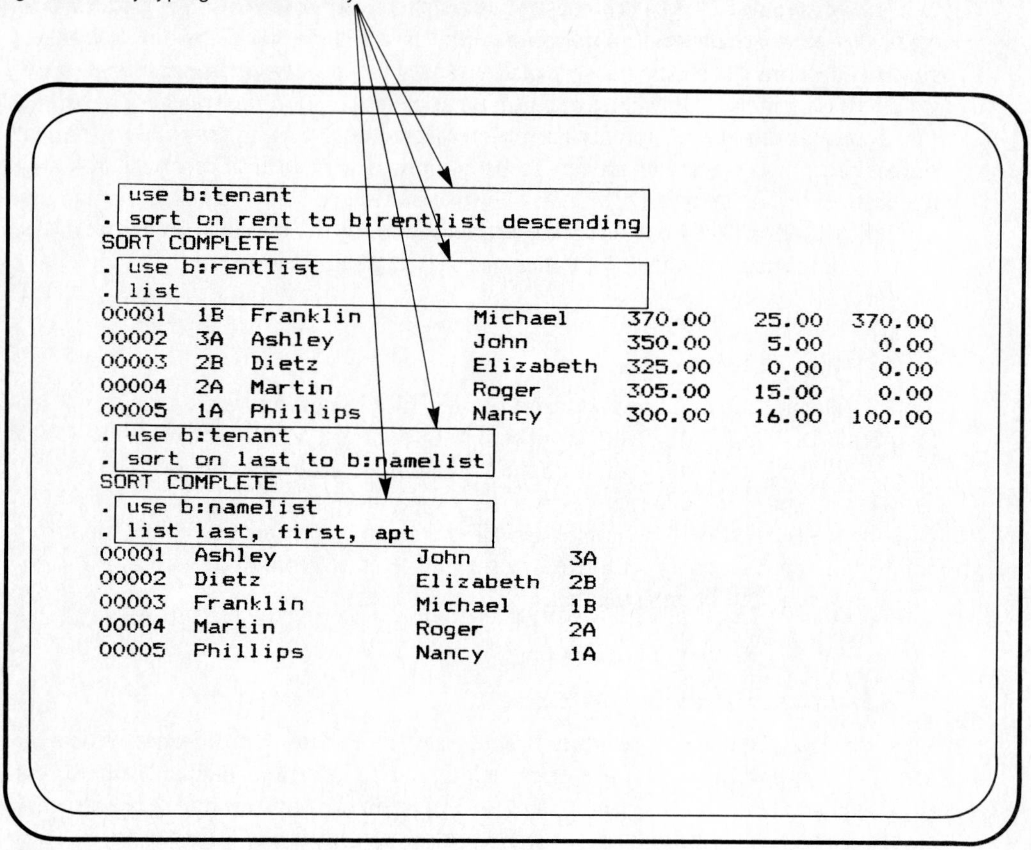

Figure 16-9 Two SORT examples with displayed result files

UNION allows combining all the records from one file followed by all the records from a second.

INTERSECTION produces a file consisting of all the records in one file which exactly match records in a second file.

DIFFERENCE is the opposite of INTERSECTION. The result file consists only of records from a file that do not match records in a second file.

UNIQUE produces a result file that deletes duplicate records.

DUPLICATE produces a file containing only the first occurrence of a duplicated record.

Other DBMSs give different names to these functions, like SUBTRACT instead of DIFFERENCE.

Ms. Jones' system offers a feature called UPDATE. The feature is useful for transaction-oriented businesses, like a sales company. One file could be a master, another could contain transactions. Transactions could be added to, or substituted for, corresponding fields in the master record. In this way, a customer invoice of items or a customer statement of monthly activity could be generated.

Because creating new files out of old ones is so flexible, applications can start simple and grow as needed. If a field is forgotten, it takes only a few minutes to add it to a file.

Ms. Jones makes an effort to keep records small. Each one deals with only one subject. Her latest one is an apartment maintenance file containing: apartment number, date last painted, and a comments column. Except for the apartment number, which is needed to JOIN or relate files, no data is duplicated. This technique adheres to good database design practice.

Database theorists would recognize her files as being in a desirable *third normal form.* In ordinary terms it means two major conditions are met. One is that there is no field duplicated in several files, except for fields needed to create new relationships. In Ms. Jones system, apartment number is duplicated in files and used for joining and otherwise manipulating records. Such a field is often called a key or index. Second, it means that all fields in a record depend entirely on the key and cannot be further decomposed to form separate records.

By adhering to good file design, she avoids *update anomalies.* An anomaly occurs when fields are duplicated in several files and an update, such as a change or deletion, is recorded in only one file.

Update Data

When Ms. Jones makes an update, she goes to the only file that the field exists in throughout the database and makes the change. For example, if tenant Nancy Phillips changed her name to Phillips-Wilkes, a change is needed to the tenant file. Had the lease file also included tenant name, it too would need updating. Ms. Jones avoids the multiple update problem by having primary data elements in only one file.

Because her DBMS creates duplicate records each time she creates new files from old ones, she does run the risk of having out-of-date result files. These secondary files are created from primary files. She makes it a habit not to reuse result files. Instead, she executes a new SORT or JOIN as needed. The new result file automatically writes over, or replaces, the old one.

Some DBMSs avoid all possible update anomalies. They handle result files differently. They never create duplicate records in result files. All result files are simply references or indexes with pointers back to records in the primary file. This means an update goes to the only file that the data exist in. All other files referencing that data are thereby automatically updated. Some DBMSs call this *virtual operations.*

RELATIONAL DBMS

Ms. Jones has a *relational DBMS.* The term relational defines how the files are structured. *Relational* files resemble tables with rows and columns. Figure 15–6 is an example of a relational file structure. Fields in one table file can be made to relate to fields in another table file. For example, apartment number in the tenant table file can be related to apartment number in the lease table file to create a new relation or relationship. Formal database theory calls a file a table or a *relation*.

The ease of data manipulation occurs because any two fields can be directly related without the need for any imposed structure. This is not the case with two other kinds of file structure used in DBMSs.

In both *hierarchical* and *network* DBMSs, records are rigidly linked by added pointer fields in records, as symbolically illustrated in Figure 16–10. Many large mainframe computer DBMSs are built with these structures. They work fine if the predictable path is always the one needed to retrieve data. If a data request is made outside the limitations of the record pointers, the request cannot be answered. Or a great deal of restructuring of pointers first must be done to get at the data. These types of systems are noted for their inflexibility and their need for experienced programmer and database administrator support.

LARGE COMPANY TRENDS

Large companies with established mainframe DBMSs are implementing small computer versions of their large systems. With a microcomputer version of a compatible DBMS at user workstations, slices of the company's database can be downloaded from the corporate mainframe. At workstations data can be used for local manipulation and analysis. No file format conversion steps are necessary since everyone uses copies of the same DBMS.

For the noncorporate user, DBMSs that function across a line of computers have advantages. They protect a user's investment regardless of how automation needs expand in the future. A migration path exists to port applications and data unchanged to a more powerful hardware environment. The main advantage of larger hardware is the massive amounts of data that can be manipulated and the increased speed of manipulation.

Mainframe and minicomputer DBMSs that are downscaled for microcomputers include, among many others, Sequitur, FOCUS, Oracle, Ingres, and MicroRIM. Prices to implement these systems vary from under $1,000 per copy to about $5,000 per copy. Some require about three days of formal user training, just as they do for large computer use. Those systems that work with command languages require some programmer orientation to use effectively.

The trend to supply users with slices of the corporate database for their own data manipulation is helping to change the role of the corporate data processing department. Its job is becoming more one of trustee rather than owner of the corporate database. Its job is to be sure user service requests are handled with dispatch and with timely updated information. Processing has moved out of the central computer department to the local user workstation.

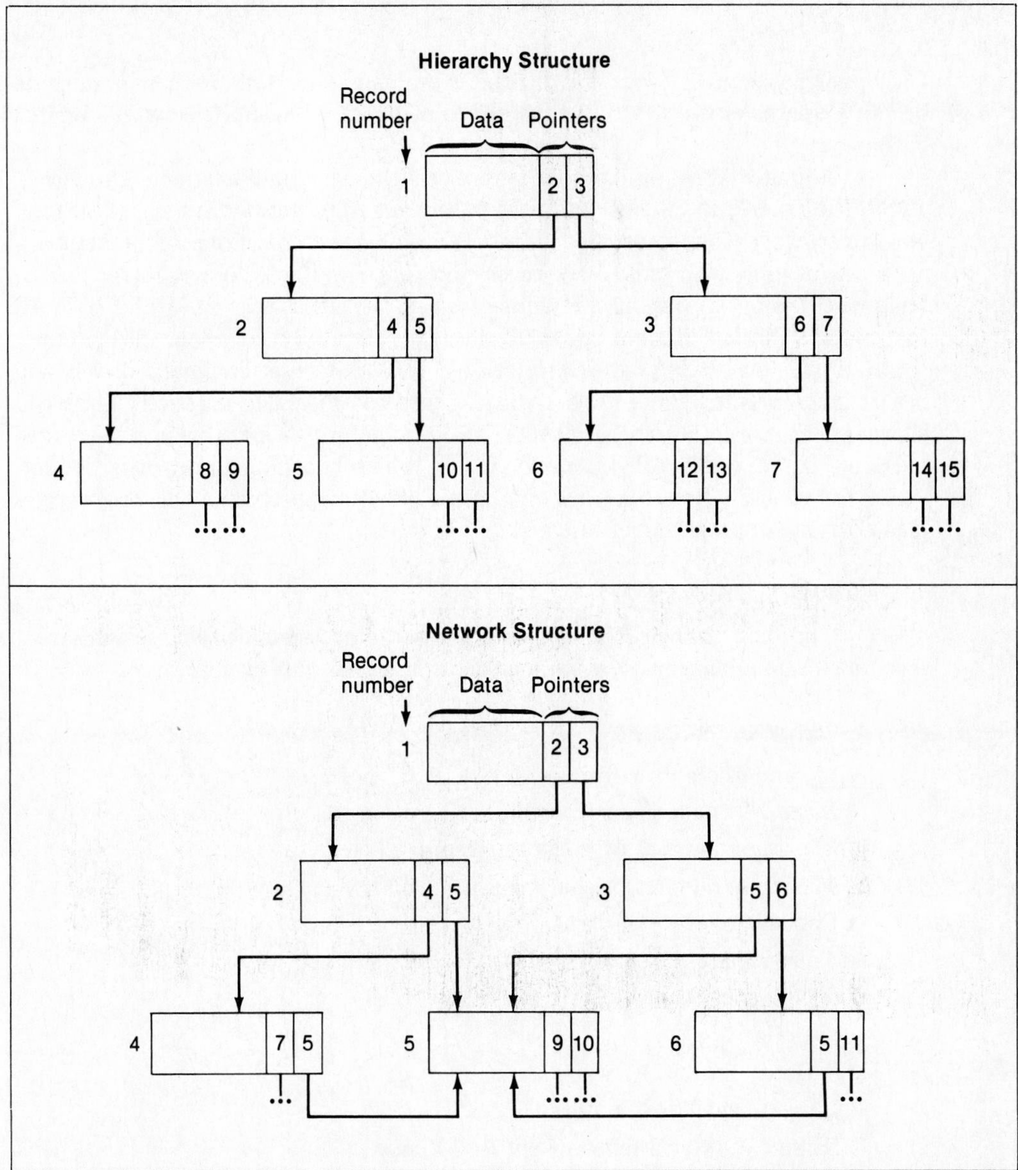

Figure 16-10 Hierarchy versus network structure

This arrangement requires that the corporate database administrator implement strong security controls. Who can get what information must be monitored. Who has the authority to update information must be extremely controlled to avoid trashing the integrity of the database.

EVALUATION

Perhaps no packaged software is as difficult to evaluate as a DBMS. Perhaps none could benefit a user as much. Ms. Jones wanted to avoid being encumbered with a limited package.

A limited DBMS is one that cannot perform data manipulation equivalent to JOIN, PROJECT, and SORT functions. Many *File Management Systems* (FMS) fall into this category. They sometimes allow only one file of records. Some of these systems are ideal for users with limited file needs who foresee no need to ever merge files or build new files out of old ones. Example systems are DB Master and PFS:FILE. All cost considerably less than relational DBMSs, which typically cost about $500 or more.

Ms. Jones felt comfortable with a DBMS that is command-driven and programmer-oriented. Since she had programmed before, she found it very flexible in allowing her to create custom calculations, reports, and forms. One programmer-oriented relational DBMS is dBASE II. Another that is primarily command-driven is Condor.

Other users, however, would find such a DBMS inappropriate. They might prefer menu-driven nonprogrammer-oriented systems.

Fulfilling Requirements

One thing that helped Ms. Jones the most to find a suitable package was having specified her requirements. Having the following detail was invaluable:

REQUIREMENT DETAIL

Maximum number of files
Maximum number of records per file
Maximum number of fields per record
Maximum number of characters per field
Data types:
  Character
  Numeric
  Dollar
  Date
Largest calculated number
Sample of typical report (Rent Roll Report)
Sample of typical form (rent statement)

She found many DBMSs have limitations in these and other areas.

To determine a package's suitability she used her tenant billing application as a test. The hands-on test unquestionably solved the problem of which packages were suitable candidates.

One of the desirable features she liked about a relational DBMS is that it adapts to an evolving application. Although she had well defined requirements, she knew that, as she became more familiar with the capabilities of the DBMS, she would want new functions implemented.

Multiuser Environments

As with operating systems, DBMSs come in three varieties. One is the familiar stand-alone single-user system. Another is a multiuser system that allows several users to be attached to one small computer; this is the computer cluster arrangement. A third is the newer local area network environment that allows small computers, attached to a common communicating cable, to have access to a common DBMS.

Any multiuse DBMS environment requires sophisticated controls to prevent two users from updating a record at the same time. A system of record locking and control is needed. So is a more sophisticated system of backup to recover from a system crash. Access security is another area of concern. These multiuser environment concerns are addressed in Chapter 13, "Local Area Networks."

Checklist

Ms. Jones used checklists to guide a systematic approach to the evaluation process. They resemble the Database Management System Checklist found in Figure 16–11 and two other supporting checklists from Chapter 4. The supporting two are the Software General Checklist and the Hands-On Test Checklist.

Figure 16-11 Database Management System Checklist

Candidate Packages Names:
A: ______________________________
B: ______________________________
C: ______________________________

Check "must have" items		Rating (Scale: 1 = poor to 10 = excellent) A	B	C
	General			
______	Menu-driven	______	______	______
______	Command-driven	______	______	______
______	Query by example	______	______	______
______	Programmer knowledge required	______	______	______
______	Formal training required	______	______	______
	Type:			
______	Single-user	______	______	______
______	Multiuser	______	______	______
______	Security adequate	______	______	______
	Record structure:			
______	Relational	______	______	______
______	Hierarchical	______	______	______
______	Network	______	______	______

Figure 16-11 (continued)

Check "must have" items		*Rating (Scale: 1 = poor to 10 = excellent)*		
		A	*B*	*C*
	Create the Database			
	Data types provided:			
____	Character	____	____	____
____	Numeric	____	____	____
____	Dollar	____	____	____
____	Date	____	____	____
____	Other ____________________	____	____	____
	Data entry:			
____	Entry form provided	____	____	____
____	Must design entry form	____	____	____
____	Checking performed like number of digits or upper and lower range limits	____	____	____
____	Duplicate records allowed	____	____	____
____	Key field indexing	____	____	____
	Query the Database			
	Search operators provided:			
____	< less than	____	____	____
____	> greater than	____	____	____
____	= equal to	____	____	____
____	< > not equal to	____	____	____
____	<= less than or equal to	____	____	____
____	>= greater than or equal to	____	____	____
____	And	____	____	____
____	Not	____	____	____
____	Or	____	____	____
____	Wildcard searching	____	____	____
____	Range searching	____	____	____
	Sorts:			
____	Numeric	____	____	____
____	Alphabetic	____	____	____
____	Ascending	____	____	____
____	Descending	____	____	____
____	Result files with duplicate records	____	____	____
____	Result files with no duplicate records (only pointers to primary files)	____	____	____
	Automatic:			
____	Count	____	____	____
____	Mean	____	____	____
____	Minimum	____	____	____
____	Maximum	____	____	____
____	Variance	____	____	____
____	Standard deviation	____	____	____
____	Other ____________________	____	____	____
	Ordering by:			
____	Item	____	____	____
____	Group	____	____	____
____	Groups with totals	____	____	____

Figure 16-11 (continued)

Check "must have" items		Rating (Scale: 1 = poor to 10 = excellent) A	B	C
	Generate Reports and Forms			
______	Design format on screen	______	______	______
______	Automatic report formatting	______	______	______
______	Save format	______	______	______
______	Revise format	______	______	______
______	All preceding query capabilities enabled	______	______	______
______	Totaling across report columns	______	______	______
	Interfacing			
______	Read files created by other applications	______	______	______
______	Write files for use by other applications	______	______	______
	Build New Files from Old Ones with			
______	Add, change, or delete fields, records, files, or databases	______	______	______
______	JOIN two files	______	______	______
______	PROJECT a result file that is a subset of another file	______	______	______
	Other features:			
______	UNION	______	______	______
______	INTERSECTION	______	______	______
______	DIFFERENCE	______	______	______
______	UNIQUE	______	______	______
______	DUPLICATE	______	______	______
	Update Data			
______	Add, change, delete	______	______	______
______	Deletion procedure	______	______	______
______	Recall a deleted record	______	______	______
______	Insert records in the middle of a database	______	______	______
______	Possibility of update anomalies	______	______	______
	Limitations			
______	Number of simultaneous databases	______	______	______
______	Number of files per database	______	______	______
______	Number of files available at one time	______	______	______
______	Maximum size per file (Kbytes)	______	______	______
______	Maximum records per file	______	______	______
______	Maximum fields per record	______	______	______
______	Maximum characters per field	______	______	______
______	Largest calculated number	______	______	______
	Subtotal	______	______	______
	Divide by number of items rated for average rating	______	______	______

Transfer Average Rating to Selection Summary: Software, Figure 5-2.

The support checklists helped to organize her evaluation of a DBMS's performance, ease of use, and documentation. Performance is a critical test area, especially if large databases are planned. A file sort, for example, that takes several hours on one DBMS versus a half-hour on another makes a significant difference.

Many DBMS suppliers offer demonstration disks to potential users. At least one offers free demo disks. Another sends demo and real system disks. They charge the full price of the package with a money-back guarantee only if the real system disk is still sealed in its package when returned.

Many others charge for documentation and demo disks. The investment is well worth it if no other way exists to hands-on test a package. Every DBMS has a different approach which a user must be comfortable with over the long-run. A hands-on test quickly settles the user-system compatibility issue.

SELF TEST

1. What is a database management system (DBMS)?
2. Give two reasons why people use a DBMS?
3. What is another name for the data entry process to create a database?
4. Describe "querying the database." Give three examples.
5. What is a wildcard search? Give an example.
6. What is a query language?
7. Describe an example sequence to create a report using a report generator.
8. Describe two program structures that are used, in one DBMS program language, to generate forms.
9. Explain the difference between HLL and VHLL.
10. Give an example of why interfacing with other non-DBMS files is a desirable feature.
11. Give two examples of DBMS sorts.
12. Describe the benefits of the JOIN and PROJECT commands
13. Give an example of an update anomaly. How is it avoided?
14. What features distinguish a database file in the so-called third normal form?
15. What is a relational DBMS? What makes it different from other DBMS structures?
16. What are large companies doing in the DBMS area?
17. What is most helpful in a search for a suitable DBMS package?

EXERCISES

1. Read three recent articles on DBMSs. Write a report summarizing what you learned from each article.
2. *CMB Apartments, Inc. Case.* Assume that Ms. Jones asks you to research a DBMS purchase. Research all the DBMS articles you can that appeared over the last few months. Write a report for Ms. Jones about your research. Identify three DBMSs you would recommend evaluating further.
3. *CMB Apartments, Inc. Case.* Research the three packages selected in exercise 2. Use the DBMS checklist from this chapter and the General Software Checklist from Chapter 4 as aids. Based on this evaluation, which package would you choose and why?

4. *CMB Apartments, Inc. Case.* Do a benchmark test of the DBMS chosen in exercise 3. Use the Hands-on Test Checklist from Chapter 4 as an aid in testing.
   a. Would you still choose the same package?
   b. Make a report about the test including what was:
      - Surprisingly easy to execute
      - Surprisingly difficult to execute
      - Impossible to execute
      - The result of PROJECT, UNION, and SORT tests
      - The procedure to create the Rent Roll Report
      - The procedure to create rent statements

RESOURCES AND REFERENCES

Books

ATRE, SHAKU, *Database Management Systems for the Eighties,* QED, 1983.
DATE, C. J., *An Introduction to Data Base Systems,* 3rd ed., Addison-Wesley, 1981.
KRONKE, DAVID, *Database: A Professional's Primer,* SRA, 1977.
KRONKE, DAVID, *Database Processing,* SRA, 1977.
KRUGLINSKI, DAVID, *Data Base Management Systems: A Guide to Microcomputer Software,* Osborne/McGraw-Hill, 1983.
MARTIN, JAMES, *Application Development Without Programmers,* Prentice-Hall, 1982.
MARTIN, JAMES, *Computer Data-Base Organization,* 2nd ed., Prentice-Hall, 1977.

Disk-Based Tutorials

Teach Yourself dBASE II, DELTAK
The dBASEII Program, Cdex

Supplement: dBASE II® Tutorial*

This supplement is a keystroke-by-keystroke tutorial on how to use the relational database management system dBASE II by Ashton-Tate, Inc. It is written to be used as a guide while sitting at a computer. If a computer is not available, a reading of the tutorial can serve as a simulation of the actual session.

dBASE II works on many brands of small computers. The IBM Personal Computer dBASE II version 2.4 is used in the tutorial. It requires either PC-DOS or MS-DOS, 128 Kbytes of memory, two floppy disk drives, and a printer.

The tutorial aims to create a database file and a Rent Roll Report for the tenant billing application described in Chapters 15 and 16. It also covers some database queries that require sorting and selective searches.

*dBASE II® is a registered trademark of Ashton-Tate.

SET-UP PROCEDURE

In order to use dBASE II, it is necessary first to boot the system with the DOS operating system. The procedure is as follows:

1. Open the left disk unit drive door (or latch) by pulling up at its bottom edge. The left drive will be known as drive A throughout this tutorial.
2. Carefully insert the DOS disk, with its label up, into the drive. The oval cutout in the square disk jacket should enter the drive first. The label should enter the drive last. Gently push the disk all the way in and close the drive door.
3. Turn the computer's power switch on. The disk drive begins to whir and click, and the red in-use light on the drive comes on. The operating system prompt A> appears on the screen.
4. Open the door of drive A and remove the DOS disk. Gently replace it with the dBASE II program disk.
5. Place a formatted disk in the right disk drive unit. The right drive will be known as drive B throughout this tutorial. It will be for user-created files.
6. Type **DBASE.** Boldface entries in this tutorial will indicate those typed by a user at the computer. Type only boldface characters. Do not type a period that ends a tutorial sentence. After every typed entry, type a carriage return to end the entry. The carriage return will be assumed and not indicated in this tutorial.

   A copyright message and a dot below it appears on the screen. DBASE II is a command-driven database management system. The dot is the constant recurring symbol to indicate that the program is waiting for a user-typed command. To quit the program, type **QUIT** at any dot command opportunity.

CREATE THE DATABASE

The familiar dot on the screen indicates that the program is ready for a command. To create the database, begin by typing function key F8 to generate the command CREATE.

In this tutorial and the exercises that follows it, three function keys are used as follows:

FUNCTION KEY	COMMAND
F3	LIST (Note: Not used for selective LISTs).
F8	CREATE
F9	APPEND

All commands can also be typed in full.

Generating CREATE results in the message ENTER FILENAME:, so type **B:TENANT,** as shown in Figure 16–2. Have the "caps lock" key on for upper case letters. The B: prefix indicates that the file will be saved on the B disk drive, or the one on the right. The normal procedure is to have the program disk in the A drive and the data disk in the B drive.

As Figure 16–2 indicates, a request for entry of the record structure is followed by typing field information. Type information as shown in Figure 16–2. If a mistake occurs, backspace to correct it before typing a carriage return. A carriage return for the seventh item indicates an exit.

If other errors occur, it is possible to start over by typing **DELETE FILE B:TENANT** at a dot command opportunity.

After successfully creating the record structure, the message ENTER RECORDS NOW (Y/N)? appears. Type **Y** for yes. A yes entry generates a blank form on the screen that resembles the one in Figure 16–3. Release the "caps lock" key to enable use of upper- and lower-case characters.

Enter the first record exactly as shown in Figure 16–3. Occasionally a beep sounds when a field is full, and the cursor moves to the next item automatically. Otherwise, just carriage return after a line is entered.

1. Type as if using a typewriter. The following keys have special actions:

KEYS	ACTION
Arrow keys	Move the cursor in all four directions without disturbing characters.
Space bar	Deletes a character where the cursor is located.
←	Backspace, same left movement as the left cursor control key.
Carriage return	Moves the cursor to the beginning of the next line. If the record is complete, it is saved and the next available record is displayed to continue. To quit adding records, type a carriage return as the first character of a new record.
CTRL R	Type these two keys simultaneously to save a record whenever information is not complete.
CTRL Q	Type these two keys simultaneously for an alternate way to stop adding records. This does not save a record.

2. Typing function key F3 for the command LIST displays all records on the screen.
3. To print a list of records on paper, type two keys at once, CTRL and P to turn the printer on. Then type function key F3 for LIST. Typing CTRL and P again turns the printer off. Turning the printer on and off this way can be done at any time while working with dBASE. Enter four more records using the test data given in the first example of Figure 16–4 before signaling completion.

CORRECT MISTAKES

Listing, as shown in Figure 16–4, displays records and reveals if any remain with errors. If any do, they can be fixed.

For example, if record number four is in error, type **edit 4.** The data entry form, as shown in Figure 16–3, appears. Revision is again possible. Experiment with changing the first name from Elizabeth to Betty.

QUERY THE DATABASE

With all records created or loaded, it is possible to pose questions to the database and get quick responses. To review record content, type F3 to generate the LIST command. The screen should resemble the first example in Figure 16–4.

Try all the example queries in Figure 16–4. If a SYNTAX ERROR message occurs, it usually indicates that there are spelling, spacing, or punctuation errors in the query statement. Retype them as shown. Notice how character field data must be typed inside quotation marks.

Experiment further by making up your own queries using available record content, as shown in the first example of Figure 16–4.

GENERATE A REPORT

To generate the Rent Roll Report refer to Figure 16–6. It identifies all questions and responses needed to get a Rent Roll Report like the one illustrated in the same figure.

Begin by setting the caps lock key to upper case. Then type **REPORT FORM B:RENTROLL.** Carriage return through the next request to enter options. From this point type the user entries as illustrated in Figure 16–6. When done, a carriage return instead of a number at entry number 007 signals the end of the report definition.

If the definition contains no errors, the report will execute immediately. The definition is automatically saved for reuse, although it cannot be modified. To reuse it, just type **REPORT FORM B:RENTROLL TO PRINT.** Eliminating the TO PRINT will send the report to the display instead of to the printer.

Typing erroneous field names during the report definition generates an automatic option to repair the error. But errors also occur in heading titles or column spacing. Since no facility exists to correct such errors, it requires beginning again from scratch by retyping **REPORT FORM B:RENTROLL.** The new report will automatically overlay the erroneous one as long as the name is the same.

SORT AND REORDER THE DATABASE

To sort the database, a SORT command is supplied. An example of use is given in Figure 16–9. Notice that the sorted file is given a new name. Also notice that the newly named file must be invoked with a **use** command. Any file invoked with **use** is considered the primary file for command purposes.

Experiment with sorting the tenant database using the examples given in Figure 16–9.

The *dBASE II Manual* should be consulted for complete user instructions. The *dBASE II User's Guide* by Adam B. Green (SoftwareBanc) is also helpful.

Exercises

1. *CBM Apartments, Inc. Case.* Implement the tenant list for the new super that was designed in exercise 2 of Chapter 15.
   a. Produce one version of the tenant list using the LIST command with the printer turned on (type CTRL P).
   b. Produce another version of the tenant list using the report generator.
2. *CMB Apartments, Inc. Case.* Add two more test records to the tenant file as follows:

Record Number	*Last Name*	*First Name*	*Apt*	*Rent*	*Other*	*Past*
6	(Your Own)	(Your Own)	3B	$365.00	$16.00	—
7	Mikes	Jo	4A	$320.00	—	$20.00

   Use the APPEND command by typing function key F9 to add the records. At a dot opportunity, type F9 and follow normal data entry procedures. Run a new Rent Roll Report to reflect the added records.
3. *Warehouse Company Case.* Assume you bought a DBMS to implement the custom application for your warehouse business.
   a. Create the customer database file using the test data given in exercise 3 of Chapter 15.
   b. Print a list of the database records using the LIST command with the printer turned on.
4. *Warehouse Company Case.* Experiment with the capability of your DBMS by executing the following:
   Find all customers that:
   - have account numbers in the 10,000 to 17,000 range
   - live in zip code 10020
   - live in the 914 telephone area code zone
   - have a past due balance greater than $150.00
5. *Warehouse Company Case.* Use the report generator feature of the DBMS to prepare the Customer Report designed in exercise 3a of Chapter 15.

17

ALTERNATE PHASE TWO: PROGRAM DESIGN

When a database management system is not used to develop a custom application, more design work remains. This chapter concentrates on the steps that lead to a program blueprint ready to be translated into code.

The life of a program has many phases, as symbolically shown in Figure 17–1. Program design is one of the critical early phases. As Figure 17–1 implies, each phase feeds its successor. Experience in the successor phase may propagate changes back to the predecessor phase. The earlier in the software life cycle that design errors are uncovered, the less expensive it is to correct them.

This chapter continues the methodology that began in Chapter 15. It uses the list of rent statement data elements created in that chapter to derive a hierarchy chart or diagram. After two levels of refinement, the chart becomes transformed into a program blueprint.

The refinement is a result of defining the process logic. Defining the process logic is the most complex step of program design. Once all blueprints, including those for file maintenance functions, are designed, they become the basis for program coding in any language and on any computer.

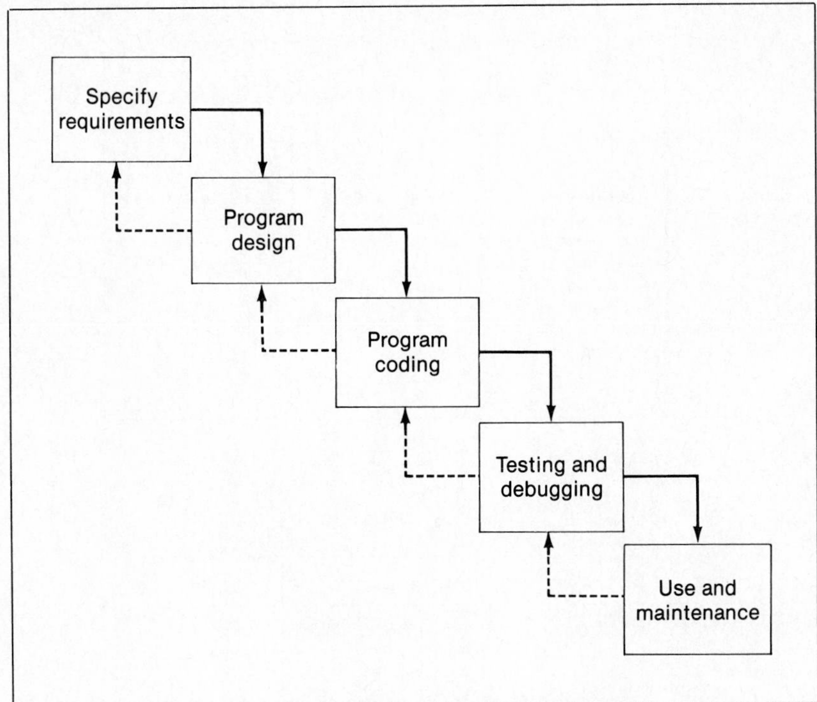

Figure 17-1 Phases in the life cycle of a program

STEP 1: REPORT HIERARCHY DEFINITION

Continuing a custom programming effort requires a so-called report hierarchy definition. When the report hierarchy is known, all items on the data elements list from Figure 15-4 need to be located on it.

Most reports and other computer outputs have an inherent structure that resembles a hierarchical or pyramidal organization. As shown in Figure 17-2, a typical company report might include totals at the department, section, and division levels. Department totals are summed to provide section totals. All section totals are summed to provide division totals. Finally, all division totals yield the grand total for the company report.

Ms. Jones' report hierarchy is simple but more readily discoverable since she added the short Rent Statement Summary Report shown in Figure 17-3. The Summary prints out totals that are accumulated during rent statement print processing. The Summary prints immediately after the last rent statement. It functions as an *audit trail,* or check, on the number of statements printed and on the dollar amounts processed. These totals should match those on the Rent Roll Report, which is run and manually checked

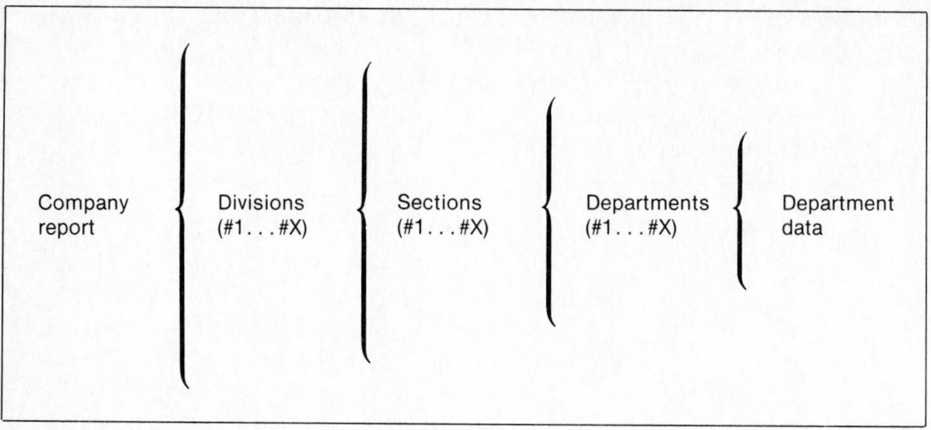

Figure 17-2 Sample company report hierarchy

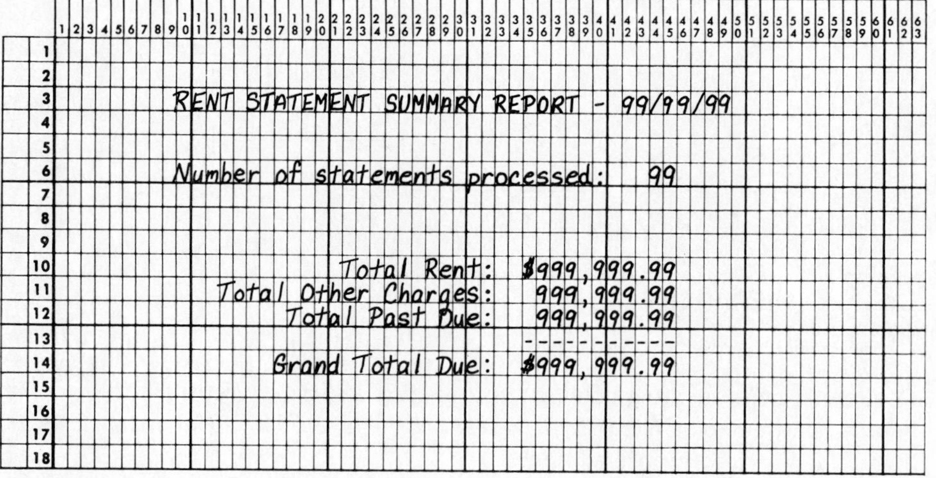

Figure 17-3 The Rent Statement Summary Report design prepared on a printer spacing layout sheet. This summary report prints immediately after the rent statements. It functions as an audit trail of processing.

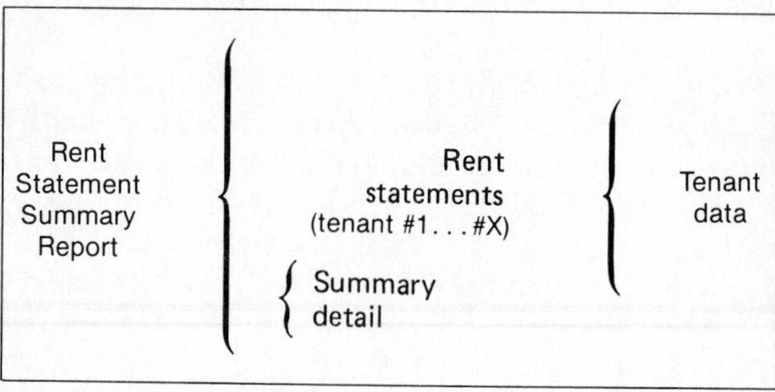

Figure 17-4 Report hierarchy

for accuracy before the statements are printed. If the totals do not match, it could signal a processing problem.

The report hierarchy for the Rent Statement Summary Report appears in Figure 17–4. A detailed version of the report hierarchy with all data elements mapped onto it appears in Figure 17–5.

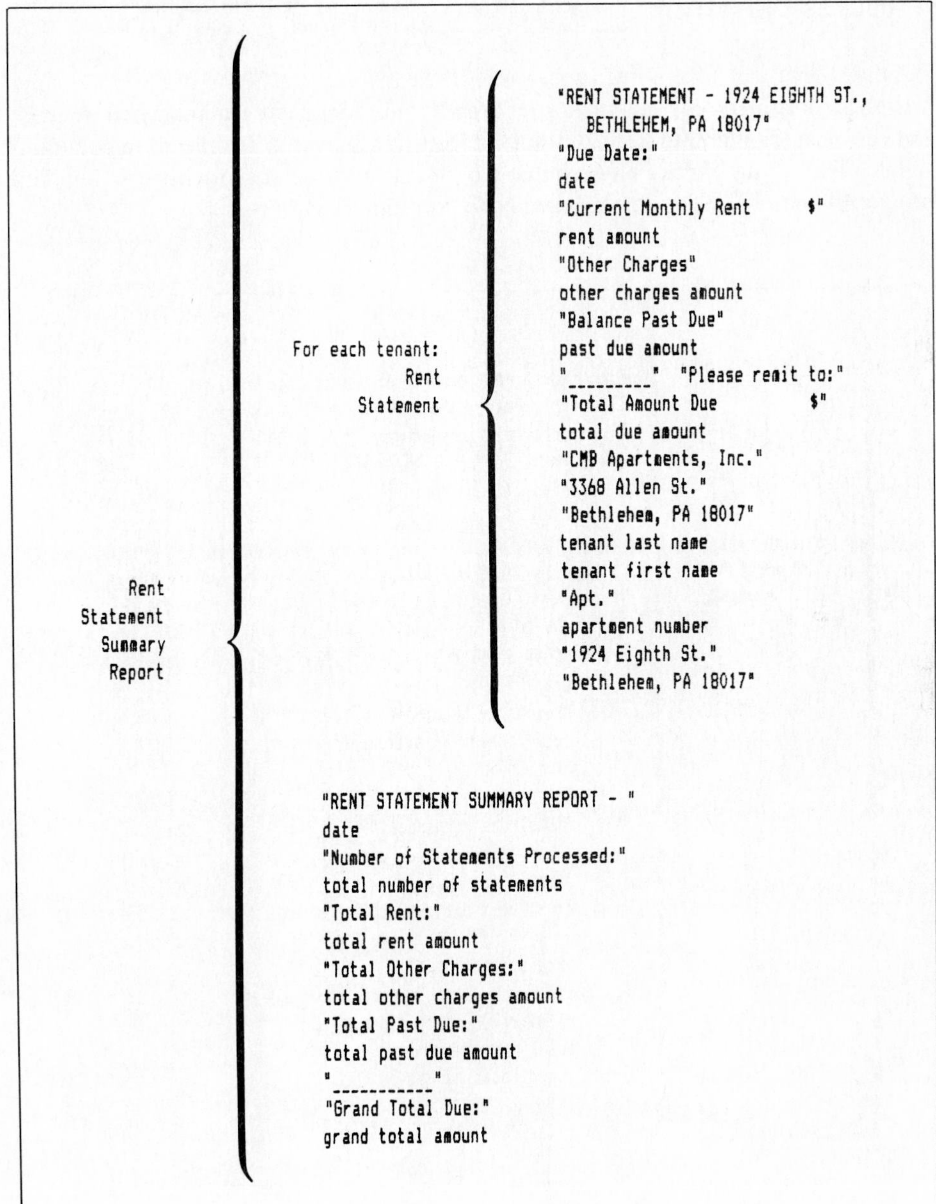

Figure 17–5 Data elements mapped onto the report hierarchy

To accurately transfer or map data elements onto the hierarchy diagram, Ms. Jones must determine where elements logically occur during report production. In her case, it is a simple mapping. More elaborate mappings occur with more complex data and report structures.

STEP 2: PROCESS DEFINITION

Defining the processes required to produce the Rent Statement Summary Report begins with the report hierarchy diagram from Step 1. This document gets modified, revised, and renamed throughout Step 2 until it emerges as a blueprint for program coding. It is much like the architect's blueprint of a building that is ready for construction. The program blueprint, when done, is ready for coding.

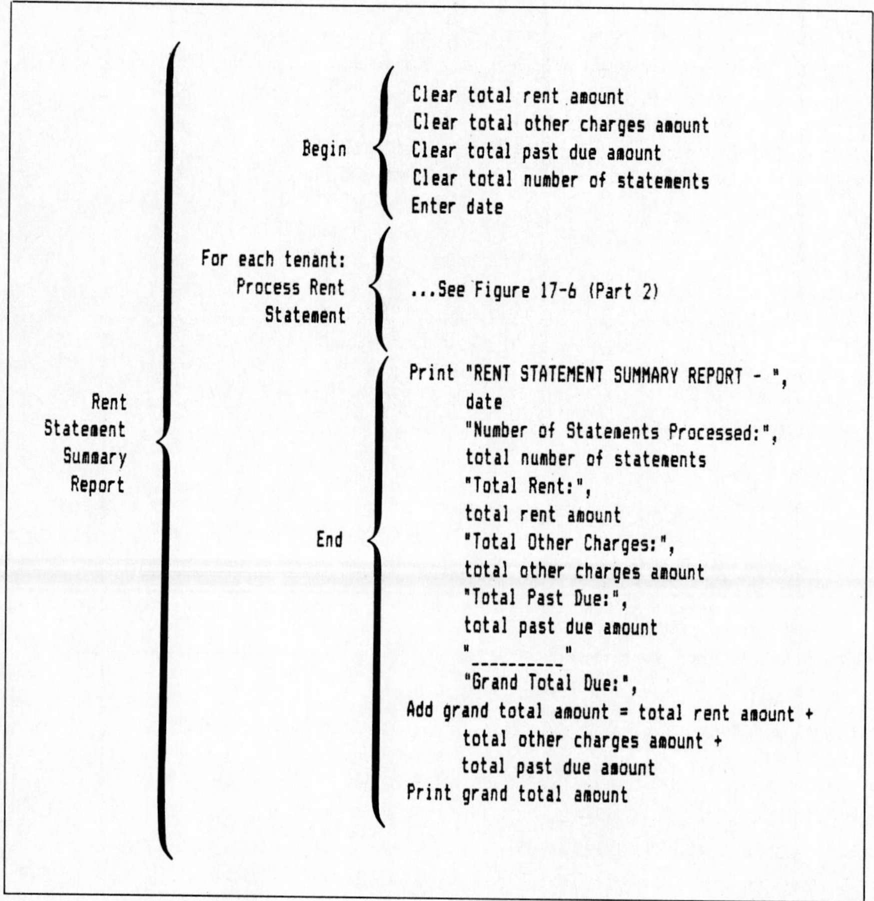

Figure 17-6 (Part 1) Preliminary program blueprint for the Rent Statement Summary Report

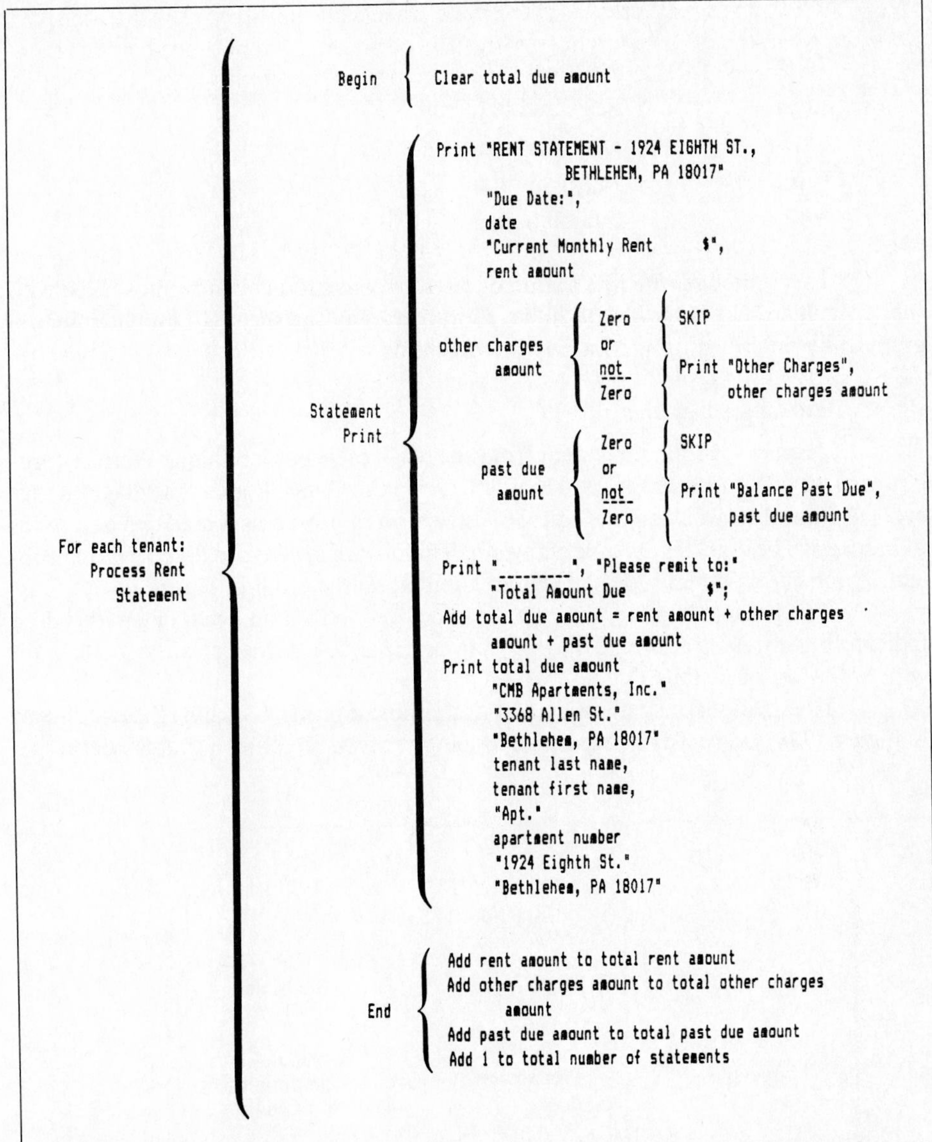

Figure 17-6 (Part 2) Preliminary program blueprint for the Rent Statement Summary Report

The program blueprint goes through two major transitions. One involves inserting details about processing logic. The other involves inserting details about the physical limitations of computer processing.

Figure 17-6 illustrates the program blueprint at the "preliminary" level. Processing logic is identified mainly by adding action words to the old report hierarchy diagram.

Some word conventions used are:

WORD	TO IDENTIFY
Clear	Set variable to zero
Enter	User keyboard entry
Print	Paper output
Add	Summation

This is the first full illustration of another convention already introduced with the report hierarchy diagram. Both the report hierarchy and the program blueprint are graphically described using Warnier-Orr diagrams.

Warnier-Orr Diagrams

Warnier-Orr diagrams stem from the work of Jean-Dominique Warnier (pronounced warn-YAY) in France and Kenneth Orr in the United States. The diagram that evolved from their work on the logical construction of programs is made up of a series of brackets. The brackets are used with a small number of symbols to decompose a problem. A schematic outline of the Warnier-Orr diagram is given in Figure 17–7.

Using this schematic, sets of actions are defined within beginning and ending indicators. Any element on the diagram can be expanded further by adding a bracket with a new set of actions.

The small set of symbols used to decompose a problem include the two shown in Figure 17–8. One defines a repetitive looping process, the other a simple alternating

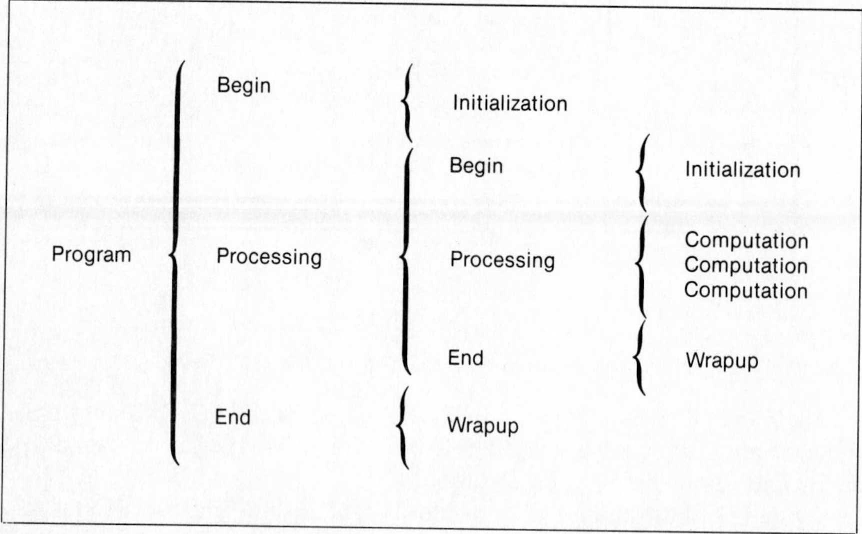

Figure 17-7 Schematic of a Warnier-Orr diagram

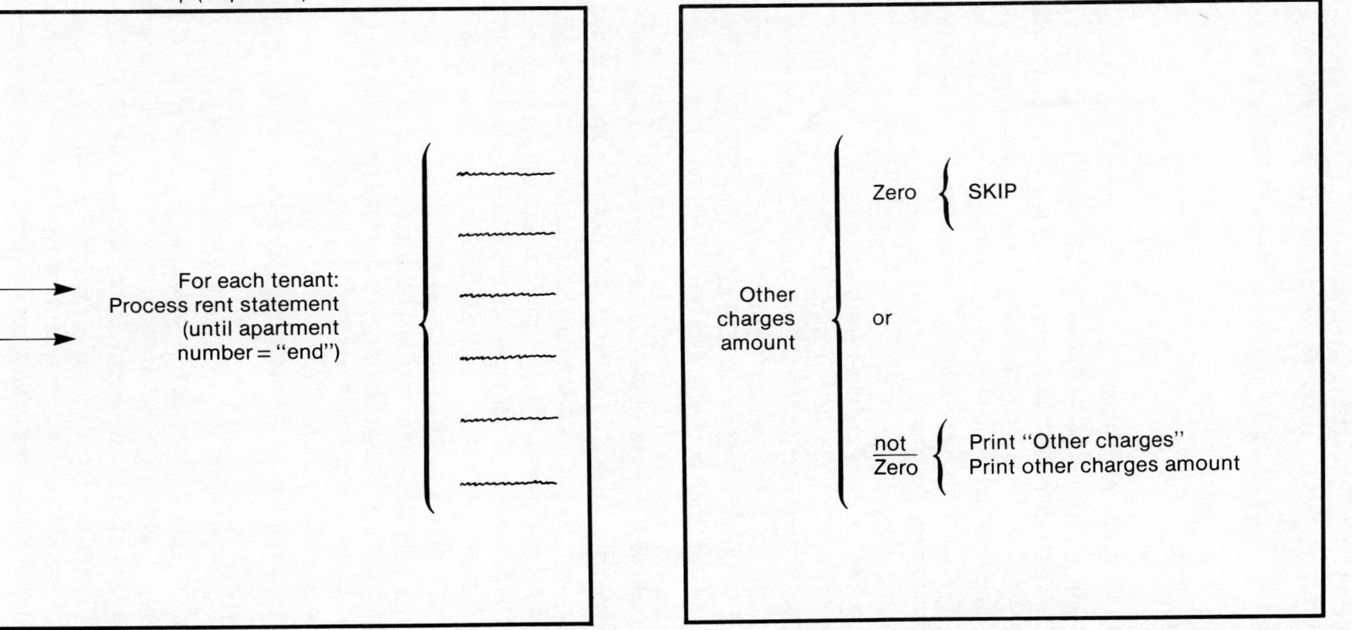

Figure 17-8 Examples of loop and decision processes

or decision process. Besides these two processing logic structures, almost everything else on a Warnier-Orr diagram represents a simple sequential, or "do one right after the other" type of process.

Program Blueprint

To begin diagramming the preliminary program blueprint, as illustrated in Figure 17–6, Ms. Jones made a fresh start. She wrote "Begin" and "End" inside each bracket on new worksheets. She worked in pencil because everything was subject to change as new details were uncovered and others were expanded. She even kept scissors handy to cut out portions of old diagrams that could be reused each time she made a fresh start.

In other words, this part of the design process never comes out right the first time. It is an iterative process where one change reflects on others. It is an orderly process, however, that moves at a controlled pace of ever increasing detail.

Ms. Jones approached the process design from the lower left "End" process on Part 1 and moved to the right to the next higher "End" process on Part 2 of Figure 17–6. The direction of process completion follows a semicircle, from the bottom of the diagram to the top. She ended at the top "Begin" on Part 1 of the diagram.

At the first "End," as shown in Figure 17–6 (Part 1), little is needed to reflect the process logic detail. The summation step requires a calculation that is indicated with the "Add" verb. Otherwise, the inclusion of "Print" to the old report hierarchy accomplishes process logic refinement at this level.

The next higher "End" process, as shown in Figure 17–6 (Part 2), has to accumulate total amounts. They will be needed at the termination of all processing to print on the Summary. "Total due amount" is the only amount not accumulated for each statement. It is calculated, as already indicated, while printing the Summary. Since the Summary requires a count of statements processed, this is a good time to add one to the accumulator or counter to prepare that necessary figure.

The next higher step takes Ms. Jones to the most detailed level of the process logic. This level has no hierarchial processing. One step is performed right after the other. Everything is familiar here except for alternate processing in two places.

Processing depends on whether or not there is data in "other charges" or "past due" amounts. If these balances are zero, the descriptive labels never even appear on the rent statement.

At the first "Begin" process, on Figure 17–6 (Part 2), the first *initialization* occurs. *Initialization* is required to insure that data variables used by a process are cleared of any old numbers. Usually accumulators and counters are candidates for initialization. Several are needed at the next highest "Begin" process on Figure 17–6 (Part 1).

At the top-most "Begin" process is the place where the redundant variable, "due date" will be entered. Once entered it can be reused for every statement processed. It is the only required human intervention in this program. Printing rent statements is essentially a *batch* operation. Batch programs require no user interaction. Most computer-printed copy is produced by similar batch processing programs.

Physical Considerations

Before the process logic definition is complete, physical characteristics of computer processing need to be considered. Things like user input prompts, file handling and page break controls need to be detailed on the final copy of a program bluepint. The physical considerations added by Ms. Jones to her program blueprint are shown in the blocked areas of Figure 17–9, Parts 1 and 2.

The largest block of additions to the final program blueprint occurs in the first "Begin" process. Mainly it concerns the interface between the program and the user. A prompt lets the user know that a due date for printing on rent statements is needed. After that is entered, the program alerts the user to align paper in the printer and to turn the printer on. Finally, the program lets the user know processing is in progress. In a multitasking system, such a message would be unnecessary since executing several tasks simultaneously is possible.

In addition to the user interface, file handling procedures are considered here. Where files are resident on disk they must be opened before individual records can be read or accessed. As apparent from Figure 17–9, physical considerations require adding a control file. It contains only one item, the last tenant record number used. The number is needed in this program to signal the end of the print process.

Before entering the repetitive print process, a record number counter is set to one. The control number is retrieved from the disk file. These two numbers will be compared each time before loop entry to determine when to terminate printing.

The loop control test condition is labeled on the left side of the main loop bracket. When the record number counter becomes greater than the control number, processing will cease. The counter is incremented by one each time through the main loop. At some point, it will register a number higher than the control number. In that case, processing *falls through,* to use a programmer phrase, to the next sequential step after the loop. In this case, it is the "End" process to print the Summary report.

The loop control test would probably be different if Ms. Jones had used a sequential tenant file. Instead she chose to use a direct access file as described in Chapter 3. It enabled her to have rapid access to any record in the file by entering its record number. This file organization requires more programmed control than a sequential file.

Ms. Jones decided to add the numeric field, record number, to each tenant record. It was done because the alphabetic apartment number field would not be directly usable to access records. Although indexing would make using the apartment number possible, she decided to implement it later when she became a more experienced programmer.

Another physical consideration concerns not printing statements for unoccupied apartments. To control printing, a check is made for "Unoccupied" in the tenant last name field. If present, the entire record is skipped and a new record is retrieved.

Another physical consideration concerns the variable spacing within each rent statement. All tenants will have two amount lines printed, one for "current monthly rent" and another for "total amount due." Some will also have one or two other lines printed. They depend on whether an amount exists in either the "other charges" or "past due" fields in a tenant's record.

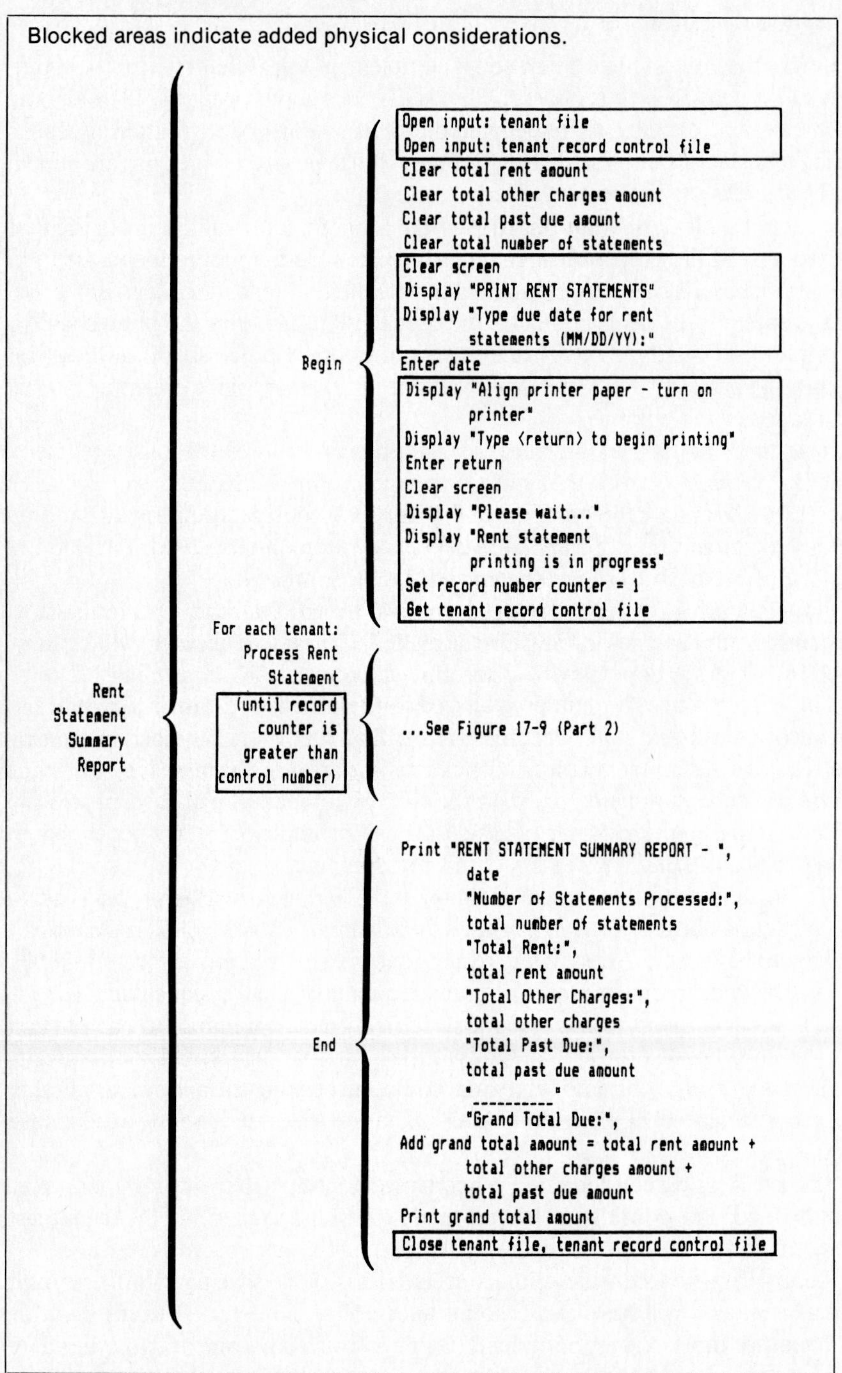

Figure 17-9 (Part 1) Final program blueprint for the Rent Statement Summary Report

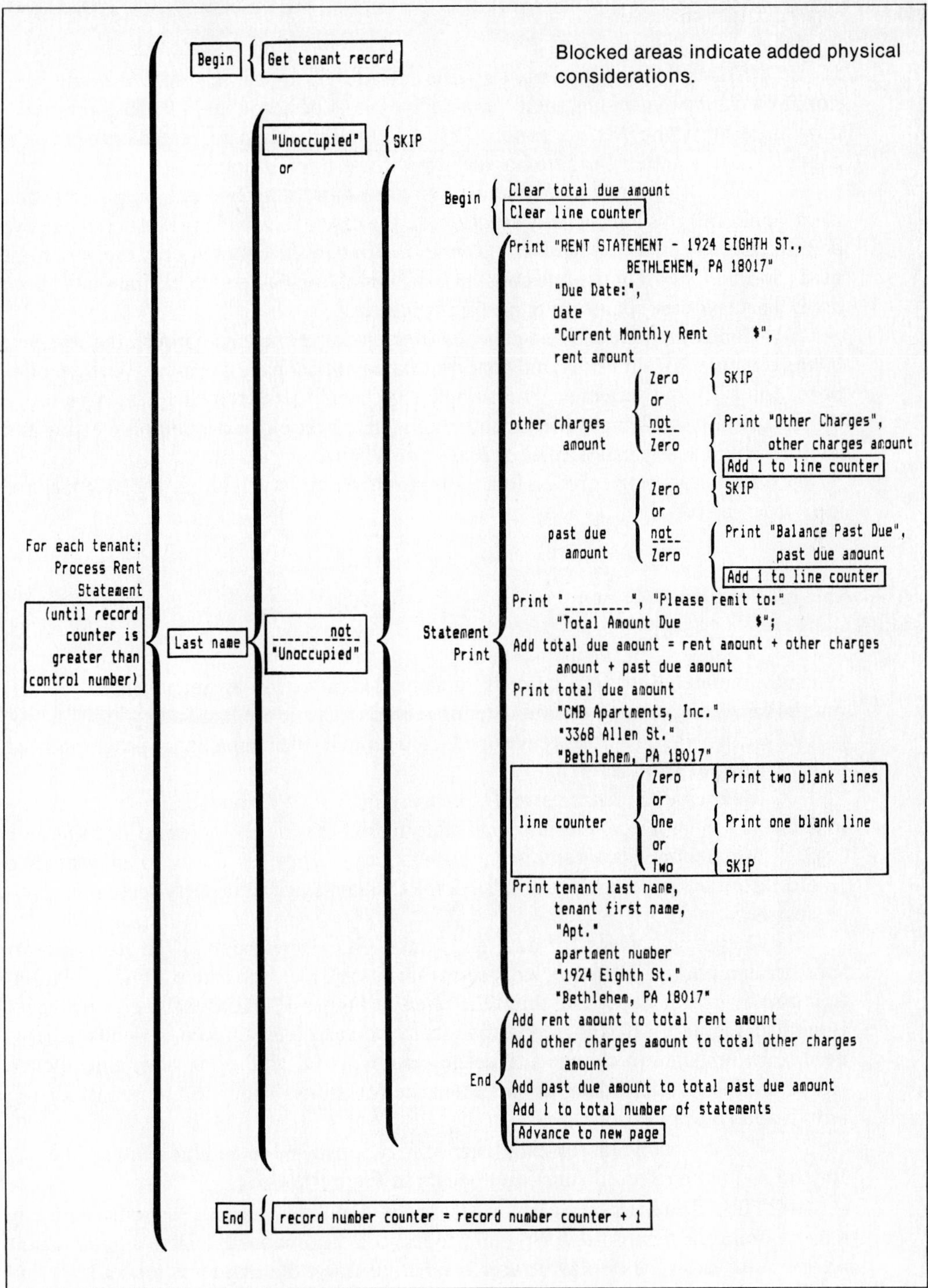

Figure 19-9 (Part 2) Final program blueprint for the Rent Statement Summary Report

In order to have the tenant's name and address appear in exactly the right position for a window envelope, these variable lines must be accounted for. To control window address printing, Ms. Jones added a line counter. It gets incremented once or twice, depending on whether "other charges" and "past due" amounts are printed.

Since a test of the line counter can have more than two outcomes, programmers would call this logic a *case structure.* In the case of a zero in the line counter, two additional lines must be added. In the case of a one in the counter, only one more line needs adding. A two in the line counter indicates all available variable lines have been used. This last case requires no specific processing.

Controlling the end of a page requires similar testing and control. In the tenant billing example, for simplicity, only one rent statement per page is printed. With a 66 line page, and a 23-line statement, it is simple to control the skip to the next page top.

Reports with many hierarchial totaling levels require more complex testing and control. It is usually called *control break processing.*

At this point the process logic definition is complete. It is ready to be translated into program code.

DATABASE MAINTENANCE DEFINITION

When the tenant billing application is implemented on a database management system, things like adding, changing, and deleting records to a file are handled by built-in programs. When an application is developed from scratch, file maintenance programs need to be developed from scratch.

Maintenance programs need to be working first. Without tenant records already available in a file, for example, it is impossible to print rent statements or do anything else.

Maintenance programs are user-interactive. They ask a user to enter or type record information through prompts on the display. Each data entry screen needs to be designed.

Designing screens for data entry takes Ms. Jones back to the requirements specification phase. To specify what screens will look like, she uses standard information display layout paper like that illustrated in Figure 17–10. Ordinary graph paper is suitable. Figure 17–10 is the screen to initialize or create a tenant record. Similar screens need to be designed to change and delete records. Add, change or view, and delete a record are the standard database maintenance functions. They need to be included in any file-based application.

The process logic for maintenance functions need to be blueprinted. The one for the add tenant record function appears in Figure 17–11.

The Add Tenants program in Ms. Jones' application is designed to be used only once to build the tenant file for rental property. It automatically places a valid tenant record number on the display. A user is asked to fill in the requested tenant information. The routine repeats until the user indicates termination by typing "end" for apartment number. Anytime after the file is built, if an apartment changes tenants, the change is entered with the change program. Record number and apartment numbers remain fixed.

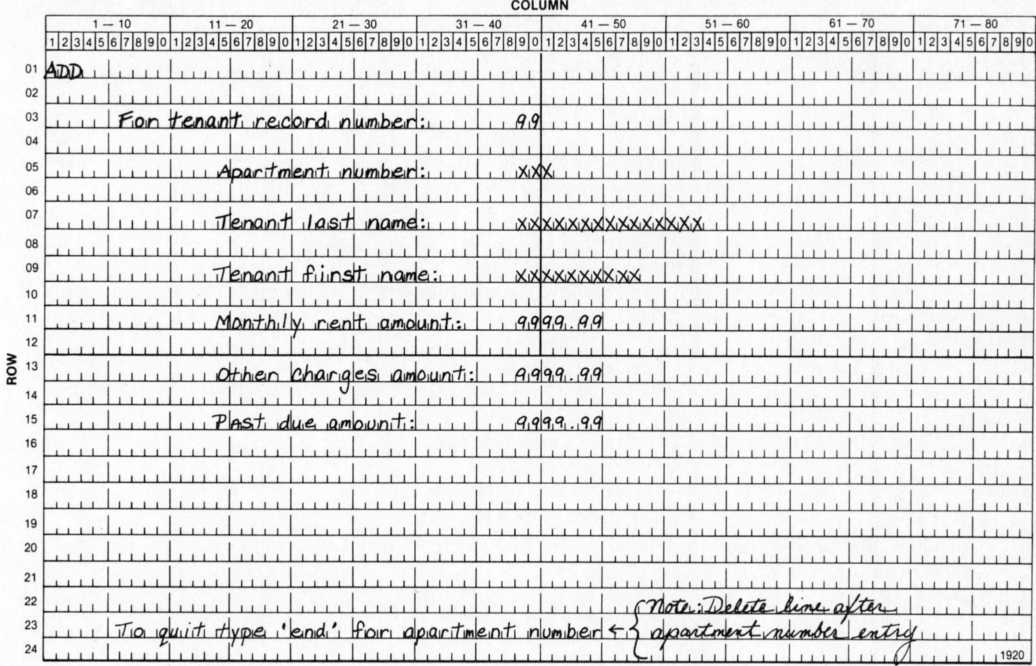

Figure 17-10 The add tenants screen design prepared on a display layout sheet.

Other more sophisticated systems handle file initialization, adding and changing routines many different ways. Separate index files can be built during file initialization to make the program more generalized than it is now. Displaying the full screen at once for data entry is more sophisticated than prompting line by line. While Ms. Jones was aware of alternatives, she decided to work in phases. At each new learning level she would try another new programming technique.

Because the process logic is not designed for a specific language on a specific computer, it could be coded in any programming language desired. This approach to design is called *language independence* by professional program designers.

TOP-DOWN IMPLEMENTATION

Another concept of professional design is top-down program implementation. It involves coding from the so-called "big picture" to the smallest refinement. It essentially duplicates the approach taken to process logic design.

To apply the top-down approach, Ms. Jones brought together the report and file maintenance programs into one program blueprint, as shown in Figure 17-12. It incorporates a main menu display as shown in Figure 17-13, which is the normal unifying device in a user-interactive application.

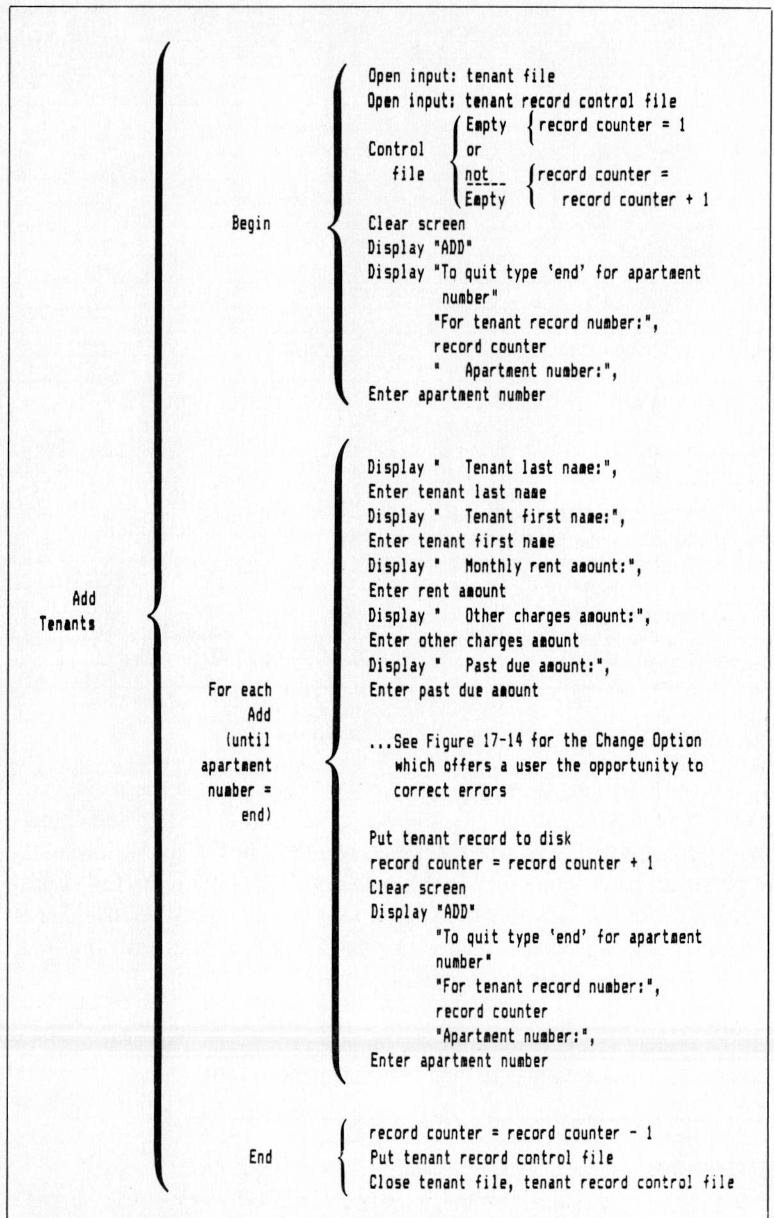

Figure 17-11 Program blueprint for adding tenant records to the file

Programming the main menu logic first, together with all interfaces to so-called subprograms, gives assurance that subprograms interface properly. While interfacing subprograms, such as Add Tenants, may not be complex in this tenant billing application, it may be in other larger applications.

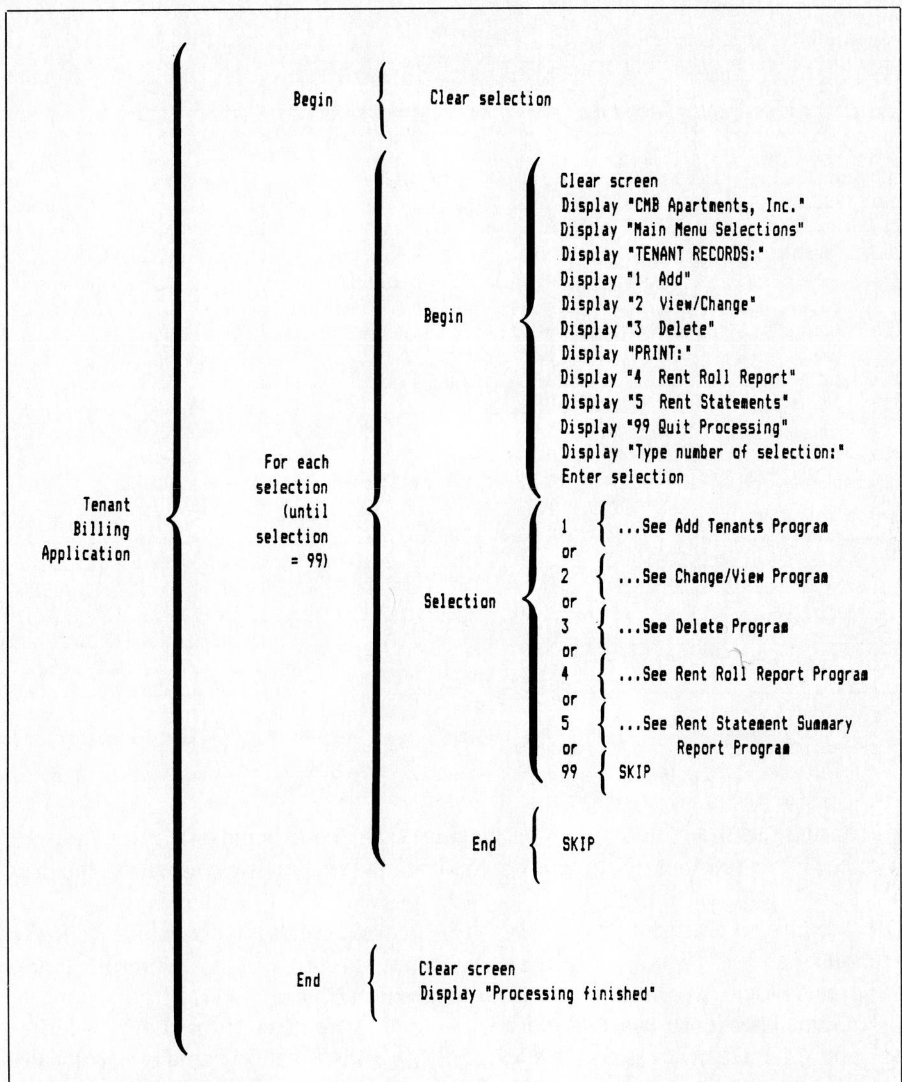

Figure 17-12 Program blueprint for the tenant billing application main menu

In large jobs subprograms are assigned to different programmers. By doing the main menu interface logic first and continuing to work from the top down, the original design plan is made to work before progressing further. If programmed from the bottom up, there is no assurance that any one programmer's work will interface with another programmer's. The probability that such an application will work harmoniously radically decreases.

Much has to be left unexplored in this simple tenant billing example. It is designed only as a first pass and assumes no errors. Typically this is how the application would be programmed to get a *prototype* working quickly. Then all error conditions, which

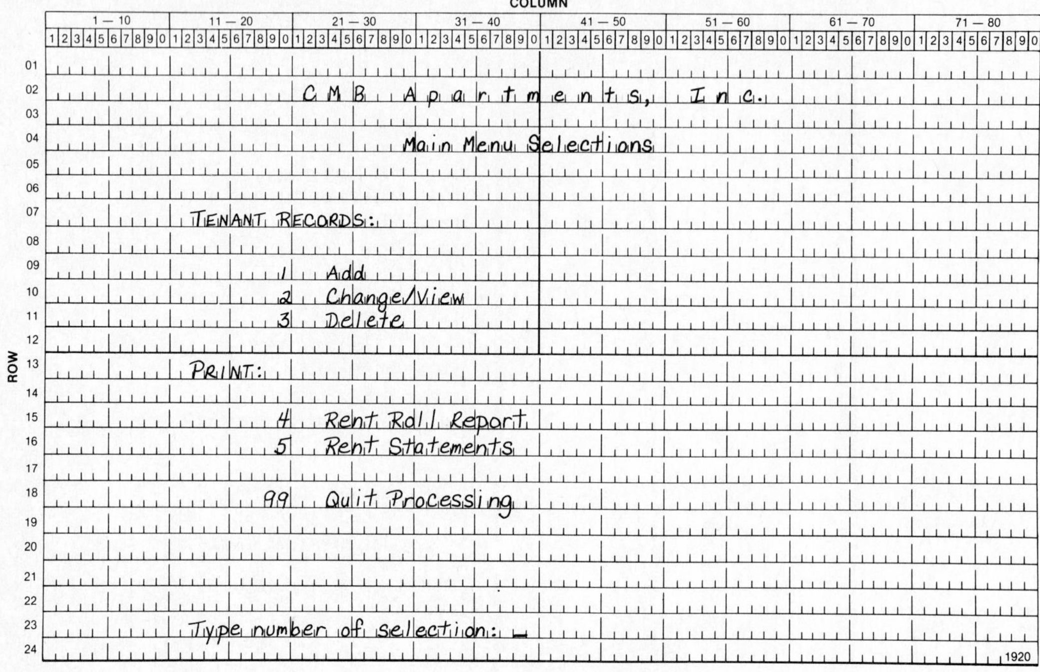

Figure 17-13 The main menu screen design prepared on a display layout sheet

often consume as much and more design time than the original programs, are implemented. Error routines inordinately complicate the process logic as well as the program code.

To give an example of an error routine, consider one to allow a user to make corrections if an error is noticed in the Add Tenants subprogram. One simple version of the process logic for this change option is given in Figure 17–14.

Some liberties to favor ease of understanding are taken throughout at the expense of program efficiency and sophisticated design. Many changes could be beneficially applied to improve the tenant billing application.

Students of program design are encouraged to examine books listed in the Resources and References sections at the end of the chapters in Part V.

SELF TEST

1. Describe the phases in the life cycle of a program.
2. Use an example to describe a typical company report hierarchy.
3. Give an example of an audit trail.

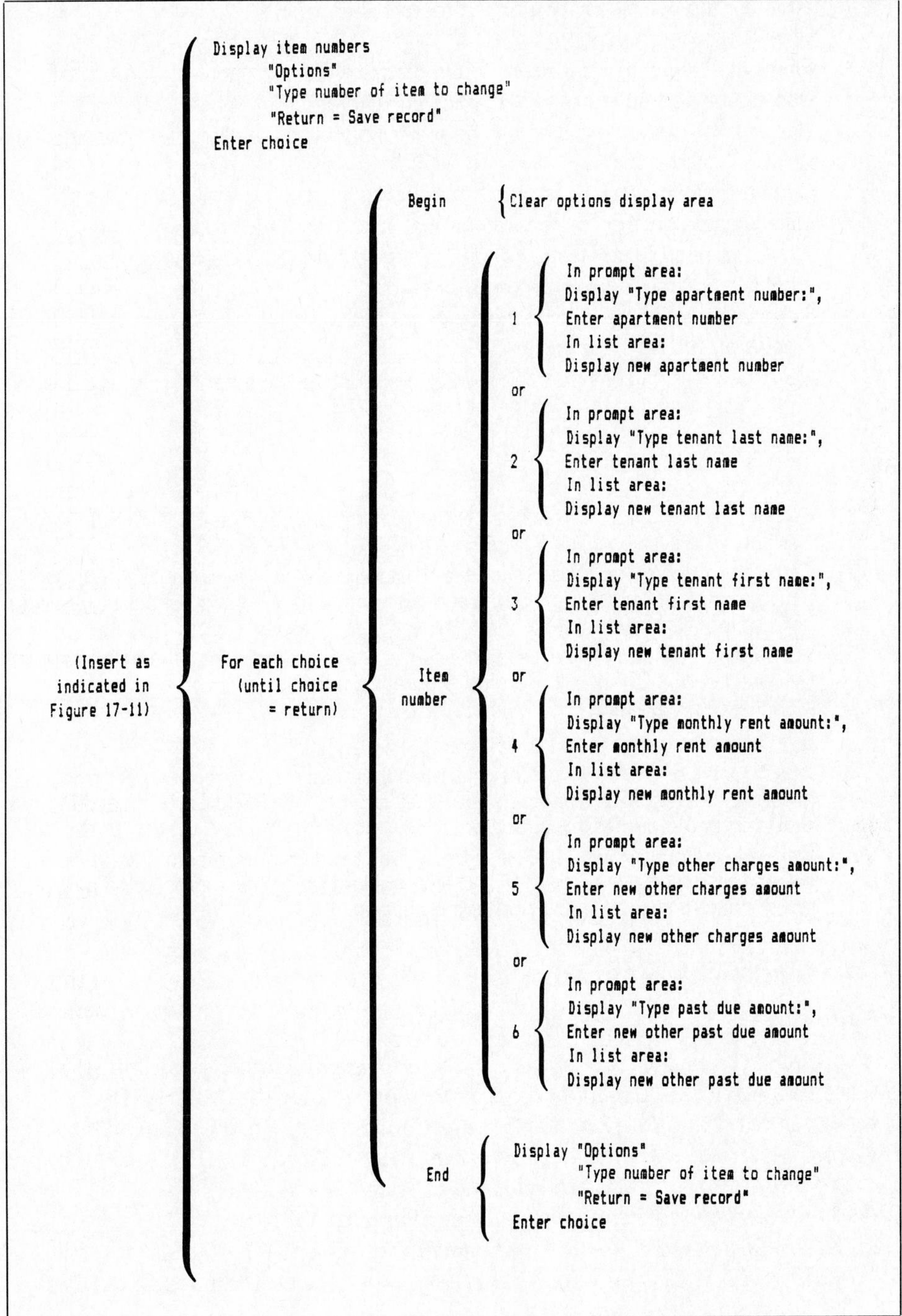

Figure 17-14 Program blueprint for changing information while adding tenant records to the file

4. What are the two steps involved in program design?
5. What is a program blueprint?
6. Identify the two major transitions that a program blueprint goes through.
7. Describe the components of a Warnier-Orr diagram.
8. Use an example to describe how the preliminary program blueprint is constructed.
9. What is initialization?
10. Compare batch with user-interactive programs.
11. Identify some physical considerations that impact the final program blueprint.
12. What program blueprints are needed to provide for database maintenance?
13. What is language independence in program design?
14. Describe how top-down implementation proceeds.
15. What is a prototype application?
16. Describe error routines that will need to be added to the tenant billing application.

EXERCISES

1. *CMB Apartments, Inc. Case.* Design the program blueprint for the Rent Roll Report. Use the data elements list created in exercise 1 of Chapter 15.
2. *CMB Apartments, Inc. Case.* The tenant list for the new superintendent also needs a program blueprint. Using the report design and data elements list from exercise 2 of Chapter 15, prepare the program blueprint for the new report.
3. *Warehouse Company Case.* Using the printer spacing layouts and the data elements lists prepared in Chapter 15, create program blueprints for the:
   a. Customer Report
   b. Customer monthly billing statement
4. *Warehouse Company Case.* Design a main menu for your warehouse company application. Use Figure 17–13 as a guide. Design the screen using a display layout sheet provided at the end of the chapter.
5. *Warehouse Company Case.* Design the screen to add a customer for the warehouse billing application. Use Figure 17–10 as a guide. Design the screen using a display layout sheet provided at the end of the chapter.

RESOURCES AND REFERENCES

See also Chapter 15, Resources and References.

CONSTANTINE, L. AND E. YOURDON, *Structured Design,* 2nd ed., Yourdon, 1978.
GALITZ, WILBERT O., *Handbook of Screen Format Design,* QED, 1981.
HIGGINS, DAVID A., *Program Design and Construction,* Prentice-Hall, 1979.
JACKSON, MICHAEL, *Principles of Program Design,* Academic, 1975.
JACKSON, MICHAEL, *System Development,* Prentice-Hall, 1983.
ORR, KEN, *Structured Requirements Definition,* Orr, 1981.
ORR, KEN, *Structured Systems Development,* Yourdon, 1977.
RICHARDSON, GARY L., CHARLES W. BUTLER, AND JOHN D. TOMLINSON, *A Primer of Structured Program Design,* Petrocelli, 1980.
WARNIER, JEAN-DOMINIQUE, *Logical Construction of Programs,* Van Nostrand, 1976.
WARNIER, JEAN-DOMINIQUE, *Program Modification,* Martinus, 1978.

COLUMN

ROW	1 — 10	11 — 20	21 — 30	31 — 40	41 — 50	51 — 60	61 — 70	71 — 80
	1 2 3 4 5 6 7 8 9 0	1 2 3 4 5 6 7 8 9 0	1 2 3 4 5 6 7 8 9 0	1 2 3 4 5 6 7 8 9 0	1 2 3 4 5 6 7 8 9 0	1 2 3 4 5 6 7 8 9 0	1 2 3 4 5 6 7 8 9 0	1 2 3 4 5 6 7 8 9 0
01								
02								
03								
04								
05								
06								
07								
08								
09								
10								
11								
12								
13								
14								
15								
16								
17								
18								
19								
20								
21								
22								
23								
24								1920

Figure 17-15 Display layout sheet

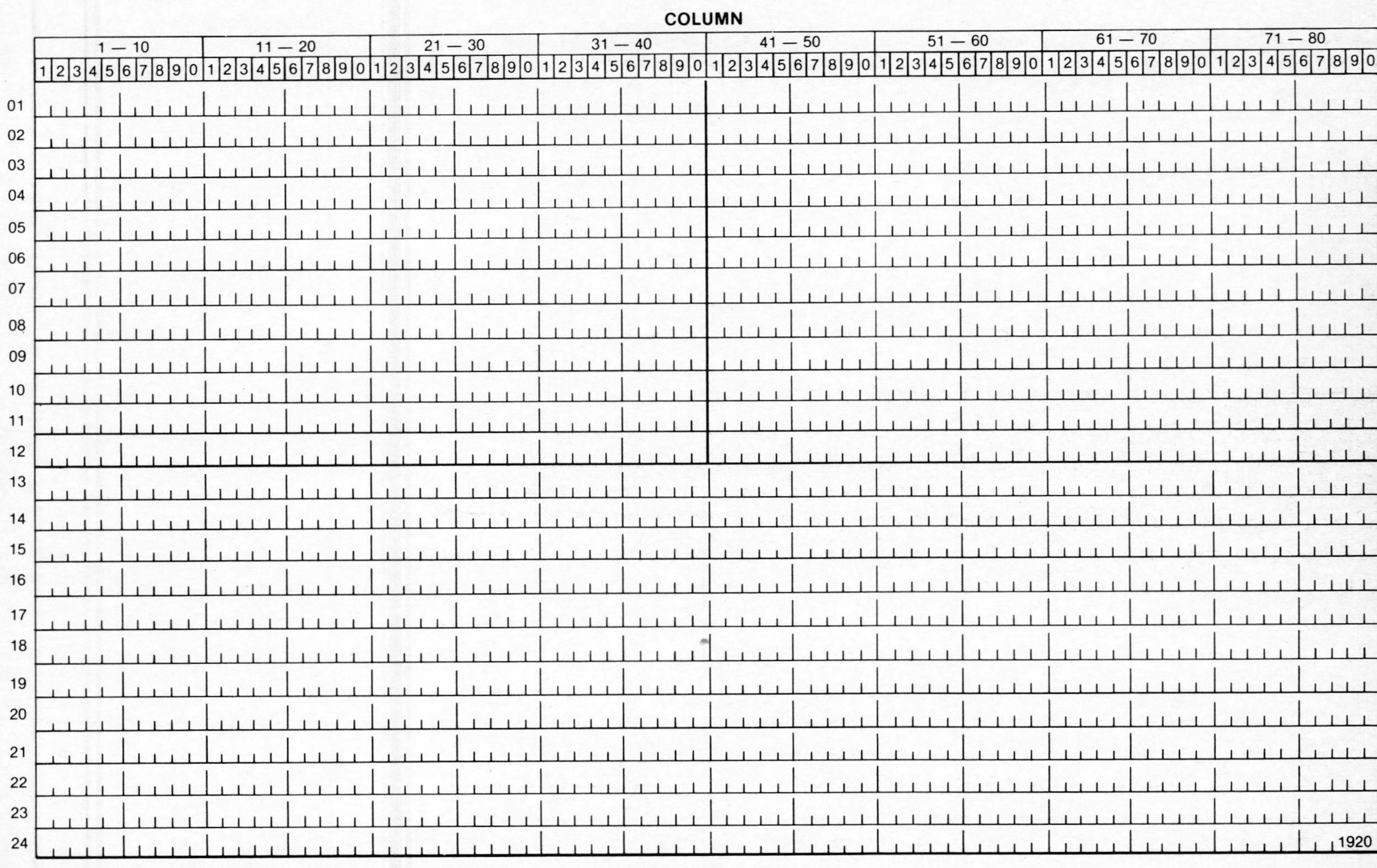

Figure 17-15 Display layout sheet

18

STRUCTURED BASIC PROGRAMMING

This chapter serves as an overview of the BASIC language. It specifically uses the language to program a prototype version of the tenant billing application specified in Chapter 15 and designed in Chapter 17.

Elementary language concepts like BASIC program line numbers, statements, commands, and variables are reviewed. Also covered are the control structures that can mold BASIC to produce a fully structured program. File handling with a random file creation example ends the chapter.

The IBM Personal Computer version of BASIC is used in this chapter.*

USING BASIC

To help refresh an understanding of BASIC, Ms. Jones tried a few simple exercises that relate to her tenant billing project. The first exercise she did helps to understand how user keyboard input occurs and how a BASIC program controls data entry. This first exercise appears in Figure 18–1.

*Used with permission of IBM

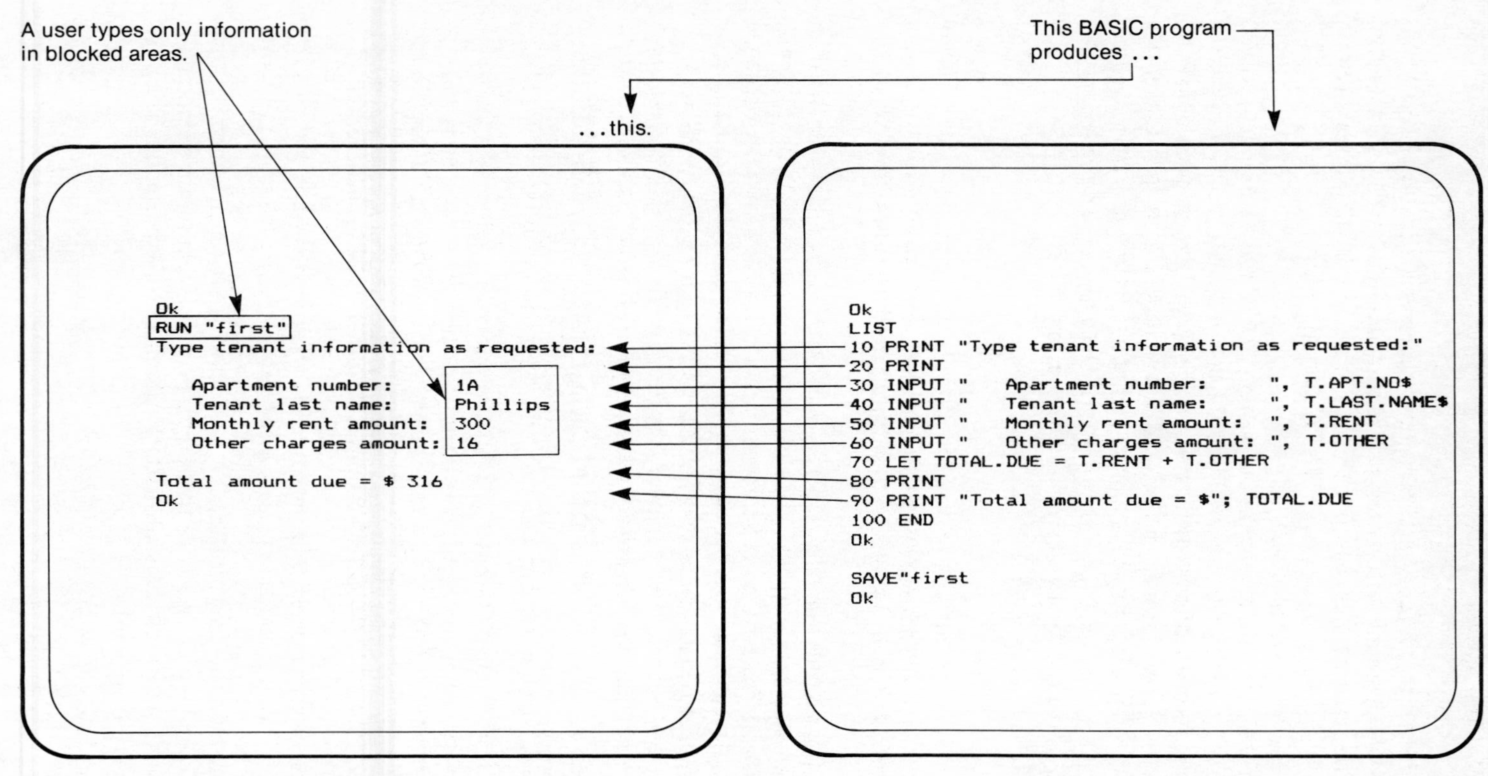

User's View:
This is what a user sees on the display when running the BASIC program on the right.

Programmer's View:
This is a program coded in BASIC as it appears on the display.

Figure 18-1 First exercise

To enter the first exercise, after turning on the computer, she types BASIC next to the familiar "A>" operating system prompt. That puts a copy of the BASIC language interpreter from disk storage into central memory. The familiar BASIC screen prompt is "OK." Anytime she wants to finish her BASIC programming, she types SYSTEM to return to the operating system level.

Some of the things she reviews about writing BASIC programs are identified in Figure 18–2. Before typing the program into the computer, Ms. Jones wrote each statement on paper. Many professional programmers preplan all program code before typing it into the computer. Some experienced programmers prefer to code right at the keyboard. Others prepare programs using a word processing application in place of pencil and paper. This has the advantage, in many cases, of being directly transferable to the BASIC program. It eliminates the need to retype program lines.

Program Line Numbers

Programs in many languages are characterized by program line numbers. Each BASIC program line starts with a number from 1 to 65529. Ms. Jones follows programming convention by leaving gaps between numbers. It provides room to insert lines later, if needed.

Following every line number is a BASIC statement word or keyword. Selected statements appear in the list given in Figure 18–3. Ms. Jones only needs four statement words to construct the first exercise. All other words in the program she makes up based on the processing logic.

If she types something incorrectly, she moves the cursor to the incorrect program line and types over the error. Sometimes she needs to insert or delete characters. The special INS insert key makes room between characters, and the special DEL delete key deletes characters. She needs to type a carriage return at every revised line to save changes.

When two lines are entered with the same line number, the new one replaces the old one. Lines could be added in any order and are automatically sorted into sequential order.

Soon Ms. Jones begins to use the AUTO command to generate program line numbers automatically. Using this command requires typing AUTO without a line number. AUTO command options are noted in the list of selected commands in Figure 18–4.

Anything typed without a line number, like AUTO, is assumed to be a command. Commands execute immediately. Even statements could be executed immediately if typed without line numbers. Consider the following two examples:

Example 1: PRINT 2+3 <RETURN>
5
Example 2: 10 PRINT 2+3 <RETURN>
RUN <RETURN>
5

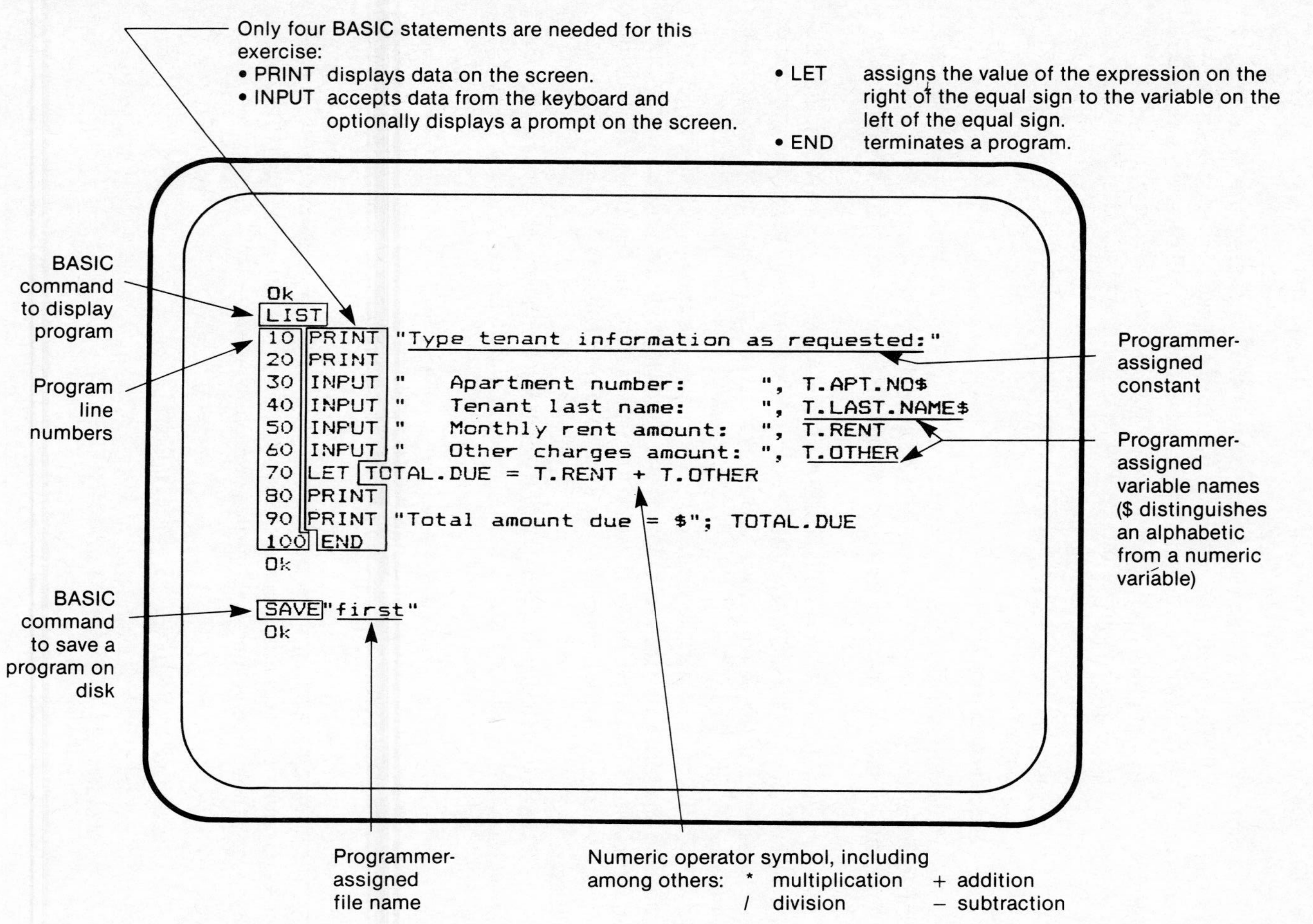

Figure 18-2 BASIC program characteristics

Figure 18-3 Selected BASIC statements (without file handling)

BASIC statements are most common in programmed mode, preceded by line numbers. They can be used in immediate mode also, without line numbers.

Keyword	*Action*	*Example*
CLS	Clears the screen.	10 CLS
CHAIN	Loads and runs the named program. In the example, B: is not part of the file name. It is a disk designation.	200 CHAIN "B:PAYCHECK"
END	Ends the program and returns to immediate mode.	500 END
GOSUB	Branches to a subprogram or subroutine located at the designated program line number (*see* RETURN).	200 GOSUB 2000
FOR/NEXT	Marks the extents of a FOR/NEXT loop.	200 FOR COUNT = 1 TO 10 ... 250 NEXT COUNT
GOTO	Branches to a designated program line number (restricted use in structured programming).	200 GOTO 500
IF/THEN/ ELSE	Controls branching in an alternative or decision process.	See text.
INPUT	Accepts keyboard input and assigns it to designated variables. A prompt is optional. A comma after the prompt suppresses a question mark, a semicolon allows it.	200 INPUT "NAME :", XNAME$
KEY OFF	Erases the function key display from the 25th line.	10 KEY OFF
LET	Assigns a designated value to the LET variable. LET is optional.	200 LET NUMBER = NUMBER + 1
LOCATE	Moves the cursor to the specified location (using row and column numbers). The example locates the cursor at row 1, column 1, the upper left-hand corner of the screen, or home position.	50 LOCATE 1,1
LPRINT	Prints data on the printer.	50 LPRINT XNAME$
PRINT	Displays data on the screen. A semicolon lets a programmer control spacing; a comma uses built-in default zone spacing.	50 PRINT "NAME = "; XNAME$
PRINT USING	Formats displayed output.	See text.
RETURN	Indicates the end of a subprogram or subroutine and returns program control to the statement following the most recent GOSUB.	2900 RETURN
WHILE/ WEND	Controls a repetitive or looping process.	See text.

Figure 18-3 (continued)

SPECIAL KEY COMBINATIONS

Keys Typed Simultaneously	*Action*
CTRL/BREAK	Stops program execution and returns to BASIC immediate mode.
SHIFT/PRTSC	Prints the displayed text on the printer.
CTRL/NUM LOCK	Used to temporarily interrupt printing or program listing. Typing a carriage return or any key ends the pause.
CTRL/ALT/DEL	Performs a system reset, similar to switching the computer power from off to on.

Figure 18-4 Selected BASIC commands

BASIC commands are most commonly used in immediate mode, without line numbers, for immediate execution.

Command	*Action*	*Example(s)*
AUTO	Generate line numbers automatically in increments of ten (use Ctrl-Break to exit).	AUTO
	Generate line numbers beginning at statement 100 in increments of twenty.	AUTO 100, 20
CLEAR	Clears all variables.	CLEAR
CONT	Continues program execution after a halt.	CONT
DELETE	Deletes specified program lines.	DELETE 100
EDIT	Displays a specified line for editing or revision.	EDIT 40
FILES	Displays files in the disk directory. The asterisk in the example represents "all." The B: is a disk designator.	FILES FILES "B:*.*"
KILL	Erases a file.	KILL "B:FIRST.BAS"
LIST	Lists program lines on the display.	LIST LIST 10 LIST 10–50
LLIST	Lists program lines at the printer.	LLIST
LOAD	Loads a program file from disk storage.	LOAD "B:FIRST"
MERGE	Merges a disk file with the program in memory.	MERGE "B:TEST"
NAME	Changes the name of a disk file.	NAME "B:FIRST.BAS" AS "B:BUILD.BAS"
NEW	Erases everything in memory.	NEW
RENUM	Renumbers program lines in increments of ten.	RENUM
RESET	Closes all open files.	RESET
RUN	Executes or runs a program in memory.	RUN

Figure 18-4 (continued)

Command	*Action*	*Example(s)*
SAVE	Saves a program with the designated name.	SAVE "B:FIRST"
	Saves a program in ASCII text format (needed for later CHAIN or MERGE use).	SAVE "B:FIRST", A
SYSTEM	Returns control to the operating system.	SYSTEM
TRON/TROFF	Traces the execution of program statements to aid in debugging (disabled with TROFF).	TRON TROFF

The first example has no line number and executes immediately. It is called *immediate* execution. The second example requires the explicit RUN command to execute. It is called *deferred* execution. Programs are generally designed for deferred execution. They require line numbers and an explicit RUN command to execute.

Typing a carriage return key after every statement or command is necessary in BASIC. It is similar to the carriage return required after any data entry in any interactive application. It signals the end of a logical entry.

When Ms. Jones types or punctuates statements incorrectly and then tries to execute them, she receives "SYNTAX ERROR" messages. Repairing the statement or punctuation error usually solves most syntax debugging problems.

Statements

Another characteristic of the BASIC language is its set of statements. Statements are most common in programs with line numbers. Someone at a later time is assumed to retrieve the program, previously saved as a file on disk, and execute it. The example in Figure 18-2 is of a deferred execution program.

As mentioned, only four statements are needed to construct the exercise program. PRINT displays data on the screen. Data could be a constant, indicated by the presence of quotation marks around the data in the program. It could also be information currently contained in a nonconstant or variable. In Figure 18-2, to pick one of many variable examples, line 90 displays whatever number is currently in the variable TOTAL.DUE.

PRINT by itself generates a blank line. Fancier print effects are possible with the PRINT USING statement as shown in Figure 18-5.

In any interactive program one of the most used statements is INPUT. It does double duty by displaying prompts and accepting keyboarded data into a waiting variable. The comma after the prompt suppresses a question mark, whereas a semicolon prints it. In programs where INPUT is used without a prompt, the question mark serves as a convenient signal that input is desired.

Another statement used is LET. It is called an assignment statement. The value of the expression on the right of the equal sign is assigned to the variable on the left of the equal sign. In line 70 of Figure 18-2, TOTAL.DUE is assigned the sum of rent and other charges. LET is optional in most BASICs and generally is not used by experienced programmers.

The final statement used is END. It terminates program execution and returns control to the immediate mode.

Figure 18-5 PRINT USING examples

The following program shows three examples of how the PRINT USING statement works.

```
10 BOOK.NUM = 12
20 TITLE$ = "BASIC"
30 PRICE = 17.5
40 FORM1$ = "The price of the & book, item ####, is $$###,.##."
50 PRINT USING FORM1$; TITLE$, BOOK.NUM, PRICE
60 PRINT USING "The price of the & book, item ####, is $$###,.##.";
        TITLE$, BOOK.NUM, PRICE
70 PRINT USING "The price of the \    \ book, item ####, is $###,.##.";
        TITLE$, BOOK.NUM, PRICE

RUN
The price of the BASIC book, item    12 is     $17.50.
The price of the BASIC book, item    12 is     $17.50.
The price of the BASIC book, item    12 is $   17.50.
Ok
```

Program lines 50 and 60 are the same, except 50 calls on a separated PRINT USING template. LIne 70 shows a fixed-length character variable, indicated with backslashes, as well as a fixed dollar sign.

TEMPLATE CHARACTERS	MEANING
	Numeric:
#######	Integer format (right-justified)
####.##	Fixed decimal format (rounded)
$	Prefix value with a fixed dollar sign
$$	Prefix value with a floating dollar sign
	Character:
\\	Two or more characters (left-justified)—to specify more characters, insert blanks between the backslashes
&	Variable length character string (entire string is printed)

Examples:	*Format*	*Variable Value*	*Result*
	##	12	12
	##.##	12	12.00
	#####,.##	1200	1,200.00
	##.#	2.36	2.4
	\ \	ALAN	ALAN
	$$###.##	12.36	$12.36

Figure 18–7 Variable naming rules and types

1. Names should be under 40 characters long. Longer na carefully chosen to be descriptive of their content.

2. The first character must be a letter.

3. An optional last character indicates variable type as fo

SYMBOL	VARIABLE TYPE
$	Character (or "string")
%	Numeric: integer
!	Numeric: single-precisio
#	Numeric: double-precisic

4. Variables without the last character symbol are assum

5. Words reserved for commands and statements canno as part of another longer name, they can be used. For but NAME is not. Variable type symbols do not affect r that cannot be used as variable names appears in Figu

6. Characters between the first and last can be any lette

PROGRAM CONTROL STRUCTURES

The first exercise program demonstrates tures. It is the sequence structure where c from the program blueprints in Chapter gram two other kinds of control. One is t is the *alternate paths* or *decision proces*

By restricting herself to three pr the practice of *structured programming*

Repetition

To experiment with repetitive pr test program. The new loop exercise prog data for several tenants, processing one fashion. This kind of processing is inevit to build the tenant database file and to p

Many other statements not covered in this chapter are important when doing other programming tasks.

Commands

Commands are mostly used in immediate mode, without line numbers, for immediate execution. Examples of commands in Figures 18–1 are SAVE, RUN, and LIST. SAVE immediately saves a copy of the program in memory as a disk file. Ms. Jones saves her exercise as a file called FIRST on the disk in drive A. Had she wanted to save the program on the disk in drive B, she would have typed "B:FIRST". Drive A is the so-called *default drive*. The drive designator does not become part of the file name.

The RUN command executes a program already in memory. If the program is on disk, it must be loaded into memory first. The LOAD "FILENAME" command gets it into memory. Then a RUN command executes it. Another possibility is RUN "FILENAME" which does both the load and run functions.

Other commands especially useful to programmers are LIST and LLIST. LIST displays a program on the display. Because a long listing scrolls up off the screen so quickly, pressing two keys simultaneously, the CTRL and NUM LOCK combination, suspends scrolling. Pressing a carriage return or any key resumes scrolling.

Alternately, an LLIST command lists program lines at the printer. This is useful to make a documentation copy of the program. Whenever extensive program revisions are needed, Ms. Jones uses a printed listing for solving coding problems away from the computer.

Two other commands, TRON and TROFF, aid in debugging work. TRON turns a program trace on. It displays line numbers as they are executed. It lets Ms. Jones see if the lines are executing as planned. She can turn the trace off with TROFF. Many of these heavily used commands are available at the touch of a single function key. A prompt line at the bottom of the screen constantly identifies function key actions.

When a function key is used, the command appears in capital letters on the screen. BASIC likes everything in capital letters. Program entry work, however, can be done in upper- and lower-case characters. Whenever LIST or RUN is typed, everything is automatically converted to upper case, except for anything in quotation marks.

Variables

As Figure 18–2 illustrates, there are a number of programmer-assigned *variables*. *Variable* data does not remain constant during computer processing. The same variable names are used for every record processed in a program. While the names assigned remain constant, their values change according to the tenant record being processed.

She thought of variables as a row of mailboxes. Mailboxes always remain in place, and each has a unique address. Each day new mail gets deposited and each day it is removed from the mailboxes. This is exactly what happens when using variables.

Inside the computer, mailboxes become sections of memory. A section is reserved each time the executing program encounters a new programmer assigned variable name.

Figure 18-8 BASIC reserved words that cannot be used as variable names

ABS	CVS	FRE	LOG	POINT	SQR
AND	DATA	GET	LPOS	POKE	STEP
ASC	DATE$	GOSUB	LPRINT	POS	STICK
ATN	DEF	GOTO	LSET	PRESET	STOP
AUTO	DEFDBL	HEX$	MERGE	PRINT	STR$
BEEP	DEFINT	IF	MID$	PRINT#	STRIG
BLOAD	DEFSNG	IMP	MKD$	PSET	STRING$
BSAVE	DEFSTR	INKEY$	MKI$	PUT	SWAP
CALL	DELETE	INP	MKS$	RANDOMIZE	SYSTEM
CDBL	DIM	INPUT	MOD	READ	TAB
CHAIN	DRAW	INPUT#	MOTOR	REM	TAN
CHR$	EDIT	INPUT$	NAME	RENUM	THEN
CINT	ELSE	INSTR	NEW	RESET	TIME$
CIRCLE	END	INT	NEXT	RESTORE	TO
CLEAR	EOF	KEY	NOT	RESUME	TROFF
CLOSE	EQV	KILL	OCT$	RETURN	TRON
CLS	ERASE	LEFT$	OFF	RIGHT$	USING
COLOR	ERL	LEN	ON	RND	USR
COM	ERR	LET	OPEN	RSET	VAL
COMMON	ERROR	LINE	OPTION	RUN	VARPTR
CONT	EXP	LIST	OR	SAVE	WAIT
COS	FIELD	LLIST	OUT	SCREEN	WEND
CSNG	FILES	LOAD	PAINT	SGN	WHILE
CSRLIN	FIX	LOC	PEEK	SIN	WIDTH
CVD	FN	LOCATE	PEN	SOUND	WRITE
CVI	FOR	LOF	PLAY	SPACE$	WRITE#
				SPC	XOR

The new exercise showed her how the WHILE / WEND statements automatically create a loop inside the program. Every time the program sequentially moves down to find the end of the WHILE structure, or WEND, it loops back on itself. A WHILE statement indicates the top of the loop. Her main job was to figure out a way to exit from loop processing.

To control loop termination, she has a user type "end" instead of an apartment number. Because the test for "end" occurs at the top of the loop, it also controls entry to the loop.

The not equal test for the loop control belongs to a group of *relational operators,* among which are:

RELATIONAL OPERATOR	TEST PERFORMED
=	Equal
< >	Not equal
<	Less than
>	Greater than
<=	Less than or equal to
>=	Greater than or equal to

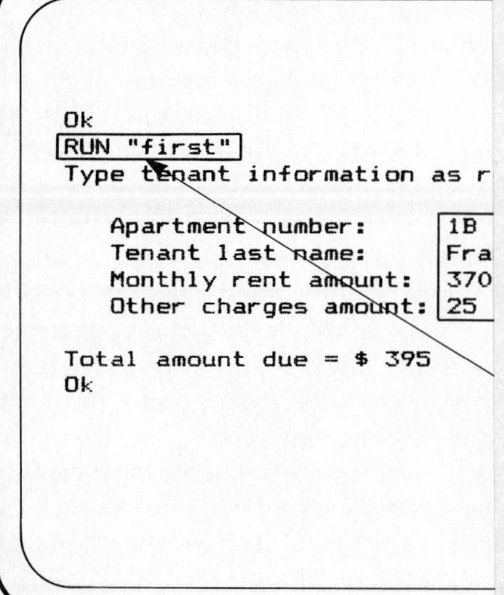

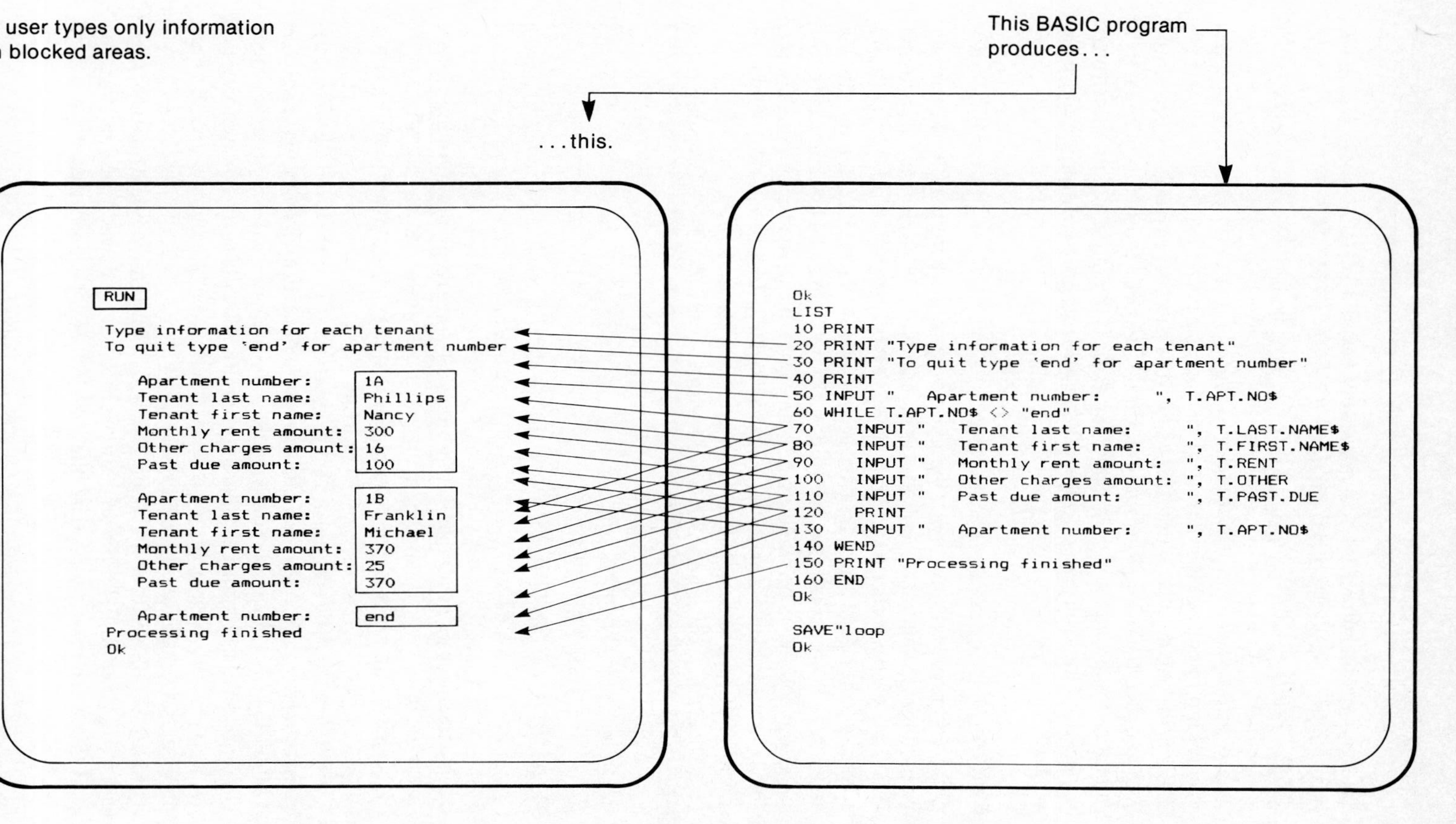

Figure 18–9 Loop exercise

After a user enters the first apartment number, the WHILE statement checks to see if it is "end." If not, the next statement executes inside the loop. Once inside the loop, no exit is possible until the entry test is failed. This makes it necessary to ask for the next apartment number inside the loop itself. The logical place to do it is at the end of the loop before recycling. Ms. Jones considered this position to mark not only the end of one loop cycle, but also the start of the next cycle.

Once inside the loop, the program resembles the first exercise. It is a simple *sequential* structure embedded in the *loop* structure. If needed, another loop could have been nested inside the existing one. The main observation is that programs are constructed like building blocks. One structure fits into another and there are only three main structures to work with.

Decision

A decision process is the only other main program structure left to experiment with. Properly aligning rent statement addresses in a window envelope, for example, requires a decision as to whether to add one or two extra lines to the body of the statement. The amount to be added depends on the accumulated total in a line counter variable.

Ms. Jones' program calls for printing two blank lines if the line counter is zero, and one line if the counter is one. No extra blank lines are needed if the line counter is 2. The line counter variable can contain three possible values 0, 1, and 2. Only two values require significant action, 0 and 1, so a value of 2 is ignored.

This program problem can be solved with two simple IF-THEN statements, for example:

```
70 IF LINE.COUNTER=0
        THEN PRINT: PRINT
80 IF LINE.COUNTER=1
        THEN PRINT
```

The colon separates multiple statements combined on one logical program line. In the case of line 70, the use of multiple statements eliminates a second test of LINE.COUNTER = 0 to generate the second blank line. As it is, both PRINTs execute if the condition is true.

Another way to program a decision process is with an IF-THEN-ELSE statement. To experiment with it, Ms. Jones developed the exercise given in Figure 18–10. Instead of blank lines, she includes some printing in order to trace the program logic.

The decision exercise runs as a *batch program*. A batch program has no significant human intervention. Most print programs, like the rent statements and the Rent Roll Report programs, execute in batch mode.

In Figure 18–10, with the line counter set to a constant of 1, the program logic falls through to the second IF-THEN structure, which is nested inside the first one. The rule is that, if the tested condition is true, the first IF-THEN is processed. If the tested condition is false, the ELSE is processed.

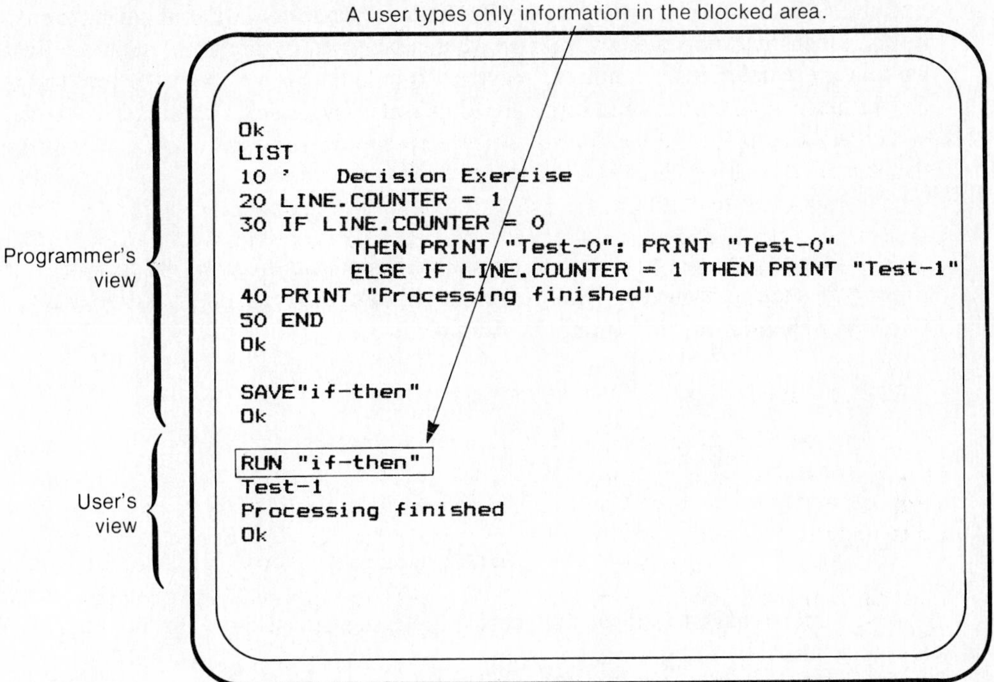

Figure 18-10 A decision structure programming exercise that requires no user intervention

To examine the decision structure further, Ms. Jones retypes a new constant of zero in line 20 and reruns the program. Her user's view on the screen this time is:

RUN
Test-O
Test-O
Processing finished
OK

The multiline, indented format of the IF-THEN-ELSE structure visually supports the logic flow. To achieve this within a single program line, Ms. Jones types a CTRL and carriage return double key sequence at the end of a line. On the next line she types the TAB key once. When finished with the logical line, she types the normal carriage return. Since one statement holds a maximum of 255 characters, it restricts how deeply she could extend logical program lines.

With the exercise in Figure 18-10, Ms. Jones begins a common professional programmer practice of internally documenting programs. In line 10, the "Decision

Exercise'' description clearly labels what the following code does without having to read it first. Documentation is easily inserted wherever desired by beginning program lines with an apostrophe. The computer ignores such lines that serve only as memos to the programmer. Apostrophes can begin anywhere on a line, even after executable code.

SUBROUTINES

Ms. Jones often uses the decision structure to send the program off to process subprograms and subroutines. They represent program code that is physically located out of the present sequential order. An example is:

```
100 IF CONTROL$ = "end"
        THEN GOSUB 2000
        ELSE GOSUB 3000
110 PRINT "CONTINUE"
```

In the preceding example, the program branches on a true condition from line 100 to line 2000. A RETURN statement placed at the end of the GOSUB subroutine sends control back to the next statement following the GOSUB. In the example, the return would be to line 110.

Many examples of GOSUB use appear in the program listing at the end of the chapter.

Subroutines often contain small sections of program code that are reused at different places in a program. A subroutine can also be an entire subprogram. Often when subprograms are merged with one controlling program, like a main menu program, they are still called subroutines or just routines.

FILE HANDLING

Tenant records in the database need to be accessed in random order for changes and viewing. BASIC provides a random access capability to do this. Ms. Jones decided to use it to create her database.

An alternative would be sequential access. With sequential access, if a request is made to view record 1,000, all records between 1 to 999 must be sequentially scanned to get to 1,000. By contrast, with random access, the requested record is retrieved immediately. With very large files, the different access techniques make a big difference in processing speed.

Create a Random File

In order to work with a random file, Ms. Jones had to become familiar with the following statements and built-in functions:

STATEMENTS		FUNCTIONS	
OPEN	CLOSE	MKI$	CVI
LSET		MKS$	CVS
PUT	GET	MKD$	CVD

Most of these are used in the program shown in Figure 18-11, which creates a tenant file. She coded most of the program directly from the Add Tenants program blueprint in Figure 17-11. As is apparent, she reused code from the earlier loop exercise.

New file handling code appears in blocked areas.

```
Ok
LLIST
10 '**************************
20 '*                        *
30 '*       Add Tenants      *
40 '*                        *
50 '**************************
60 '
70 OPEN "R", #1, "Tenant.dat"
80 FIELD #1,  2 AS T.REC.NO$,         3 AS T.APT.NO$, 15 AS T.LAST.NAME$,
             10 AS T.FIRST.NAME$,  4 AS T.RENT$,     4 AS T.OTHER$,
              4 AS T.PAST.DUE$
90 CLS        '(Clear screen)
100 PRINT "Type information for each tenant"
110 PRINT "To quit type 'end' for apartment number"
120 PRINT
130 REC.NO = 1
140 PRINT "For tenant record number: ", REC.NO
150 INPUT "   Apartment number:             ", XT.APT.NO$
160 WHILE XT.APT.NO$ <> "end"
170     INPUT "   Tenant last name:             ", XT.LAST.NAME$
180     INPUT "   Tenant first name:            ", XT.FIRST.NAME$
190     INPUT "   Monthly rent amount:          ", XT.RENT
200     INPUT "   Other charges amount:         ", XT.OTHER
210     INPUT "   Past due amount:              ", XT.PAST.DUE
220     LSET T.REC.NO$ = MKI$(REC.NO)
230     LSET T.APT.NO$ = XT.APT.NO$
240     LSET T.LAST.NAME$ = XT.LAST.NAME$
250     LSET T.FIRST.NAME$ = XT.FIRST.NAME$
260     LSET T.RENT$ = MKS$(XT.RENT)
270     LSET T.OTHER$ = MKS$(XT.OTHER)
280     LSET T.PAST.DUE$ = MKS$(XT.PAST.DUE)
290     PUT #1, REC.NO
300     REC.NO = REC.NO + 1
310     PRINT
320     PRINT "For tenant record number: ", REC.NO
330     INPUT "   Apartment number:             ", XT.APT.NO$
340 WEND
350 CLOSE #1
360 PRINT "Processing finished"
370 END

Ok
SAVE"add",a
```

Figure 18-11 A program to add tenant records to a random access file

To test the program, she used prepared test data shown in Figure 15-6. The new numeric tenant record number field is added because, to use a random access file, record numbers must be known. They also must be numeric. Using the record number is one solution to random file access.

In Ms. Jones' sample program, the tenant record is not typed by a user. The program automatically generates it. With each pass through the loop, the record number counter is incremented by one.

When she became a more experienced programmer, she created a separate index file to hold record numbers. It allowed the indirect access to tenant records based on a user entry of either last name or apartment number.

Blocked areas on the program listing in Figure 18-11 highlight Ms. Jones' file handling code. The OPEN statement opens a file called Tenant.dat for processing. The "R" identifies it as a random access file. The "#1" is an arbitrarily assigned file reference number that is reused each time the same file is referenced elsewhere in the program. If other files would be used, they would be given other reference numbers. The CLOSE statement at the end of the program closes the open file.

The FIELD statement reserves a section in memory especially for transferring records to and from the disk. It is often called a record *buffer* area. The buffer only transfers character information, so all FIELD variables are noted with $ suffix. LSET statements are used to get information into the buffer before the PUT statement physically creates or writes a disk record.

Numeric information first must be converted to character format before the buffer accepts it. The MKI$, MKS$, and MKD$ are built-in functions that *make in*teger, *s*ingle- and *d*ouble-precision numbers, into characters. The ground rules followed are listed in Figure 18-12.

One thing Ms. Jones had to get used to was that variable names used in a FIELD statement cannot be reused as INPUT variable names. Nor can they be assigned values (with or without a LET statement). Breaking either rule means the program cancels the FIELD association.

Figure 18-12 Ground rules for numeric variables used in random access records

		USE		
		Use To Convert To		*Use For FIELD Statement*
If Number Is . . .	*variable is . . .*	*Character*	*Numeric*	
Up to 32767	Integer	MKI$	CVI	2
Less than 9999.99	Single-precision	MKS$	CVS	4
Over 9999.99	Double-precision	MKD$	CVD	8

To make INPUT names different from FIELD names, she simply adds an initial X to the variable name. This clearly distinguishes INPUT from FIELD variables while it also retains the common association between the two.

Access a Random File

The program to print the rent statements and Rent Statement Summary Report accesses the random access file. The code Ms. Jones wrote appears in Figure 18–13. The printed output is given in Figure 18–14.

```
10 '*************************
20 '*                       *
30 '* Print Rent Statements *
40 '*                       *
50 '*************************
60 '
70 '
80 'This program is saved as "B:Bills.bas".  It is chained to
90 'from main menu selection "5" of the program "B:Mainmenu.bas."
100 'When complete it chains back to the main menu program.
110 '
120 '
130 '((( Open files )))
140 '
150 OPEN "R", #2, "B:Tenant.dat"
160 FIELD #2,  2 AS T.REC.NO$,        3 AS T.APT.NO$,   15 AS T.LAST.NAME$,
              10 AS T.FIRST.NAME$,  4 AS T.RENT$,       4 AS T.OTHER$,
               4 AS T.PAST.DUE$
170 '
180 '
190 OPEN "R", #1, "B:Control.dat"  'A one-record control file
200 FIELD #1, 2 AS RECORD.CTR$     'Contains the last tenant record number
210 '
220 '((( Initialize accumulators )))
230 '
240 TOT.RENT = 0
250 TOT.OTHER = 0
260 TOT.PAST.DUE = 0
270 STMT.CTR = 0
280 '
290 '((( Ask for date and paper alignment )))
300 '
310 CLS
320 LOCATE 1: PRINT "PRINT RENT STATEMENTS"
330 LOCATE 21,11
340 PRINT "Type due date for rent statements"
350 PRINT
360 LOCATE 23,11: INPUT "(MM/DD/YY): ", X.DATE$
370 LOCATE 21,11
380 PRINT "Align printer paper - turn on printer"
390 PRINT
400 LOCATE 23,11: INPUT "Type <return> to begin printing", X.BEGIN$
```

Figure 18–13 The program listing to print rent statements and the Rent Statement Summary Report based on the program blueprint in Figure 17–9

```
410 LOCATE 21: PRINT SPACE$(79)
420 LOCATE 21,11: PRINT "Please wait..."
430 PRINT
440 LOCATE 23,11: PRINT "Rent Statement printing is in progress"
450 '
460 '((( Set record count control )))
470 '
480 REC.NO = 1        'Begin at record number one
490 GET #1, 1         'Retrieve the last number used
500 '
510 '((( For each tenant )))
520 '
530 WHILE REC.NO <= CVI(RECORD.CTR$)
540     GET #2, REC.NO
550     IF T.LAST.NAME$ <> "Unoccupied      "
             THEN GOSUB 860      'Print subroutine
560     REC.NO = REC.NO + 1
570 WEND
580 '
590 '((( Print a summary report )))
600 '
610 LPRINT: LPRINT
620 LPRINT TAB(10) "RENT STATEMENT SUMMARY REPORT - "; X.DATE$
630 LPRINT: LPRINT
640 LPRINT TAB(10) "Number of statements processed:    "; STMT.CTR
650 LPRINT: LPRINT: LPRINT
660 FORMR$ = "                      Total Rent:  $######,.##"
670 FORMO$ = "             Total Other Charges:   ######,.##"
680 FORMP$ = "                  Total Past Due:   ######,.##"
690 FORMG$ = "                 Grand Total Due:  $######,.##"
700 LPRINT USING FORMR$; TOT.RENT
710 LPRINT USING FORMO$; TOT.OTHER
720 LPRINT USING FORMP$; TOT.PAST.DUE
730 LPRINT TAB(35) "-----------"
740 GRAND.TOT = TOT.RENT + TOT.OTHER + TOT.PAST.DUE
750 LPRINT USING FORMG$; GRAND.TOT
760 '
770 CLOSE #1, #2
780 CHAIN "B:Mainmenu"
790 '
800 '
810 '---------- Rent Statement Subroutines ----------
820 '
830 '
840 '
850 '--------------------
860 'Print rent statement
870 '--------------------
880 '
890 '
900 '((( Initialize accumulators )))
910 '
920 TOT.DUE = 0
930 LINE.CTR = 0
940 LPRINT
950 LPRINT
960 '
```

Figure 18-13 (continued)

```
970 '((( Print heading )))
980 '
990 LPRINT TAB(11) "RENT STATEMENT - 1924 EIGHTH ST., BETHLEHEM, PA 18017
1000 LPRINT: LPRINT
1010 LPRINT TAB(11) "Due Date:    "; X.DATE$
1020 LPRINT
1030 '
1040 '((( Print statement amounts )))
1050 '
1060 FORMA$ = "              Current Monthly Rent      $ ####.##"
1070 FORMB$ = "              Other Charges               ####.##"
1080 FORMC$ = "              Balance Past Due            ####.##"
1090 FORMD$ = "              Total Amount Due          $ ####.##"
1100 '
1110 LPRINT USING FORMA$; CVS(T.RENT$)
1120 IF CVS(T.OTHER$) > 0
     THEN LPRINT USING FORMB$; CVS(T.OTHER$)
1130 IF CVS(T.PAST.DUE$) > 0
     THEN LPRINT USING FORMC$; CVS(T.PAST.DUE$):
     LINE.CTR = LINE.CTR + 1
1140 '
1150 LPRINT TAB(36) "---------"; TAB(54) "Please remit to:"
1160 TOT.DUE = TOT.DUE + CVS(T.RENT$) + CVS(T.OTHER$) + CVS(T.PAST.DUE$)
1170 LPRINT USING FORMD$; TOT.DUE
1180 '
1190 '((( Print remit address )))
1200 '
1210 LPRINT TAB(54) "CMB Apartments, Inc."
1220 LPRINT TAB(54) "3368 Allen St."
1230 LPRINT TAB(54) "Bethlehem, PA 18017"
1240 IF LINE.CTR = 0
     THEN LPRINT: LPRINT
     ELSE IF LINE.CTR = 1 THEN LPRINT
1250 '
1260 '((( Print tenant information )))
1270 '
1280 LPRINT TAB(11) T.LAST.NAME$; TAB(26) T.FIRST.NAME$; TAB(36)"Apt. ";
     T.APT.NO$
1290 LPRINT TAB(11) "1924 Eighth St."
1300 LPRINT TAB(11) "Bethlehem, PA 18017"
1310 LPRINT
1320 LPRINT
1330 LPRINT
1340 LPRINT "         ---------------------------------------------------
-----"
1350 '((( Accumulate totals )))
1360 '
1370 TOT.RENT = TOT.RENT + CVS(T.RENT$)
1380 TOT.OTHER = TOT.OTHER + CVS(T.OTHER$)
1390 TOT.PAST.DUE = TOT.PAST.DUE + CVS(T.PAST.DUE$)
1400 STMT.CTR = STMT.CTR + 1
1410 '
1420 '
1430 '((( Advance printer to a new page )))
1440 '
1450 LINES = 23
1460 WHILE LINES < 66
```

Figure 18-13 (continued)

```
1470     LPRINT
1480     LINES = LINES + 1
1490 WEND
1500 '
1510 RETURN
1520 '
1530 '
```

Figure 18-13 (continued)

```
RENT STATEMENT - 1924 EIGHTH ST., BETHLEHEM, PA 18017


Due Date:    04/21/8X

Current Monthly Rent        $  300.00
Other Charges                   16.00
Balance Past Due               100.00
                             ---------
                                            Please remit to:
Total Amount Due            $  416.00
                                            CMB Apartments, Inc.
                                            3368 Allen St.
                                            Bethlehem, PA 18017


Phillips        Nancy       Apt. 1A
1924 Eighth St.
Bethlehem, PA 18017
```

```
RENT STATEMENT SUMMARY REPORT - 04/21/8X


Number of statements processed:     5



              Total Rent:  $  1,650.00
     Total Other Charges:        61.00
         Total Past Due:        470.00
                             -----------
        Grand Total Due:  $  2,181.00
```

Figure 18-14 Sample rent statement and Rent Statement Summary Report printed by the program listed in Figure 18-13

A GET statement reads the desired record and automatically places it in the FIELD buffer area. Data must be retrieved from the buffer to be used elsewhere in the program. The CVI, CVS, and CVD functions *C*on*v*ert numeric information back to *I*nteger, *S*ingle- and *D*ouble-precision numbers for normal program use.

In this program Ms. Jones uses the PRINT USING statement to format printed output. It is one of the more difficult BASIC statements she learned to work with. The program also shows the use of total accumulators.

Evident also is the use of a second file. It is the control file that contains a single record. The record has one field that contains the last tenant record number used. Having this number available enables the program to know when to stop printing statements. The last tenant record number is captured in another program that adds tenant records to the file.

PROGRAM CONSTRUCTION

While Ms. Jones follows top-down program design techniques as used by professional program designers, she begins constructing her application from the bottom up. She needs a database to drive the rest of the program development effort, so she builds the database file first.

This is normal procedure. After programming the Add Tenants program, which builds the file, she does the Rent Statement Summary Report program, which uses the file.

One way to link programs to the main menu requires using the MERGE and RENUM commands. MERGE provides for combining the separate programs into one, and RENUM enables renumbering program lines into an orderly sequence. A listing of the main menu program is given at the end of the chapter in Figure 18–15.

Her rent statement print program is CHAINed to and from the main menu program. In this way it remains a separate stand-alone program. When done executing, therefore, it has to CHAIN back to the main menu program.

Had the final program been too large to fit into memory all at once, she could have used CHAIN statements instead of GOSUBs for all main menu selections. The two work much the same way except the CHAIN command goes to a separate disk file instead of to a separate place in the same program. Also, a CHAINed program could CHAIN itself to another program. In this way a program of unlimited size could be executed without regard for actual memory size.

Subprograms that are not yet implemented display dummy messages when selected from the main menu. One might display "Arrived at Delete Subprogram, not yet implemented." All subprograms are first implemented as stand-alone programs. When fully debugged, they are merged into the master main menu program.

DEBUGGING

Ms. Jones finds writing program code and debugging the problem code a tedious and time-consuming task. Problems in code could be as simple as typing PRNT for PRINT. The language processor recognizes only PRINT and anything else causes a SYNTAX ERROR to flash on the display. Errors often are misspellings as well as misused variable names. Problems are uncovered when RUN is typed to execute the code.

Some error messages are not for syntax errors. These often involve incorrect process and file handling logic. Many require looking up the problem in the section of the BASIC manual on error messages. The manual describes the causes and possible solutions to problems, but usually lets users resolve bugs with a lot of detective work. During coding and debugging, Ms. Jones spends much time with the BASIC manual learning all the nuances of how the language works.

Process logic problems are harder to detect. For example, if a total due calculation involves four variables, but only three are programmed, it might go undetected. The program might execute perfectly if all the code is correct. This kind of logic error requires careful checking for logic accuracy.

The program code in the final listing is created using code and techniques described in this chapter. It also uses four special built-in BASIC functions. The first is the LEN(X$) function, which returns the number of characters in variable X$. It is used frequently to test whether or not a user enters a carriage return. If no entry is made and only a carriage return is entered, LEN equals zero. It is a useful way to accept and test for a carriage return response to selection options.

The second built-in function, LOF(X), is used once. It is used to see if the tenant file is empty. If empty, the program starts with number one to assign tenant record numbers automatically. If not empty, it starts with whatever number exists in the control file plus one. The X refers to the file reference number used in the file OPEN statement.

The other two built-in functions are TAB(X) and SPACE$(X). TAB functions exactly like a typewriter TAB key to move the printhead or cursor position a designated number of spaces. SPACE$(X) allows spaces in a print line for X characters.

As mentioned elsewhere, various data entry techniques, editing, error trapping, control, and other BASIC coding topics are beyond the scope of this chapter. The final listing is considered only a first pass or a working prototype. Much can be done to refine the code and program efficiency. This occupied Ms. Jones in a subsequent project.

The printed program listings and the blueprint diagrams become permanent application documentation. Ms. Jones copied them all and saved one copy in a safe place. Whenever a revision is needed, the blueprints are updated, as is the code. With this documentation, either she or another programmer has a model on which to base further application modifications or revisions.

```
10 'CMB APARTMENTS INC.
20 '
30 'Tenant billing application:
40 '   .maintains a file of apartments
50 '   .produces monthly rent statements
60 '   .produces a Rent Roll Report
70 '
80 'Programmer:  Irene K. Jones
90 'Saved as "B:Mainmenu.bas"
100 'Last revision: 06/06/8X
110 '
120 'All user entries are identified
130 'by the prefix "X" as in X.SELECT.
140 '
150 KEY OFF       'Erase the 25th display line
160 '
```

Figure 18-15 Tenant billing application—main menu program listing

```
170 '
180 '*****************************************
190 '*                                       *
200 '*          Main Menu Selections         *
210 '*                                       *
220 '*****************************************
230 '
240 '
250 X.SELECT = 0
260 WHILE X.SELECT <> 99
270     CLS
280     PRINT
290     PRINT "                         C M B   A p a r t m e n t s,  I n c."
300     PRINT
310     PRINT "                                   Main Menu Selections"
320     PRINT: PRINT
330     PRINT "            TENANT RECORDS:"
340     PRINT
350     PRINT "                    1   Add"
360     PRINT "                    2   Change/View"
370     PRINT "                    3   Delete"
380     PRINT
390     PRINT "            PRINT:"
400     PRINT
410     PRINT "                    4   Rent Roll Report"
420     PRINT "                    5   Rent Statements"
430     PRINT: PRINT
440     PRINT "                   99   Quit Processing"
450     LOCATE 23: INPUT "         Type number of selection: ", X.SELECT
460 '
470 '
480 '   ((( Find the appropriate routine )))
490 '
500     IF X.SELECT = 1
             THEN GOSUB 710                 'Add
510     IF X.SELECT = 2
             THEN GOSUB 1760                'Change/View
520     IF X.SELECT = 3
             THEN GOSUB 2580                'Delete
530     IF X.SELECT = 4
             THEN CHAIN "B:Rentroll.bas"    'Rent Roll Report
540     IF X.SELECT = 5
             THEN CHAIN "B:Bills.bas"       'Rent Statements
550 '
560 WEND
570 '
580 CLS: LOCATE 12,11
590 PRINT "Processing finished"
600 END
610 '
620 '
630 '
640 '
650 '*************************
660 '*                       *
670 '*     Add Tenants       *
680 '*                       *
690 '*************************
```

Figure 18-15 (continued)

```
700 '
710 '
720 '((( Op
730 '
740 OPEN "R
750 FIELD #
760 GOSUB 3
770 '
780 '((( Ch
790 '
800 GET #1,
810 IF LOF(
       THE
       ELS
820 '
830 '((( Se
840 '
850 CLS
860 LOCATE
870 LOCATE
880 LOCATE
890 '
900 '((( En
910 '
920 PRINT "
930 PRINT
940 INPUT "
950 WHILE X
960      GOS
970      LOC
980      INP
990      PRI
1000     INP
1010     PRI
1020     INP
1030     PRI
1040     INP
1050     PRI
1060     INP
1070 '
1080 '    (((
1090 '
1100     LSE
1110     LSE
1120     LSE
1130     LSE
1140     LSE
1150     LSE
1160     LSE
1170 '
1180 '    (((
1190 '
1200     LOC
1210     LOC
1220     LOC
1230     LOC
1240     LOC
```

Figure 18-15 (con


```
1760 '**************************
1770 '*                        *
1780 '*      Change/View       *
1790 '*                        *
1800 '**************************
1810 '
1820 '
1830 GOSUB 3370      'Open tenant file
1840 GOSUB 2460      'Display prompts
1850 WHILE XT.REC.NO <> 99
1860 '
1870 '   ((( Display the asked for record )))
1880 '
1890    CLS
1900    GET #2, XT.REC.NO
1910    GOSUB 4230       'Display record
1920 '
1930 '   ((( Display the item numbers )))
1940 '
1950    LOCATE 1: PRINT "CHANGE/VIEW"
1960    LOCATE 7,11: PRINT "1"
1970    LOCATE 9,11: PRINT "2"
1980    LOCATE 11,11: PRINT "3"
1990    LOCATE 13,11: PRINT "4"
2000    LOCATE 15,11: PRINT "5"
2010 '
2020 '   ((( Display options )))
2030 '
2040    LOCATE 19,7: PRINT "Options"
2050    PRINT "            Type number of item to change"
2060    PRINT "              99 = Exit to main menu"
2070    PRINT "              Return = View another record"
2080 '
2090 '   ((( Change an item -or- view another record -or- exit to main menu )))
2100 '
2110    LOCATE 23,11: INPUT CHOICE$
2120    IF LEN(CHOICE$) = 0 THEN GOSUB 2460
              ELSE IF CHOICE$ <> "99" THEN GOSUB 2260
                    ELSE XT.REC.NO = 99
2130 WEND
2140 '
2150 CLOSE #2
2160 RETURN
2170 '
2180 '
2190 '---------- Change/View subroutines ----------
2200 '
2210 '
2220 '-----------------------------------------
2230 'Select item and perform appropriate change
2240 '-----------------------------------------
2250 '
2260 WHILE LEN(CHOICE$) <> 0
2270    GOSUB 4430      'Clear prompt area
2280    LOCATE 22,1
2290    IF CHOICE$ = "1"
              THEN GOSUB 3590      'Change last name
```

Figure 18-15 (continued)

```
2300    IF CHOICE$ = "2"
                THEN GOSUB 3720      'Change first name
2310    IF CHOICE$ = "3"
                THEN GOSUB 3850      'Change rent
2320    IF CHOICE$ = "4"
                THEN GOSUB 3980      'Change other
2330    IF CHOICE$ = "5"
                THEN GOSUB 4100      'Change past due
2340    GOSUB 4430    'Clear prompt area
2350    LOCATE 20,7: PRINT "Options"
2360    PRINT "          Type number of item to change"
2370    PRINT "          Return = Save record"
2380    LOCATE 23,11: INPUT CHOICE$
2390 WEND
2400 PUT #2, CVI(T.REC.NO$)
2410 GOSUB 2460     'Display prompts
2420 RETURN
2430 '
2440 '
2450 '-------------------------
2460 'Change/View screen prompts
2470 '-------------------------
2480 '
2490 CLS
2500 PRINT "CHANGE/VIEW"
2510 LOCATE 20,7: PRINT "Options"
2520 PRINT "          Type tenant record number"
2530 PRINT "          99 = Exit to main menu"
2540 LOCATE 23,10: INPUT XT.REC.NO
2550 RETURN
2560 '
2570 '
2580 '*************************
2590 '*                       *
2600 '*    Delete a Record    *
2610 '*                       *
2620 '*************************
2630 '
2640 '
2650 GOSUB 3370     'Open tenant file
2660 CLS : PRINT "DELETE"
2670 LOCATE 20: PRINT "       Options"
2680 PRINT "           Type tenant record number to delete"
2690 PRINT "           99 = Exit to main menu"
2700 LOCATE 23,11: INPUT XT.REC.NO
2710 WHILE XT.REC.NO <> 99
2720 '
2730 '   ((( Display the asked for record )))
2740 '
2750    GET #2, XT.REC.NO
2760    CLS : PRINT "DELETE"
2770    GOSUB 4230      'Display record
2780 '
2790 '   ((( Ask for confirmation )))
2800 '
2810    LOCATE 23,7
2820    INPUT "To delete please confirm (y/n): ", X.CONFIRM$
```

Figure 18-15 (continued)

```
2830      CLS: PRINT "DELETE"
2840      IF X.CONFIRM$ = "y"
                  THEN GOSUB 3020       'Purge record
2850 '
2860 '    ((( Display options )))
2870 '
2880      LOCATE 20,7: PRINT "Options:"
2890      PRINT "            Type tenant record number to delete "
2900      PRINT "            99 = Exit to main menu"
2910      LOCATE 23,11: INPUT XT.REC.NO
2920 WEND
2930 '
2940 CLOSE #2
2950 RETURN
2960 '
2970 '
2980 '---------- Delete subroutines ----------
2990 '
3000 '
3010 '----------------------
3020 'Purge record from file
3030 '----------------------
3040 '
3050 ZERO = 0
3060 LSET T.LAST.NAME$ = "Unoccupied"
3070 LSET T.FIRST.NAME$ = "            "
3080 LSET T.RENT$ = MKS$(ZERO)
3090 LSET T.OTHER$ = MKS$(ZERO)
3100 LSET T.PAST.DUE$ = MKS$(ZERO)
3110 PUT #2, CVI(T.REC.NO$)
3120 '
3130 '((( Display confirmation )))
3140 '
3150 LOCATE 10,7: PRINT "Tenant information for"
3160 PRINT
3170 LOCATE 12,7: PRINT "Record no."; XT.REC.NO; "has been deleted"
3180 '
3190 RETURN
3200 '
3210 '
3220 '
3230 '
3240 '
3250 '///////////////////////////////////////////////
3260 '/                                             /
3270 '/               Common Subroutines            /
3280 '/                                             /
3290 '///////////////////////////////////////////////
3300 '
3310 'These routines are shared by more than one of
3320 'the main menu selection options.
3330 '
3340 '
3350 '
3360 '-----------------------
3370 'Open tenant record file
3380 '-----------------------
```

Figure 18-15 (continued)

```
3390 '
3400 OPEN "R", #2, "B:Tenant.dat"
3410 FIELD #2, 2 AS T.REC.NO$,        3 AS T.APT.NO$,   15 AS T.LAST.NAME$,
              10 AS T.FIRST.NAME$,  4 AS T.RENT$,       4 AS T.OTHER$,
               4 AS T.PAST.DUE$
3420 RETURN
3430 '
3440 '
3450 '-----------------------
3460 'Change apartment number
3470 '-----------------------
3480 '
3490 LOCATE 23,11: INPUT "Type apartment number: ", XT.APT.NO$
3500 LSET T.APT.NO$ = XT.APT.NO$
3510 LOCATE 5,39
3520 PRINT SPACE$(13)
3530 LOCATE 5,39
3540 PRINT XT.APT.NO$
3550 RETURN
3560 '
3570 '
3580 '----------------
3590 'Change last name
3600 '----------------
3610 '
3620 LOCATE 23,11: INPUT "Type tenant last name: ", XT.LAST.NAME$
3630 LSET T.LAST.NAME$ = XT.LAST.NAME$
3640 LOCATE 7,39
3650 PRINT SPACE$(13)
3660 LOCATE 7,39
3670 PRINT XT.LAST.NAME$
3680 RETURN
3690 '
3700 '
3710 '-----------------
3720 'Change first name
3730 '-----------------
3740 '
3750 LOCATE 23,11: INPUT "Type tenant first name: ", XT.FIRST.NAME$
3760 LSET T.FIRST.NAME$ = XT.FIRST.NAME$
3770 LOCATE 9,39
3780 PRINT SPACE$(13)
3790 LOCATE 9,39
3800 PRINT XT.FIRST.NAME$
3810 RETURN
3820 '
3830 '
3840 '------------------
3850 'Change rent amount
3860 '------------------
3870 '
3880 LOCATE 23,11: INPUT "Type monthly rent amount: ", XT.RENT
3890 LSET T.RENT$ = MKS$(XT.RENT)
3900 LOCATE 11,39
3910 PRINT SPACE$(13)
3920 LOCATE 11,38
3930 PRINT XT.RENT
```

Figure 18-15 (continued)

```
3940 RETURN
3950 '
3960 '
3970 '---------------------------
3980 'Change other charges amount
3990 '---------------------------
4000 '
4010 LOCATE 23,11: INPUT "Type other charges amount: ", XT.OTHER
4020 LSET T.OTHER$ = MKS$(XT.OTHER)
4030 LOCATE 13,39
4040 PRINT SPACE$(13)
4050 LOCATE 13,38
4060 PRINT XT.OTHER
4070 RETURN
4080 '
4090 '----------------------
4100 'Change past due amount
4110 '----------------------
4120 '
4130 LOCATE 23,11: INPUT "Type past due amount: ", XT.PAST.DUE
4140 LSET T.PAST.DUE$ = MKS$(XT.PAST.DUE)
4150 LOCATE 15,39
4160 PRINT SPACE$(13)
4170 LOCATE 15,38
4180 PRINT XT.PAST.DUE
4190 RETURN
4200 '
4210 '
4220 '--------------
4230 'Display record
4240 '--------------
4250 '
4260 LOCATE 3
4270 PRINT "              Tenant record number:   "; CVI(T.REC.NO$)
4280 PRINT
4290 PRINT "              Apartment number:         "; T.APT.NO$
4300 PRINT
4310 PRINT "              Tenant last name:         "; T.LAST.NAME$
4320 PRINT
4330 PRINT "              Tenant first name:        "; T.FIRST.NAME$
4340 PRINT
4350 PRINT "              Monthly rent amount:    "; CVS(T.RENT$)
4360 PRINT
4370 PRINT "              Other charges amount:   "; CVS(T.OTHER$)
4380 PRINT
4390 PRINT "              Past due amount:        "; CVS(T.PAST.DUE$)
4400 RETURN
4410 '
4420 '
4430 '-----------------
4440 'Clear prompt area
4450 '-----------------
4460 '
4470 LOCATE 19,1
4480 PRINT SPACE$(79)
4490 PRINT SPACE$(79)
```

Figure 18-15 (continued)

```
4500 PRINT SPACE$(79)
4510 PRINT SPACE$(79)
4520 PRINT SPACE$(79)
4530 RETURN
4540 '
4550 '
```

Figure 18-15 (continued)

SELF TEST

1. How does a programmer know when the computer is in the BASIC language versus the operating system software level?
2. What convention is followed by programmers in assigning program line numbers?
3. What is the major difference in use between BASIC statements and commands? Between deferred and immediate execution?
4. How are erroneous program lines corrected?
5. Identify and describe three frequently used statements and three frequently used commands.
6. Use an example to describe how variables work in a program.
7. Describe how the LET assignment statement works in a program.
8. Use an example to show how math operators have a built-in precedence rule.
9. What are the three main program control structures?
10. List common relational operators.
11. Give an example of how a repetitive loop is programmed in BASIC.
12. Describe, using several examples, how the decision process is programmed.
13. What is internal program documentation? Give some examples.
14. Using an example, describe how a GOSUB works in a BASIC program.
15. Compare how a request to view record 1000 would be handled using sequential versus direct access file organizations.
16. What is the function of the FIELD statement in a direct access file.
17. How does bottom-up program construction proceed?
18. Compare the use of CHAIN and GOSUB in a BASIC program.
19. Compare syntax and logic program error types.
20. Give examples of two BASIC built-in functions.

EXERCISES

1. Type the first exercise into the computer exactly as shown in Figure 18–1. Make a list of the debugging problems encountered and how they are solved. Use the data given in Figure 15–6 to test the exercise. Save the program to reuse in exercise 2.
2. Modify a copy of the first exercise program to match the loop exercise in Figure 18–9. Use the data given in Figure 15–6 to test the exercise. Also test the program using your own test data. Save the program to reuse in exercise 6.

3. Type the decision exercise into the computer exactly as shown in Figure 18–10.
   a. Run the exercise as is.
   b. Change the variable data in line 20 to zero and rerun the exercise.
   c. Change the variable data in line 20 to 2 and rerun the exercise.
   d. Make up your own decision exercise and get a printed copy of the program (use LLIST).
4. Create your own BASIC program exercise that incorporates a loop and relates to a business subject. LLIST your program to the printer to get a hardcopy of the programmer's view. To get a printed copy of the user's view, do a screen dump. It requires typing two keys simultaneously, the SHIFT and PRT SCR print screen keys.
5. Modify a copy of the loop exercise program to parallel the Add Tenants exercise, as shown in Figure 18–11. Make up your own test data, patterned after Figure 15–6, to load the random access file created.
6. *CMB Apartments, Inc. Case.* Write a BASIC program that prints the Rent Roll Report blueprinted in exercise 1 of Chapter 17. Modify the program created in exercise 2 to create the tenant file. All program listings in this chapter provide guidance on how to code the program. Be sure the program is well documented internally with descriptions of what the code is doing.

   To simplify the exercise, control the print loop with a constant that is the last record number used in exercise 5. Establish a new program line that sets LOOP.CONTROL to the last number used before entering the loop. There is no need to use a control file.

   The loop control code should be WHILE REC.NO < = LOOP.CONTROL.
   a. LLIST the program code at the printer.
   b. Produce a hardcopy of the Rent Roll Report.
7. *CMB Apartments, Inc. Case.* Repeat exercise 6 to program the new Tenant List blueprinted in exercise 2 of Chapter 17.
8. *Warehouse Company Case.* Using Figure 18–15 as a guide, write a BASIC program to create a direct access file of customer records for (your name) Warehouse Company. Use the data given in exercise 3 of Chapter 15 to load the file. The screen and program blueprint created in Chapter 17 should direct the code required.
9. *Warehouse Company Case.* Write a BASIC program that prints the Customer Report blueprinted in exercise 3 of Chapter 17. Use the customer data file created in exercise 8 of this chapter. Run the program to get a hardcopy of the report. LLIST the program to the printer.
10. *CMB Apartments, Inc. Case.* When Ms. Jones acquired new buildings, she had to generalize the application programs. Two main changes were needed. The apartment building address on rent statements had to vary based on the building processed. Also, the apartment address had to be included in the Rent Roll Report heading to distinguish one building report from another. Describe how these changes would be implemented in the existing application programs.

RESOURCES AND REFERENCES

See also Chapters 16 and 17, Resources and References.

Programming

DAHL, O., E. DIJKSTRA AND C. HOARE, *Structured Programming,* Academic, 1972.

DIJIKSTRA, E. W., *A Discipline of Programming,* Prentice-Hall, 1976.
PARIKH, GIRISH, *Techniques of Program and System Maintenance,* QED, 1982.

BASIC Language

AMSBURY, WAYNE, *Structured BASIC and Beyond,* Computer Science Press, 1980.
CLARK, JAMES F. AND WILLIAM O. DRUM, *BASIC Programming: A Structured Approach,* South-Western, 1983.
CORTESI, DAVID E., *Your IBM Personal Computer: Use, Applications, and BASIC,* Holt, Rinehart, 1982.
FINKEL, LEROY AND JERALD R. BROWN, *Data File Programming in BASIC,* Wiley, 1981.
JOHNSTON, RANDALPH P., *BASIC Using Micros,* Mitchell, 1983.
KITCHEN, ANDREW, *BASIC by Design,* Prentice-Hall, 1983.
KNECHT, KEN, *Microsoft BASIC,* 2nd ed., Dilithium, 1983.
LIEN, DAVID, A., *Learning IBM BASIC,* CompuSoft, 1982.
MILLER, DAVID, *IBM Data Files: A BASIC Tutorial,* Reston, 1983.
PARKER, ALAN J., *BASIC for Business for the IBM Personal Computer,* Reston, 1983.
POOLE, LON, *Using Your IBM Personal Computer (BASIC),* Sams, 1983.
SEBESTA, ROBERT W. AND JAMES M. KRAUSHAER, *Computer Concepts Structured Programming and Interactive BASIC,* Mitchell, 1982.

BASIC Language Disk-Based Tutorials

ATI Training Power—MBASIC, ATI.
BASIC Primer, IBM.
Teach Yourself BASIC, DELTAK.

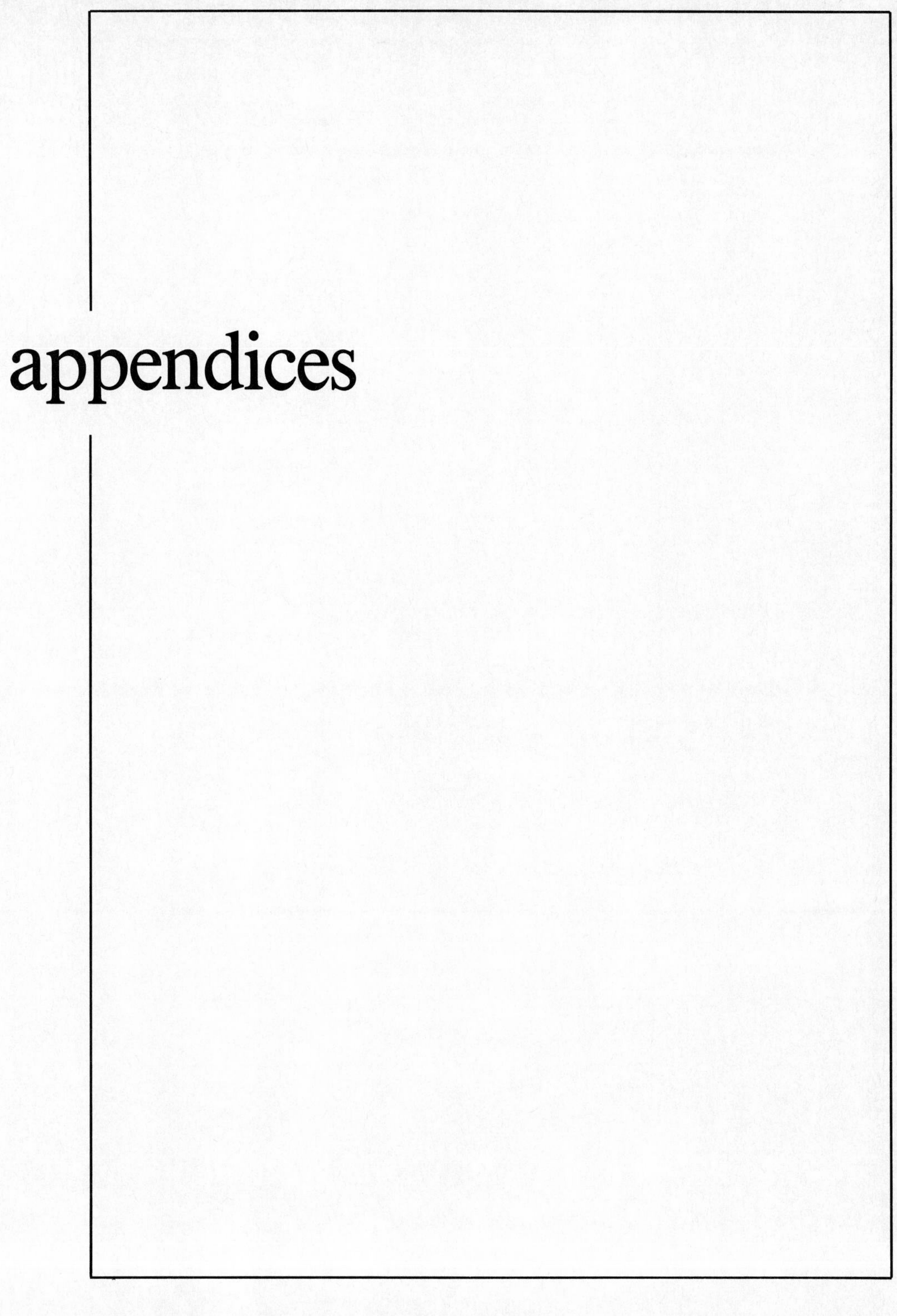

appendices

ADDRESS INFORMATION AND TRADEMARK ACKNOWLEDGMENTS

1-2-3, Lotus
8088, 8086, Intel
Absolute Reference, The Journal for 1-2-3 Users, Que
Academic Press, 111 Fifth Ave., New York, NY 10003
Addison-Wesley Publishing Co., Reading, MA 01867
Advanced Local Area Network, Interactive Systems/3M, 3M Center, Buidling 225–5, St. Paul, MN 55144
Alpha Software Corp., 12 New England Executive Park, Burlington, MA 01803
Amdek, 2201 Lively Blvd., Elk Grove Village, IL 60007
Anderson Report, Anderson Publishing Company, 4505 E. Industrial St., Suite 2J, Simi Valley, CA 93063
Apple Computer Inc., 20525 Mariani Ave., Cupertino, CA 95014
ASCOM, Dynamic Microprocessor Associates, 545 Fifth Avenue, New York, NY 10017
Ashton-Tate, 10150 West Jefferson Blvd., Culver City, CA 90230
Aspen Software Co., P.O. Box 339–P, Tijeras, NM 87059
Association for Computing Machinery, 11 West 42nd St., New York, NY 10036
Association of Computer Users, PO Box 9003, 4800 Riverbend Rd., Boulder, CO 80301
Association of Consulting Management Engineers (ACME), 230 Park Ave., New York, NY 10169

Association of Management Consultants (AMC), 331 Madison Ave., New York, NY 10017
Asynchronous Communication Software, IBM
ATI, American Training International, Inc., 3770 Highland Ave., Suite 202-Q, Manhattan Beach, CA 90266
Auerbach, Philadelphia Operations Center, 6560 N. Park Dr., Pennsauken, NJ 08109
Battery Lane Publications, P.O. Box 30214, Bethseda, MD 20014
The Benchmark Spelling Checker, Metasoft, 711 East Cottonwood, Suite E, Casa Grande, AZ 85222
Boardroom Books, 330 W 42nd St., New York, NY 10136
BPS Business Graphics, BPS, Inc., 143 Binney Street, Cambridge, MA 02142
Brady, Robert J. Co., Bowie, MD 20715
Brown, William C., 2460 Kerper Blvd., Dubuque, IA 52001
Business Graphics System, Peachtree
Byte, 70 Main Street, Peterborough, NH 03458
Caere Corp., 100 Cooper Court, Los Gatos, CA 95030
CalcStar, MicroPro
Calligraphy, Datamost, Inc., 8943 Fullbright Ave., Chatsworth, CA 91311
Canadian Information Processing Society, 243 College Street, Toronto, Ontario, M5T 2U1 Canada
Carnegie Press, 100 Kings Road, Madison, NJ 07940
Cdex, Cdex Corporation, 5050 El Camino Real, Los Altos, CA 94022
Character Generator, Ensign Software, 7337 Northview, Boise, ID 83704
Chart-Master, Decision Resources, P.O. Box 309, Westport, CT 06881
College Placement Council, 62 Highland Ave., Bethlehem, PA 18017
COMMLINK, Edge Technology, Inc., 2735 S.E. Raymond, Portland, OR 97202
Computer Graphics News, Scherago Associates, Inc., 1515 Broadway, New York, NY 10036
Computer Graphics World, Pennwell Publishing Co., 1714 Stockton St., San Francisco, CA 94133
Comprehensive Software Support, PO Box 90833, Los Angeles, CA 90009
CompuServe, 5000 Arlington Centre Blvd., PO Box 20212, Columbus, OH 43220
CompuSoft Publishing, Box 19669, San Diego, CA 92119
Computer Decisions, Hayden Publishing Co., PO Box 1417, Riverton, NJ 08077
Computer Law Journal, 530 West Sixth St., Los Angeles, CA 90014
Computer Science Press, 11 Taft Ct., Rockville, MD 20850
Concurrent CP/M-86, Digital Research
Condor, Condor Computer, 2051 S. State St., Ann Arbor, MI 48104
Consultant Brokerage, 1104 Blue Lake Square, Mountain View, CA 94040
Context MBA, Context Management Systems, 23864 Hawthorne Blvd., Suite 101, Torrance, CA 90505
CP/M, CP/M-86, Digital Research
Crosstalk, Microstuf, Inc., 1845 The Exchange #205, Atlanta, GA 30339
Dartnell, 4660 Ravenswood Ave., Chicago, IL 60640

Data Communications, McGraw-Hill
Data Processing Digest, P.O. Box 1249, Los Angeles, CA 90028
Data Resources, Inc., 1114 Ave. of the Americas, New York, NY 10036
Datamation, 875 Third Ave., New York, NY 10022
Datapro Research Corp., 1805 Underwood Blvd., Delran, NJ 08075
Datec., Inc., 200 Eastowne Dr., Suite 116, Chapel Hill, NC 27514
DAX (Data Exchange), Ungerman Bass, 160 Wilbur Place, Bohemia, NY 11716
DB Master, Stoneware, 50 Belvedere St., San Raphael, CA 94901
dBASE II, Ashton-Tate
Dekotek, 2248 Broadway, New York, NY 10024
DELTAK Microsystems, East/West Technological Center, 1751 West Diehl Rd., Naperville, IL 60566
Desktop Computing, Green
DesQ, Quarterdeck Office Systems, 1918 Main St., Suite 240, Santa Monica, CA 90405
Diagram-Master, Decision Resources, 21 Bridge Square, Westport, CT 06880
DIALOG, DIALOG Information Services, Inc., 3460 Hillview Ave., Palo Alto, CA 94304
Digital Equipment Corp., Maynard, MA 01754
Digital Research, Inc., P.O. Box 579, 160 Central Ave., Pacific Grove, CA 93950
Dilithium Press, 11000 S.W. 11th St., Ste. E, Beaverton, OR 97005
Directory of Management Consultants, Templeton Rd., Fitswilliam, NH 03447
Douthett Enterprises, Inc., 906 North Main, P.O. Box 3266, Suite 1, Wichita, KS 67201
Dow Jones News Retrieval Service, P.O. Box 300, Princeton, NJ 08540
Duncan-Atwell, 1200 Salem Ave., Hillside, NJ 07205
EasySpeller, Information Unlimited
EasyWriter, Information Unlimited
E-COM, U.S. Postal Service, E-Com Management, Operations Center, 197 S. Main St., Wilkes Barre, PA 18703
E-COM Connection, Fogle Computing Corp., 357 East Blackstock Rd., PO Box 5166, Spartanburg, SC 29304
ECOMNET, Palmetto Software, PO Box 5063, Spartanburg, SC 29304
Electrohome Electronics, Emes Systems, 1201 Broadway, New York, NY 10001
Electronic Information Exchange System (EIES), New Jersey Institute of Technology, 323 High Street, Newark, NJ 07102
Elsevier Service Publishing Co., Inc., 52 Vanderbilt Ave., New York, NY 10017
E-Mail, Jones Engineering Associates, Inc., PO Box 26134, Charlotte, NC 28221
Ethernet, Digital, Xerox and Intel
EtherSeries, 3COM, 1390 Shorebird Way, Mountain View, CA 94133
Exec/BUS, Executec Corp., 12200 Park, Central Dr., Dallas, TX 75251
Fast Graphs, Innovative Software
Fingraph Associates, 960 Tower Dr., Suite G, Springfield, IL 62704
FOCUS, Information Builders, Inc., 1250 Broadway, New York, NY 10001
Fortune Systems Corp., 1501 Industrial Rd., San Carlos, CA 94070
Fox & Geller, 604 Market St., Elmwood Park, NJ 07407

Geyer-McAllister Publications, 51 Madison Ave., New York, NY 10010
GrafTalk, Redding Group, Inc., 609 Main St., Ridgefield, CT 06877
Grammatik, Aspen
Graphic Communications, Inc., 200 Fifth Avenue, Waltham, MA 02254
GraphPower, Ferox Microsystems, 1701 N. Ft. Myers Dr., Suite 611, Arlington, VA 22209
Graphwriter, Graphic Communications
Green, Wayne, Inc., 80 Pine St., Peterborough, NH 03458
Hayes Microcomputer Products, Inc., 5923 Peachtree Industrial Blvd., Norcross, GA 30092
Hewlett Packard, Personal Computer Group, 11000 Wolfe Rd., Cupertino, CA 95014
Holt, Rinehart and Winston, Inc., 383 Madison Ave., New York, NY 10017
HOSTCOMM, N.F. Systems, Ltd., PO Box 76363, Atlanta, GA 30358
Houston Instruments, 8500 Cameron Rd., Austin, TX 78753
IBM, International Business Machines, PO Box 1328, Boca Raton, FL 33432
IBM Personal Computer, IBM
IEEE Computer Graphics and Applications, IEEE Computer Society, 10662 Los Vaqueros Circle, Los Alamitos, CA 90720
Imprint Software, 1520 South College Ave., Fort Collins, CO 80524
Independent Computer Consultants Association, PO Box 27412, St. Louis, MO 63141
InfoPro, Inc., P.O. Box 22, Bensalem, PA 19020
Information Industry Association, 316 Pennsylvania Ave., S.E., Suite 400, Washington, DC 20003
Information Sources, 1807 Glenview Rd., Glenview, IL 60025
Information Unlimited Software, Inc., 2401 Marinship Way, Sausolito, CA 94965
InfoStar, MicroPro
InfoWorld, 375 Cochituate Rd., Framingham, MA 01701
Ingres, Relational Technologies, 2855 Telegraph Ave., Berkeley, CA 94705
Innovative Software, 9300 W. 110th St., Suite 380, Overland Park, KS 66210
INSPEC Tape and Online Services, IEE, Station House, Nightengale Rd., Hitchin, Herts, SG5 IRI, England
Institute of Management Consultants (IMC), 19 W. 44 St., New York, NY 10036
Interface Age, McPheters, Wolfe & Jones, 16704 Marquardt Ave., Cerritos, CA 90701
Integrator, The, Alpha Software
Intel Corporation, 3065 Bowers Ave., Santa Clara, CA 95051
Intermec, 4405 Russell Rd., Lynnwood, WA 98036
International Computer Programs, Inc., P.O. Box 40946, Indianapolis, IN 46240
International Information/Word Processing Assoc., 1015 North York Rd., Willow Grove, PA 19090
LEXIS, Meade Data Central, P.O. Box 933, Dayton, OH 45401
Lifetime Learning Publications, Ten Davis Dr., Belmont, CA 94002
Lifetree Software, Inc., 411 Pacific St., Suite 315, Monterey, CA 93940
Lisa, Apple
LogiCalc, Software Products International, 10343 Roselle St., #A, San Diego, CA 92121
Lotus 1-2-3, Lotus Development Corp., 161 First St., Cambridge, MA 02142

Management Information Sources, 1626 N. Vancouver Ave., Portland, OR 97227
Martinus Nijhoff Social Sciences Division, 160 Old Derby St., Hingham, MA 02043
MBASIC, Microsoft
McGraw-Hill, Inc., 1221 Avenue of the Americas, New York, NY 10020
McMullen & McMullen, Inc., P.O. Box 230, Jefferson Valley, NY 10535
MEDLARS, National Library of Medicine, 8600 Rockville, MD 20209
Micro Business Software, Inc., Dover Rd., Willow Hill Building, Chichester, NH 03263
Microcomputer Index, 2464 El Camino Real, Suite 247, Santa Clara, CA 95051
Microcomputing 80, Green
Micro Decision Systems, PO Box 1392, Pittsburgh, PA 15219
Micronix, Morrow Designs, 600 McCormick St., San Leandro, CA 94577
MicroPro International Corp., 33 San Pablo Avenue, San Rafael, CA 94903
MicroRIM, Microrim, 1750 112th St., N.E., Bellevue, WA 98004
Microsoft, Inc., 10700 Northrup Way, Bellevue, WA 98004
Micro-Software Services, 11781 Lee Jackson Highway, Fairfax, VA 22033
Microsoft Word, Microsoft
Mini-Micro Systems, Cahners Publishing Co., 221 Columbus Ave., Boston, MA 02166
MIS Week, Fairchild Publications, 7 East 12th St., New York, NY 10003
Mitchell Publishing, Inc., 915 River St., Santa Cruz, CA 95060
Mouse House, The, 1741 Eighth St., Berkeley, CA 94710
MP/M, MP/M-86, Digital Research
MS-DOS, Microsoft
MultiPlan, Microsoft
National Computer Graphics Asso., 8401 Arlington Blvd., Ste. 601, Fairfax, VA 22031
NEC Information Systems, 5 Militia Dr., Lexington, MA 02173
New York Zoetrope, 80 East 11th St., New York, NY 10003
NewsNet Action Letter, NewsNet, Inc., 945 Haverford Rd., Bryn Mawr, PA 19010
Notepad, Infomedia Corp., 801 Traeger Ave., Suite 275, San Bruno, CA 94066
Office Administration and Automation, Geyer-McAllister
Office, The, Office Publications, 1200 Summer St., Stamford, CT 06904
Online, Inc., 11 Tannery Lane, Weston, CT 06883
OnTyme Electronic Message Network Service, Tymnet
Open Systems, Inc., 430 Oak Grove, Minneapolis, MN 55403
Oracle, 3000 Sand Hill Rd., Menlo Park, CA 94025
Orr, Ken and Associates, Inc., 1725 Gage Blvd., Topeka, KS 66604
Osborne/McGraw-Hill, 630 Bancroft Way, Berkeley, CA 94710
Oyez Publishing, 212 Colgate Ave., Kensington, CA 94707
Pacific Software Manufacturing, 2608 Eighth St., Berkeley, CA 94710
Para Publishing, PO Box 4232-P, Santa Barbara, CA 93103
PC-BBS, Miracle Computing, 313 Clayton Court, Lawrence, KS 66044
PC Clearinghouse, Inc., 11781 Lee-Jackson Highway, Fairfax, VA 22033
PC-DOS, IBM
PC Magazine, One Park Ave., New York, NY 10016
PCNET, Orchid Technology, 487 Sinclair Frontage, Milpitas, CA 95035

PC-TALK, The Headlands Press, Inc., PO Box 862, Tiburon, CA 94920
PC World, PC World Communications, Inc., 555 DeHaro St., San Francisco, CA 94107
Peachtree Software, Inc., 3445 Peachtree Road, N.E., Suite 800, Atlanta, GA 30326
Perfect Software, Inc., 702 Harrison St., Berkeley, CA 94710
Perfect Speller, Perfect Software
Perfect Writer, Perfect Software
Personal Computer Age, 1981 Locust St., Pasadena, CA 91107
Personal Computing, 4 Disk Drive, Box 1408, Riverton, NJ 08077
Petrocelli Books, Inc., 1101 State Rd., Princeton, NJ 08540
PFS:FILE, Software Publishing Corp., 1901 Landings Dr., Mountain View, CA 94043
Pick, Pick Associates, 17911 Skypark Circle, Suite D, Irvine, CA 92714
PlannerCalc, Comshare, 1935 Cliff Way, Atlanta, GA 30329
Polaroid Corporation, Cambridge, MA 02139
Popular Computing, PO Box 307, Martinsville, NJ 08836
Prelude Press, Box 69773, Los Angeles, CA 90069
Prentice-Hall, Inc., Route 9W, Englewood Cliffs, NJ 07632
Proofreader, Aspen
QED Information Sciences, Inc., PO Box 181, Wellesley, MA 02181
QNX, Quantum Software Systems, Inc., 7219 Shea Court, San Jose, CA 95139
Que Corp., 7960 Castleway Dr., Indianapolis, IN 46250
Qume Corp., 2350 Qume Dr., San Jose, CA 95131
Random House Dictionary of the English Language, Random House, 201 East 50th St., New York, NY 10022
Reference, PO Box 100, Milford, NH 03055
Reston Publishing Co., 11480 Sunset Hills Rd., Reston, VA 22090
Sams, Howard W. & Co., Inc., 4300 W. 62 St., Indianapolis, IN 46268
Sequitur, Pacific
Shenson, Howard L., Inc., 20121 Ventura Blvd., Suite 245, Woodland Hills, CA 91364
Small Business Computers, Ahl Computing, Inc., PO Box 789-M, Morristown, NJ 07960
Small Systems World, Hunter Publishing Co., 950 Lee St., DesPlaines, IL 60016
Sofstar, Inc., 13935 U.S. 1, Juno Square, Juno Beach, FL 33408
SofTech Microsystems, Inc., 16885 West Bernardo Dr., San Diego, CA 92127
Software Arts, Inc., 27 Mica Lane, Wellesley, MA 02181
Software Fitness Program, Open Systems
Software Solutions, Inc., 305 Bic Dr., Milford, CT 06460
SoftwareBanc, 661 Massachusetts Ave., Arlington, MA 02174
Solomon Series Software, TLB, Inc.
Sorcim Corp., 2310 Lundy Ave., San Jose, CA 95131
Source Telecomputing Corp., 1616 Anderson Rd., McLean, VA 22102
South-Western Publishing Co., 5101 Madison Rd., Cincinnati, OH 45227
SpellStar, MicroPro
Supercalc, Sorcim
St. Martin's Press, 175 Fifth Ave., New York, NY 10010
Standard and Poors, 25 Broadway, New York, NY 10004
StarBurst, MicroPro

Strobe, Inc., 897-5A Independence Ave., Mt. View, CA 94043
Sybex, 2344 Sixth St., Berkeley, CA 94710
System 16, Tandy
Tandy Corporation, Fort Worth, TX 76102
TCS Software, 3209 Fondren Rd., Houston, TX 77063
Technology and Business Communications, Inc., 730 Baton Post Rd., Suite 25, Box 89, Sudbury, MA 01776
Telecommunications, 610 Washington St., Dedham, MA 02026
Telenet, GTE: Telenet, 8229 Boone Blvd, Vienna, VA 22180
Telex, Western Union
Texas Instruments, PO Box 2909, Austin, TX 78769
TLB, Inc., PO Box 414, Findlay, OH 45840
Today's Office, PO Box 619, Garden City, NY 11530
Tymnet, Inc., 20665 Valley Green Dr., Cupertino, CA 95014
UCSD p-System, SofTech
Uninet, 2 Pennsylvania Plaza, New York, NY 10001
Universal Operating System, SofTech
Unix, Bell Laboratories, Murray Hill, NJ 07974
United Press International, 220 E. 42nd St., New York, NY 10017
U.S. Government Printing Office, North Capitol & H Streets N.W., Washington, D.C. 20401
U.S. National Bureau of Standards, Washington, D.C. 20234
Van Nostrand Reinhold Books, 135 W. 50th St., New York, NY 10020
Venix, VenturCom, Inc., 139 Main St., Cambridge, MA 02142
Videotex, IBM
VisiCalc, VisiCorp
VisiCorp, Inc., 2895 Zanker Rd., San Jose, CA 95134
VisiOn, VisiCorp
VisiPlot, VisiCorp
VisiWord, VisiCorp
Volkswriter, Lifetree
Volkswriter Deluxe, Lifetree
Western Union Telegraph Co., 1 Lake St., Upper Saddle River, NJ 07458
Westlaw, PO Box 3526, 50 W. Kellogg Blvd., St. Paul, MN 55165
Wiley, John and Sons, 605 Third Ave., New York, NY 10158
WordStar, MicroPro
World Computer Graphics Asso., 2033 M Street, N.W., Suite 250, Washington, D.C. 20036
Xenix, Microsoft
Xerox Corporation, 701 S. Aviation Blvd., El Sequndo, CA 90245
Yourdon Press, 1133 Ave. of the Americas, New York, NY 10036
Z80, Zilog
Ziff-Davis Publishing Co., One Park Ave., New York, NY 10016
Zilog Corp., 1315 Dell Ave., Campbell, CA 95008

ASCII code chart

The following chart is a standard way to represent the ASCII character set. When writing ASCII code combinations in binary, it is conventional to number the bits from one through seven and to place the least significant bit on the right.

b_7	b_6	b_5	b_4	b_3	b_2	b_1

b_4 b_3 b_2 b_1	b_7 → 0, b_6 → 0, b_5 → 0	0 0 0	0 0 1	0 1 0	0 1 1	1 0 0	1 0 1	1 1 0	1 1 1
0 0 0 0		NUL	DLE	SPACE	0	@	P		p
0 0 0 1		SOH	DC1	!	1	A	Q	a	q
0 0 1 0		STX	DC2	″	2	B	R	b	r
0 0 1 1		ETX	DC3	#	3	C	S	c	s
0 1 0 0		EOT	DC4	$	4	D	T	d	t
0 1 0 1		ENO	NAK	%	5	E	U	e	u
0 1 1 0		ACK	SYN	&	6	F	V	f	v
0 1 1 1		BEL	ETB	′	7	G	W	g	w
1 0 0 0		BS	CAN	(	8	H	X	h	x
1 0 0 1		HT	EM	)	9	I	Y	i	y
1 0 1 0		LF	SUB	*	:	J	Z	j	z
1 0 1 1		VT	ESC	+	;	K	[	k	{
1 1 0 0		FF	FS	′	<	L	\	l	II
1 1 0 1		CR	GS	–	=	M	]	m	}
1 1 1 0		SO	RS	.	>	N	^	n	~
1 1 1 1		SI	JS	/	?	O	—	o	DEL

Printable character (NUL–SI in column 000 otherwise shaded as follows)

Printable character — Auxiliary device control character

Printer control character — Other control characters

Abbreviations of ASCII code

ACK	Acknowledge	FF	Form feed
BEL	Bell	FS	Form separator
BS	Backspace	GS	Group separator
CAN	Cancel	HT	Horizontal tab
CR	Carriage return	LF	Line feed
DC1	Direct control 1	NAK	Negative acknowledge
DC2	Direct control 2	NUL	Null
DC3	Direct control 3	RS	Record separator
DC4	Direct control 4	SI	Shift in
DEL	Delete	SO	Shift out
DLE	Data link escape	SOH	Start of heading
EM	End of medium	SP	Space
ENQ	Enquiry	STX	Start text
EOT	End of transmission	SUB	Substitute
ESC	Escape	SYN	Synchronous idle
ETB	End transmission block	US	Unit separator
ETX	End text	VT	Vertical tab

POWERS OF 2 CHART

Powers of 2

$2^0 = 1$	
$2^1 = 2$	$2^{17} = 131{,}072$
$2^2 = 4$	$2^{18} = 262{,}144$
$2^3 = 8$	$2^{19} = 524{,}288$
$2^4 = 16$	$2^{20} = 1{,}048{,}576$
$2^5 = 32$	$2^{21} = 2{,}097{,}152$
$2^6 = 64$	$2^{22} = 4{,}194{,}304$
$2^7 = 128$	$2^{23} = 8{,}388{,}608$
$2^8 = 256$	$2^{24} = 16{,}777{,}216$
$2^9 = 512$	$2^{25} = 33{,}554{,}432$
$2^{10} = 1024$	$2^{26} = 67{,}108{,}864$
$2^{11} = 2048$	$2^{27} = 134{,}217{,}728$
$2^{12} = 4096$	$2^{28} = 268{,}435{,}456$
$2^{13} = 8192$	$2^{29} = 536{,}870{,}912$
$2^{14} = 16{,}384$	$2^{30} = 1{,}073{,}741{,}824$
$2^{15} = 32{,}768$	$2^{31} = 2{,}147{,}483{,}648$
$2^{16} = 65{,}536$	$2^{32} = 4{,}294{,}967{,}296$

INDEX